The Gospel of
JOHN

Also by James Montgomery Boice

The Gospel of

JOHN

Volume 1

The Coming of the Light

John 1–4

JAMES
MONTGOMERY
BOICE

Baker Books

A Division of Baker Book House Co
Grand Rapids, Michigan 49516

© 1985, 1999 by James Montgomery Boice

Published by Baker Books
a division of Baker Book House Company
P.O. Box 6287, Grand Rapids, MI 49516-6287

Third printing, February 2002

Printed in the United States of America

Library of Congress Cataloging-in-Publication Data

Boice, James Montgomery, 1938–
  [Gospel of John]
  The Gospel of John / James Montgomery Boice.
      p.   cm.
  Includes bibliographical references and indexes.
  Contents: v. 1. The coming of the light, John 1–4.
  ISBN 0-8010-1182-5 (hardcover)
  1. Bible. N. T. John Commentaries. I. Title.
  BS2615.3.B55   1999
  226.5'077—dc21   99-22764

For current information about all releases from Baker Book House, visit our web site:
http://www.bakerbooks.com

To him who is light,
in whom is no darkness at all

The Coming of the Light

1

Introducing John's Gospel

John 1:1

In the beginning was the Word, and the Word was with God, and the Word was God.

The Gospel of John has blessed the hearts of God's people through the centuries. It has been called "God's love letter to the world." Luther wrote of it, "This is the unique, tender, genuine chief Gospel. . . . Should a tyrant succeed in destroying the Holy Scriptures and only a single copy of the Epistle to the Romans and the Gospel according to John escape him, Christianity would be saved." Luther must have especially loved the Gospel because he preached on it for many years from the pulpit of the parish church of Wittenberg.

Some of the most widely known and best-loved texts in the Word of God are from this Gospel—John 3:16: "For God so loved the world that he gave his one and only Son, that whoever believes in him shall not perish but have eternal life"; John 6:35: "I am the bread of life. He who comes to me will never go hungry, and he who believes in me will never be thirsty"; John 10:11: "I am the good shepherd"; John 11:25: "I am the resurrection and the life"; John 15:1: "I am the true vine." There is the beloved fourteenth chapter: "Do not let your hearts be troubled. Trust in God; trust also in me. In my Father's house are many rooms; if it were not so, I would have told you. I am going there to prepare a place for you. And if I go and prepare a place for you, I will come back, and take you to be with me that you may also be where I am. You know the way to the place where I am going. . . . I am the way and impact of their discovery is continuing even now as the scrolls are being unrolled, assembled, translated, and published.

Before the scrolls were discovered, scholars evaluated the differences between John and the synoptic Gospels in a way that was highly unfavorable to John. For instance, they noticed the unique language of John's Gospel, with its contrasts between light and darkness, life and death, the world below and the world above, and so on. They noticed that the contrasts were generally lacking in Matthew, Mark, and Luke. "Well," they said, "it is obvious that the first three Gospels are Jewish and reflect a Jewish setting. But it is also obvious that John's work is not. John's Gospel must come from a Greek setting. Therefore, we must seek the origin of these unique terms not in the actual speech of Jesus of Nazareth but in Greek thought and particularly in Hellenistic Gnosticism."

Then the Dead Sea Scrolls were discovered. These revealed a whole world of nonconformist Judaism that had simply not been known to scholars previously. The home of the scrolls was Qumran, not far from Jerusalem, in the very area where John placed the earliest events of Christ's ministry. And what was most significant, the literature revealed the same use of the so-called Greek terms (*logos,* light, darkness, life, death) that are found in John's Gospel and actually provided a far closer parallel to them.

One scholar, A. M. Hunter of Aberdeen University in Scotland, writes of these discoveries: "The dualism which pervades the Johannine writings is of precisely the same kind as we discover in the Dead Sea Scrolls."[1] John A. T. Robinson writes: "I detect a growing readiness to recognize that this [the historical background of John's gospel] is not to be sought at the end of the first century or the beginning of the second, in Ephesus or Alexandria, among the Gnostics or the Greeks. Rather, there is no compelling need to let our gaze wander very far, either in space or time, beyond a fairly limited area of southern Palestine in the fairly limited interval between the crucifixion and the fall of Jerusalem." He adds that the Dead Sea Scrolls "may really represent an actual background, and not merely a possible environment, for the distinctive categories of the Gospel."[2]

Other Factors

The historical trustworthiness of John's Gospel is also supported by John's accurate knowledge of the geography of Palestine. This has been vindicated increasingly by archaeological discoveries.

To be sure, John mentions many places that are also mentioned by the synoptic Gospels, so critics could say that these were only known secondhand from their writings. For instance, John could hardly tell the story of Jesus without mentioning Bethsaida (1:44; 12:21), the praetorium (18:28, 33; 19:9), Bethany (11:18), and so on. But John also speaks accurately of Ephraim (11:54), Sychar (4:5, which is probably to be identified with Shechem at Tell Balatah), Solomon's Porch (10:23), the brook Kidron, which Jesus crossed to reach Gethsemane (18:1), and Bethany beyond Jordan, which John carefully distinguished from the other Bethany near Jerusalem (1:28). All of these places are now known, and John himself has again and again been demonstrated to be accurate.

Two archaeological discoveries are particularly interesting. In 5:2, John mentions a pool called Bethesda that, he says, had five porches. For years no one had even heard of this pool. What is more, since John's description made it sound like a pentagon, and since there had never been any pentagon-shaped pools in antiquity, the existence of this pool was thought by many New Testament scholars to be doubtful. Now, however, approximately fifty to seventy-five feet below the present level of the city of Jerusalem, archaeologists have uncovered a large rectangular pool surrounded by four covered colonnades and having an additional colonnade crossing it in the middle somewhat like a bridge. In other words, there was a pool with five porches, as John said. It is conclusive evidence of John's accurate knowledge of the city of Jerusalem as it was before its destruction by the Roman general Titus in A.D. 70.

The second archaeological discovery involves the probable identification of Aenon near Salim, which John mentions in 3:23, as having "plenty of water" in the Jordan valley. It was obviously the place where John the Baptist found adequate water for his baptizing.

These three lines of evidence—the evidence of the manuscripts, the discovery of the Dead Sea Scrolls, and the knowledge of ancient geography—are also supported by other lines of discoveries. There has been an attempt to show that the author of the fourth Gospel (whoever he may have been) must have spoken in Aramaic because, according to those who are experts in this field, Aramaic idiom underlies John's Gospel. Careful study of the text has convinced other scholars that the material preserved by John may be as old as Pauline theology or the traditions preserved by the Synoptics. Thus, a better knowledge of the author of the fourth Gospel and his times has succeeded in pushing scholars away from the critical postures they once held, and has caused them to admit not only the possibility of apostolic authorship but to speak even more surely of an early and very reliable tradition that underlies and is in fact preserved in the writing of the Gospel.

John's Purpose

What does this have to do with a study of what is obviously a spiritual Gospel? Just this: John himself insists upon the reliability of the things about which he writes. Take 1 John 1:1, 3 as an example. There John writes, "That which was from the beginning, which we have heard, which we have seen with our eyes, which we have looked at and our hands have touched—this we proclaim concerning the Word of life. . . . We proclaim to you what we have seen and heard that you also may have fellowship with us. And our fellowship is with the Father and with his Son, Jesus Christ." In other words,

John says that he is writing to them about a person whom he has heard, seen, and touched. Hence, he is writing about something objectively true that will bear the brunt of historical investigation.

John sounds the same note in the Gospel: "Jesus did many other miraculous signs in the presence of his disciples, which are not recorded in this book. But these are written that you may believe that Jesus is the Christ, the Son of God, and that by believing you may have life in his name" (John 20:30–31).

There are always people who will say that faith is something that must be entirely divorced from evidence. But that is not stated in the Bible. Faith is believing in something or someone *on the basis of evidence* and then acting upon it. In this case, John has provided evidence for the full deity of Jesus so that readers, whether in his age or ours, might believe it and commit their lives to Jesus as their Savior.

In John's Gospel we have an accurate record of things that were said and done in Palestine almost 2,000 years ago by a Jew named Jesus of Nazareth and that are presented to us as evidence for his extraordinary claims. If one will believe this and approach the record honestly with an open mind, God will use it to bring that person to fullness of faith in the Lord Jesus as God's Son and his Savior. This was John's purpose in writing his Gospel. It is my primary purpose in writing these studies.

What will happen in your case? It all depends on whether or not you open your mind to John's teaching. Sometime ago I was talking to a young man who was very critical of Christianity.

"Have you investigated the evidence?" I asked him.

"What do you mean? How does one do that?" he asked.

"Go home this week and begin to read John's Gospel," I answered. "But before you begin, take a moment to pray something like this: 'God, I do not know if you exist or, if you do, whether you hear me. But if you exist and if you hear me, I want you to know that I am an honest seeker after truth. If this Book of John can really speak to me and show me that Jesus is the Son of God and is God, I ask you to prove that to me while I read it. And if you prove it, then I will believe in him and serve him forever.'" I told him that if he did that, God would speak to him and that he would be convinced that all the things that are written about Jesus of Nazareth in this book are true and that he is the Son of God and our Savior.

The young man went home. I saw him a week later, and I asked, "Did you read the book?"

He answered, "Well, I have to admit that there are other things to which I give a higher priority."

Here is another case. A Christian at the University of Pennsylvania entered into a series of Bible studies in John's Gospel with a young woman who was not a Christian. The two young women went through several chapters where Jesus is declared many times to be God, but none of it clicked with the non-

(v. 2). With these words the highly emphatic and unequivocal statement of the full divinity of the Lord Jesus Christ is ended.

Knowledge of God

At this point we need some practical applications. What does it matter to say that Jesus Christ is God?

First, to say that Jesus Christ is God is to say that we can now know *the truth about God*. We can know what he is like. The counterpart to this statement is that apart from Jesus Christ we really cannot know him. Is God the god of Plato's imagination? We do not know. Is he the god of Immanuel Kant, the German philosopher? Is he the god of other philosophers? Is he the god of the mystics? The answer is that apart from Jesus Christ we do not know what God is like. But if Jesus Christ is God, then we do know, because to know the Lord Jesus Christ is to know God. There is no knowledge of God apart from a knowledge of the Lord Jesus Christ, and there is no knowledge of the Lord Jesus Christ apart from a knowledge of the Bible.

One of the saddest stories in the Word of God concerns this theme. It is in John's Gospel. Toward the end of his ministry, Jesus explained carefully that he was going away from the disciples but that he was going to prepare a place for them and would one day return. The disciples were depressed at the thought of his leaving them. He went on to say that if they had really known him, they would have known the Father. At this point Philip, who was one of the disciples asked him, "Lord, show us the Father and that will be enough for us" (John 14:8). In other words, Philip was saying, "If I could just see God, I would be satisfied." How sad! The disciples had been with Jesus for almost three years and now were nearing the end of his ministry. Still they had not fully recognized that Jesus is God and that they were coming to know God through him. Jesus then had to answer by saying, "Don't you know me, Philip, even after I have been among you such a long time? Anyone who has seen me has seen the Father. How can you say, 'Show us the Father'?" (v. 9).

If you want to know what God is like, study the life of Jesus Christ. Read the Bible! The things recorded there of Jesus Christ are true. What is more, if you read them, you will find that the Holy Spirit of God, who is the Spirit of truth, will interpret and explain them to you.

Always Like Jesus

The second practical application of the truth that Jesus Christ is God is that God was always like Jesus. William Barclay, who knew this truth, writes, "If the Word was with God before time began, if God's Word is part of the eternal scheme of things, it means that God was always like Jesus. Sometimes we tend to think of God as just and holy and stern and avenging; and we tend to think that something that Jesus did changed God's anger into love, and altered God's attitude to men. The New Testament knows nothing of that idea. The whole New Testament tells us, and this passage of John especially tells us, that God has always been like Jesus."[2]

Does Jesus Christ hate sin? Yes! So God has always hated sin also. Does Jesus Christ love the sinner? Yes! Therefore, God loves him also. Barclay says, "What Jesus did was to open a window in time that we might see the eternal and unchanging love of God."[3] In fact, God so hates sin and so loves the sinner that in eternity he planned the way in which he would redeem the race. We read the Old Testament and we find God saying, "There *must be* an atonement for sin." We read the accounts of Christ's life and death, and we find God saying, "There *is* the atonement for sin." We come to our time and as the Word of God is preached we find God speaking to our hearts and saying, "That *was* the atonement for sin. Believe it and be saved." God has always been like Jesus.

An Acceptable Sacrifice

Third, the truth that Jesus Christ is God means that his death on the cross was significant. It means that in this way he himself became the one sufficient and acceptable sacrifice for man's sin. If you or I were to be so foolish as to make a statement that we would die for another man's sins and then were somehow to lose our lives, in terms of sin our death would mean nothing. We are sinners. If we were to die for sin, or pretend to do it, the only sin we could die for would be our own. But Jesus had no sin. Being God, he is sinless. Hence, when he died, he died for the sins of others, in their place; he removed forever the burden of sin from those who believe on him.

Finally, because Jesus Christ is God, it means that he is able to satisfy all the needs of your heart. God is infinite. Jesus is also infinite. Therefore he is able to satisfy *you* out of that inexhaustible immensity.

There is a story that illustrates this truth. Do you remember the verses in Ephesians in which Paul prays that the Christians to whom he is writing might "have power, together with all the saints, to grasp how wide and long and high and deep is the love of Christ, and to know this love that surpasses knowledge—that you may be filled to the measure of all the fullness of God" (Eph. 3:18–19)? These verses speak of the four dimensions of God's love— breadth, length, depth, and height—and they say that out of that fullness God is able to satisfy the one who comes to him. During the Napoleonic period in Europe some of the emperor's soldiers opened a prison that had been used by the Spanish Inquisition. There were many dungeons in the prison, but in one of them the soldiers found something particularly interesting. They found the remains of a prisoner, the flesh and clothing all long since gone and only an ankle bone in a chain to tell his story. On the wall, however, carved into the stone with some sharp piece of metal, there was a crude cross. And around the cross were the Spanish words for the four dimensions of Ephesians 3:18–19. Above was the word "height." Below was the word "depth." On one side there was the word "breadth." On the other there was the word "length." Clearly, as this poor, persecuted soul was lying in chains and was dying, he comforted himself with the thought that God who in himself contains the breadth, length, depth, and height of all things was able to satisfy him fully. He is able to satisfy you fully whatever your need or your longing.

"Who Is This?"

This is John's thesis. We are going to see the evidence for it as we go on in these studies. But even here we must raise the question with which we began and which is above all questions: What do you think of Jesus Christ? Who is he?

This was the question that was raised all through Christ's earthly ministry. When Jesus rode into the city of Jerusalem on a donkey on what we call Palm Sunday the people turned to one another and asked, "Who is this?" (Matt. 21:10). The disciples asked the question after Jesus had stilled the storm on the Lake of Galilee: "Who is this? Even the wind and the waves obey him!" (Mark 4:41). Herod asked, "I beheaded John. Who, then, is this I hear such things about?" (Luke 9:9). When Jesus forgave the sins of the paralytic, the scribes and Pharisees asked themselves, "Who is this fellow who speaks blasphemy? Who can forgive sins but God alone?" (Luke 5:21).

This is the question. Is Jesus only a man? If he is, you can afford to forget him. Or is he God? If he is God, then he demands your belief and your total allegiance. Do you believe that Jesus is God? You should be able to say with doubting Thomas, in the story that is really the spiritual climax of the fourth Gospel, "My Lord and my God." To draw back from making that confession is to perish. To believe it is to enter into eternal life.

3

Jesus Christ Is Man

John 1:1, 14

In the beginning was the Word, and the Word was with God, and the Word was God.

The Word became flesh and made his dwelling among us. We have seen his glory, the glory of the One and Only, who came from the Father, full of grace and truth.

The last study looked at the first two verses of John's Gospel, the verses that declare so unequivocably that Jesus is God. We now want to skip ahead to the verse that goes with them and that says in equally certain terms that Jesus is man. That verse is John 1:14. "The Word became flesh and made his dwelling among us. We have seen his glory, the glory of the One and Only, who came from the Father, full of grace and truth." Jesus is God. Jesus is man. Properly understood, these are the two most important truths to be made about Christ's person.

A Biblical Doctrine

It is not only in John's Gospel that we encounter such teaching, of course. These themes are found throughout Scripture. What is more, although they are very profound they are taught in the most natural way and in a totally artless manner.

Take the three places where God the Father describes the Son's nature by means of two complementary verbs. In the Old Testament prophecy of

26

theories to explain the phenomena that they and others have observed. Some devise myths or philosophies or make scientific statements to explain the workings of the natural world. Some observe the sky by eyesight; others build telescopes. Still others send space probes to investigate what even their best telescopes are unable to reveal to them. Man is always exploring, questioning, trying to understand. He never grows out of the child's questioning "Why?"

It is the same in the spiritual life. Man has always wanted to know about God and to understand his purposes with men. The universality and diversity of the world's religions prove this. But when we turn our minds to God, apart from God's self-revelation, our minds are baffled. We can devise theories, but in the realm of metaphysics there is no data on which to operate. Men see effects, but they cannot see the cause. They see natural phenomena, but they cannot observe the phenomena of the spiritual world. The Reformers observed this and were led to speak of the *deus absconditus,* the hidden God. They knew that man is finite and sinful and that no exercise of will, no stretching of his mind will lift him up the towering ladder of understanding to explore the mind of God.

The Bible also recognizes this. One of Job's comforters asks, "Can you fathom the mysteries of God? Can you probe the limits of the Almighty?" (Job 11:7). The answer is that this is impossible. Thus, men would forever remain in ignorance, were God not to take steps to disclose himself to man. A motion picture by Ingmar Bergman of Sweden speaks about half of this problem. It is called *The Silence.* It portrays the plight of three characters who do not hear the voice of God and who believe that God is silent. The truth, however, is that God is not silent. God has spoken. And he has spoken in terms that are perfectly clear and that, therefore, remove all human excuses for failing to know and worship him.

The Logos

This leads to a study of one of the most important words in the opening chapter of John's Gospel. We have already mentioned it several times in the preceding studies. In English it is the word "word" itself. In Greek it is the word *logos.* It occurs in verses 1 and 14. "In the beginning was the Word, and the Word was with God, and the Word was God. . . . The Word became flesh and made his dwelling among us." This term refers to Jesus Christ, for he is the one who became flesh and dwelt among men. Still we must ask (and indeed biblical scholars have been asking ever since the Gospel was written), why is Jesus Christ called "The Word"? What is the significance of this title? The answer has to do with God's revealing of himself.

To understand this term, we need to ask what meaning it would have had for those to whom the Gospel of John was first written. For instance, what meaning would it have had for a person of Jewish background who was just beginning to hear and understand the gospel?

The first verses of this Gospel, including the term "Word," would refer a Jewish person to the first words of the Book of Genesis where we are told that in the beginning God spoke and all things came into being. In other words, to the Jewish mind Jesus would somehow be associated with the creative power of God and with the self-disclosure of God in creation. We can get a feeling for what this would have meant to a Jew by imagining ourselves to be reading a book that began "When in the course of human events" and included the words "self-evident" and "inalienable rights." Clearly the author would be trying to remind us of the Declaration of Independence and of the founding principles of the American republic.

We need to add to this, however, that the idea of "word" would also have meant more to a Jewish mind than it does to us today. To the Jew a word was something concrete, something much closer to what we would call an event or a deed. A word spoken was a deed done. This way of thinking resulted from the Jew's Old Testament theology. What happens when God speaks? The answer is that the thing is instantly done. God said, "Let there be light," and there was light (Gen. 1:3). God said, "So is my word that goes out from my mouth: It will not return to me empty, but will accomplish what I desire and achieve the purpose for which I sent it" (Isa. 55:11). Thus, the Jew would be somewhat prepared for the thought that the Word of God could somehow be seen and touched as well as heard and that the "Word" might somehow find expression in a life. It would not be entirely strange for a Jew to learn, as the author of Hebrews puts it, that "In the past God spoke to our forefathers through the prophets at many times and in various ways, but in these last days he has spoken to us by his Son" (Heb. 1:1–2).

In a very brief way, then, we have seen what the description of Jesus Christ as the "Word" might have meant to a Jew. But we must remember that the Jews were not the only ones who would be reading John's Gospel. The Gospel would also be read by Greeks and by those who spoke Greek and were influenced by Greek thought. What would the word *logos* mean to them?

For the Greeks, the answer to this question is found, not in religion but in philosophy. Almost 2,600 years ago, in the sixth century B.C., a philosopher by the name of Heraclitus lived in Ephesus. He was the man who said that it is impossible to step into the same river twice. He meant that all of life is in a state of change. Thus, although you step into the river once, step out, and then step in a second time, by the time you have taken the second step the water has flowed on and it is a different river. To Heraclitus, and to the philosophers who followed him, all of life seemed like that. But, they asked, "If that be so, how is it that everything that exists is not in a state of perpetual chaos?" Heraclitus answered that life is not a chaos because the change that we see is not mere random change. It is ordered change. And this means that there must be a divine "reason" or "word" that controls it. This is the *logos,* the word that John uses in the opening verse of his Gospel.

However the *logos* also meant more than this to Heraclitus. For once he had discovered, as he thought, that the controlling principle of matter was God's *logos,* then it was only a small step for him to apply it also to all the events of history and to the mental order that rules in the minds of men. For Heraclitus, then, the *Logos* became nothing less than the mind of God controlling this world and all men.

By the time John came to write his Gospel, the age of Heraclitus was nearly seven hundred years in the past. But the ideas of Heraclitus had been so formative for Greek thought that they had survived, not only in his own philosophy but also in the philosophy of Plato and Socrates, the Stoics, and others who had built upon it. They were discussed by many persons much as we discuss the atomic theory or evolution today. The Greeks knew all about the *Logos.* Therefore, it was with a stroke of divine genius that John seized upon this word, one that was as meaningful to the Greeks as it was to the Jewish people, and said by means of it, "Listen, you Greeks, the very thing that has most occupied your philosophical thought and about which you have all been writing for centuries—the *Logos* of God, this word, this controlling power of the universe and of man's mind—this has come to earth as a man and we have seen him."

Plato, we are told, once turned to that little group of philosophers and students that had gathered around him during the Greek Golden Age in Athens and said to his followers, "It may be that some day there will come forth from God a Word, a *Logos,* who will reveal all mysteries and make everything plain." Now John is saying, "Yes, Plato, and the *Logos* has come; now God is revealed to us perfectly."

Do you believe it? John is declaring that the unknown God of the Greeks, the hidden God of the Middle Ages, the silent God of the twentieth century, is neither unknown, hidden, nor silent. He is fully revealed in Jesus. "It is true that no one has ever seen God at any time. Yet the divine and only Son, Who lives in the closest intimacy with the Father, has made Him known" (John 1:18 PHILLIPS).

A Previous Revelation

This is a natural stopping point for our study, of course, but we cannot really stop here. For the point John is making is not only that Jesus is the revelation of God, but that Jesus was always active in revealing God. Hence, even before the incarnation, there was no excuse for failing to believe.

This is seen first of all in the emphasis John places upon Christ's role in creation. Creation reveals God, and Jesus was God's agent in creation. Thus, John can say, "Through him all things were made; without him nothing was made that has been made" (v. 3). What has God revealed about himself in creation? Paul answers by saying, "For since the creation of the world God's invisible qualities—his eternal power and divine nature—have been clearly seen, being understood from what has been made, so that men are without excuse" (Rom. 1:20). This means that when Jesus Christ began by revealing God in creation he revealed him in two important aspects—his existence and his power—and that these are sufficient to condemn all men for their failure to bow down and worship him.

We know the force of this verse from things in our own experience. When we see a leaf blowing down the street, we do not attribute powers of self-motivation to the leaf. We assume that a power equal to the effect is behind the leaf and has put it in motion. We call that power wind. When we examine a watch of fine Swiss workmanship, we do not assume that the steel and glass and small bearings possess the ability of organizing themselves into a watch. We posit the existence of a watchmaker. So it should be in the realm of nature. Jesus intended that we should recognize God's existence and power through nature.

But nature is not enough. For one thing, no one has ever come to an obedient faith in the God of creation through nature. For another, the revelation of God in nature is not specific in terms of God's plans, and it is not personal. Hence, Jesus Christ was also active in revealing God through Scripture. It may be true that God has revealed his existence and his power in nature, but it is equally true that this is all he has revealed there. Men may recognize the power of God, but if they would know his plans, they must consult the Bible.

You will remember that when the apostle Paul preached the gospel to the men of Athens, he preached to men who had the knowledge of God through nature but did not know who he was. An altar in Athens was inscribed, "To the unknown God." Other altars that have been discovered since are even more indefinite; they say, "To whomever it may concern." How wonderful that this form of address need never be made by anyone. For Paul, who was instructed in the Scriptures and knew the God whom the Greeks worshiped ignorantly, proclaimed, "Now what you worship as something unknown I am going to proclaim to you" (Acts 17:23). He went on to show that God, the creator of the world, was no blind deity, to be worshiped blindly, but a personal God who has willed that all men should live in harmony with one another and come to know and worship him. "In the past God overlooked such ignorance, but now he commands all people everywhere to repent" (v. 30).

The First and the Last

Preeminently, however, Jesus has revealed God through the incarnation, and it is there that God is known personally. God has spoken to men indirectly through his creation and directly through the Scriptures, but there is a more wonderful truth than this. God has spoken to man personally through Jesus Christ. Jesus is his best and greatest word to lost men. If we know God's power in creation and his plans in the Scriptures, we know his personality in the Son. As we look to Jesus we see God himself. "Anyone who has seen me has seen the Father." We discover a God of infinite love and perfect holiness, possessing a desire wonderful enough and a power adequate enough to save rebellious men and women from sin.

Do you believe that? Have you found the fullness of God's glory in Jesus? If you have not yet found it, let me caution you that Jesus is not only the first and most important and all-inclusive word of the Father, he is also God's last word. You will not find God apart from him. If you do not receive him, the last word you will hear from him will be the word of your judgment. Jesus said, "I am the Alpha and the Omega, the First and the Last, the Beginning and the End" (Rev. 22:13). He will either say, "Come, you who are blessed by my Father; take your inheritance, the kingdom prepared for you since the creation of the world" (Matt. 25:34), or he will declare, "I never knew you. Away from me, you evildoers!" (Matt. 7:23).

5

Jesus Christ Is Life

John 1:4

In him was life, and that life was the light of men.

In this verse John introduces two of the greatest themes of his narrative. Often at the beginning of an important work of literature or music, a writer or composer will declare a theme and then allow it to recur again and again throughout the book or composition. This is sometimes done through a visual image, as in a Hardy novel. Sometimes it is through a musical motif, as in a Beethoven symphony. Sometimes it is done by means of a word or a concept, as we have here. John's themes are "light" and "life." And they occur in such a variety of contexts and so frequently that we need to take some time to examine them at the outset.

In this study we will look at the claim that Jesus is the *life* of the world. In the next study we will look at the claim that he is the *light*.

A Prominent Theme

It is quite obvious to any careful reader of the Gospel that the word "life" is an important one, for John speaks often of life in connection with Jesus Christ and of the eternal life that he offered and, indeed, still offers to men and women.

To some extent the Gospel begins and ends with this theme. John begins by declaring, "In him was life, and that life was the light of men" (1:4). In 20:30–31, he concludes, "Jesus did many other miraculous signs in the presence of his disciples, which are not recorded in this book. But these are written that you may believe that Jesus is the Christ, the Son of God, and that by believing you may have life in his name." In John 14:6 Jesus declares that he is the source of life: "I am the way and the truth and the life. No one comes to the Father except through me." John 5:40 shows that men will not come to him that they might have life. In John 10:28 Jesus says of those who do come, "I give them eternal life, and they shall never perish; no one can snatch them out of my hand." John 10:10 says, "The thief comes only to steal and kill and destroy; I have come that they may have life, and have it to the full." In all, the word "life" occurs more than thirty-five times in the Gospel. And the related verb "to live" increases that total by at least fifteen more instances.

Physical Life

But what does it mean to say that Jesus is the source of life or that he is the life? The first answer to that question is one that takes us back to the opening pages of the Book of Genesis and therefore to the role of the Lord Jesus Christ in giving life to all living things in the world. We have already seen in our previous studies that the writer intends a reference to the first chapters of Genesis in his introductory verses; this is also the case here. "In the beginning" (v. 1) reminds us of the sentence: "In the beginning God created the heavens and the earth" (Gen. 1:1). The *Logos* or "Word" of God reminds us of the way in which God spoke in creation: "And God said, 'Let there be light,' and there was light" (Gen. 1:3). In the same way, when John says of the Lord Jesus Christ, "Through him all things were made; without him nothing was made that has been made. In him was life" (John 1:3, 4), every Bible student should think instantly of the life that went forth out of God to bring life to inanimate matter at the beginning of the creation of the world. In other words, John is saying that our physical life comes from God through the Lord Jesus.

This is suggested in the early chapters of Genesis. For we read that "the LORD God formed the man from the dust of the ground and breathed into his nostrils the breath of life, and the man became a living being" (Gen. 2:7).

All the terms in this verse from Genesis are important. In the first place, we are told that God formed man of the dust of the earth. Once, in a message on Christ's statement that we are the salt of the earth, I pointed out that when God does a work in human history he uses common substances or common people so that the glory might be to his name and not to man's. We see this in his choice of Abraham, Moses, David, the prophets, Mary and Joseph, John the Baptist, and the disciples to do certain things. We have it stated in 1 Corinthians 1:26–29, "Brothers, think of what you were when you were called. Not many of you were wise by human standards; not many were influential; not many were of noble birth. But God chose the foolish things of the world to shame the wise . . . so that no one may boast before him." We have the same principle in the opening chapters of the Bible.

When God formed man, what did he use? Did he use gold, silver, iron, uranium, platinum? No, he used dust—a common substance. But he breathed into it the breath of his life. Thus, even though we may be "fearfully and wonderfully made," as the psalmist says (Ps. 139:14), nevertheless, the glory is God's and there is nothing in us about which man can boast. "So low is the dust," writes Donald Grey Barnhouse in *Genesis,* "that God gave it to the serpent for the food of his curse. Job uses the word twenty times to describe the littleness of man in his misery. It is to dust that all bodies return in death. But we can look up to the Lord in confidence because 'he knows our frame and he remembers that we are dust' (Ps. 103:14, RSV)." The writer then adds, "Dust that exalts itself is hateful, but dust that acknowledges its dustiness finds favor in the sight of the Lord."[1]

There is a lesson for us in the dust; but we must stop our examination of the verse at this point, because for our present exposition of John 1:4 the important term in Genesis 2:7 is "breath." It is the breath of God that makes the dust live.

What is God's breath? It is that which goes forth out of his mouth. It is his Spirit, the Holy Spirit, and it is associated with his spoken word. When we speak about these three terms in English—breath, Spirit, and word—they seem to be unrelated. But this is not true in the Hebrew language. In Hebrew the same word that is used for Spirit is also used for "breath." It is the word *ruach,* which even has a breathy sound. And what is more significant, in Hebrew thought the breath of God or the breath of a man is associated with the person's spoken words. For a man speaks, as we know, by means of it. When we put these ideas together, we find that God brought forth life in man by speaking the word of life (which John has already identified with Jesus Christ) in such a way that the Spirit of life (which is his Holy Spirit) passes into man and causes him to breathe. In other words, these terms provide an illustration of the role of each member of the Trinity in creation.

The significance of man's created nature is seen most clearly when he is contrasted with the Lord Jesus Christ. In the great resurrection chapter, 1 Corinthians 15, there is a verse toward the end that says, "'The first man Adam became a living being'; the last Adam, a life-giving spirit" (v. 45). In other words, even though we live by the breath of God, we do so only by inhaling. Christ lives by exhaling. Thus, we know that we are his creatures and that he is the Creator.

Spiritual Life

However, this is only the beginning of our understanding of what John intends by the use of the word "life" in the Gospel. He is speaking of Christ's role in creation, in one sense. But this is only the groundwork for the spiritual interpretation of the word that he unfolds in the pages of the Gospel. It is true that John speaks of physical life here, but as the book goes on he speaks increasingly of spiritual life. And the point is that just as Jesus is the source of physical life, so is he the source of the spiritual life that we receive when we believe on him.

To appreciate the importance of the gift of spiritual life, we must realize first that apart from it we are dead spiritually. Or you might say, we are as unresponsive to God as was the dust of the earth before God breathed his Spirit into it.

We can say this, of course, because God says it. Take the verses from the second chapter of Ephesians for an example. Here Paul writes to the Christians at Ephesus, reminding them that before God made them alive they were totally dead in everything spiritual and were in rebellion against him. "As for you, *you were dead* in your transgressions and sins, in which you used to live when you followed the ways of this world and of the ruler of the kingdom of the air, the spirit who is now at work in those who are disobedient. All of us also lived among them at one time, gratifying the cravings of our sinful nature and following its desires and thoughts. Like the rest, we were by nature objects of wrath. But because of his great love for us, God, who is rich in mercy, *made us alive* with Christ even when we were dead in transgressions—it is by grace you have been saved. And God raised us up with Christ and seated us with him in the heavenly realms in Christ Jesus" (Eph. 2:1–6).

What a past is described in these verses! And what a condition! In our natural state we can do nothing to improve ourselves spiritually. Apart from Christ no man has ever breathed one breath toward God, nor had one spiritual heartbeat. Man is dead in sin. He needs a new life. That is why we must be born again. Being born again means receiving a new life from God through the Lord Jesus Christ by faith in him.

One might add here, however, that when the Bible declares that all men are dead spiritually, it does not imply that all are in an identical state of corruption. In his book, *In the Heavenlies*, Harry A. Ironside points to three instances in the life of Christ that illustrate clearly what the Bible is saying. He writes, "The beautiful little maid, the daughter of Jairus, had been dead only a few minutes when the blessed Lord reached her father's house, but she was dead, she was lifeless. Fair to look upon, lovely and sweet, no doubt, in the eyes of her beloved parents, like a beautiful marble statue, but although there was not the corruption that there might have been, she was dead nevertheless. Turn over to Luke's gospel and you find that as the blessed Lord came to the village of Nain they were carrying a young man out to bury him. He was dead. Dead perhaps a day or two. . . . This young man was dead longer than the little maid, but life was just as truly extinct in her case as in his. Then you have the blessed Lord at the grave of Lazarus. The sisters told Him not to roll the stone away, for their brother had been dead four days and would already be offensive. Corruption had set in, but the Lord Jesus brought new life to that man"[2] as well as to the others. In the same way, we are all genuinely dead apart from the life-giving Spirit of Jesus Christ. There may be degrees of corruption so that relatively speaking some men are far less offensive than others. But all men are dead spiritually. All need the divine life.

Where does it come from? It comes from Jesus Christ. He is the life of the world. Because we were dead in our sins, God sent Jesus Christ to give us new life. Because we were guilty of sin, God sent Jesus to be the propitiation for our sins by bearing them in his own body on the tree.

Eternal Life

There are two more truths that should be noticed before concluding this study. First, the life that God gives through Jesus Christ is not merely an earthly life or a life of such quality that it can be lost, but *eternal* life. It can never be lost. Thus the life that we receive from God in the moment of our belief in Jesus Christ is the same life that we will be living with God in eternity in what we would call unending millions of years from now.

What is eternal life? It is life without end, the life of God. If it could be lost, as some persons think is the case, then it would not be eternal life. For instance, what would eternal life be if it could be lost at the end of one million years? It would not be eternal life. It would be one-million-years life. But if God said that it was going to last for one million years, then it could not be lost before the expiration of that period. If God said that he was going to give us one-thousand-years life, then the life could not be lost before the end of one thousand years. If he said that it was one hundred-years life, it could not be lost before one hundred years had expired. But we thank God that he has not given us merely one-hundred-, one-thousand-, or even one-million-years life. He has given us eternal life. It is truly eternal or everlasting. Thus, the apostle John writes, "And this is the testimony: God has given us eternal life, and this life is in his Son" (1 John 5:11).

The second truth is that God has not only given us eternal life (which no one can take from us); he has also given us a life that is meant to be abundant even in our present circumstances. The Lord Jesus Christ once said, "The thief comes only to steal and kill and destroy; I have come that they may have life, and have it to the full" (John 10:10).

It is unfortunate that many Christians, though they have eternal life, nevertheless do not have life abundantly. This was not meant to be. Instead of living a miserable life and always complaining, Christians are meant to live lives of such joy and exuberance that their lives will be a blessing to others.

There is a magnificent picture of this abundant life in the first verses of the beloved Twenty-third Psalm. "The LORD is my shepherd, I shall not be in want. He makes me lie down in green pastures, he leads me beside quiet waters, he restores my soul. He guides me in paths of righteousness for his name's sake" (Ps. 23:1–3). I believe that the reason this psalm has been so beloved by Christians throughout all the ages of church history is that it sets forth as something quite practical the abundant life that is ours because of God's care for us. We know that we were once sheep that were lost. Even now we wander away from Christ's fold. But still we are his, and we know that the abundant life is ours whenever we will leave our wandering and lie down in the company of our Shepherd.

Did you know that a sheep will not eat or drink when it is lying down? Most people have never heard this. But it is a fact, and it gives special meaning to the phrase, "He makes me lie down in green pastures." If a sheep is lying down, even in the greenest of pastures and even with the most tender morsel of grass within an inch of its nose, the sheep will not eat the grass. Instead, if it is hungry, it will scramble to its feet, bend over, and then eat the morsel that was much easier to reach before. Thus, when the psalm tells us that the Lord Jesus Christ, our Shepherd, makes us lie down in green pastures, it means that he is able to satisfy us so completely that we cannot possibly yearn for anything more.

Oh, the joys of living out the abundant life of Christ! They are the joys of increasingly finding him to be the bread of life that satisfies all our hunger and the water of life that quenches our deepest thirst.

6

The Light of the World

John 1:4–5

In him was life, and that life was the light of men. The light shines in the darkness, but the darkness has not understood it.

Several years ago an old woman in the bush country of southern Rhodesia in Africa said to a missionary, "You have brought us the light, but we don't seem to want it. You have brought us the light, but we still walk in darkness." She was speaking only of the life she knew in Africa. But her words aptly describe the reaction of people everywhere to the light of Jesus Christ when he first shone upon the world. He was the light of the world. In one sense he had always been the light of the world. Yet, when he appeared the world rejected him because it preferred darkness.

This great image—the image of Christ as the light of the world—is the second theme that John the evangelist introduces in the fourth and fifth verses of his opening chapter. Later we are told quite pointedly by Jesus, "I am the light of the world" (8:12). Here we read, "In him was life, and that life was the light of men. The light shines in the darkness, but the darkness has not understood it."

God Is Light

What does John mean when he declares that Jesus Christ is the light of men? By this title, Jesus is revealed as the One who knows God the Father and who makes him known. Light is a universal image for the illumination of the mind through understanding. Before Christ came into the world, the world was in darkness. The world did not know God. Christ came. His light shone before men. Then men had light of the knowledge of the glory of God in the face of Jesus Christ.

The context for the significance of this image lies in the fact that God is pictured as light throughout the Old and New Testaments. David writes in one psalm, "The LORD is my light and my salvation" (Ps. 27:1). Psalm 36:9 says, "For with you is the fountain of life; in your light we see light." Another psalm says: "Praise the LORD, O my soul. O LORD my God, you are very great; you are clothed with splendor and majesty. He wraps himself in light as with a garment; he stretches out the heavens like a tent" (Ps. 104:1–2). John writes, "God is light; in him there is no darkness at all" (1 John 1:5).

God is light! We recognize this truth personally every time we sing some of our most beautiful hymns:

> Eternal light! Eternal light!
> How pure the soul must be
> When, placed within Thy searching light,
> It shrinks not, but with calm delight
> Can live, and look on Thee!

Or this great hymn by Walter Chalmers Smith:

> Immortal, invisible, God only wise,
> In light inaccessible hid from our eyes,
> Most blessed, most glorious, the Ancient of Days,
> Almighty, victorious, Thy great name we praise.

How perfect the image seems to be! And how appropriate as a term for the One who makes the Father known! E. M. Blaiklock, former professor of classics at Auckland University in New Zealand, makes these comments: "God is light. The image is satisfyingly complete. Light penetrates the unimaginable depths of space, far beyond the limits of human vision. In all the vastness of the great globe of vanished millennia into which the telescope can probe, the gleaming galaxies float, or tell in light how once they floated, when the effulgence which we see today began its endless journey.

"Without light there is no vision, no view of reality, no confident journeying, no growth save of chill and evil things, no health, no life. The hand shrinks from the cold and slimy life which survives sluggishly in dark caves. When some plant of the open day strikes root in such places, it becomes a pale and flaccid thing distorted beyond recognition, as it reaches for a gleam through some chink or crevice in the rock.

"But light, like God, exists by itself, apart from that which it illuminates. . . . Light on earth is a medium, a means by which we see this and that object. It picks up and reveals the loveliness of shape and color. But light exists by itself and apart from that which it gilds and glorifies. It is an environment, a condition, a wonder which fills and floods the whole immensity of space."[1]

Blaiklock is right. The image is rich, and it is totally appropriate to describe the Lord Jesus Christ. God the Father is light. So also is Christ the Son. He is the image of the invisible God, the One who fills all in all. In him we see and know the Father.

Light and Darkness

The image also teaches that by his coming into the world Jesus exposed the works of darkness. For he shone in the darkness, and the darkness did not like it. B. F. Westcott, in *The Revelation of the Father*, has written, "The light which reveals the world does not make the darkness, but it makes the darkness felt. If the sun is hidden, all is shadow, though we call that shadow only which is contrasted with the sunlight; for the contrast seems to intensify that which is, however, left just what it was before. And this is what Christ has done by his coming. He stands before the world in perfect purity, and we must feel as men could not feel before he came, the imperfection, the impurity of the world. The line of separation is drawn forever, and the conscience of men acknowledges that it is rightly drawn. Whether we know it or not the light which streams from Christ is ever opening the way to a clearer distinction between good and evil. His coming is a judgment. The light and the darkness are not blended in him, as they are in us, so that opinion can be doubtful."[2]

The coming of Jesus into the world exposed the world's darkness, even where men thought they had most light. When I was very young I spent a number of summers at a Christian camp in Canada. At this camp during the course of each summer my friends and I took several camping trips. The trips were fun, as I remember, but the sleeping conditions were not. The ground was hard. Often it was damp and cold. Sometimes it rained. I remember often lying awake for most of the night talking or fooling around with the other campers. During a particularly long night we would play with our flashlights. We would shine them in one another's eyes, and the game was to see which was the brightest. Generally, the one with the brightest reflector or the largest number of batteries won. Of course, the game could be played only in the dark, for eventually the sun came up, and after that the differences between the flashlights faded into insignificance by comparison to the strong light of the sun.

That is the experience people have when they come face-to-face with Jesus Christ. So long as we live in the darkness of this world you and I are able to compare the relative merits of human goodness or righteousness. We are able to see the difference between a three-battery character, a two-battery character, and one whose battery has almost gone out. We rate men accordingly. But all these distinctions fade away in the presence of the white light of the righteousness of Jesus Christ. His coming reveals the profundity of the darkness.

What is your reaction to that? It can be one of two things. You can hate Christ for it, as many people have done. You can try to get rid of his presence in your life. This is what John implies when he says that the darkness did not overcome the light. He could not say that unless the darkness had tried to overcome it. You can do that. Or you can do what God wants you to do. You can say, "Lord, I see now that my own good works are far from perfect. In fact, they seem quite dark, almost nonexistent, by comparison with your righteousness. I realize that they will never take me to heaven. But you have the goodness which I do not have, and you have promised to give it to all who will believe on your Son and receive him as Savior. That is what I do now. I trust you to remove my sin and accept me as your child forever."

If you will say that, God will do as he has promised. For this is the reason why the Lord Jesus Christ came. We are told, "God made him [Jesus Christ] who had no sin to be sin for us, so that in him we might become the righteousness of God" (2 Cor. 5:21).

Light Victorious

The third important point to note in studying this image is the fact that the light of the Lord Jesus Christ has not been overcome by the darkness. In fact, John says, "The light *still shines* in the darkness, and the darkness has never put it out" (PHILLIPS).

The word that occurs most prominently in the second part of this verse—the word that is translated "comprehend" in the King James Version of the Bible and is translated as "put it out" by Phillips in the paraphrase that I have just quoted—is a word with at least three meanings. Thus, there has been a wide diversity of interpretations of the verse by translators. On the most literal level the word means "to seize" or "to apprehend," whether physically (as in John 8:4, where the scribes and the Pharisees claimed that they had seized the woman taken in adultery), or intellectually, in which case it would mean "to understand." This is the interpretation given to the verse by the King James translators, who rendered the verse, "and the darkness comprehended it not," as well as by the Latin Vulgate that says, *"tenebrae eam non comprehenderunt."*

However, the word can also mean "to overtake" and, thus, by extension "to overtake in pursuit" or "to overcome." This is the clear meaning of the verb in the only other place where it occurs in John's Gospel—John 12:35—where we read, "Walk while you have the light, before darkness overtakes you." In this sense the word passed into the sports vocabulary of antiquity and was used when a wrestler was said to have "taken down" his opponent. This is the meaning adopted by Williams, who says that the darkness "never overpowered" the light, and by the New Scofield Bible and the Revised Standard Version, which use the verb "overcome."

All these translations are right. The darkness certainly did not understand the light. It did not overcome it. And yet, there is another meaning of the word that I believe comes even closer to John's true meaning and is more appropriate. It is "to quench," "to extinguish," or "to eclipse," the concepts employed by J. B. Phillips and the New English Bible. Thus, to use the terms of astronomy, which may certainly be involved here, we can say that God's light is shining in the darkness and that it has never been eclipsed.

We do not see this on earth in the unending natural cycles of light and darkness. Here darkness always overcomes light. You can be in the gloomiest country on earth, or the brightest, and night will always follow upon day. It can be retarded by artificial means, but night comes eventually. I have often noticed how long daylight lasts on evening flights to this country from one of the European capitals. The flights take only six or seven hours, and there is a gain of three hours in flying the 3,000 miles from east to west. The planes fly high, and one can follow the sun for a greater distance over the horizon. On such a flight dusk lingers for almost four hours. Yet the night comes at last, and the plane eventually settles into the blackness that shrouds the eastern seaboard of the United States.

What the physical darkness does each evening, spiritual darkness tried without success to do in the case of Jesus Christ. He simply overcame it. One man who learned this truth rather late in life is Malcolm Muggeridge, England's well-known satirist and social critic. In his words, "Having seen this other light [the light of God revealed in Jesus Christ], I turn to it, striving and growing toward it as plants do toward the sun. . . . Though, in terms of history, the darkness falls, blacking out us and our world, You have overcome history. You came as light into the world in order that whoever believed in You should not remain in darkness. Your light shines in the darkness, and the darkness has not overcome it. Nor ever will."[3]

"You Are the Light"

In order to see the full teaching of the Gospel of John about light, we need to add to these truths that there is a sense in which in our day Jesus is no longer the light of the world directly but is so only as his light is reflected to the world by Christians. It is true that John uses the present tense in describing Christ's light—"the light *shines* in the darkness"—but John would be the first to say that Christ shines in our day only through Christians (cf. 1 John 2:7–11). Thus, when Jesus was in the world he said, "As long as I am in the world, I am the light of the world." But when he turned to those who had believed on him, he said, "You are the light of the world" (Matt. 5:14). He did not mean that they were to glow in their own right like fireflies. Rather, they were to be kindled lights, like John the Baptist, whom Jesus termed a "lamp that burned and gave light" (John 5:35).

To those who did not believe he said, "You are going to have the light just a little while longer. Walk while you have the light, before darkness overtakes you" (12:35).

Do you see what Christ is saying? He is saying that today Christians are the light of the world. But they can be the light of the world only because he is their light and they reflect him. It is as Paul wrote to the Corinthians, "For God, who said, 'Let light shine out of darkness,' made his light shine in our hearts to give us the light of the knowledge of the glory of God in the face of Christ" (2 Cor. 4:6).

Do men see Christ in you? They will not find him in the world today—not in the world's literature, culture, or pastimes. They will see him only as you look to Jesus, as he increasingly becomes your light, and as he is reflected from your life to others.

Is Jesus your light? He is if he does for you what light always does when it issues forth from the Father. First, it puts confusion to flight. This is the picture that we have in the opening chapter of Genesis where we are told how God moved upon the formless void that existed before the world began and said, "Let there be light." The light of God dispelled the darkness and brought forth life and order. If Jesus is the light of your life, he also dispels the darkness and places your life in order.

Second, the light of Jesus Christ is revealing. That is, it penetrates the darkness and shows us what has always been there. If the light of the Lord Jesus has had this effect in you, then you will not be playing the part of the hypocrite. You will have seen your heart. You will have been able to say with Isaiah, "Woe to me! . . . I am ruined! For I am a man of unclean lips, and I live among a people of unclean lips" (Isa. 6:5); or with Peter, "Go away from me, Lord; I am a sinful man!" (Luke 5:8); or with Paul, "I am the worst" of sinners (1 Tim. 1:15).

Finally, if Christ is your light, you will have guidance in the midst of darkness and, with the guidance of God, true liberty.

> Long my imprisoned spirit lay,
> Fast bound in sin and nature's night:
> Thine eye diffused a quickening ray,
> I woke, the dungeon flamed with light:
> My chains fell off, my heart was free, .
> I rose, went forth, and followed Thee.

7

John the Baptist

John 1:6–8

There came a man who was sent from God; his name was John. He came as a witness to testify concerning that light, so that through him all men might believe. He himself was not the light; he came only as a witness to the light.

In the previous studies we have been looking at the person of Jesus Christ and at the things John the evangelist says about him in the first five verses of his Gospel. Now we want to turn to the second person John mentions—John the Baptist. He is mentioned in order that we might learn about his witness to Jesus Christ. John writes, "There came a man who was sent from God; his name was John. He came as a witness to testify concerning that light, so that through him all men might believe. He himself was not the light; he came only as a witness to the light."

The Forerunner

Most of us tend to overlook the importance of the ministry of John the Baptist. For we focus on the ministry of Jesus Christ, as we should, and we remember that John the Baptist was only the forerunner of the Lord. John says that the Baptist came to bear witness to Jesus Christ. This was his reason for existing. John himself said, "He [Christ] must become greater; I must become less" (John 3:30). And yet, if John the Baptist had not lived in that age and if the preparation of Christ's way had not been his primary ministry, we would no doubt look back on him with the highest praise, much as we look back on Isaiah, Daniel, Jeremiah, Amos, or any of the other great Old Testament figures.

Certainly John was a charismatic figure. We read that droves of people went out to him, much as they later did to hear the Lord Jesus Christ. This following was so substantial that it even disturbed the priests and Levites in Jerusalem who sent delegates to investigate John's teaching. Some of these were also convicted, repented, and were baptized as a sign that they had turned from their sins (Mark 1:4–5).

In some sense, too, John was the pivot of biblical history, for we read in Luke that "the Law and the Prophets were proclaimed until John" (Luke 16:16). This means that John was the last of the Old Testament prophets and, hence, the last of the representatives of the old order. After this Jesus came preaching the Kingdom of God, which was entered from that time forward by faith in his person. John was also the herald of the new dispensation. So he earned the praise of the Lord Jesus Christ, who said, "I tell you the truth: Among those born of women there has not risen anyone greater than John the Baptist; yet he who is least in the kingdom of heaven is greater than he" (Matt. 11:11).

This last verse probably refers primarily to the fact that those who came after John and who believed in Jesus would receive the Holy Spirit. But it might also refer to John's extraordinary humility. Jesus said that the one who humbles himself shall be exalted, and John certainly did that. He called himself a voice crying in the wilderness. You cannot see a voice; you can only hear it. Thus, it was John's role and pleasure merely to be the herald of the Lamb who takes away the sin of the world. Like Paul, who came later, John's concern was solely that Jesus be magnified, whether by his life or his death (Phil. 1:19, 20), and in this he was a true and faithful forerunner.

A Witness

John was also known for his ministry of baptism, and for the fact that he baptized the Lord Jesus Christ. However, when John the evangelist refers to John the Baptist in the first chapter of the Gospel, he does so not for the sake of his ministry itself or his baptism of Jesus but solely for the sake of his testimony to Jesus. In this sense, the witness of John the Baptist takes its place in the first chapter of the Gospel as an established, historical testimony—so that we might learn that the One who was the light of the world was identified historically for the response of faith and obedience of men.

We see this emphasis upon John's testimony by the way in which the evangelist handles the material relating to Christ's forerunner. Most noticeable perhaps is the absence from John's Gospel of many aspects of John the Baptist's ministry that are present in the synoptic Gospels—Matthew, Mark, and Luke. For example, John eliminates all references to his preaching of repentance and all mention of him as the herald of God's kingdom. He does not issue a call to repentance in John's Gospel, as in the others (Matt. 3:8; Mark 1:4; Luke 3:8), and he does not engage in water baptism, although several references to baptism in the Gospel show that the evangelist was aware and knew his readers to be aware of this part of the Baptist's activity (1:26; 3:22–26). Moreover, as I have pointed out in my book, *Witness and Revelation in the Gospel of John*, "When John meets the priests and Levites in Matthew's Gospel, he denounces their hypocrisy, terming them a 'brood of vipers' and pointing to his own baptism as a way of repentance and of salvation from the wrath to come (Matt. 3:7–10). In the fourth Gospel, by contrast, a similar encounter appears in an official character without apparent conflict and is the occasion for the formal presentation of the Baptist's testimony (1:19–34)."[1]

Even more significant than these changes and omissions is the fact that the evangelist does not report the baptism of Jesus himself, even though he shows Jesus to be present in the area of the Jordan during John's ministry and even though the baptism is the crowning point of John's ministry in the synoptic Gospels. Apparently the actual baptism did not have much interest for John the evangelist. Instead, everything is focused on Jesus Christ. In place of the baptism there is Jesus. In place of an act there is the verbal proclamation.

We can find a good illustration of what this means by imagining that we have been reading an article dealing with Abraham Lincoln. The article speaks of his Gettysburg Address, but there is no reference to the actual battle of Gettysburg or to the fact that Lincoln traveled there in its aftermath to give this eulogy. Suppose further that the article goes on to discuss the president's Second Inaugural Address but again without any reference to the fact that the Civil War was now over and that this address was designed to bind up the nation's wounds. If that were the case, we would recognize at once that the article was interested in Lincoln as a writer and not primarily as a general or a statesman. The article would probably be entitled something like, "Lincoln: The Writer" or "Abraham Lincoln in Prose." It is exactly the same type of selection that is present in the handling of the Baptist's witness in John's Gospel.

Moreover, while it is the case that John's account of the Baptist's ministry is lacking in many of the themes found in Matthew, Mark, and Luke, it is no less striking that it is also lacking in themes peculiar to the fourth Gospel. Thus, although John tells us that the Baptist was sent to bear witness to the Light, nowhere does the forerunner actually identify Jesus as the Light. And neither does he term Jesus the vine, the bread from heaven, the shepherd, the door, the way, the truth, the life, or any of the other themes that occur later on in John's narrative.

The same point can be made another way. That is, just as the words of the Baptist do not develop the themes of the Gospel, neither does the Gospel develop the themes that are present in the Baptist's witness. If John had wanted to do this, the obvious starting place would have been the Baptist's reference to Jesus as God's Lamb. But in spite of the fact that the evangelist seems to make clear that Jesus was crucified in Jerusalem at precisely the moment when the lambs were being sacrificed for the Jewish Passover, the theme of the sin-bearing lamb does not recur. On the basis of such observations, we are justified in believing that John the evangelist preserved the witness of the Baptist word for word so that he might present it almost as what we would call "legal evidence" for the benefit of the readers of the Gospel.

The final proof of this unique interest on the part of John is that the words for "witness" replace those for "preaching" (Matt. 3:1; Mark 1:4; Luke 3:3) and "exhortation" (Luke 3:18), which the synoptic writers use of the Baptist's ministry. Thus, in John's evaluation the Baptist emerges as the first and greatest witness to the person and ministry of the Lord. John indicates his interest in him precisely as a witness to the Lord.

A Faithful Witness

We are going to be studying the actual testimony of John the Baptist later on. But even at this point we should notice that we have here an outline of what made the witness of Christ's forerunner effective. This is important because it tells us how we too can be effective as we also seek to bear a testimony to our Lord.

The outline is stated quite clearly in verses 7 and 8, although, to be sure, it is clearer in the Greek text than it is in the English. It has three parts. John writes that the Baptist, who was sent from God (1) was not the Light but (2) was sent to bear witness to the Light in order that (3) men might believe through him. This outline was pointed out quite clearly by Professor C. H. Dodd of Cambridge University, England, who also shows that this is precisely the outline that the evangelist employs in the verses immediately following the prologue. That is, verses 19–28 show that the Baptist was not the Light; verses 29–34 picture him pointing to the Light; and verses 35–51 show how that witness resulted in the first men coming to believe in Christ's person.

Think what this means personally. In the first place, John the Baptist was aware that he was *not* the Light. This is important simply because all successful witnessing to Jesus Christ must start with this self-realization. Whenever a Christian layman, minister, writer, teacher, or whoever it might be, gets to thinking that there is something important about him, he or she will always cease to be effective as Christ's witness. The testimony will stop. Unfortunately, this has been true of many Christians and of many important Christian movements.

Second, John bore witness to the Light. This is important also, because there are always many shy or uncertain Christians who feel that they are bearing a witness simply because they are "living" the Christian faith or refusing to do certain things and doing others. They "live" it at work, at school, in their homes. Unfortunately, important as it may be, this is not in itself witnessing. It is what Paul Little, the author of the helpful and stimulating little book *How to Give Away Your Faith,* calls "pre-evangelism." Living the faith is a most essential basis for any effective witness. If we do not live what we profess, the profession will be discredited. Yet, living the faith is not itself witnessing.

Witnessing is speaking to others about Jesus Christ. This is implied in the very word itself, for witnessing is a legal term that points to verbal testimony rendered in a court of law. If we are to do this effectively, we must be able to tell who Jesus Christ is, what he said about the depravity of man's nature, why his death and resurrection are the essential elements in the solution to the problem of man's sin and depravity, and how one comes into a relationship with Jesus personally.

Finally, the witness must be given with the belief of other persons in Jesus Christ as its object. John, we are told, bore witness to the Light "that through him all men might believe." It should be almost unnecessary to mention this, of course, for it is obvious. Yet it is necessary simply because it is possible for a person to become so mechanical in his witness that he can go through all the motions of witnessing without actually looking and praying for the response to Christ in faith by the other person. If we could remember this, we would find witnessing exciting, and we would learn that winning the argument often becomes far less important than winning the person to the Lord.

The Results

Two conclusions follow. First, when a witness is so given—that is, with the awareness on the part of the one witnessing that he or she is not the Light but is only pointing to the Light in order that men and women might believe—then men and women *will* believe. This is God's way of doing things. He says that he has chosen to save men by the foolishness of preaching, and this means by the foolishness of verbal proclamation. It is foolish, as men think of it. But it is the power of God unto salvation for those who will believe.

We have a demonstration of this in the remainder of the chapter, in the verses referred to earlier. For after John has borne his witness to the Light, declaring, "Look, the Lamb of God, who takes away the sin of the world" (1:29), the evangelist records that there was a whole string of disciples who followed Jesus as the result of this testimony. First, there were two disciples, one of whom was Andrew. Andrew found his brother Simon, and Simon became a follower. After this there was Philip, then Nathanael. Then there were others. Clearly, when a witness to Jesus Christ is given in the way John the Baptist gave it, people will believe.

The second conclusion is related to this. It is simply that if you will witness in this way, men and women will believe as the result of *your* testimony.

There are seven different kinds of witness mentioned in the pages of John's Gospel. The most important is the witness of Jesus Christ himself. Jesus said, "Even if I testify on my own behalf, my testimony is valid, for I know where I came from and where I am going. But you have no idea where I come from or where I am going" (John 8:14). The second witness is the witness of the Father. Again Jesus noted, "I am one who testifies for myself; my other witness is the Father, who sent me" (8:18). There is the witness of the Holy Spirit who "will not speak on his own; he will speak only what he hears, and he will tell you what is yet to come. He will bring glory to me by taking from what is mine and making it known to you" (16:13–14). In addition to the testimony of the three persons of the Trinity, there are also these: the witness of the Scriptures, the witness of Christ's works, and the witness of John the Baptist, which we have just been considering. That makes six witnesses, but there is one more. It is the witness of ordinary men and women. The first of these very human testimonies is given by the Samaritan woman, and her witness is followed by the testimony of the multitude that had seen the raising of Lazarus; the special witness of the eleven disciples; and the testimony of the beloved disciple who was an eyewitness of the crucifixion. You and I are, therefore, included in this last category of witnesses.

What does that mean? It means that God regards your testimony as being important enough to be included among all those other monumental testimonies to the person and work of the glorious Lord Jesus Christ. Your testimony may not have a very wide scope. It is certainly not as world embracing as the testimony of the Scriptures. It may not be spectacular, as was the testimony of John the Baptist. Still it is most important. You know a special aspect of Christ's personality or work to which only you can point adequately. And what is more, as you do point to it and witness to him, men and women will come to know him personally as their Savior.

8

Light for Every Man

John 1:9

The true light that gives light to every man was coming into the world.

What was the greatest moment in the history of the world? The traditional answer would be either the discovery of fire or the invention of the wheel. A historian might refer to the flowering of the intellectual life of Greece in the fifth century B.C. Another might argue for the imposition of world law under the authority of the Roman Empire. A modern person might refer to the discovery of atomic energy or, in our own time, to travels beyond the earth—to the moon and perhaps one day to the planets.

These moments in the history of the human race are interesting, of course, and important. In their own way they are very significant. But no thinking Christian would ever answer the question by pointing to one of these happenings. The only answer that a Christian can give would be the coming into human history of the Lord God Almighty in the person of Jesus Christ. Beside that event all other events fade into insignificance by comparison. This moment alone is preeminent. It is about this moment that our text speaks when it points to the coming of Jesus Christ during the days of John the Baptist. "The real light which enlightens every man was even then coming into the world" (John 1:9 NEB).

56

The Light Was Coming

If we are to understand this verse properly, we need to understand at the outset that it is talking about the coming of the Lord Jesus Christ and not, as some versions of the Bible indicate, the coming of light into the lives of all men.

In the Greek text that stands behind our English Bibles, the word translated "coming" occurs in such a place and with such endings that the reference itself is ambiguous. This ambiguity was noticed as far back in church history as the time of the early church writer Origen, in the second century. On the one hand, the word "coming" could refer to the phrase "every man." In that case, the words should be translated the way we find them in the King James Bible ("That was the true Light, which lighteth every man that cometh into the world") or in the paraphrase of the New Testament by J. B. Phillips, which makes it even clearer ("That was the true light that shines upon every man as he comes into the world"). In this form the text is a proof text for the doctrine of natural revelation, the teaching that God has given all men sufficient illumination to come to him. The early Quakers, who believed in natural revelation, were so fond of this text that some of them even called it "the Quakers' text."

There are some difficulties with this interpretation, however, even though the Greek text makes it theoretically possible. For one thing, in this form the verse is redundant. Thus, it is hardly necessary to add that the light shines on every man as he *comes into the world*, for that much is implied by his very existence. For another thing—and this is even more significant—the phrase "coming into the world" is not used elsewhere by John of a man being born. It always has an entirely different meaning, as we shall see.

Another interpretation suggests that "coming" refers, not to "every man" but to the "Light." In this form the reference is to the incarnation of the Lord Jesus Christ, and it is far better. This is the view of all the major commentators, including Frederick Godet, B. F. Westcott, J. H. Bernard, and others, and it is the view reflected in translations of the Revised Standard Version, the New English Bible, and the New International Version.

There are several reasons why this translation should be preferred, besides the fact that the Bible does not elsewhere support the idea of an inner light for every man. First, the phrase "coming into the world," while not used elsewhere in John of the birth of a man, is used frequently for the coming into human history of Jesus Christ. Thus, at the multiplication of loaves and fishes the multitude exclaimed, "Surely this is the Prophet who is to come into the world" (6:14). Martha told Jesus, "I believe that you are the Christ, the Son of God, who was to come into the world" (11:27). Jesus said, "I came from the Father and entered the world; now I am leaving the world and going back to the Father" (16:28). To Pilate's remark, "You are a king then!" the Lord Jesus replied, "You are right in saying I am a king. In fact, for this rea-

son I was born, and for this I came into the world, to testify to the truth.
Everyone on the side of truth listens to me" (18:37).

Second, the verse in this form fits perfectly into the context of John's prologue, which proceeds from the ministry of Jesus before the incarnation,
through the preparatory work of John the Baptist, to a description of the
incarnation itself and of men's response to it. Without this interpretation
John would be speaking of the reaction of men to Christ's coming in verses
10–12 before he actually says that Jesus came into the world. With it the passage flows along perfectly. When John wrote his first epistle he could say,
"The true light is already shining" (1 John 2:8), but here he acknowledges
that the true Light was only coming when the ministry of John the Baptist
began. We should therefore translate the passage, "John the Baptist was not
that Light. He was only sent to bear witness to the Light. Nevertheless, the
true Light, which shines upon every man, was even then (i.e., during the lifetime of John the Baptist) coming into the world."

A Genuine Light

John 1:9 is interesting for several reasons. First, it says that the Light that
was even then coming into the world was the "true" or "genuine" Light. In
the Greek language there are two different but related words that are almost
always translated "true" in our Bibles. The first is the word *alēthēs* which means
"true" as opposed to "false." That is, if you were to make a statement in a
court of law, it would be either true or false, right or wrong. But that is not
the word that John uses here.

Here John uses the word *alēthinos*. This word means "true" as opposed to
"partial" or, as we would say, "the truth, the whole truth, and nothing but
the truth" as opposed to part of it. A better way of translating this word would
be by use of the terms "real" or "genuine." Thus, we should say that the light
of the Lord Jesus Christ was the real light beside which all other lights were
imperfect or misleading.

This is of great importance. Every now and then we hear a Christian say
that there is no good to be found in anything that has its origin in the world.
But that is not entirely true. It is true that no good coming out of man or
out of his world will ever please God, but still there are good things in life
when they are seen from man's perspective. The things I referred to earlier
fall into this category—inventions, philosophy, law, atomic energy, adventure, and so on—and we would be poorer without them. John is not denying that these things have value in a limited way. However, he is saying that
these lights are only partial lights and are misleading if followed exclusively.
Christ alone is the Light that enlightens all darkness and gives illumination
spiritually.

Unfortunately, men will always mistake the partial lights for the real one.
Take a few current examples. One light that men followed, particularly in
the nineteenth century and well into this one, was the light of "progress." A

belief in "progress" was based upon the discoveries of science and diplomacy, and it was linked at least psychologically to the theory of evolution. Men followed this light by droves. But the dream of progress burst like a bubble in the history of two world wars. Before the Second World War men would laugh at those who spoke literally of the judgments recorded in the Book of Revelation—massive destruction and the loss of life, great plagues, geological catastrophes, and signs in the heavens. But now, since the advent of the world's nuclear arsenals, the subject is not so humorous. Most persons are willing to admit that the doctrine of inevitable progress was illusory.

Another partial light is the pursuit of material prosperity. We follow the dream to great excess in America. Thanks to us, much of the world now follows it also, or would like to. This is the idea that happiness comes through an annual wage hike, second car, summer home, four-day workweek, or round-the-world vacations. Once again, these things have a limited benefit. They are at least relatively better than the kind of abject poverty we find in much of India or in the Far East. They are better than death by starvation, better than illiteracy and unemployment. Still they are not the way to contentment. They do not make the heart of a man right with God. Thus, a few years ago, in the midst of the most prosperous age this world has ever known, *Time* magazine spoke of ours as "the age of anxiety" and could find no cure for its malaise.

The world's lights are not necessarily false lights. But they are imperfect lights. They are partial. They do not provide that which men most need for the satisfaction of the inner hunger of their souls. John is saying that the place where men and women can find adequate illumination about themselves and about life under the eye of an almighty and righteous God is Jesus. We are to look to him. Those who will do that will find that he is the One able to guide them through the darkest night, who will enable them to distinguish between the lights that are better and the lights that are worse, and who will cause them to grow spiritually and in every other way.

Every Man

The second important teaching in this verse is that today the light of the Lord Jesus Christ shines on *every* man. Here we are helped by realizing that John is writing out of a definite historical situation. John was writing toward the end of the apostolic era, and he had known the conflicts that had come about as the result of preaching the gospel to the Jews. The Jews, like some modern American Christians, thought that because God had blessed them in a certain historical way they were therefore the only ones whom God could be blessing. They looked back to their religious heritage and boasted in it. They considered the light that God had shed abroad to be their property exclusively. John writes that Jesus came to shine upon all men so that Greeks and Romans, as well as Jews, might share in his kingdom.

That is glorious, of course. But it also has a somber side. For we ask our-selves, "What does the light do when it shines, as it does, on every man?" We must answer, "It brings the works of darkness to light." When Jesus Christ came into the world he was a light such as the world had never seen before, and men hated him for existing simply because he revealed how dirty and vile their lives were morally. He did that then and he does that today. Hence, if you will allow his light to shine upon you, the first thing you will discover is that you are at heart a child of the darkness.

Suppose for a moment that in your town some soap manufacturer would hold a huge contest and invite the homemakers to come together and wash their linen tablecloths. The cameras would be there to record it for televi-sion commercials. One manufacturer would be pushing his product as "the hungry detergent." Another would be saying that his was "enzyme active." A third would say his had "punch." The homemakers wash their linen in these products and when the washing is over and the linen is dry, they spread the tablecloths on the grass to get the benefit of the natural light. Just as they are getting around to the judging, it snows. Isn't it true that in spite of the washing, every tablecloth there would seem to be dirty yellow?

It is the same spiritually. Between persons there is some ground for com-parison. We can say that Joe is better than Sam and that Bill is worse than both. John is so-so. George is not bad. But next to the Lord Jesus Christ all that we are appears to be dirty, and God says that at best "all our righteous acts are like filthy rags" (Isa. 64:6). Have you seen that? If you have, then you are ready to yield to Christ for your cleansing, your transformation, and your true growth.

Not long ago a longtime missionary to Korea named Archibald Campbell wrote a book comparing Korea as he found it with Korea now. He had served in Korea for more than forty years. "In Korea . . . there was spiritual dark-ness until the gospel of Christ was brought in. Men sold their daughters, their sisters, and sometimes their wives into prostitution without a qualm of conscience. Better-class women were not to be seen on the streets. Young girls had to wear great hats, made of reeds, four feet across, which completely hid their faces from view. Wife beating was commonplace. I have seen a man dragging his wife along the street by the hair. Onlookers shrugged their shoulders and said, 'That thing's going to die.' My own frantic appeal to the Chief of Police proved useless. There was little that could be called integrity. . . . Selfishness was in the very physical make up. . . . Medicine men were in business for a living, but hospital service for the sick and afflicted was beyond comprehension. If they can't pay for it, let 'em die! Lepers were outcasts. The blind were beggars."[1]

It is a grim picture, although one not without parallels elsewhere. But then, as Campbell shows, the gospel of God's grace through the Lord Jesus Christ arrived, and in the space of just two generations the country began to be transformed. Values changed, and this was true even though the light of Christ had begun to shine in only a small percentage of the vast population.

The effect can be seen by the following story. In one of the refugee camps that came into being as the result of the Korean War, there was a Korean couple who had a son named Oh In Ho. Oh In Ho had a chance to come to America, an almost unbelievable opportunity at that time, and he chose to come to Philadelphia where he enrolled at the University of Pennsylvania. One evening, on the way to mail a letter, he was attacked by a gang of teenage thugs and was killed. His refugee parents were miles away in Korea. They were living in a hovel made of scrap lumber. But they were Christians, and they were surrounded by Christian friends. From their friends and from their own almost nonexistent savings, these Korean Christians collected hundreds of dollars. Then they sent it to America with the request that the murderers of their son be forgiven and that, with this money, they be sent to a Christian school where they might learn about the Lord Jesus Christ.

What a judgment that act was on so-called "Christian" America. It is an example of the transforming light of the Lord Jesus Christ who in the lifetime of John the Baptist was even then beginning to shine upon our world.

9

Jesus, the Unknown

John 1:10

He was in the world, and though the world was made through him, the world did not recognize him.

Have you ever heard the story of the medieval king who left his kingdom in the hands of servants and rode away to battle? He was gone for years. During those years the kingdom became more and more corrupt. When he returned at last, the king discovered that those whom he once had commanded had quite forgotten him and wherever he went he was unrecognized. This is what happened when the King of kings, the Lord Jesus Christ, first entered human history. He had made the world, the apostle John says, but the world had forgotten him. Thus, although "he was in the world, and though the world was made through him, the world did not recognize him" (John 1:10).

Jesus, the unknown! It is a puzzling and astonishing idea. I suppose that in our century the best-known person in the whole history of the world is Jesus Christ. His name is known, not only in the Western world but also in the East and, indeed, in the farthest corners of our globe. His name is on millions of tongues daily. Yet John is telling us that for some thirty years, from the birth of Jesus until the time of the public ministry of John the Baptist, the Lord of glory was in the world of men but was unknown by them. This fact points a most instructive finger at the extent of the depravity of man, for it shows that men were (and are) spiritually blind.

Depravity of Man's Will

Why was it that the world did not know and recognize the Lord Jesus Christ when he was present? The first answer to that question is that the world did not want him. We know from experience that if a man does not want to see a truth (or an injustice either, for that matter), he will not see it. So, in exactly the same way, men and women did not recognize the Lord Jesus Christ primarily because they did not want to recognize him.

Of course, this runs counter to the estimate most people have of themselves. Some time ago a well-known Bible teacher was interviewed on a Christmas television program by a young woman who was apparently very ignorant of spiritual things. She wanted to add a religious note to her program. So she began by saying how much the spirit of Christmas is needed in our day, just as it was at the birth of Jesus nearly two thousand years ago. She noted how eagerly the whole world waited for the coming of the baby Jesus. The Bible teacher replied that he did not want to seem contradictory but that he was obliged to say that her statement was far from the truth. In fact (and he gave the details) even the various elements of the Christmas story show that the world actually wanted to go about its merrymaking and cupidity without being disturbed by any thoughts about God.

We ourselves can see the truth of this statement. In our Bibles we have the story of Mary and Joseph traveling from Nazareth to Bethlehem when Jesus was about to be born. What happens? We find that the innkeeper does not want him, and so the Lord of glory is born in a stable. Perhaps as much as two years later wise men come to Jerusalem inquiring after the one born King of the Jews, and Herod doesn't want him. He has the babies of Bethlehem murdered, thinking by that means to eliminate a potential rival to his earthly throne. The same story shows the religious leaders correctly answering Herod's question concerning the birthplace of the Messiah: "In Bethlehem in Judea," they replied, "for this is what the prophet has written" (Matt. 2:5). But it is the wise men from the East and not the spiritual leaders of Jerusalem who travel to Bethlehem and there fall down and worship Jesus. The world will always miss the real Christmas because it does not want to be disturbed in its affairs.

A text that puts this great fact theologically is found just two chapters later in John's Gospel: "This is the verdict: Light has come into the world, but men loved darkness instead of light because their deeds were evil" (3:19). Jesus was the Light of the world. When he came into the world his light shone upon men's darkness and revealed the darkness for what it was. Men hated him for it. Thus, they would not acknowledge him to be God's Son, the Lord of glory.

Men and women simply did not want to acknowledge Christ, and they do not want to acknowledge him now. So the corruption that was in the world at Christ's first coming continues. I remember how shocked and astonished I was at my discovery of the moral depravity of the Roman world of Christ's day the first time I visited the remains of the ancient Roman city of Pompeii.

Pompeii was buried by an eruption of Vesuvius in A.D. 79. Today it has been uncovered, and a person can therefore visit the city and come away with the feeling that he has almost seen life as it was during the first century. I remember my visit, and I remember my shock at discovering the visual record in Pompeii of the city's moral and sexual depravity. But it is the same today. The point of John's statement is that men and women are so in love with their sins that they do not want anyone to dissuade them from them.

Today, in so-called "Christian" America, identical things are practiced; the same kinds of pictures are sold. And the heart of man is again demonstrated to be "deceitful above all things and desperately wicked," as God declares it to be. Men do not want Jesus Christ.

Spiritual Blindness

The second reason why the world did not know the Lord Jesus Christ at his coming is that the world was unable to recognize him; that is, not only did men not want to see him, they also were spiritually blind. Thus we read in Paul's two great letters to the Corinthians, "And even if our gospel is veiled, it is veiled to those who are perishing. The god of this age has blinded the minds of unbelievers, so that they cannot see the light of the gospel of the glory of Christ, who is the image of God" (2 Cor. 4:3–4), and "The man without the Spirit does not accept the things that come from the Spirit of God, for they are foolishness to him, and he cannot understand them, because they are spiritually discerned" (1 Cor. 2:14).

What happened when man fell into sin? How far did man fall? There are only four answers to that question theologically, and only one of them is biblical. The first view is that man fell upward. This idea has entered Western thought largely through the impact of the evolutionary theory, and it is held by those who believe that just as man is supposed to have evolved from lower forms of life to higher forms so also has his understanding of God and his morality moved upward. This is entirely false, however, and we must see that man is no better today because, instead of being able to pick up one stone hammer and hit one other man over the head so that he kills him, he is now able to pick up a nuclear bomb and annihilate thousands. Our own recent history of wars and violence should be enough to teach us that, whatever man did when he fell, he certainly did not fall upward.

The second answer is that man fell but that he only fell part way. It says that he fell over the edge, but that he caught the edge with his fingers and dangles there until someone comes along and helps him back up. This is where religion comes in; sometimes the tools that are used are the sacraments. This view is obviously found in the Christian church. But it is not biblical.

The third view is that man fell over the edge but that he got stuck on a shelf halfway down. Those who believe in this doctrine would be quick to admit, verbally at least, that man is a fallen being. They would even use biblical language to insist that he is indeed "dead in trespasses and sins."

Nevertheless, if you press them closely, you will find that they believe that even though a man is dead spiritually he is still capable of doing something. In other words, as Donald Grey Barnhouse once said, you might say that such persons believe that although man is in his coffin he nevertheless has one arm outside of it working for himself. Clearly this is not the biblical view either. The biblical view is that when man fell into sin he fell all the way to the bottom and there he lies hopelessly lost, blind to all spiritual truth, and unable to help himself until God reaches down by grace, lifts him up, sets him on the edge, and then says, "Now, this is the way, walk in it." This is a true picture of man's spiritual inability or blindness, and it is as a result of such blindness as well as man's willfullness that the Lord Jesus Christ was unrecognized.

When we understand that this is an accurate picture of man as God sees him, then we also understand why it was that John the Baptist had to appear as Christ's forerunner. What was the Baptist's ministry? John tells us that the Baptist came to bear witness to the Light. And the point is that if he had not come to bear witness to the Light, no one, including Christ's disciples, would have noticed him.

A story about Donald Grey Barnhouse perfectly illustrates John's function. Dr. Barnhouse was preaching in Ireland at the beginning of the Second World War at a time when, because of the German bombing, a blackout was imposed at a certain hour each evening. It happened that this hour occurred in the midst of Dr. Barnhouse's evening studies. One evening after he had been preaching in the dark for about twenty minutes, someone in a back room accidentally threw the main switch that turned on all the lights in the church. Instantly, there was considerable commotion in the congregation. In particular, a man in the front row began to paw at the person next to him and ask in a loud whisper, "What happened? Why did he stop?" He was quite agitated until his friend explained that the lights had come on accidentally. The man, of course, was blind. He was the one person in the auditorium who could not see the light.

This man is a picture of all men when the light of Jesus Christ first shone upon the world. He was the Light. He was in the world. But the world went about its business until John the Baptist came, crying, "The light is on! The light is on!" When that was said the world looked up with its sightless, sunken eyes, and asked, "What is light?" And they did not respond until God reached down and began to touch their eyes so that some of them might see. To some of these the apostle Peter later wrote, "But you are a chosen people, a royal priesthood, a holy nation, a people belonging to God, that you may declare the praises of him who called you out of darkness into his wonderful light" (1 Peter 2:9).

If we have understood the significance of the fact that men and women did not recognize the Lord Jesus Christ when he came into the world, then we have also begun to understand three of the most important teachings of John's Gospel. The first is the glory of Jesus Christ. The second is the total depravity of man, which, indeed, is taught throughout Scripture. The third is the necessity of God's sovereign and unconditional election as the basis of our salvation.

Everything we have said up to this point substantiates the first two of these teachings. The glory of Jesus Christ is evident, and the spiritual depravity of our race is demonstrated by the willfullness and spiritual blindness of all men apart from the unmerited grace of God in their lives.

If there is any doubt of this, we need only to ask, "After the Light of the world was pointed out to men by John the Baptist, what did men do about him?" and then weigh the answer. The answer is that after the Lord Jesus Christ had been forced upon man's gaze, both by the ministry of the forerunner and by Christ's own public ministry, men responded not by falling down and worshiping him as they ought to have done but by crucifying him. The cross of the Lord Jesus Christ is the response of fallen men to God's goodness.

The third of John's teachings—the need for the sovereign and unconditional election of men by God as the basis of their salvation—flows from the first two and, in fact, is taught just three verses farther on in John's Gospel. If it is true (as it is) that people are totally unable to seek or find God, then the only basis on which anyone ever finds God is that God comes *first of all* seeking him. And isn't that what we are taught quite openly and repeatedly in the Bible? What happens in the opening pages of the Book of Genesis? Man sins and immediately reveals the nature and extent of that sin by running away from God. He hides. But then—marvelous truth—God comes to him, seeking him out. The first recorded question of God in the history of the universe is this one: "Where are you?" In the same way today he comes calling.

You may be saying, "But I am an exception. I have not run away from God. I have sought God. I sought God in the Presbyterian church; and when I couldn't find him in the Presbyterian church, I joined the Methodist church. When I couldn't find God there, I became a Baptist. After that I became a Christian Scientist. Now I am hunting for God by means of drugs through mysticism." The answer to that is that you have not been seeking God; you have been running away from him. When God got close to you in the Presbyterian church you left it and became a Methodist. When he got close to you in the Methodist church you became a Baptist. So it was. You went from church to church to church. And God is calling out, "When are you going to stop running away from me, my child? I want you, and I want to take you to myself."

Let us learn that the first great word that God has to speak to us is that we—you and I—do not naturally want him. But his second word is that in spite of that fact, in spite of our sin, he still loves us and comes to us in the person of the Lord Jesus Christ, his Son, to draw us back to himself. If you believe that, God is already at work in your heart and will in time add to that faith a full measure of spiritual understanding.

10

His Own Received Him Not

John 1:11

He came to that which was his own, but his own did not receive him.

The opening verses of John's Gospel have already introduced us to two very significant themes: the glory of the Lord Jesus Christ, and the depravity of man. These themes are foils to one another. For in this magnificent prologue to the Gospel, the depravity of man is seen precisely in the fact that men failed to recognize the Lord Jesus Christ when he came among them. No sooner has this been said, however, than someone will ask, "But certainly there should be an exception to this blanket description of human depravity. Haven't you forgotten about the Jews, his own people? They had the prophecies of his coming; they had the law; they even had John the Baptist. He came to them especially. Surely they must have recognized him?" But John answers that this is no exception; for, "He came to that which was his own, but his own did not receive him" (John 1:11). In fact, John would say, it is in the light of this inexplicable rejection of Jesus by the Jews that we see the depravity of man most clearly.

From early Greek history comes the story of Agamemnon, the king who (according to Homeric lore) commanded the expedition against Troy. There were three great figures on the Greek side: Agamemnon, Achilles, and Odysseus. Of the three, only Agamemnon returned home quickly with honor after the long war. Achilles was killed at Troy. Odysseus returned only after many years of wandering and many hardships. Agamemnon alone returned in triumph and in safety. But then tragedy struck. For Agamemnon was killed by his wife, who had in the meantime proved unfaithful to him.

This was the great story of infidelity in ancient times. For most ancients it was the sum of perfidy. But it was far less significant and far less dramatic than the rejection of the Lord Jesus Christ by Israel. He had created them, called them into existence as a nation, and foretold his coming to them. Then, when he came, he was rejected by Israel and was crucified. John states it very simply. "He came to that which was his own, but his own did not receive him" (John 1:11). This is now the supreme demonstration of the wickedness of the heart of man.

Past History

This is not surprising, of course. For it was only an act illustrated many times previously in Jewish history. Indeed, throughout the Old Testament we find that the people of Israel despised the men who brought them the blessings of God and spoke for him, and they chose instead the counsels of their own hearts.

We see the principle first in the patriarchs. Abraham had been told by God that he and Sarah were to have a son through whom Abraham would become a great nation and all the families of the earth would be blessed. But Abraham followed his own way instead of God's. He had a son by Hagar, Sarah's Egyptian slave girl. When God came to him again to repeat the promise, Abraham replied, "If only Ishmael might live under your blessing!" (Gen. 17:18). His heart, like our hearts, did not naturally want God's way. In the same way, Isaac tried to bless Esau instead of Jacob, in spite of the fact that God had chosen Jacob to carry on the line of Israel. God was obliged to overrule him. A generation later we find the sons of Jacob trying to murder their brother Joseph because God had revealed that he was going to exalt Joseph and use him for a special purpose.

Moses was the first leader to find out what this tendency on the part of the people was to mean nationally. God had delivered them from Egypt and had done so through ten great miracles, beginning with the changing of the waters of the Nile into blood and ending with the death of Egypt's firstborn. But the people had no sooner left Egypt—in fact, they had not yet crossed the Red Sea—than they began to murmur against Moses and the Lord. They said, "Was it because there were no graves in Egypt that you brought us to the desert to die? What have you done to us by bringing us out of Egypt? Didn't we say to you in Egypt, 'Leave us alone; let us serve the Egyptians'? It would have been better for us to serve the Egyptians than to die in the desert!" (Exod. 14:11–12). Later, when they were actually in the wilderness, they rebelled again, crying, "You have gone too far! The whole community is holy . . . why then do you set yourselves above the LORD's assembly?" (Num. 16:3).

When Jeremiah preached to the southern kingdom of Judah the people said, "We will not listen to the message you have spoken to us in the name of the LORD!" (Jer. 44:16). When Amos came to Bethel to preach against the corruption of the northern kingdom, Amaziah, the court priest, reported his activities to the king saying, "Amos is raising a conspiracy against you in the very heart of Israel" (Amos 7:10). He told Amos, "Get out, you seer! Go back to the land of Judah. Earn your bread there and do your prophesying there. Don't prophesy anymore at Bethel, because this is the king's sanctuary and the temple of the kingdom" (Amos 7:12–13).

Christ's Parable

When the Lord Jesus Christ came he was received with the same contempt and disdain. Thus, toward the end of his ministry but before his crucifixion he summed up their reaction in the parable of the landowner and his vineyard.

"There was a landowner who planted a vineyard. He put a wall around it, dug a winepress in it and built a watchtower. Then he rented the vineyard to some farmers and went away on a journey. When the harvest time approached, he sent his servants to the tenants to collect his fruit.

"The tenants seized his servants; they beat one, killed another, and stoned a third. Then he sent other servants to them, more than the first time, and the tenants treated them the same way. Last of all, he sent his son to them. 'They will respect my son,' he said.

"But when the tenants saw the son, they said to each other, 'This is the heir. Come, let's kill him and take his inheritance.' So they took him and threw his out of the vineyard and killed him.

"Therefore, when the owner of the vineyard comes, what will he do to those tenants?"

"He will bring those wretches to a wretched end," they replied, "and he will rent the vineyard to other tenants, who will give him his share of the crop at harvest time."

Jesus said to them, "Have you never read in the Scriptures:

> "'The stone the builders rejected
>   has become the capstone;
> the Lord has done this
>   and it is marvelous in our eyes'?

"Therefore I tell you that the kingdom of God will be taken away from you and given to a people who will produce its fruit."

Matthew 21:33–43

Later we read that when "the chief priests and Pharisees heard Jesus' parables, they knew he was talking about them" (v. 45).

In this parable God himself is the householder. The earth is the vineyard. The people of Israel are the tenant farmers. The prophets are the servants who came with the Lord's message and were beaten, stoned, and murdered. The son is the Lord Jesus Christ. The murder of the son is Christ's crucifixion. The casting out of the wicked servants is the replacement of Israel as a special people by the Church in this age of Gentile blessing. Clearly this is a picture in the Lord's own language of the truths preserved for us in John's prologue. "He [Jesus] was in the world, and though the world was made through him, the world did not recognize him. He came to that which was his own, but his own did not receive him. Yet to all who received him, to those who believed in his name, he gave the right to become children of God" (John 1:10–12).

No Excuse

At this point we naturally want to go on to describe the free offer of the gospel to people in our age. But before we do we need to answer one more objection. It is an important objection. Someone will say, "But surely they must have had an excuse? There must have been a failure of communications." But this is only the way men think, not God, and the objection is invalid.

Men are always ready to make excuses for their conduct, even when it is obviously wrong. Sometime ago I heard a story of a little boy who was at home several days before Christmas and who knew that all the presents had been brought in and were hidden away in his father's closet. He was not supposed to go into that closet. But the time came when he could no longer resist the temptation. So he slipped up to his father's room, opened the closet door, and began pulling the presents out and unwrapping them. Suddenly, in the midst of his unwrapping, he heard the front door open and his father's footsteps ascending the stairs. Quickly he pushed the wrappings inside the closet. Then, since he had nowhere else to go, he stepped in after them and closed the door. He stood there breathless as his father entered the room and approached the closet. When his father opened the door, there he stood with wrapping paper all around him, feeling guilty. His father asked, "What are you doing here?" And the little boy said, "Everybody's got to be someplace."

That is a revelation of the human heart. We make excuses for our conduct. But God will not allow us to get away with excuses and will force us instead to face up to the reality of our situation. Thus, we are not allowed to make excuses for any rejection of the Lord Jesus Christ on the part of Israel.

We say, "But surely there must have been an excuse for Israel." But there was no valid excuse. And there is no excuse for people who reject the Lord Jesus Christ today. Think of the reasons why Israel should have recognized their Messiah. In the first place, they had the prophecies of his coming. These included the prophecies of his suffering and death just as much as the forecast of his glorious reign. They are found in Psalm 22, Isaiah 53, and so on. Like all men, Israel found what they wanted to find in the Word of God and ignored the rest. They opened the Old Testament: there were the prophecies that told how the Messiah was to be beaten and killed, bearing the iniquities of the people. They should have understood, for they had the history of the sacrifices in Israel to help them interpret these things. Yet they flipped over these pages and instead chose ones that spoke of Christ's triumph. That they talked about and anticipated.

Also they had the evidence of Christ's miracles. To some extent the evidential value of the miracles is overrated by Christians; that is, the miracles are taken as having more value in leading a person to faith in Christ than they were intended to have. People have said that the miracles prove Christ's divine origin, but that does not necessarily follow. For one thing, in Christ's own day some saw his miracles and attributed them to Satan, and even Jesus did not deny that as a possible conclusion. He only pointed out that it was invalid in his case since his miracles were directed against the power of Satan himself. For another thing, the miracles do not in themselves prove any more than that Jesus was a miracle worker.

For the gentile world, then, the miracles are of only very limited value and interest. But this is not the case within Judaism. In Judaism the miracles had exceptional value. And this was true precisely because they were prophesied in the Old Testament about the Messiah. When Jesus came he fulfilled them; thus, he should have been recognized by Israel on this basis.

It was just as though a spy, who wanted to be able to identify a person bearing a message from his friend, should tear a dollar bill in half and give one half to his friend to be given later to the messenger. When the messenger came, the two halves of the dollar bill would be matched perfectly. In the same way, God declared beforehand to Israel what the Messiah would do. When Jesus came he did it, miracles and all. Thus, they should have received him. Interestingly enough, this was precisely the argument that Jesus used with the disciples of John the Baptist who came to him at one point with John's question, "Are you the one who was to come, or should we expect someone else?" (Luke 7:20). Jesus answered, "Go back and report to John what you have seen and heard: The blind receive sight, the lame walk, those who have leprosy are cured, the deaf hear, the dead are raised, and the good news is preached to the poor. Blessed is the man who does not fall away on account of me" (vv. 22–23). In other words, "You may judge by that whether or not I am fulfilling Scripture."

The third reason why the Jews of Christ's day should have believed on him is the ministry of John the Baptist. John was an extraordinary figure, and he attracted a great deal of attention, so much so, in fact, that the leaders of the nation sent priests and Levites to ask him if he was himself the Messiah. This was an official delegation, and John's answer was an official response. He said, "I am not the Christ." The following day he pointed to

Jesus and said, "Look, the Lamb of God." Israel should have followed John's testimony and received Jesus.

All Are Guilty

But where does this leave us—in some sort of privileged, protected position? Can we say, "Well, the Jews are guilty, but thank God we're not like that"? Not at all. In fact, if we really understand the Jews' reaction, we will understand the Gentiles' reaction also. And we will learn that the reaction of Israel is only typical of the reaction of all mankind to Christ's coming.

The Jews had prophecies of Christ's coming, but so does the world today. In fact, the Scriptures of the Old Testament are far more widely translated and circulated in our age than in any age previously. And for us there is the added advantage that we are told in the New Testament how Jesus of Nazareth fulfilled them. The Jews of Jesus' day saw the miracles, but we also have a record of the miracles. What is more, we have evidence of the miraculous power of Jesus Christ in the lives of countless millions of Christians, many of whom have demonstrated Christ's ability to be victorious in them over the worst that life can offer. Finally, we also have the witness of John the Baptist and of that great host of men and women since him whose lives have been transformed by Jesus and who have been called by him to proclaim the eternal gospel.

Where do you stand? If you are running away, saying, "Well, those things are interesting as myths or stories, but I won't take them seriously," you are trying to escape reality. You cannot get away with it permanently. You must face these truths now or at the judgment seat of Christ. On the other hand, you need not continue to run. You need not be identified with those, both Jews and Gentiles, who will not receive Christ. Receive him, and thereby become a child of God by faith in his name.

11

The Free Offer of the Gospel

John 1:12

Yet to all who received him, to those who believed in his name, he gave the right to become children of God.

We have seen two very important themes in the prologue to John's Gospel: the glory of Jesus Christ, and the depravity of man. The glory of Jesus is described in verses 1–9. The depravity of man is shown by man's rejection of Jesus when he came. These two themes leave us at the end of verse 11, with a very depressing picture. Men as a whole did not know Jesus; and, by and large, his own people, the Jews, who should have known better, rejected him. Are we to think then that no one believed? No, that would be a false inference. So John hurries to point out that although the Lord of glory was unknown by the world at large and was rejected by the nation of Israel, nevertheless, there were some who did receive him. He writes, "Yet to all who received him, to those who believed in his name, he gave the right to become children of God" (John 1:12).

This is a glorious verse, especially since it comes, as it does, after the dismal picture of the preceding verses. It is a verse for you personally. It reminds us here at the very beginning of the Gospel—even before the account of the crucifixion and the resurrection—that the gospel of salvation by grace apart from the keeping of the law is today offered freely to all men, and it points to the glorious privilege of those who receive it.

God's Children

We need to look at this statement in parts, beginning with the part declaring that those who believe become God's children. How are we to understand this? If we are to understand it rightly, we need to recognize first that people are not (or do not become) God's children naturally. The ideas of the universal fatherhood of God and the universal brotherhood of man have been popular themes in the past. But this is not biblical teaching. It is true that Paul told the men of Athens: "We are his offspring" (Acts 17:28), but that is not the same thing as saying that we are God's legitimate children. And what is more, in that verse Paul was actually only quoting a Greek poet, either Aratus or Cleanthes, obviously in order to establish a point of contact with his Greek hearers. In his own teaching, by contrast, he stresses that we become God's children only by means of the new birth.

It is also true that there are verses in the Old Testament that speak of the nation of Israel as God's child or of the Jews as God's children. In Exodus 4:22 Israel is called the "firstborn" son of God. David says in the Psalms: "As a father has compassion on his children, so the LORD has compassion on those who fear him" (Ps. 103:13). Isaiah has written, "O LORD, you are our Father" (Isa. 64:8). Jeremiah says, "I thought how I would set you among my sons, and give you a pleasant land, a heritage most beauteous of all nations. And I thought you would call me, My Father, and would not turn from following me. Surely, as a faithless wife leaves her husband, so have you been faithless to me, O house of Israel, says the LORD" (Jer. 3:19–20 RSV). Although this is true, we must note that these verses are not talking about the Babylonians, Egyptians, Syrians, or even Americans. They are talking about God's relationship to Israel and, thus, about a special relationship that they had to God and that was possessed by no other people at that time. Moreover—and this is much to the point—not one of these verses makes the relationship of father to son the relationship of God to any *individual* Israelite.

The true biblical teaching is seen most clearly in the great discussion of this theme by Jesus Christ as recorded in the eighth chapter of the Gospel. The starting point of the discussion, as John records it, was the question of freedom. Jesus had said, "Then you will know the truth, and the truth will set you free" (John 8:32). Because this was a touchy theme in a country that was then under the rule of the Roman armies, Jesus' Jewish hearers reacted to Christ's words violently, saying, "We are Abraham's descendants and have never been slaves of anyone. How can you say that we shall be set free?" (v. 33). Jesus did not bother to refute their absurd contention although he could have. They had been slaves to the Egyptians, Babylonians, Syrians, Moabites, Edomites, Ammonites, Philistines, Greeks, and Romans. There had almost never been a power in the ancient Near East to which they had not been in bondage at some time or other. But Jesus did not speak about this. He was speaking of a slavery to sin.

Even this was a sore spot with Jesus' hearers, as it is to people today. So they answered by becoming vicious, probably accusing Jesus of being illegitimate. "We are not illegitimate children," they protested. "The only Father we have is God himself" (v. 41). At this point Jesus nailed down the whole subject by denying that they were in any sense God's children. For, "If God were your Father, you would love me. . . . You belong to your father, the devil, and you want to carry out your father's desire" (vv. 42, 44).

Now if the Jews, who had a special historical relationship to God, could not be called his children even by Jesus Christ, who was himself a Jew, how much less can this be true of the rest of us. It is true that not all men are children of the devil. A person becomes a child of the devil in the same way that another becomes a child of God; that is, by a moral commitment to him and to his principles. Nevertheless, a man is not naturally a child of the Father of the Lord Jesus Christ either. According to the Bible he becomes a child of God only through a new birth.

By Whose Authority?

The second important part of the verse is the part that declares that we become God's children not on the basis of any human authority but on the authority of the Lord Jesus Christ. The verse says, "Yet to all who received him, to those who believed in his name, he gave the right to become children of God."

The importance of this is that it gives the one who believes on the Lord Jesus Christ great boldness. On one of the military campaigns of the emperor Napoleon, when Napoleon had dropped the reins of his horse in order to read papers, the horse reared up and nearly unseated him. A corporal of the grenadiers, a very lowly soldier, leaped forward and caught the bridle of the emperor's horse so that in a few seconds he had brought the animal under control. Napoleon turned to the corporal and said, "Thank you, Captain."

"Of what company, sire?" asked the soldier who had just been called a captain.

"Of my guards," answered Napoleon.

In an instant the young man threw aside his musket and walked across the field toward the headquarters of the general's staff, tearing off his corporal's stripes as he went. He took his place among the emperor's officers. Someone asked what he was doing, and he replied that he was a captain of the guards.

"By whose authority?" they asked him.

"By the authority of the emperor," the young man answered.

It all depends upon the authority of the commander involved. If one of the soldier's friends had called him a captain, the two corporals might have had a good laugh together, but that would have been all. The title bestowed by the friend would have meant nothing. However, when the emperor gave the order, the corporal seized upon it instantly and was then received as a

captain by the staff. In the same way, our position before God as God's children depends upon the highest authority in the universe, the authority of
the Lord Jesus Christ, the King of kings and Lord of lords, before whom
every knee shall bow. And we can be as bold in seizing our rank as Napoleon's
soldier was.

Will we step back into the ranks and boast, "Jesus has called me God's
child," but fail to assume the privileges and responsibilities of that position?
Or will we take him at his word and come to God to enjoy all the privileges
of being his own? If you have believed on the Lord Jesus Christ and understand this verse properly, then you will come to God as his child with great
boldness.

Faith in Christ

At this point someone might say, "That is wonderful. It must be a great
privilege to be God's child. But how do I become God's child? How does this
special relationship become mine?" The answer, which is the same answer
given throughout the New Testament, is that you become a child of God
through faith. This means that you must believe in the Lord Jesus Christ as
the Son of God, and also believe that by means of his death and resurrection he is your Savior.

The letter to the Hebrews says: "Without faith it is impossible to please
God" (Heb. 11:6). Romans tells us that "a righteousness from God is revealed,
a righteousness that is by faith from first to last, just as it is written: 'The righteous will live by faith'" (Rom. 1:17). Ephesians says, "For it is by grace you
have been saved, through faith" (Eph. 2:8). In Romans 10 we read, "If you
confess with your mouth, 'Jesus is Lord,' and believe in your heart that God
raised him from the dead, you will be saved. For it is with your heart that you
believe and are justified, and it is with your mouth that you confess and are
saved" (vv. 9–10). It is the same in the opening verses of John's Gospel.

There is one more truth to be seen. When you believe in Jesus Christ there
must be also a verbal expression of that belief. The Bible does not acknowledge any such thing as secret discipleship. On the contrary, it teaches that
Christ must be professed publicly. The reason, of course, is that verbal testimony indicates the reality of that faith, just as the cry of the newborn child
reveals the existence of life to the doctor and the mother. The verses just
quoted, Romans 10:9–10, say that if we "confess" with our mouth the Lord
Jesus and "believe" in our hearts that God has raised him from the dead we
shall be saved. Confession is proof that belief in the Lord Jesus Christ is
genuine.

Have you confessed your faith in the Lord Jesus Christ publicly? One of
the most famous characters in the New Testament was a man who came to
Jesus by night and held a long conversation with him, yet left Christ's presence without any outward confession of faith. As a result, we do not know
whether he was genuinely converted or not. His name was Nicodemus.

Nicodemus came to Jesus as a result of Christ's preaching, as many people travel to hear great preaching today. We know this because he referred to Christ's teaching and miracles in his opening remarks: "Rabbi, we know you are a teacher who has come from God. For no one could perform the miraculous signs you are doing if God were not with him" (John 3:2). In other words, he was very impressed. This alone was no evidence of his conversion, however, and Christ's reply to him was in essence a rebuke. The one thing that Jesus was not was a teacher sent from God. There had been thousands of teachers sent from God in the previous history of the world, and there have been thousands of teachers since. He was not one of them. He was God sent to teach, and to die, and to rise again. So he corrected Nicodemus by telling him that unless he was born again, he would never be able to understand things that were spiritual.

Nicodemus was puzzled. "How can a man be born when he is old?" he asked. "Surely he cannot enter a second time into his mother's womb to be born!" (v. 4). Jesus answered by showing that the new birth was spiritual and that it would express itself as faith in his death and resurrection. How much of this entered into the heart of Nicodemus? We do not know, for Nicodemus left no outward expression of his belief. He had heard great preaching, but so have thousands of other unbelievers. Later he would say to the Jewish leaders who were plotting against Jesus, "Does our law condemn anyone without first hearing him to find out what he is doing?" (John 7:51). But many unbelievers have argued for the due process of law and for civil liberties. We even see him bringing spices to Joseph of Arimathaea in order to embalm the body of Jesus on the day of his crucifixion (John 19:39), but many a guilty, unbelieving conscience has donated a stained-glass window or a chapel to Jesus.

Was he one of God's children? We do not know. His witness to the Lord of glory is missing, and we search in vain for his confession.

How different, on the other hand, is the account John gives us of the woman of Samaria, just one chapter later. Donald Grey Barnhouse, in *Epistle to the Romans,* has pointed out that the contrast between these two personalities is striking. "The one is the story of a man, the other of a woman. The one is seemingly a seeker, the other is found by Christ, almost by accident, but definitely by design. The first was a Jew, the second a Samaritan. The one was an aristocratic Pharisee, the other a village harlot. The one wanted Jesus to talk to him, the woman tried to avoid the probing truth and attempted to change the subject. The one came at midnight, the other at noon."[1]

Both Nicodemus and the woman heard great truths during their conversation with the Lord Jesus, but the effect of his words on them was different. Nicodemus questioned Christ, but he showed no verbal response to Christ's teaching. The woman tried to evade Christ's questions. But at last she believed and thereafter showed signs of her faith and transformation. Who was Jesus? To the woman he was revealed to be God's Messiah. So we read, "Then, leaving her water jar, the woman went back to the town and said to the people, 'Come, see a man who told me everything I ever did. Could this be the Christ?'" (John 4:28, 29). We are told that the men then went to Jesus and asked him to remain with them, and that as the result of his words and of the testimony of the woman many others believed in him also.

The importance of public confession arising out of true faith in the Lord Jesus Christ can hardly be overestimated. It is true that there is a type of confession that is insincere. It is this type of confession that the apostle James refers to when he speaks of a faith without works that is dead (James 2:20, 26). But there is also a sincere confession that will always arise out of a life transformed by Jesus. Have you told others of your faith in him?

12

Rebirth

John 1:13

Children born not of natural descent, nor of human decision or a husband's will, but born of God.

Several years ago I talked to a young man who was experiencing many difficulties in his life. He had difficulties with his family, in his work, and in many of his social relationships. He was at that time involved in an extramarital relationship. As I talked with him I discovered that he tended to blame all his troubles on his background and his birth. According to him the fault lay with his parents, and with his place in society. To this young man I had the opportunity of pointing out that, no matter what his birth may or may not have been, there was always the possibility of a new birth through faith in Jesus Christ.

This great possibility, the possibility of beginning anew, is something that came into the world with the Lord Jesus. It is one of the main themes of John's Gospel. Thus, in John 1:12–13, where John has been speaking of the ones who believed in the Lord Jesus Christ when he came, he adds in the same connection that the ones who received him did so because they had experienced rebirth. He writes that these were "born not of natural descent, nor of human decision or a husband's will, but born of God" (John 1:13).

Not of Blood

Before we can speak about the possibilities of the new birth, we need to look first at the ways in which a person cannot be born again. We need to do this to clear away false ideas that hinder our understanding of this aspect of God's truth. Sometimes it is imperative that we do this. If you were a building contractor and wanted to build a twenty-story building in the heart of New York City on a lot that already had a two-story brownstone on it, you would have to go with your bulldozers to clear away the brownstone before you could erect the higher building. It is the same in theology. Thus, in order to build an enduring structure of God's truth regarding the new birth, it is necessary to clear away the false ideas that some men and women have about it.

One false idea confuses spiritual birth with physical birth—the mistake of Nicodemus (John 3:4). It is the thought that a person can be reborn by means of some human agency. To deny this false premise is the main burden of our text, for the verse tells us that it is "not of blood, nor of the will of the flesh, nor of the will of man"—all human agencies—that a man is reborn, "but of God" (KJV).

We need to look at each of these three negative phrases individually. What does John mean when he says that we are not born into God's family by "blood"? The various commentators on this verse are fairly well agreed that it refers to physical birth. We would not refer to human birth in this way in English idiom, of course, but the reference is a natural one in the thought patterns of Judaism. For instance, in Leviticus 17:11, we read, "For the life of a creature is in the blood." This means that in Jewish thought, to refer to blood was nearly the equivalent of referring to human life. Thus, to deny that spiritual birth comes by blood is to deny that it can come about by any process of human regeneration.

I have said that we would not refer to human birth in this way in English. Yet there is a way of speaking that comes quite close. We speak of a person's "noble blood." Or we call someone a "blue blood," meaning that he comes from a privileged position in society. If we were, therefore, to use this idiom to express our denial of the first of these false ideas, we could say that no one is able to claim a position in God's family on the basis of his relationship to the important people of this earth. Even the children of Martin Luther or John Calvin or John Wesley were not saved on the basis of their family relationships. Kings as well as paupers need to confess with their mouths the Lord Jesus and believe on him with their hearts.

A great example of people believing they are right with God because of their birth is the Jews. In Christ's time they boasted to him of their physical ancestry, saying, "We are children of Abraham." How proud they were of that! Abraham had received the promises and the covenant from God, so they naturally thought they had it made just because they were descended from him physically. Jesus pointed out, however, that God was interested in a spiritual relationship and that they were indicating by their actions that they were really children of the devil.

In what are you trusting for your salvation from sin and for a right relationship with God? This verse was written to teach you that, among other things, you must not make the mistake of trusting in the fact that your parents were Christians, or that you were born in a so-called Christian country. The Bible teaches that nothing that relates to your physical birth will save you.

An Emotional High

The second negative phrase in our text is "nor of the will of the flesh." What does this mean? Various explanations of this phrase have been given. One of the earliest was that of St. Augustine, who took the phrase "not of blood" to refer to human birth (as we have already done ourselves), the phrase "nor of the will of the flesh" to refer to the woman's part in reproduction, and "nor of the will of man" to refer to the man's part in procreation. But these last two points seem to me highly unlikely. And so, too, do views that see it as a reference to adoption (Luther), the sensual imagination (Godet), or willpower (Calvin).

The clue to the true meaning of this phrase is to be found in all that is signified by the word "flesh" in the New Testament. The New Testament uses the word "flesh" to signify all that we are in terms of our natural appetites. This involves our emotions. Hence, John is saying that a person cannot become a child of God by exercising his emotions any more than he can become God's child by being born of privileged parents.

Many people believe themselves to be Christians simply because they get an emotional kick out of attending a certain kind of church service. This comprises much of popular religion today, and it is also a fair description of the kind of mystical religion that is connected with the drug cult. Are such experiences valid? Not according to the teaching of the Bible! The Bible teaches that a surge of the emotions does not produce rebirth. You can be moved to tears in a meeting, but that alone will not transform you into one of God's children.

Not by Determination

There is also a third phrase. For God not only says that those who become his children are not born by blood or by the will of the flesh, they also are not born by the will of man. This means that no one can become a child of God by determination or by the powers of positive thinking.

Someone may say, "But certainly a man can get ahead in life by the power of human determination? In this life, yes, but not spiritually. It is possible for a man with a powerful will to move ahead in this world. He may start from a family that has nothing to offer him either in terms of this world's goods or in basic values or encouragement. He may have no education or skills. Nevertheless, he can set doggedly to work, earning a living by day and going to school at night. In this way he can earn a high school diploma, and later a B.A. or a B.S. When he finishes that, he can use his training to get a good job to earn more money. He can collect a fortune and use his fortune to launch himself in politics. From there, he could move from alderman to mayor, to state senator, to United States congressman, and perhaps even to president! A man can do that by willpower, plus (we must admit it) a little "luck."

In the same way a man can achieve certain things for himself morally and ethically. He can found a new religion. But even this will not make him a child of God. In order to become a child of God a man needs to be given God's life, and this comes only from God and is imparted to a man only on the basis of God's grace. The Bible says, "He chose to give us birth through the word of truth, that we might be a kind of firstfruits of all he created" (James 1:18). It is true that a person must believe in Jesus Christ in order to become a Christian. John says that Jesus gives power to become children of God "even to them that believe on his name." You must believe. At the same time, however, you must know that if you do believe, it is only because God has already taken the initiative to plant his divine life within you. In other words, you must learn that man never makes the first move toward God and that no one would be saved unless God operated in this way.

God's Children

Moreover, isn't this exactly why the Bible speaks of our conversion to Christ as rebirth? Why does God use this image? He could have said merely that we must gain an intellectual understanding of these things. That would be legitimate in some sense, because an intellectual understanding is part of it. He could have said that we must attain a certain degree of commitment. The idea of commitment is valid. Instead, God, in the Bible, speaks of life—eternal life—and rebirth. Jesus told Nicodemus, "You must be born again." Clearly God uses this image because it alone shows that the initiative lies with the Father entirely and not with the son or the daughter who is engendered.

What did you have to do with your birth? Did you say, "I would like to be a boy and be born to Mr. and Mrs. Smith; they seem like a nice couple"? Did you say, "I'd like to be a girl, five feet, six inches tall, and have blond hair"? Of course, you didn't! You had absolutely nothing to do with it! Instead, your father met your mother and between them they produced you, and you only realized what had happened afterward. It is obvious, therefore, that when God uses this image he does so to show that he alone is responsible for your salvation and that you believe only because he first created the life within you to do it. Many verses support this truth by showing that the basis of our sonship lies in God's electing love. John writes: "How great is the love the

Father has lavished on us, that we should be called children of God!" (1 John 3:1). Paul declares that God has "predestined us to be adopted as his sons through Jesus Christ" (Eph. 1:5). James says, "He chose to give us birth through the word of truth" (James 1:18).

There are reasons why God has done things in this manner, of course, and the first reason is simply that we might become aware of God's great love and mercy and serve him because of it. In other words, we are to read a passage like Romans 9:14–16—"What then shall we say? Is God unjust? Not at all! For he says to Moses, 'I will have mercy on whom I have mercy, and I will have compassion on whom I have compassion.'"—and we are to say, "Lord God, if it is not of anything human but solely of your mercy that we are saved, then how great is your mercy!" We are to serve him better because of it.

Many people (even Christians) will not like what I am saying because it detracts from man's efforts. But that is exactly the point. The biblical doctrine of rebirth takes everything away from man and gives everything to God. It is the principle of the "seesaw" in theology. It is the principle that you cannot have both ends of the seesaw—God and man—up at the same time. You know how a seesaw operates. When Johnny is at the bottom, Suzie is at the top. And when Suzie is down, Johnny is up. In the same way, you can never have God and man up or down at the same time. If you exalt man in your thinking so that he is able to take care of himself spiritually and eventually inch his way into heaven, then God will be down and there will not be much need for him. But if man is down where he should be and where the Bible places him, dead in trespasses and sins, with a depraved will and utterly without any genuine spiritual potential, then God will be up where he belongs. He will be great and mighty and altogether lovely, as he is. And the Christian, who has come to see these things, will look up from the dung heap of this world, still covered with much of the world's refuse, and say, "Oh, my God, how could you love me?" And when he gets to that point the love of Christ will begin to constrain him, and he will begin to learn that God has set things up this way so that it will be with the bonds of love and not the whip of the law that we are drawn to holiness through the Lord Jesus Christ.

We have this thought stated in the fourth stanza of that great hymn written by Isaac Watts, "When I Survey the Wondrous Cross":

> Were the whole realm of nature mine,
> That were a present far too small;
> Love so amazing, so divine,
> Demands my soul, my life, my all.

The Uncommitted

It is a pity that we are not able to give an exposition of the whole Gospel of John at one time, because someone could conceivably stop at this point and go away, saying, "Well, then, there is nothing for us to do at all." But I am not saying exactly that. I am saying that the initiative is with God in salvation, and that no one—absolutely no one!—would believe in the Lord Jesus Christ unless God had taken the first step by planting his own life within those persons. At this point, however, I must add (and, indeed, I will be adding it more and more as we go on in our studies) that when God does take the first step in saving us, we then become what I would call "free spiritual agents" so that thereafter we are able to obey him and follow his leading. By our rebirth we are initiated into an entirely new series of relationships and duties within his family.

No one who has believed on Jesus Christ is to take these doctrines as an excuse for going out and living as he or she pleases. Paul says, "God forbid" that any true child of God should do that. At the same time, it should not be an excuse for spiritual inactivity on the part of the uncommitted either. Every time I come to such themes and preach them I know that there will be some persons who will react by saying, "Well, if the entire initiative is with God in salvation, then I obviously can do nothing. I'll just sit back and wait to see if he will save me." That does not follow. It is true that you cannot give yourself divine life, but you can expose yourself to the claims of the Christian faith and ask God (if there is a God) to reveal himself to you.

Let me make two suggestions. If you have never honestly faced the claims of the Lord Jesus Christ and of Christianity, begin by reading a Gospel. It doesn't really matter which one, but John is an excellent one with which to start. Read it slowly, and ask yourself what kind of a man could speak and act as Jesus did and have the kind of effect he had upon his contemporaries. I can assure you that this will not be wasted motion, because God says that it is through reading the Word that one is converted. The Bible says that we are "born again, not of perishable seed, but of imperishable, through the living and enduring word of God" (1 Peter 1:23).

Second, you can pray. You do not even need to be convinced of God's existence to do this. For you can merely say, "God (if there is a God), I want you to know that I am an honest seeker after the truth concerning you—or at least I would like to be. And I know that I come to spiritual things as if I were blind. Still, I come. I am as open to the truth as I can be. If you exist, I want you to speak to me. And, furthermore, I want you to know that if you do exist and if you convince me that Jesus Christ is really your Son and died for my sin, then I promise to submit myself to him and follow him all the days of my life." That you can do if you are an honest seeker after truth. If you do that, God will already have taken the initiative in saving you and will already be leading you out of darkness into his light.

13

God with Us

John 1:14

The Word became flesh and made his dwelling among us. We have seen his glory, the glory of the One and Only, who came from the Father, full of grace and truth.

I wish it were possible to approach John 1:14 as though reading it for the first time. The verse contains something that was new and quite startling when it was first written, and yet for us who read it nearly two thousand years later it has become commonplace. We read: "The Word became flesh and made his dwelling among us. We have seen his glory, the glory of the One and Only, who came from the Father, full of grace and truth." This was the great sentence for which the Gospel of John was written. It tells us—inexplicable as it may be—that God became man. Nevertheless, because we have heard that verse from childhood, we read it and are often strangely unmoved.

The Church Fathers

Fortunately, we can capture a sense of the original, shattering newness of this sentence from the writings of the church fathers, particularly those who were converted to Christianity out of paganism. Augustine, who became the greatest theologian of the early church, was no mean scholar. He had drunk deeply at the spring of Platonic philosophy. He had spent years soaking up the religious and philosophical system of the Manichaeans. Yet, as he said later, although he had read all about the Word in non-Christian books—that the Word was God and had been active in the creation of the world—nevertheless, that the "Word became flesh" he had not read there.

Another church father, Junius the younger, has also written of his reaction to first reading these verses. "My father, who was frequently reading the New Testament, and had long observed with grief the progress I had made in infidelity, had put that book in my way in his library, in order to attract my attention, if it might please God to bless his design, though without giving me the least intimation of it. Here, therefore, I unwittingly opened the New Testament thus providentially laid before me. At the very first view, although I was deeply engaged in other thoughts, that grand chapter of the evangelist and apostle presented itself to me—'In the beginning was the Word, and the Word was God.' I read part of the chapter, and was so affected that I instantly became struck with the divinity of the argument, and the majesty and authority of the composition, as infinitely surpassing the highest flights of human eloquence. My body shuddered. My mind was in amazement, and I was so agitated the whole day that I scarcely knew who I was. Nor did the agitation cease, but continued till it was at last soothed by a humble faith in him who was made flesh and dwelt among us."

This was the astounding new thing—that the Word of God could enter into our history as a man so that men could see him. In him men could behold God's glory.

He Pitched His Tent

Actually, as John wrote this verse he was doubtlessly referring to the great days of Israel's desert wanderings; and he was making the point that, although those days were great days for Israel, in our day something much better has happened. It involves all men. We know that John was making this contrast, because of an unusual word that occurs in the verse. In English it is the word "dwelling." We have it in the phrase, "The Word became flesh and made his dwelling among us." Literally, the phrase means "to dwell in a tent." So we could also translate the verse: "The Word became flesh, and pitched his tent among us," or "The Word became flesh, and tabernacled among us." This last translation is particularly significant because the word refers beyond any question to the portable wilderness tabernacle or temple of the Hebrew nation. The tabernacle was the center of their worship and the most important single object in their camp.

In all, the tabernacle was about forty-five feet long and about fifteen feet wide; that is, it was three times as long as it was wide. And it was divided into two distinct parts, the inner section being in the form of a square fifteen feet by fifteen feet, and the outer section being twice as long as it was wide. It was made of boards covered with curtains. The inner chamber contained the ark of the covenant. The outer chamber contained the golden altar of incense, the table of shewbread, and the golden candlestick. This entire

structure stood in a courtyard surrounded by curtains of pure linen rising
to a height of over eight feet. The courtyard measured 175 feet long and
about 87 feet wide. In the courtyard there was a great brazen altar for sacrifices and a laver for purifications.

Everything about the tabernacle—its dimensions, furnishings, colors, functions, and arrangement—was designed to communicate spiritual truth.
Hence, many of its functions were previews of the functions Jesus Christ
would fulfill when he eventually pitched his tent among us. We can list several of the more obvious parallels.

1. The tabernacle was *the center of Israel's camp*. We see this in the laws ordering the distribution of the various tribes in the Jewish encampment as
recorded in the early chapters of the Book of Numbers. On the eastern side
of the tabernacle were the tribes of Judah, Issachar, and Zebulun. These set
out first when the nation began to break camp. On the south were Reuben,
Simeon, and Gad. These marched second. After these tribes came the Levites,
who surrounded the tabernacle in the encampment. Ephraim, Manasseh,
and Benjamin were on the west. Dan, Asher, and Naphtali always camped to
the north. These came last when the people were on the move. We see this
position of the tabernacle reinforced by the instructions given to the Levites
for their place in the march; for we read in Numbers 2:17, "Then the Tent
of Meeting and the camp of the Levites will set out in the middle of the
camps. They will set out in the same order as they encamp, each in his own
place under his standard." This is highly significant in reference to Jesus
Christ, for he is the center of the Christian encampment. He is our gathering place. This is why Jesus could say, "But I, when I am lifted up from the
earth, will draw all men to myself" (John 12:32). He told his disciples: "For
where two or three come together in my name, there am I with them" (Matt.
18:20).

2. The tabernacle was *the place where the law of Moses was preserved*. The first
two tables of stone, which had been given to Moses by God, were broken
(Exodus 32); but the second set was deposited in the ark of the covenant
within the Holy of Holies of the tabernacle for safekeeping. This also speaks
to us of Christ Jesus. Speaking of his perfect obedience to God and of his
perfect keeping of the law, the Lord Jesus Christ said, "for I always do what
pleases him" (John 8:29). In the same manner Psalm 40 is prophesying
Christ's perfect obedience when it reports him as saying, "I desire to do your
will, O my God; your law is within my heart" (Ps. 40:8).

3. The tabernacle was *the dwelling place of God*. This was no doubt largely
symbolic during the Old Testament period, although it was symbolized in a
very striking way. Within the Holy of Holies, between the wings of the cherubim that stretched out over the covering of the ark of the covenant, there
was the shekinah glory that symbolized God's presence. The shekinah was
what we would call "light." At times it was hidden by the cloud that spread
out over the tabernacle. At other times it flashed out in judgment against

some evil in the camp of Israel. The glory within the Holy of Holies symbolized the presence of God. Thus, John, who knew that God had been revealed in the flesh in Jesus, could write, "We have seen his glory, the glory of the One and Only, who came from the Father."

4. Because the tabernacle was the place where God dwelt among his people, it was also *the place of revelation*. It was the place where God met with men and spoke to them. For this reason the tabernacle was also called "the tent of meeting," a phrase that occurs scores of times in the Old Testament.

The second tabernacle, Jesus Christ, is the place where God meets with men today and speaks to them. If you have ever visited a mint, you know that the coins manufactured there are produced by large presses that stamp out a whole sheet of coins at one time. A sheet of silver or alloy is fed into the machine, there is a clump, and a shower of coins tumbles out into a basket. I am told that a skilled engraver can take a coin, examine it under a magnifying glass, and tell not only the actual die from which the coin came but even the condition of the die, which cannot be seen where it is within the press. It is on the basis of such an examination that the dies are replaced when they show signs of wear. In the same way, we cannot see God. The Bible reports God as saying to Moses: "You cannot see my face, for no one may see me and live" (Exod. 33:20). Yet God is revealed to us perfectly in Jesus, in whom we see the Father. The Bible tells us that, like the coin from the mint, he is the "exact representation" of God's invisible person (Heb. 1:3).

5. The tabernacle was also *the place where sacrifices were made*. In the outer court of the tabernacle, on the east side near the only opening into the courtyard, stood the brazen altar on which sacrifices burned continually. For anyone approaching the tabernacle from outside, this was the first of the furnishings of the tabernacle seen by him. This was significant, for it indicated that there is no approach to God except by means of the sacrifice. "Without the shedding of blood there is no forgiveness [of sin]" (Heb. 9:22; cf. Lev. 17:11). In the same way, today there is no approach to God except through faith in the sacrifice provided by Jesus Christ, who in the tabernacle of his flesh offered himself up on Calvary.

This is the answer to the supreme question of man in all ages of human history. It is far more important than any scientific question or political question. How can a sinful man, corrupt by nature, approach a holy God? We all need God, but how can we find him? How can we come close enough to him to understand him? How can we become acceptable before him? How can we know forgiveness for sin? How can we know God's peace? How can we find fellowship with the One in whom we live and move and have our being? The answer is in the tabernacle and in the Christ whom the tabernacle prefigures. At the cross of Christ the perfect sacrifice is performed; Jesus dies in our place. He is the Lamb of God that takes away the sin of the world. On the basis of his sacrifice, we who were once children of wrath have now become God's children and can approach God the Father.

6. Finally, the tabernacle was *the place where the people of Israel worshiped.* We worship in the presence of the Lord Jesus Christ today. The people of Israel brought their sacrifices to the tabernacle, gave their gifts there, and asked their questions. On occasion they were summoned to hear the voice of God. Their priests ministered in the temple enclosure. In the same way, we gather around the person of our Lord, who regulates our worship and receives our homage. It is through Jesus alone that we have access by one Spirit unto the Father (Eph. 2:18).

> Thou art the Way: to thee alone
>   From sin and death we flee;
> And he who would the Father seek
>   Must seek him, Lord, by thee.
> Thou art the Truth: thy Word alone
>   True wisdom can impart;
> Thou only canst inform the mind,
>   And purify the heart.
> Thou art the Life; the rending tomb
>   Proclaims thy conquering arm,
> And those who put their trust in thee
>   Nor death nor hell shall harm.
> Thou art the Way, the Truth, the Life:
>   Grant us that Way to know,
> That Truth to keep, that Life to win,
>   Whose joys eternal flow.

Christ's Glory Beheld

The final point of our study is that when Jesus Christ pitched his tent among us, he did so in order that men and women might see him and thus come to know God. John indicates this when he observes: "And we beheld his glory."

This happened in a very literal way with the first disciples about whom John is certainly speaking in this verse, for they saw the glory of Jesus during the days of his flesh. We must not miss the point that John has constructed his account of the first momentous week in the earthly ministry of Jesus Christ to emphasize this great truth. Beginning with the nineteenth verse of this chapter, John begins an account of the most important events of seven consecutive days, beginning with the day on which John the Baptist received the delegation of priests and Levites from Jerusalem and ending on the day in which Jesus changed the water into wine at Cana of Galilee in the presence of his disciples. Significantly enough, the story of the wedding (and therefore also the story of the events of this first week) ends with the statement: "This, the first of his miraculous signs, Jesus performed at Cana in Galilee. He thus revealed his glory, and his disciples put their faith in him" (John

2:11). This was the reason for his coming. He came that men might see his glory and believe on him.

It is also true, however, that the experience of the early disciples is duplicated in all who believe in the Lord of glory today, for Paul writes of the experience of all Christians when he says that "we, who with unveiled faces all reflect the Lord's glory, are being transformed into his likeness with ever-increasing glory, which comes from the Lord, who is the Spirit" (2 Cor. 3:18).

Is that your experience? Have you beheld the glory of the eternal Son of God who tabernacled among us and who is revealed to us today by means of his Holy Spirit? If it is, then you are called upon to bear a witness to him, as John and the other disciples did. Can you testify to what he has done for you and in your life? I can testify to what Christ has done for me. I look at the second chapter of Ephesians and find myself placed among those who were "dead in . . . transgressions and sins . . . gratifying the cravings of our sinful nature and following its desires and thoughts" but of whom it can now be said, "But because of his great love for us, God, who is rich in mercy, made us alive with Christ even when we were dead in transgressions" (Eph. 6:1-6). He lifted my vision to see Christ, who is altogether lovely, and has drawn me toward himself with bonds of love, so that now I seek to serve him and exalt his name before men.

You say, "Is that something special?" Not at all. It is merely the experience of every true believer. To the giving of such a testimony each of us is called. What a vision! The glory of Jesus Christ! What a task! To make him known to a darkened and sinful world!

14

Grace and Truth

John 1:14

The Word became flesh and made his dwelling among us. We have seen his glory, the glory of the One and Only, who came from the Father, full of grace and truth.

Dr. Francis Schaeffer, founder of the L'Abri Fellowship in Switzerland, tells a story about a prominent American government leader. He had been invited to address a group of student leaders in Washington and had chosen to speak on the theme of restoring values in our culture. When he had finished there was a moment of silence. Then one student arose—a man from Harvard University—and asked, "Sir, upon what base do you build your values?" It was a brilliant question but a tragic moment for the speaker, for he simply looked down and replied, "I do not know." Here was a man who was calling upon the youth of America to return to a system of moral values, but he was offering them nothing to build upon. As Dr. Schaeffer remarks, he was a man trying to tell his hearers not to steal the company funds and run off to Morocco and yet giving no reason why they should not.

We miss the point of the illustration if we think that the experience of the speaker was unique. It is not unique at all. In fact, it is typical of millions of persons in our day who earnestly want to believe in a system of values and yet have no real basis for their beliefs. They are confused about life. They do not know what is right or wrong, true or false. They want to believe that there is a thing called truth. They want to believe that there is a God who is full of love and is gracious. They want to believe that life has meaning. But they have no valid basis for any of these beliefs. To these people the Bible speaks with special relevance when it says that there is a basis for the demands of ethics, belief in goodness, and truth.

What is the basis? This is the point of what is perhaps the most important theological statement in John's Gospel, the statement contained in the verse that we have already been considering: "The Word became flesh and made his dwelling among us. We have seen his glory, the glory of the One and Only, who came from the Father, full of grace and truth" (John 1:14). The verse states that Jesus Christ is the basis on which we can know that God is good and that the universe has meaning.

God's Grace

The first thing that John says was revealed in Jesus Christ was grace, God's grace. Because of this we know that God is gracious. What is grace? Grace is simply the unmerited favor of God toward humanity. The New Scofield Bible says, "Grace is the kindness and love of God our Savior toward man." Dr. Harry A. Ironside wrote, "Grace is the very opposite of merit. . . . Grace is not only undeserved favor, but it is favor shown to the one who has deserved the very opposite." The Bible expresses it when it says that "God demonstrates his own love for us in this: While we were still sinners, Christ died for us" (Rom. 5:8). In other words, God is gracious toward us, not on the basis of what we have done but solely because it is his nature to be gracious.

In one sense, of course, all men are recipients of God's grace. That is what theologians have called "common grace." When the human race sinned in Adam, the entire race came under judgment. The race deserved nothing. God did not owe it anything. If God had simply taken Adam and Eve in the moment they had sinned and cast them into the lake of fire, he would still have been just; and the angels could still have sung,

Holy, holy, holy
is the Lord God Almighty,
who was, and is, and is to come.
Revelation 4:8

Moreover, if God had allowed the race to increase to an extent similar to what it has increased to today, and then had brushed it aside into everlasting torment and judgment, God would have been just even then. This is a most important truth. God does not owe man anything. Consequently, all the blessings that people enjoy are the result of God's grace.

Let me put this as clearly as I am able to before we move on. If you are not a believer in the Lord Jesus Christ, you are a recipient of God's common grace whether you acknowledge it or not. If you enjoy good health, that is common grace. If you are not on the poverty rolls but instead enjoy the comfort of a home and plenty to eat, that is common grace. If you have a good job and are able to hold it down because of your natural abilities and hard work, that is common grace. The list could be endless. There is no person living who has not been the recipient of God's common grace in some way. If you think that it is not of grace that you receive your blessings but that you deserve them, you are merely showing your ignorance of spiritual things.

Yet, if such grace is wonderful, the grace that is shown in Jesus Christ is even more wonderful. This is "saving grace," for this is a grace that does not spare men merely for a certain limited time; it redeems them for time and eternity. It transforms them from what the Bible calls "children of wrath" into God's sons.

A great example of such a transformation is John Newton. In his very early years Newton had been raised in a Christian home in England; but his parents died when he was only six years old and he was sent to live with an unbelieving relative. There Christianity was mocked, and he was abused. Finally, to escape these conditions, Newton ran away to sea, joining the British navy. He fell into gross sin; it gained a hold on him. He eventually deserted the navy and went to one of the worst areas of Africa. As he tells it, he went there for only one purpose and that was "to sin his fill."

In Africa Newton fell in with a Portuguese slave trader. When the trader went away on slave-hunting expeditions, as he often did, the power in the compound passed to the slave trader's African wife. She hated white men and took out her venom on Newton. He was cruelly abused, so much so that at times he was forced to eat his food off the dusty floor like a dog.

After a time Newton fled from the compound and made his way to the coast, where he signaled a slave ship. The captain of the ship was disappointed at first when he learned that Newton had no ivory to sell. But when he found that Newton could navigate a vessel, he made Newton a shipmate. Even then Newton got into trouble. One day he broke into the ship's supply of rum and got so drunk that he fell overboard and would have drowned if an officer had not saved him by thrusting a harpoon into his thigh and hauling him back into the ship. The harpoon made such a wound that years later Newton could still put his hand into the fist-sized opening.

Near the end of one voyage, as they were nearing Scotland, the ship ran afoul of bad weather, was blown off course, and began to sink. Newton was sent down into the hold to work the pumps. He was terrified. He thought surely the ship would sink and he would drown. For days he worked the pumps, and as he pumped the water out of the hold he began to cry out to God. Bible verses about God's love and the death of Christ that he had heard as a child and thought he had forgotten came to his memory, and as he remembered them he was miraculously transformed. He was born again. When the storm had passed and he was again in England, he went on to become a highly educated preacher and teacher of the Word of God in that country, even preaching before the queen. It was of this storm and this conversion that William Cowper, the poet, wrote:

> God moves in a mysterious way
> His wonders to perform;
> He plants his footsteps in the sea
> And rides upon the storm.

Newton himself, who, through this experience, became in England a great proclaimer of God's grace, declared:

> Amazing grace! How sweet the sound,
> That saved a wretch like me!
> I once was lost, but now am found,
> Was blind, but now I see.

Newton was a great preacher of grace, and the fact is not at all surprising. For he had learned, as all Christians have learned, that God is exceedingly gracious. He had been assured of this as he had thought upon the death and resurrection of the Lord Jesus Christ through whom God's grace is known.

Truth

The second aspect of God's nature that John speaks of in this verse is truth. John tells us that this too is revealed in Jesus Christ. Truth is a great word in John's writings. In all it occurs about twenty-four times. This is the first reference, and in almost every case (including this one) it is related to the character of God.

We find this in the rest of the Bible also. For instance, we read in Deuteronomy and Isaiah that God is truth (Deut. 32:4; Isa. 65:16). We read that God desires truth in our inward parts (Ps. 51:6). We are told that the Lord hates a lying tongue (Prov. 6:17). Jesus declared that he was himself the truth: "I am the way and the truth and the life" (John 14:6). Jesus called the Holy Spirit the Spirit of truth (John 14:17; 15:26; 16:13). He spoke of the Word of God as the truth (John 17:17). When we put all these statements together we find that God the Father is truth, that God the Son is truth, that God the Holy Spirit is truth, and that everything that takes its nature from God is also characterized by truth. In other words, truth is of the character of God. We who are Christians must, therefore, for that very reason, take our stand upon it.

We do not deal with the opinions of men when we deal with Christian doctrine. We deal with truth. Thus, a person's eternal destiny depends upon his relationship to the eternal truth in Jesus Christ.

I have been impressed by the extent to which we have seen the opposite of this in our day. That is, we have entered a period of history in which truth is supposed to be relative and in which no system of ideas is recognized by the majority of all men to be binding. I am impressed too by the fact that all the great present-day apologists have seen this.

One man who has been pointing this out is Francis A. Schaeffer. He points out that people no longer believe in truth. They did believe in truth before the impact of the philosophy of Hegel. In that day, if one fact was true, the opposite of that fact was believed to be false. There was antithesis, and what was true or false then was believed to be true or false forever. After Hegel, the idea grew that reality was to be represented not by what is true as opposed to what is false but rather by what is true *now* or, worse yet, by what is true only for the *individual*. Under this system *my* truth is not necessarily *your* truth, and what is true for me *now* may not be true for me *tomorrow*.

"But what does that mean for our day?" you may ask. The answer is that we are dealing with truth, real truth, when we present the claims of Jesus Christ and of Christianity. What happens most often when you testify to the saving power of the Lord Jesus Christ today? Isn't it true that the most common reaction is simply: "Fine; that's good for you. I'm glad it helps you, but, after all, what you say is only relatively true. If something else helps me, then that is perfectly valid also." This is the view we need to fight against.

C. S. Lewis is another Christian apologist who saw the changing attitudes toward truth. Here is an example of his insight from the first of *The Screwtape Letters,* in which a senior devil named Screwtape gives some basic instruction to a junior tempter named Wormwood: "I note what you say about guiding your patient's reading and taking care that he sees a good deal of his materialist friend. But are you not being a trifle naive? It sounds as if you supposed that *argument* was the way to keep him out of Enemy's clutches. That might have been so if he had lived a few centuries earlier. At that time the humans still knew pretty well when a thing was proved and when it was not; and if it was proved they really believed it. They still connected thinking with doing and were prepared to alter their way of life as the result of a chain of reasoning. But what with the weekly press and other such weapons we have largely altered that. Your man has been accustomed, ever since he was a boy, to have a dozen incompatible philosophies dancing about together inside his head. He doesn't think of doctrines as primarily 'true' or 'false,' but as 'academic' or 'practical,' 'outworn' or 'contemporary,' 'conventional' or 'ruthless.' Jargon, not argument, is your best ally in keeping him from the Church."[1]

That is true. For today, even in the books of theology, we are presented with the idea that Christian doctrine is not so much true as it is helpful. And the conclusion is that you can take it or leave it, sift it or drop it, all according to its practical value to you personally. This is diabolical. It is not the philosophical basis of Christianity.

Instead, when you come to the gospel of the Lord Jesus Christ, you come to a declaration that certain things are really true for all time, whatever they may mean to you personally. And furthermore, we are told that it is on the basis of such truth that you as an individual will be forced to give a reckoning.

You say, "But what are these truths?" Let me give you a summary. First, there is the truth about man. We have been hearing for generations that man is doing better and better, and that given time enough things will turn out all right and all his problems will be solved. How foolish! Given enough time things will turn out exactly as they have been turning out since the beginning of the world. The reason for this is that there is something wrong in the heart of man. The Bible calls it sin. It may also be called rebellion, selfishness, pride, or any number of similar words. It is the same principle. The truth about man is that man carries his greatest problem about within him.

People always want to blame someone else, even the devil. There is a wonderful story about a little girl called Mary Ann who one day got into a fight with her brother. The mother stopped the fighting by yanking Mary up sharply and sitting her down in a corner. She asked, "Mary Ann, why did you let the devil put it into your heart to pull your brother's hair and kick his shins?" Mary Ann thought a minute and then said, "Well, maybe the devil did put it into my head to pull brother's hair, but kicking his shins was my own idea." That was tremendous theology, and it shows what is wrong with the world. It is not what the devil, the environment, or our history makes us do that makes the world such a bad place, but it is what *we* do. The truth about the problems of man is that man himself is the problem.

The second truth that we receive from Christianity is the truth about God. This is most necessary, for there are profound misconceptions about him. People think of God as removed, arbitrary, unconcerned, indulgent. But God declares that he is love and truth and justice and that he cares enough about men and women to die for them in order to bring them back to himself.

There is the truth about the atonement. People look to the death of Jesus and call it an example of a man who was deluded but who meant well. Others call it a tragedy. Some call it a demonstration of outstanding courage. That is not what the atonement means. It is true that there are aspects of Christ's death that relate to us as a moving example. Peter writes to encourage those who were suffering from persecution in his day, saying, "Christ suffered for you, leaving you an example" (1 Peter 2:21). But even as he says this he takes pains to point out the real meaning of the death of Christ by showing that it was essentially a death for others. "Christ suffered *for you.*" And he immediately adds, as if to give that meaning, "He himself bore our sins in his body on the tree, so that we might die to sins and live for righteousness; by his wounds you have been healed" (1 Peter 2:24). That is the truth about the atonement. Christ died for us in order that "whoever believes in him shall not perish but have eternal life" (John 3:16).

Do you believe these things? The truth about them did not come to the world through philosophy or through any other form of human speculation. Truth came into the world through Jesus Christ. It is recorded for men in the Bible. Your eternal destiny will depend upon the way you respond to it and upon whether or not you will commit yourself to Jesus Christ. Will you do it? To do it is to learn that God is indeed gracious and to uncover the only valid basis for truth and sound morality.

15

The Unique Christ

John 1:15-18

John testifies concerning him. He cries out, saying, "This was he of whom I said, 'He who comes after me has surpassed me because he was before me.'" From the fullness of his grace we have all received one blessing after another. For the law was given through Moses; grace and truth came through Jesus Christ. No one has ever seen God, but God the One and Only, who is at the Father's side, has made him known.

In France every child who goes to Sunday school learns John 3:16, as children do the world over. He recites it like this: "Car Dieu a tant aimé le monde qu'il a donné son Fils unique." Literally translated this means: "For God loved the world so much that he gave his *unique* Son." Unique means being without a like or equal, single in kind or excellence, matchless. It is an important word, and it is particularly important at just this point in our study since it occurs twice in the space of five verses. In Greek the word is *monogenes;* the New International Version says "One and Only"; the French say *unique.* In each case, however, the same teaching is in view.

In verse 14 John speaks of having beheld Christ's glory, "the glory of the *One and Only,* who came from the Father." In verse 18 we are told, "No one has ever seen God, but God the *One and Only,* who is at the Father's side, has made him known." We see at once, then, that Jesus is unique because there is no one quite like him (in fact, with the exception of the Father himself, not at all like him) and because he can do for men what no one else can do.

97

Jesus is unique in every aspect of his being. He is unique in his person, birth, doctrine, works, miracles, death, resurrection, and future triumphs. In the verses that are included within these two uses of the word in John's first chapter (vv. 15–18), four things are singled out particularly: (1) Jesus is unique in his origins; (2) he is unique as the channel of God's blessings; (3) he is unique as the source of grace and truth; and (4) he is unique because he is the only one in whom you and I may see God. We need to look at each of these carefully.

Unique in His Origin

In the first place, Jesus Christ is unique in his origins, for John the Baptist, who is actually speaking these words, declares, "This was he of whom I said, 'He who comes after me has surpassed me because he was before me'" (v. 15).

It is possible on a theoretical level at least that this verse could have three meanings. William Barclay points out that since Jesus was actually six months younger than John, the Baptist could be saying, "He who is my junior in age has been advanced before me." John could also be saying, "I was in the field before Jesus, I occupied the center of the stage before he did; my hand was laid to the work before his was; but all that I was doing was to prepare the way for his coming; I was only the advance guard of the main force and the herald of the king." John could have been saying either of those two things. But in actual fact it is highly unlikely that these were any more than fleeting thoughts in his mind. John the Baptist was impressed with the uniqueness of Christ's person, and the phrase should therefore mean (as the evangelist intends it to mean) that Jesus was entirely without historical origins. He was preexistent. This is clearly the equivalent of declaring him to be God.

Unique in his origins! How exalted this makes the Lord Jesus! Donald Grey Barnhouse has written in *The Cross through the Open Tomb:* "The history of every other human being begins at birth: but the Lord Jesus Christ exists eternally as the Second Person of the Godhead. Before He was born at Bethlehem, He lived; He was one with the Father in essence and being. Before He came to earth as a baby, He walked among men and revealed Himself to them. The Old Testament, which was completed four centuries before His birth, contains many stories of His appearing among men before He came as babe, child, and man."[1] Abraham saw Christ in his day; for Jesus declared, "Abraham rejoiced at the thought of seeing my day; he saw it and was glad" (John 8:56). He later added, "before Abraham was born, I am" (v. 58). Isaiah saw Jesus when he had his vision of the Lord high and lifted up (Isa. 6:1–3), for John refers to this vision, saying, "Isaiah said this because he saw Jesus' glory and spoke about him" (John 12:41). There were others.

It is no wonder, therefore, that in almost every instance in which the writers of the New Testament refer in depth to Christ's person they refer almost instinctively to his preexistence. The author of Hebrews begins by writing: "In the past God spoke to our forefathers through the prophets at many times and in various ways, but in these last days he has spoken to us by his Son, whom he appointed heir of all things, and through whom he made the universe" (Heb. 1:1–2). Paul in the Book of Philippians writes: "Your attitude should be the same as that of Christ Jesus: Who, being in very nature God, did not consider equality with God something to be grasped, but made himself nothing, taking the very nature of a servant, being made in human likeness. And being found in appearance as a man, he humbled himself and became obedient to death—even death on a cross!" (Phil. 2:5–8).

Some people consider Jesus Christ only a man, and indeed he is a man. Some point to him only as an example, and he is that also. But if that is all you can see in Jesus Christ, then your view of him is entirely misleading. For the first and most important thing to be said about him is that he is without any historical beginnings and that this is the equivalent of calling him God. Everything he did and said takes its meaning from this great truth and flows from it.

Source of All Blessings

The second point made in these verses is that Jesus is the unique channel of all God's material and spiritual blessings. This is what is meant when we are told, "From the fullness of his grace we have all received one blessing after another" (v. 16).

On one level this verse is a statement that all men have been recipients of God's grace. This is "common grace," the type of grace discussed previously. Everything truly good that comes into your life—health, prosperity, knowledge, friendships, good times, whatever it is—comes from God. This is true whether or not you recognize him as the source of such blessings.

In the Book of Hosea there is a story that illustrates this truth. Hosea was a preacher, and God had told Hosea to marry a woman who was to prove unfaithful to him. He was to do this as an illustration of the relationship between God and Israel because God had taken Israel to himself as a wife and she had proved unfaithful spiritually. The object and goal of the illustration was that Hosea was to remain faithful to her and love her, even after she had left him, because God remains faithful even when people turn from him to serve other gods.

The time came, some years after Hosea's wife had left, that she fell into poverty and ended up living with a man who no longer had enough money to take care of her. At this point God said, "Hosea, I want you to go down to the marketplace and buy the things she needs, because that is the way I do with my people. They run away from me, and I pay the bills." So we read in Hosea, "Their mother has been unfaithful and has conceived them in disgrace. She said, 'I will go after my lovers, who give me my food and my water, my wool and my linen, my oil and my drink.' . . . She has not acknowledged that I was the one who gave her the grain, the new wine and oil, who lavished on her the silver and gold" (Hos. 2:5, 8).[2] So it is! We run from God, but he pays the bills; he still takes care of us. He takes care of you. We need to learn that Jesus Christ is unique as the source of all material and spiritual blessings, even when we fail to acknowledge his goodness or thank him for them.

There is another sense in which Jesus is the source of all blessing, however. He himself is a blessing; and the true Christian—not the non-Christian—has an opportunity to be enriched by him personally. We are apt to tire of his presence because of the sin in us and to be lured by the pleasures of the world. The world does have pleasures. The trouble is simply that they do not satisfy us long or satisfy us completely. They are much like a Chinese dinner: you eat it, it tastes good, but an hour later you are hungry again. Jesus Christ is not like that. He said, "If you are thirsty, come to me and I will give you satisfying water. If you are hungry come to me; I am the bread of life. He who drinks of me and feeds on me will never hunger and never thirst." Have you done that? Are you doing that today?

If you have once known the Lord Jesus Christ and have turned back to the world's pleasure for a time, I guarantee that the world will prove increasingly insipid and empty to you. One hymnwriter knew this experience at one point in his life, and he has left us a poignant verse about it. He wrote:

> How tedious and tasteless the hours
> When Jesus no longer I see!
> Sweet prospects, sweet birds, and sweet flowers,
> Have all lost their sweetness for me!

Is that your experience? It need not be, for you can turn to Christ again and find him truly satisfying. Another hymn writer composed a verse which tells the other side of the story.

> Hast thou heard Him, seen Him, known Him?
> Is not thine a captured heart?
> Chief among ten thousand own Him,
> Joyful, choose the better part.
> What has stript the seeming beauty
> From the idols of the earth?
> not a sense of right or duty,
> But the sight of peerless worth.
> Draw and win and fill completely,
> Till the cup o'er flow the brim;
> What have we to do with idols
> Who have companied with Him?

Jesus! Unique in his origins, unique as the source of all material and spiritual blessings.

Knowledge of God

Finally, in verses 17 and 18 the apostle John records two other things about the uniqueness of Jesus. First, he says that Jesus is unique as the source of grace and truth. "For the law was given through Moses; grace and truth came through Jesus Christ" (v. 17).

This verse suggests a contrast that gives the words "grace and truth" a slightly different meaning than they had three verses earlier. The contrast is between the law with all its regulations and the new era of salvation by grace through faith apart from the works of the law that has come with Jesus Christ. It is a great contrast. Under the law, God demands righteousness from people; under grace, he gives it to people. Under law, righteousness is based on Moses and good works; under grace, it is based on Christ and Christ's character. Under law, blessings accompany obedience; under grace, God bestows his blessings as a free gift. The law is powerless to secure righteousness and life for a sinful race. Grace came in its fullness with Christ's death and resurrection to make sinners righteous before God.

Then, in the last place, we are told that the Lord Jesus Christ is unique because he is the only One in whom you and I may see God. John puts it like this: "No one has ever seen God, but God the One and Only, who is at the Father's side, has made him known" (v. 18).

No one in the ancient world would have disagreed with the first part of that statement—"No one has ever seen God"—for, as William Barclay notes in his commentary, "In the ancient world men were fascinated and depressed and frustrated by what they regarded as the infinite distance and the utter unknowability of God. . . . Xenophanes had said, 'Guesswork is over all.' Plato had said, 'Never man and God can meet.' Celsus had laughed at the way that the Christians called God 'Father,' because 'God is away beyond everything.' At the best, Apuleius said, men could catch a glimpse of God as a lightning flash lights up a dark night—one split second of illumination, and then the dark."[3] Even the Jews would have thought this way, for they knew that God had spoken to Moses in the Old Testament, saying, "You cannot see my face, for no one may see me and live" (Exod. 33:20). There would have been no disagreement at all when John the Baptist declared that no one could see God.

Yet John did not stop with that statement. It is true that no man can see God and live, as God said to Moses; but it is also true that in Christ God came to men in a way that enabled men to know him. In Jesus Christ the character of God may be known. There is no true knowledge of God apart from him. Do you want to believe that God is loving? Good! But do not base your belief on some fantasy of your imagination. What could be less reliable than that? Instead, base it on the revelation of God's love in Christ and at Calvary. Do you want to believe that God is powerful, able to bring a transformation in your life? If so, do not depend on your own wishful thinking. Look to Jesus Christ. He will reveal it; because the same One who died for your sin also rose again in power and now lives to apply that same death-conquering power to the lives of those who follow him. Are you searching for wisdom? Look to the One who has become for us wisdom from God—that is, our "righteousness, holiness and redemption" (1 Cor. 1:30).

Three Problems

What is your reaction to these things? Do you know the truth of them personally? One of the most memorable sermons that I have ever come across was preached by the late Emil Brunner at the Fraumünster Kirche in Zurich, Switzerland. It was based on the phrase "faith, hope, and love." The points were these. Every man has a past, a present, and a future. Every man has a problem in his past, a problem in his present, and a problem in his future. The problem in our past is sin, but God has an answer to that problem. The answer is faith, faith in the death and resurrection of the Lord Jesus Christ. The problem in our future is death, but God has an answer to that problem also. The answer to that problem is hope, hope in Christ's return based on the fact of his historical resurrection and his promises. The problem in our present is hate, and God's answer to that problem is love. It is the love of Christ lived out in the lives of those who trust him.

Brunner was entirely right. And he was right not only in highlighting the three great problems; he was right in pointing to the unique Christ as the answer. Has Christ become the answer to the problems in your life? He is the only One who will ever answer them completely.

16

How to Witness for Jesus Christ

John 1:19–28

Now this was John's testimony when the Jews of Jerusalem sent priests and Levites to ask him who he was. He did not fail to confess, but confessed freely, "I am not the Christ."

They asked him, "Then who are you? Are you Elijah?"

He said, "I am not."

"Are you the Prophet?"

He answered, "No."

Finally they said, "Who are you? Give us an answer to take back to those who sent us. What do you say about yourself?"

John replied in the words of Isaiah the prophet, "I am the voice of one calling in the desert, 'Make straight the way for the Lord.'"

Now some Pharisees who had been sent questioned him, "Why then do you baptize if you are not the Christ, nor Elijah, nor the Prophet?"

"I baptize with water," John replied, "but among you stands one you do not know. He is the one who comes after me, the thongs of whose sandals I am not worthy to untie."

This all happened at Bethany on the other side of the Jordan, where John was baptizing.

We come now to the first major division in the Gospel of John. The material of the prologue goes through verse 18. With verse 19 the reader is launched at last into the events of the first momentous week of Jesus' ministry.

In all, seven days are involved, beginning with the day John the Baptist met with the delegation that had come to him from Jerusalem and ending with the day Jesus attended the wedding in Cana. On the first day (vv. 19–28), John the Baptist confesses that he is not the Messiah; that is, he denies that he possesses any independent importance of his own. On the second day (vv. 29–34), John identifies Jesus as the Lamb of God, for whom he had come

103

to prepare the way. On the third day (vv. 35–39), John's testimony causes two of his own disciples to follow Jesus. On the fourth day (vv. 40–42), one of these disciples, Andrew, finds his own brother, Peter, and brings him to Jesus. On the fifth day (vv. 43–51), Jesus calls Philip, and Philip calls Nathanael. The journey to Galilee occurs on the sixth day. The seventh day (2:1–11) centers around Jesus, his mother, and his disciples at the wedding.[1]

In no other Gospel are the marks of the passing of time so clearly noted as in John. And what is perhaps even more significant, in no other Gospel are the opening events of the narrative fraught with such lasting significance.

The very fact that the tone of the Gospel changes at this point means that our handling of it must change also. Up to verse 19 we have been studying the Gospel almost verse by verse, and the eighteen verses we have considered so far have required no less than fifteen separate studies. From this point on we will move faster. In five studies we will cover the remaining half of the first chapter to see what it teaches about the way a believer can witness to the Lord Jesus Christ. We will then return to the same general ground in four more studies to uncover the teaching of the chapter about baptism. Finally, we will return once more to pick up several of the themes remaining.

In this study we begin with the witness of John the Baptist to the Lord Jesus Christ, and ask the question: How can a believer in the Lord Jesus Christ witness for him? This is an important question, particularly since the writer of the Gospel so obviously had it in mind as he composed this narrative section.

Chosen to Witness

I suppose that the greatest mistake a person can make as he reads about the witness of John the Baptist is to think that the task of the witness was somehow peculiar to John. No doubt there are many who think this, just as there are many who think that the task of witnessing today should be fulfilled primarily by ministers. But this is an error, and a serious one at that. Witnessing is every Christian's job. When Jesus Christ spoke to his disciples, saying, "You did not choose me, but I chose you and appointed you to go and bear fruit—fruit that will last" (John 15:16), it was evident that salvation consisted not so much in the fact that they had chosen him but that he had chosen them and commissioned them and us to the task of telling others about him.

An acceptance of this task was, many believe, the single most important factor in the astounding outreach and expansion of the early Christian church. It was not simply that Paul and the other leaders carried the gospel to the farthest corners of the Roman world. In fact, many of the early leaders were not particularly zealous about the missionary effort. It was rather that all Christians—small and great, rich and poor, slaves and freedmen—made it their consuming passion to tell others about the Lord.

Tertullian, writing slightly before and after the year A.D. 200, declared in his *Apology:* "We are but of yesterday, and we have filled every place among you—cities, islands, fortresses, towns, marketplaces, the very camp, tribes, companies, palace, senate, forum—we have left nothing to you but the temples of your gods."[2] How did this happen? Gibbon suggests how in the *Decline and Fall of the Roman Empire,* noting that in the early church "it became the most sacred duty of a new convert to diffuse among his friends and relations the inestimable blessing which he had received."[3] Harnack, the church historian, declared in his *Expansion of Christianity:* "We cannot hesitate to believe that the great mission of Christianity was in reality accomplished by means of informal missionaries. Justin says so quite explicitly."[4]

Informal missionaries! That is what the early Christians were; it is what all Christians should be. Moreover, when John the evangelist tells us in thirty-three verses of the first great witness to the Lord Jesus Christ and of its effect upon Christ's first followers, it is evident that he does so that we might be encouraged by the account and instructed in the matter of our own "informal" witnessing.

The Witness of John

We have already seen in an earlier study that the evangelist has a specific outline in mind as he presents these events from John's ministry. The outline is given to us in verses 6–9: "There came a man who was sent from God; his name was John. He came as a witness to testify concerning that light, so that through him all men might believe. He himself was not the light; he came only as a witness to the light." If we outline these verses, we see at once that they contain three statements about John the Baptist's testimony: (1) he was not the Light but (2) was sent to bear witness to that Light in order that (3) all men through him might believe. This outline is then followed quite closely in the narrative section of the chapter. Thus, in verses 19–28 we have John denying that he is the Light; that is, that he has any personal, independent importance. In verses 29–34 we have him bearing witness to the Light, a section that concludes with the formal statement: "I have seen and I testify that this is the Son of God." Finally, the remainder of the chapter shows the results of John's testimony as the first disciples begin to believe in Jesus.

No doubt there are many other important things that can be said about witnessing for Jesus Christ. Yet I believe that if only these three points are followed, the witness of any Christian, no matter how halting it may be, will be effective. First, the believer must recognize in the depths of his being that he is not the answer to other people's problems, that *he* is not the Light. Second, he must know that Jesus is the Light and must point men to him. Third, he must do it with the express intention of having men and women believe. Sometimes we hear that it is only the giving of a testimony that is important, not the results. But this is not entirely right. It is true that we cannot produce the results. That is God's job. So, in a sense we are not responsible for them. Nevertheless, we must want them and look for them just as earnestly as a man who pulls the fire alarm anxiously awaits the evacuation of the building.

The Workman's Voice

The evangelist begins, then, by telling us of John's confession that he was not the Christ. The section begins with the sentence: "Now this was John's testimony." If we were composing the Gospel today, this phrase would be a subheading, or what we might call a chapter title. It indicates that we are beginning a new and important section of the narrative.

The story goes on in verses 19–23: "Now this was John's testimony when the Jews of Jerusalem sent priests and Levites to ask him who he was. He did not fail to confess, but confessed freely, 'I am not the Christ.' They asked him, 'Then who are you? Are you Elijah?' He said, 'I am not.' 'Are you the Prophet?' He answered, 'No.' Finally they said, 'Who are you? Give us an answer to take back to those who sent us. What do you say about yourself?' John replied in the words of Isaiah the prophet, 'I am the voice of one calling in the desert, "Make straight the way for the Lord."'" These verses anchor the testimony of John firmly in the context of first-century Judaism, just as our testimony (if it is to be effective) must be anchored in our own century.

The delegation from Jerusalem could think of three things that John might claim to be, and the first of these quite obviously was "the Messiah." Was he the Messiah? We must remember as we read these words that the Jews were a people living under the dominion of Rome and that they were looking with great expectation for their deliverer, as any captive people do. If we want a feeling of this from our own time, we need only think of the Philippines under Japanese rule during World War II. At the start of the war General Douglas MacArthur had been in the Philippines, but he had been forced to abandon his base there in the face of the Japanese attack. As he left, however, he gave a speech in which he uttered a promise. The promise was: "I shall return." It was a simple promise. MacArthur was not even a Filipino. Yet, this promise sustained the island people during the days of the occupation as they waited for their deliverance. In fact, they remember MacArthur by these words today. In the same way, the Jews of John's day waited for the deliverer that had been promised to them in the Old Testament.

Moreover, there had been many messianic pretenders. We know of some of them through such works as the *Antiquities* of Josephus or his account of *The Jewish War*. Other false messiahs are mentioned in the New Testament (Acts 5:36–37; 21:38). It would have been easy for John, who by this time had received quite an impressive following, to have announced that he was the Messiah. But not only did he reject the temptation, he even rejected it with the hint that the One who actually was the Messiah was present. By this time he knew that Jesus was there, for the baptism of Jesus by John must have taken place before the events that John the evangelist narrates. Hence, when he rejects the title "Messiah," John does so by emphasizing the first person pronoun "I." It occupies a prominent place in the Greek text. It is as though John had said, "*I* am not the Messiah, but the One who is the Messiah stands among you."

The delegation of priests and Levites next asked him whether he was Elijah. Why should they have asked him this? The answer is that the Jews of John's time believed that the prophet Elijah would appear on earth once more before the coming of the Messiah. This idea is evident from several passages in the Gospels. For instance, in Matthew 16 there is an account of Christ asking the disciples, "Who do people say the Son of Man is?" There is the answer, "Some say John the Baptist [who had been killed by Herod in the interval]; others say Elijah; and still others, Jeremiah or one of the prophets" (vv. 13–14). In chapter 17, after the disciples had seen the Lord glorified in the transfiguration, they asked Jesus, "Why then do the teachers of the law say that Elijah must come first?" (Matt. 17:10).

The Jews had a reason for their expectation, of course, for in Malachi 4:5–6, in the very last verses of the Old Testament, there was the promise: "See, I will send you the prophet Elijah before that great and dreadful day of the LORD comes. He will turn the hearts of the fathers to their children, and the hearts of the children to their fathers; or else I will come and strike the land with a curse." This was the basis of their belief. John the Baptist was not an entirely unlikely candidate for the fulfillment of this prophecy. He was rugged like Elijah. He resembled Elijah in his work (cf. Matt. 17:12). Nevertheless, John was not Elijah, and he refused this designation.

Finally, the interrogators asked him whether he was "that prophet." This was a reference to the prophet predicted by Moses in Deuteronomy 18: "The LORD your God will raise up for you a prophet like me from among your own brothers. You must listen to him" (Deut. 18:15; cf. v. 18). But John denied that he was "that prophet" also.

Who then is John? John says that he is "a voice" who has come to prepare the way of the Lord, as Isaiah had prophesied. "A voice of one calling: In the desert prepare the way for the LORD; make straight in the wilderness a highway for our God. Every valley shall be raised up, every mountain and hill made low; the rough ground shall become level, the rugged places a plain. And the glory of the LORD will be revealed, and all mankind together will see it. For the mouth of the LORD has spoken" (Isa. 40:3–5).

You cannot see a voice. You can only hear it. No one looks much at the workman who is only preparing the road for the coming of the king. Yet, this was what John the Baptist declared himself to be: a voice and a workman. The last thing in the world that he wanted was for men to look at him. He said elsewhere, "He [Jesus] must become greater; I must become less" (John 3:30). John wanted men to forget him and see only the King.

In the Service of the King

This should be true of every good preacher, Christian worker, and witness. If we are to witness for Jesus Christ, we must first of all forget ourselves— our likes, our dislikes, our needs, our personal interests, our free time, even at times our work or our ambitions. We must think first of the other person and of his need for the Savior.

What is it that will make a person forget himself in order to point to Jesus? Only an awareness of Jesus' worth and his glory! I read a story some time ago of an African convert who told many people about Jesus, despite his great suffering from elephantiasis. This is a terribly painful disease, causing enlargement and thickening of body tissues, specifically the enormous enlargement of a limb. The disease had affected this man's legs so that it was extremely difficult for him to walk. Yet he thought nothing of making his way around the village to introduce others to the One who had transformed his life.

After a period of several months, during which he had visited all the huts in his village, this man began to take the gospel to another village that lay two miles away through the jungle. Every morning he started out painfully on his monstrous legs, and every night he returned, having visited as many homes in the second village as he possibly could. Then he would remain in his own village for several weeks before he once more became restless.

He asked the missionary doctor if another village he had visited as a child had heard the gospel. The missionary said, no, it had not. The African Christian wanted to take the Good News there, but the missionary advised against it because the village lay more than twelve miles away, over dangerous jungle paths. The burden so grew upon the African Christian that one day he slipped away quietly before dawn. The missionary learned later that the convert, arriving in the new village some time after noon, his legs bruised and scratched, had begun immediately to tell the people about Jesus. He went to everyone there, and it was not till the sun was sinking low in the sky that he began his lonely and dangerous trip through the jungle toward home. At midnight he arrived, bleeding and almost unconscious, at the house of the missionary doctor, who tended to him and dressed his feet.

Here was a man, sent by God to point people to Jesus, who was effective because he had forgotten himself in the service of his King.

17

Witnessing to Jesus Christ

John 1:29-34

The next day John saw Jesus coming toward him and said, "Look, the Lamb of God, who takes away the sin of the world! This is the one I meant when I said, 'A man who comes after me has surpassed me because he was before me.' I myself did not know him, but the reason I came baptizing with water was that he might be revealed to Israel."

Then John gave this testimony: "I saw the Spirit come down from heaven as a dove and remain on him. I would not have known him, except that the one who sent me to baptize with water told me, 'The man on whom you see the Spirit come down and remain is he who will baptize with the Holy Spirit.' I have seen and I testify that this is the Son of God."

How can a believer witness to Jesus Christ? It is an important question, not only because each of us is called upon to witness (as we have already seen) but also because the expansion of the gospel in our time (as in all ages of the Christian church) depends in no small measure upon whether or not we will do it and, if we do, how well.

We have already looked at the first great principle for being a witness: the witness must recognize that he has no independent importance in himself. The evangelist expresses this in the case of John the Baptist, whose witness has been the basis of our story, by reminding us that he was not the Light. This teaches us, among other things, that a Christian will never be an effective witness if he is placing either himself or his own needs first in his thinking. Our own needs possess a certain degree of importance, of course. But we will never be able to focus on the needs of others if our own needs dom-

109

inate us. For one thing, there is a sense in which our own needs are already met, whether we recognize it or not, for Paul wrote to the Philippians, saying, "And my God *will meet* all your needs according to his glorious riches in Christ Jesus" (Phil. 4:19). Our needs are met in Christ, and we have little to testify of if we do not see that clearly. Besides, we cannot really show love to the other person, which is the essence of witnessing, if we are not placing his needs before our own.

All that is true. Yet, we must go on from this point to see that our recognizing that we are not the Light is not in itself witnessing. That is only the first and preliminary principle.

A Verbal Witness

The second great principle for witnessing is that we must bear witness to the Light, and this means that we must witness verbally. Our witness must move out of the area of life and into the area of words. If it does not, we will be like the young man who went from a Christian home to a secular college. His parents were concerned how he would make out. So when he arrived home at Christmas they asked him anxiously, "How did you get along?" He answered, "Oh, I got along great. No one even knows that I'm a Christian." I am not denying the importance of the Christian life, of course. There must be the kind of upright character and true commitment to Christ that will back up the witness by words. We will see more about this in our next study. But, important as it is, the living of the Christian life by itself is not enough for a *complete* witness; there must also be a verbal witness.

We can easily see why this must be so. For one thing, a nonverbal witness is at best merely puzzling to the non-Christian, and it can be totally misunderstood. Some time ago, after I had mentioned witnessing in the context of a message I was giving in a church other than my own, a woman came up to me to tell how she was bearing a witness in her place of employment. She apparently worked in a large office. Just that morning, so she said, as she was going out to lunch, one of the other workers handed her fifty cents and asked her to pick up a packet of cigarettes for him. What did she do? She returned the money, saying that she did not believe in smoking. She said to me that she believed God had helped her to bear a witness for Christ in that situation.

I do not want to be too hard on this woman. She had a right, if she wished, to disapprove of smoking. In view of the warnings being given in our day about smoking, probably more non-Christians than ever before are taking this position. Still, the point that I want to make here is that in this case the "witness" to Christ that the woman thought she was giving was really no witness at all. For had I been the man who had asked the favor and been refused, I would probably have considered her rude and never even have thought of her views in terms of Christianity.

The second reason why a nonverbal witness is inadequate is that, if it is effective at all, it should lead to a verbal witness. That is, if you are attempting to honor Christ by the way you are living, the things you are doing should lead to conversation about Jesus Christ and what he has meant in your experience.

Someone will say, "Oh, but isn't it true that many persons have been led to Jesus Christ by means of the conduct of some Christian?" That is quite true; many have! The conduct of Christians has been an important step, even an essential step, in the salvation of many thousands of persons. But I am convinced that the matter has never stopped on that level and that these thousands would never have come to Christ unless the witness through the lives of Christians had not moved beyond actions at some point to a consideration of the person and claims of Jesus Christ as these truths were presented to them verbally.

People who have greatly moved the world for Christ have been ready to speak at any opportunity. In his book *Henceforth,* Hugh E. Hopkins tells of Douglas Thornton, an English believer who was being seen off at a railway station in Egypt. With some difficulty his friend found him an empty compartment on the train: "An empty compartment!" Thornton exclaimed. "Why, man, I want to fish." He moved into a crowded compartment. It is also recorded that, when exploring the Great Pyramid on the outskirts of Cairo, Thornton redeemed the time by evangelizing the guide who was then crawling up a narrow passage on his hands and knees behind him.

We find another example in the conversion experience of John Wesley, the father of the Methodist church. Wesley had been a preacher for years before he was genuinely born again, and during this time (as might be expected) his ministry was a failure. After a particularly discouraging experience in the United States, as he was returning from Georgia to England by ship, he came into contact with a body of Moravian Christians. He was very much impressed with the calm they maintained in the midst of a storm at sea. It was not on the ship, however, but later at a meeting in the little chapel at Aldersgate in London, while someone was reading from Luther's exposition of the letter to the Galatians, that Wesley "felt his heart strangely warmed" and was converted. After that he became one of the greatest evangelists in church history.

A verbal witness is a true witness. Thus, throughout the Gospel of John, the stories of those who are reached by Jesus Christ almost without exception end with a spoken profession of their belief. The man born blind is last seen in an attitude of worship, voicing the confession: "Lord, I believe" (John 9:38). The woman of Samaria grows in her understanding of Jesus. At the beginning of the narrative she regards him merely as a Jew (John 4:9). In verse 12 she raises the possibility that he may be greater than the patriarch Jacob. In verse 19 she calls him a prophet. The conclusion comes in her testimony to her neighbors when she argues that he is the Messiah (v. 29). In the same way John the Baptist testifies to the One who takes away the sin of the world.

The Message

Now, if we are to bear a witness to Jesus Christ, clearly we must know something about him. And this means that we must have a message. What is our message? The major parts of the answer to this question are suggested in our story. They are: 1) a witness to *who Jesus Christ is;* 2) a witness to *what he has done;* and 3) a witness to *how a man or woman can come to know him personally.*

First, we witness to who Jesus Christ is. John did this when he testified, "This is the one I meant when I said, 'A man who comes after me has surpassed me because he was before me'" (v. 30). Again, "I have seen and I testify that this is the Son of God" (v. 34). This is where we begin in our witness, because most of the points of Christian doctrine gain their significance from the fact that Jesus Christ is God. If Christ were only a man, then his death on the cross might have been inspiring as an example or a means by which we are excited to good works. We might say, "I never want such a tragedy to happen again" and become a great social worker. But if this is all that Christ is, then his death was in no sense an atonement; he did not die for our sin, and we are still under the condemnation of God and are still the children of wrath. In the same way, if he is not God, then we have no living God to worship, for we cannot know God apart from Jesus Christ.

As you begin to witness, let me suggest that you begin here. Begin with Christ's claims about himself. You might refer to John 5:18, which tells us that Jesus "was even calling God his own Father, making himself equal with God." He said, "I and the Father are one" (John 10:30). He told the disciples: "Anyone who has seen me has seen the Father" (John 14:9). Most non-Christians have never actually faced these claims, and many have never even heard them.

Second, we witness to what Jesus Christ has done. In one sense, of course, this is an overwhelming topic. For if Jesus is God, then all that God has done, and does, Christ does. He has been active in the creation of the world, in guiding the history of redemption, in giving us the Old and New Testaments, in helping us today in temptation, and in other things. Yet there is a sense in which the work of Christ focuses on something much more limited and therefore much easier to share. The focus of Christ's work is to be found in his death on the cross. Hence, we want to share the meaning of his death when we try to tell others about him.

In his day, John the Baptist did this by reference to the Jewish sacrifices. He said, "Look, the Lamb of God, who takes away the sin of the world" (v. 29). Have you ever given thought to what must have been involved in that statement—for John and for his hearers? For centuries Israel had known all about the sacrificial lamb. They had learned about it first from the story of Abraham, who was the father of their nation. At God's command Abraham had been going up the mountain to sacrifice his son Isaac when Isaac had turned to him and asked, "Father, . . . Behold the fire and the wood, but where is the lamb?" Abraham had answered, "My son, God will provide himself a lamb for a burnt offering." And God did! Israel had also known about the lamb as a result of the institution of the Passover. On that occasion the blood of the lamb on the doorposts of the house was the sign for the angel of death to pass by. Moreover, they knew that daily in the services of the temple lambs and goats were sacrificed. They knew that in every instance the sacrifices meant the death of an innocent substitute in place of the one who had sinned.

On this basis John the Baptist came along and exclaimed, "Look, the Lamb of God." He recognized that the sacrifices were to be fulfilled in Jesus and that he would bear our sin as Isaiah had said. "Surely he took up our infirmities and carried our sorrows. . . . he was pierced for our transgressions, he was crushed for our iniquities; the punishment that brought us peace was upon him, and by his wounds we are healed" (Isa. 53:4–5).

I like to think, as many other commentators have suggested, that as John identified Jesus as the sin-bearing Lamb, there may have been passing by the flocks of lambs that were driven up to the walls of Jerusalem each year to serve as sacrificial lambs for the Passover. The Passover feast was not far off (John 2:12–13). Perhaps John was led to refer to Jesus in this fashion because it showed vividly that he was able to deliver from death those who believed on him.

Do you believe that? Jesus is able to deliver us from death today. There is that final death, the second death, which is the separation of the soul of the individual from God. He delivers from that. But there are also the little deaths that we experience daily because of our natural alienation from God. Jesus is the answer to those deaths also. If you are a Christian, it is your privilege to tell others of the means by which sin is removed—through faith in the person and death of Jesus Christ—and that the one who believes in him is given new life, peace, joy, and freedom of access to God.

Finally, we also witness to the way in which a person can come to know and trust Jesus for himself. John did it by pointing to the fact that Jesus is the giver of the Spirit. He said, "I would not have known him, except that the one who sent me to baptize with water told me, 'The man on whom you see the Spirit come down and remain is he who will baptize with the Holy Spirit'" (v. 33). What does that mean? It means that Jesus Christ was the One who would give of his Spirit to those who should follow him. Or, to put it another way, it means that Jesus would come to live within the lives of his followers. Thus, when we bear witness to Jesus today, we talk not only of who Jesus is and of what he has done but also of how a person can come to have him enter his life and fill it.

Opening the Door

Someone will ask, "You say that Christ must enter our lives, but you have not told us how that can happen. How does that happen?" The answer is that it happens by faith as we "receive" him or "open" the doors of our lives to his knocking. One statement of that principle occurs in this same chapter in the verse that says: "Yet to all who received him, to those who believed in his name, he gave the right to become children of God" (v. 12). Another verse is Revelation 3:20: "Here I am! I stand at the door and knock; if anyone hears my voice and opens the door, I will come in and eat with him, and he with me." According to these verses there are two steps to the process. There is the step in which we first "hear" his voice or "believe" in him. Then there is the step in which we "receive him" or "open" to his call.

We do this by praying. We say, "Lord Jesus Christ, I admit that I am a sinner and in need of the salvation that you bring to men. I believe that you died for me, so that my sin is atoned for and borne away forever. I now open the door and invite you into my life and ask that you will cleanse me and rule my life forever. Amen." It is as simple as that, but it must be a definite commitment. The act itself is indispensable.

Have you done that? If you have not, you are not a real Christian. It is not enough merely to know about Christ; you must belong to him. On the other hand, if you have done that, then let me ask whether you have ever invited another person to make the same commitment. I can tell you on the basis of my own experience—and that of many others—that there are few joys equal to that which is ours when the invitation is given to believe in Jesus and the person to whom we are witnessing responds and comes to him.

18

Family Evangelism

John 1:35–51

The next day John was there again with two of his disciples. When he saw Jesus passing by, he said, "Look, the Lamb of God!"

When the two disciples heard him say this, they followed Jesus. Turning around, Jesus saw them following and asked, "What do you want?"

They said, "Rabbi" (which means Teacher), "where are you staying?"

"Come," he replied, "and you will see."

So they went and saw where he was staying, and spent that day with him. It was about the tenth hour.

Andrew, Simon Peter's brother, was one of the two who heard what John had said and who had followed Jesus. The first thing Andrew did was to find his brother Simon and tell him, "We have found the Messiah" (that is, the Christ). And he brought him to Jesus.

Jesus looked at him and said, "You are Simon son of John. You will be called Cephas" (which, when translated, is Peter).

The next day Jesus decided to leave for Galilee. Finding Philip, he said to him, "Follow me."

Philip, like Andrew and Peter, was from the town of Bethsaida. Philip found Nathanael and told him, "We have found the one Moses wrote about in the Law, and about whom the prophets also wrote—Jesus of Nazareth, the son of Joseph."

"Nazareth! Can anything good come from there?" Nathanael asked.

"Come and see," said Philip.

When Jesus saw Nathanael approaching, he said of him, "Here is a true Israelite, in whom there is nothing false."

"How do you know me?" Nathanael asked.

Jesus answered, "I saw you while you were still under the fig tree before Philip called you."

Then Nathanael declared, "Rabbi, you are the Son of God; you are the King of Israel."

Jesus said, "You believe because I told you I saw you under the fig tree. You shall see greater things than that." He then added, "I tell you the truth, you shall see heaven open, and the angels of God ascending and descending on the Son of Man."

Not long ago I heard of a group of people who disseminate their beliefs in a very unfortunate and, in my opinion, unbiblical way. Having memorized a presentation of their doctrine, they buttonhole a person, unload their presentation, and then dart away as if to say, "Well, that's finished; now it's up to the person either to believe it or go to hell." If you have ever found yourself doing that or even something close to that as you present the gospel of Jesus Christ, then these verses deserve your special consideration.

In the last few chapters we have learned two very important principles for witnessing. Both have been illustrated by the witness of John the Baptist to Jesus during the earliest days of Christ's ministry. The first, quite simply, is that John did not bear witness to himself. He confessed that he was not the Light. The second principle is that he did bear witness to the Light. The Light was Jesus, and John bore witness to him verbally. These two points lead now to a third great principle, which is, if we understand it properly, the direct antithesis to the distorted idea of witnessing that I have described above. John bore witness to Jesus; but he did so not to unload a certain amount of information but to lead others to believe in Jesus personally. This means that he had their life and destiny in view when he was witnessing.

We see this in two ways in John's Gospel. It is presented doctrinally, and it is illustrated clearly in the narrative. The doctrinal statement is found in the verses we have already referred to several times previously (verses 6–8), although it is somewhat hidden in the English translation. In English we read that John "came as a witness to testify concerning that light, so that through him all men might believe" (v. 7). In Greek the flow of thought is emphasized by a succession of relative clauses that build the thought in a characteristic Greek construction. The Greek says that John came for a witness *in order that* (as a specific and immediate object) he might identify the Light and *in order that* (as a final and ultimate object) all men might believe. These were the two objects of his witnessing.

Moreover, no sooner is the witness of John given in the narrative section of the Gospel (vv. 19–34) than we find this doctrinal statement illustrated by the account of the conversion of those who actually did believe as the result of John's witness. In brief, they are Andrew and an unnamed disciple (whom I believe to be the apostle John), and then, through their witness and the witness of Philip, also Peter and Nathanael. The story of these conversions occupies the next three days of the first week of Christ's ministry and fills out the next seventeen verses.

A Brother

The lesson of the verses at this point is that the witness-giving of John was immediately picked up by those who believed as the result of his testimony, so that Andrew and Philip, and eventually John the evangelist, Peter, and Nathanael, became the next witnesses. What is more, they followed the same pattern of witnessing that John the Baptist had followed. That is, (1) they did not attract attention to themselves, (2) they bore a verbal witness to Jesus, and (3) they did so in order that those to whom they were speaking might believe in him also.

This is the story. As John the Baptist was standing with two of his disciples near the place where they had been baptizing, Jesus walked by. Presumably Jesus had returned only the day before from his forty days in the wilderness and his temptation by Satan (recounted in Matt. 4:1–11; Mark 1:12–13; Luke 4:1–13). John said, "Look, the Lamb of God!" (v. 36). The two disciples heard John speak and followed Jesus.

Jesus turned when he saw them following and said to them, "What do you want?"

They answered, "Rabbi [which John tells us means 'Teacher'], where are you staying?"

Jesus said, "Come, and you will see." So they went with him and remained with him the rest of that day, for by the time they had arrived at the place where Jesus was staying, it was already four o'clock in the afternoon.[1]

We do not have a record of what was said that evening, but whatever it was it must have been tremendously exciting for these two original disciples, for when morning came one of the two who had followed Jesus (Andrew) immediately set out to find Simon Peter, his brother. We are told that when he had found Peter he said to him simply, "We have found the Messiah" (that is, the Christ), and he brought Peter to Jesus (v. 41).

We should stop at this point, I believe, to think of the significance of this first example (John the Baptist's being excluded) of a normal human witness. It was the witness of Andrew to his brother. And it was therefore a witness that began, as all true witnessing should begin, at home. Donald Grey Barnhouse has written of this passage: "Even before the Lord Jesus told His disciples that He would make them fishers of men, Andrew witnessed to his brother and landed the big fisherman, Simon Peter. Many who think that they can be used in far fields have never begun where the Lord Jesus meant them to begin—right at home."[2]

This is doubly important, first because it introduces us to a whole sphere and order of evangelism that is often overlooked in missionary conferences and missionary appeals, and second because it is through the home that the great majority of believers in the Lord Jesus Christ come to faith in him.

Barnhouse, in *First Things First,* has also written, "Oh, it is true that the first generation of believers in any tribe come straight out of heathenism, generally by the witness of some foreigner who has brought the witness to that particular tribe. And so it is that most of church history is the story of some alien who entered a tribe with little knowledge of the language, and who preached Christ in the power of the Holy Spirit so that people were saved. Paul, the Greek Jew, took the gospel to the tribes of Asia Minor, to Macedonia, and to Greece. Irenaeus, a Greek, was the first to take the gospel to Gaul, which is now France. A Latin from Rome, the second St. Augustine, was the first missionary to England, while an Englishman, Boniface, was the first to carry the gospel to Germany. Young Patrick, of high family, was kidnapped by marauders and carried to Ireland at the age of sixteen, later to become the instrument of the conversion of Ireland. In modern times the list of similar instances crosses the world. Henry Martyn took the gospel to Hindustan and to Persia. We have Adoniram Judson of Burma; Hudson Taylor of China; Mary Slessor of Calabar; Livingstone of Central Africa; and the list goes on until we have Betty Elliot of the Aucas, as well as Wycliffe Bible Translators in many other tribes.

"But in spite of all this list, which grows longer every year, these pioneers win but a small proportion of those who come to Christ. The informant who teaches his language to that strange creature, the missionary, usually ends up by coming to know the missionary's Savior. He has seen Christ in the missionary first of all, and then the informant goes and finds his own brother! That is a *first* in countless tribes. The God of Abraham became the God of Sarah, Abraham's wife, and then the God of Isaac and the God of Jacob. Household salvation is a very precious truth, and while there are definite promises which give positive assurance only of the salvation of our children, other statements give us large hope that the gospel will penetrate throughout our households."[3]

Charles Spurgeon once observed that although grace does not run in the blood, and regeneration is not of blood or of birth, yet it often happens that God uses one of a household to draw the rest to himself. He calls an individual, and then uses him as a sort of spiritual decoy to bring the rest of the family into the gospel net. Has God used you in that way? Have you a brother or a sister still outside of Christ? Do you have a husband who does not know him? A wife? I do not see how you can ever consider yourself a true witness to the Lord Jesus Christ if you are not making a maximum effort to lead to him these whom you know best.

But perhaps you are saying, "I have no brother. I have no sister. In fact, I am quite alone in this world." If that is the case, then you must go on to see that the story of the opening week of Christ's ministry also includes the witness of Philip, who had no brother, but who brought his friend to Jesus. We are told that on the next day when Jesus was about to depart for Galilee, he called Philip, saying, "Follow me." And Philip, who did follow, then went to his friend Nathanael with the report: "We have found the one Moses wrote about in the Law, and about whom the prophets also wrote—Jesus of Nazareth, the son of Joseph."

At first Nathanael was skeptical. He asked, "Nazareth! Can anything good come from there?"

Philip replied, "Come and see."

When Nathanael came and had his meeting with Jesus, he then concluded for himself: "Rabbi, you are the Son of God; you are the King of Israel" (vv. 43–49).

If you have no brother or sister (or any other family), then you must begin, as Philip did, with your friend or your neighbor. He is the one whom God has placed in your path; it is a witness to him that God has most entrusted to your charge.

"Come and See"

It is clear that if we are to witness successfully in the circles where we are best known, then we must meet certain conditions. What are they? In the first place, there must be a change in our manner of life, and this must be seen in our willingness to take second place in order that the ones to whom we are witnessing might see Jesus.

If you are sitting in a waiting room somewhere with a packet of tracts in your pocket and a person sits down next to you whom you do not know, you can witness to him and it will hardly cost you anything. That is not difficult. But if you are going to witness effectively to your brother, there must be a change in your life.

Unlike the man on the seat next to you, your brother knows you. He knows whether the thing you are professing has affected you personally. He knows whether you take your turn drying the dishes at home or whether you try to wiggle out of the responsibility. He knows whether you put thought into caring for other members of the family. He knows whether or not you are touchy and anxious above all to defend your own interests. In short, he knows whether the faith you profess is real or ineffectual. He knows whether Christ occupies the highest point in your life or whether you do.

Andrew was one who placed himself second in order that he might bring others to Jesus. We do not know a great deal about Andrew because he was not terribly well known. In fact, he was so little known that he is often introduced to us in the New Testament as Simon Peter's brother. Everyone knew who Peter was; Andrew was the man who was related to Peter. There are only three stories in the Gospels in which Andrew plays a significant role. There is the story recorded here. There is the time in which he brought to Jesus the lad with the five loaves and two small fishes (John 6:8–9). And there is the incident in which the Greeks were brought to Jesus (John 12:22). In each case Andrew put himself second in order that he might introduce others to the Savior.

The second condition for an effective witness to those who know us best is that we must be willing to let Jesus win them through us and not depend on our clever techniques or our arguments. There is no record of Andrew arguing with Peter or of Philip arguing with Nathanael. They merely invited the one to whom they were witnessing to "Come and see."

Where did they learn this technique, if we may call it that? They learned it from Jesus. When Jesus turned around and saw them following him, he first asked the question, "What do you want?" We can always begin with that question, for the gospel always relates to the needs and longings of men. When they then expressed an interest in knowing more about him, he replied with the invitation: "Come and see." It was this approach that Andrew and Philip then emulated, and Philip actually used the identical words in his approach to Nathanael (v. 46).

William Barclay tells us in his commentary on this passage how the great nineteenth-century agnostic Aldous Huxley was once profoundly moved by the gospel. He had been at a weekend house party in the midst of which, on Sunday morning, most of the guests proposed to go to church. Huxley did not intend to go and instead approached a rather plain man who, nevertheless, was known to have a very simple and radiant faith. He said to the man, "Suppose you don't go to church today and instead stay home and tell me quite simply what your Christian faith means to you and why you are a Christian."

The man replied, "Oh, I can't do that. You could demolish my arguments in a minute; I'm not clever enough to argue with you."

"I don't want to argue with you," Huxley replied. "I just want you to tell me simply what this Christ means to you." The man then stayed home and told Huxley of his faith. When he had finished, there were tears in the eyes of the brilliant agnostic. He said, "I would give my right hand if only I could believe that." What touched his heart? It was not arguments. It was a genuine faith expressed by one who knew Jesus and was not ashamed to invite others to come to him.

Time with Jesus

There is just one more point that comes out of this story, although it is clearly related to everything that has been said previously. We return to the story and find that before Andrew and the other disciple became witnesses, they had first spent time with Jesus. John tells us that they arrived about the tenth hour at the place where Jesus was staying—that is, about four o'clock in the afternoon—and that they spent the night there. What do you suppose they talked about until nightfall? We are not told, but the story reminds us of that other story in Luke where Christ spoke to the Emmaus disciples, showing them from the Old Testament how it was necessary for him "to suffer these things and then enter his glory?" after which they confessed, "Were not our hearts burning within us while he talked with us on the road and opened the Scriptures to us?" (Luke 24:26, 32). After such time spent with Jesus, when the heart burns, one is constrained to go out and find his brother.

This is the secret of all effectual witnessing. If we spend time with Christ, the other matters—knowing that we are not the Light, pointing to the Light, desiring men and women to believe—will come naturally. Moreover, we will find ourselves going to the other one to say simply, "I have found Christ. He has changed me. Come with me to Jesus."

19

Credibility: Bridging the Gap

John 1:35–51

The next day John was there again with two of his disciples. When he saw Jesus passing by, he said, "Look, the Lamb of God!"

When the two disciples heard him say this, they followed Jesus. Turning around, Jesus saw them following and asked, "What do you want?"

They said, "Rabbi" (which means Teacher), "where are you staying?"

"Come," he replied, "and you will see."

So they went and saw where he was staying, and spent that day with him. It was about the tenth hour.

Andrew, Simon Peter's brother, was one of the two who heard what John had said and who had followed Jesus. The first thing Andrew did was to find his brother Simon and tell him, "We have found the Messiah" (that is, the Christ). And he brought him to Jesus.

Jesus looked at him and said, "You are Simon son of John. You will be called Cephas" (which, when translated, is Peter).

The next day Jesus decided to leave for Galilee. Finding Philip, he said to him, "Follow me."

Philip, like Andrew and Peter, was from the town of Bethsaida. Philip found Nathanael and told him, "We have found the one Moses wrote about in the Law, and about whom the prophets also wrote —Jesus of Nazareth, the son of Joseph."

"Nazareth! Can anything good come from there?" Nathanael asked.

"Come and see," said Philip.

When Jesus saw Nathanael approaching, he said of him, "Here is a true Israelite, in whom there is nothing false."

"How do you know me?" Nathanael asked.

Jesus answered, "I saw you while you were still under the fig tree before Philip called you."

Then Nathanael declared, "Rabbi, you are the Son of God; you are the King of Israel."

Jesus said, "You believe because I told you I saw you under the fig tree. You shall see greater things than that." He then added, "I tell you the truth, you shall see heaven open, and the angels of God ascending and descending on the Son of Man."

W e live in an era in which credibility, or the lack of it, has become a significant issue. We talk about the credibility gap. It exists between parents and children, between those who are in authority and those under them, between races, between governments, between the electorate and those who seek public office. Credibility is also an issue when you and I attempt to bear a witness for the Lord Jesus Christ.

The law of the Jewish people always demanded two witnesses to any fact submitted in a legal proceeding. This is quite generally known, primarily because of the well-known phrase "at the mouth of two or three witnesses" that occurs often in the Old Testament. It is not so generally known that Jewish law, like contemporary law, also demanded that all the witnesses be credible. That is to say, it demanded that the witnesses be in a position in which they had knowledge of the facts involved, that they be morally above reproach, and that they possess a reputation for accuracy.

These factors were utilized on one occasion by the Lord Jesus Christ when he was called on to be a judge by those who actually desired to accuse him. They brought a woman to him who had been taken in adultery and who was quite possibly known to them because of their own participation in her sins. They asked him if he would uphold the law of Moses, which commanded that a person guilty of adultery be stoned, or if he would ignore the law and allow her to go free. Whichever way he answered they had him trapped, they thought. Instead of answering them immediately, however, the Lord Jesus stooped and wrote on the ground. Then he told the woman's accusers that the one who was without sin among them should cast the first stone at her. When they had been discredited as witnesses in their own eyes by their own consciences and had slipped away one by one, he turned to the woman and asked where her accusers were. She answered by saying that there was no one there to accuse her, and Jesus was able to dismiss the case under even the most demanding strictures of the law and deal with her in grace by means of his own righteousness.

Thus far in our study of witnessing we have dealt with only the first of these legal requirements. That is, we have shown that there must be witnesses so that what is established by one witness might be confirmed by God himself as he adds to that witness by his twos and threes and twelves and seventies. However, there is still the question of the witness's character, and this is also important. Luke recognized this indirectly in the opening verses both of his Gospel and the Book of Acts when he stressed that the facts concerning the life of Jesus Christ had been established by credible eyewitnesses chosen by God to bear testimony.

What about the credibility of the witnesses? What about your credibility and mine? What must you be and what must you know if your witness to the Lord Jesus Christ is to be validated?

I believe that at least eight things must be true of you if your witness to unbelievers is to be credible. (1) You must know that God's saving work has been done in your life and that it has been done forever. (2) You must know that you are a sinner and that in yourself you do not want to do God's will. (3) You must be surrendered to God. (4) You must spend time with Jesus. (5) You must be grounded in the great truths of Scripture. (6) You must be planted if you are to bear fruit. (7) You must be willing to do hard work. (8) Everything you do must be characterized by love. We now need to look at each of these requirements individually.

Assurance

The first principle is that you must know that God's saving work has been done in your life and that it has been done forever. It is easy to see why this is so. If you are uncertain about your salvation, or if you are afraid you might lose it, then all your efforts must be expended in solving these problems for yourself, and you won't be worth anything as a witness to others.

Take Martin Luther as an example. If there was ever a man who was concerned about the state of his soul, it was Martin Luther. It was this that drove him to the Erfurt Convent of the Augustinian Eremites and allowed him to submit himself to all sorts of rigors for the sake of his soul's salvation. He starved himself, beat himself, gave himself to a deep and systematic study of the Scriptures. These endeavors caused the other, less disciplined monks to regard him somewhat as a miracle of piety. His reputation for being a "young saint" spread throughout the other monasteries of Germany, even as far distant as the monastery at Grimma. Yet, at this stage of his life, in spite of his efforts and discipline, Luther was uncertain about the state of his own soul and consequently was of no use to anyone. It was only after Luther had come to the knowledge of the gospel of grace and was assured of his own salvation that he became a witness to others. Then God was able to take him out of the monastery at Erfurt and use him to shake a continent.

It is the same with you. If you are uncertain about your own relationship to God, you will never be worth anything as a witness. You may be saved. I do not mean that you cannot be a Christian and be uncertain of your salvation at the same time. That is true of far too many believers, though it should not be. But the point I am making is that if you are uncertain about your salvation, you will not be able to witness about the Lord Jesus Christ to others.

Let me pause at this point in order to ask whether the gospel itself has become real for you. We have read about Jesus Christ being the Light. Well, is he the Light for you? We have read about him being the Lamb of God that takes away the sin of the world. Has he taken away your sin? Is he your Teacher, your Lord, your Savior? If he is, then you must stand firmly upon the Word of God, which declares: "We accept man's testimony, but God's testimony is greater because it is the testimony of God, which he has given about his Son. . . . And this is the testimony: God has given us eternal life, and this life is in his Son. He who has the Son has life; he who does not have the Son of God does not have life" (1 John 5:9, 11–13). If these things are true for you and if you are assured of them, then you have taken the first important step toward becoming a believable witness.

Still a Sinner

The second step is to realize that you are still a sinner, even after your conversion, and that in yourself you do not want God's will. Naturally, that also includes witnessing about him to others. Do you want God's will? Do you want to witness? If you know your own heart, you will know that basically you prefer to be left alone to your own ways and reasoning.

We are like the Israelites during their march to the Promised Land. They rebelled against God's ways at almost every conceivable stage of their journey. God had taken them from Egypt when they were nothing but slaves, and he had brought them out of the country with signs and great miracles. Yet no sooner were they in the desert than they rebelled against Moses, saying, "If only we had died by the LORD's hand in Egypt! There we sat around pots of meat and ate all the food we wanted, but you have brought us out into this desert to starve this entire assembly to death" (Exod. 16:3). When God provided the manna to eat and water to drink, they rebelled against the menu. They said, "We remember the fish we ate in Egypt at no cost—also the cucumbers, melons, leeks, onions and garlic. But now we have lost our appetite; we never see anything but this manna!" (Num. 11:5–6). Later, when they were instructed to enter and possess the land they protested that it was impossible because of the giants that lived there. Then, when God commanded them to remain in the desert, they tried to go into the land and were defeated.

In everything the Israelites rebelled against God's counsel. But God kept at them so they would eventually learn that nothing matters but the purposes of God and so they would determine to do his will even though they did not naturally want to do it. So it is with us. We are not paragons of faith or faithfulness. Left to ourselves we too would go back to Egypt. But we must learn that. And we must determine for this reason to pursue God's will in spite of our natural inclinations.

Surrendered to God

The third thing that must be true of you if your witness is to be believable is that you must be surrendered to God. Someone will say, "But isn't that a contradiction? You have just said that we must know that we do not want God's will and now you say that we must be surrendered to him. Doesn't that mean that we must want it?" Yes, in one sense! There are doctrines in the Christian life that appear as contradictions. Nevertheless, if we are to be effective witnesses for Christ, we must come to the point where we are willing to say, "Even though I do not naturally want your will, nevertheless I have come to the point where I want it even though I do not want it."

To be able to say that, we must recognize that we do not belong to ourselves. We are bought with a price. Therefore, we are to glorify God in our body and in our spirit, which are God's (1 Cor. 6:20).

How we bargain with God at this point! We want to give God anything but ourselves. We will give him our money, even though it sometimes hurts us to do so. We will give him our children—sometimes. I know of some husbands who would even give their wives, and wives who would gladly give their husbands. But we will not give *ourselves!*

We are like Jacob at the brook Jabbok. Jacob had been gone from his homeland for many years because of fear of his brother Esau whom he had cheated out of his birthright. But he had come back with the herds and servants and family with which the Lord had blessed him during the intervening years. He had started out boldly, but the closer he came to Esau's territory, the more frightened he became. He wondered whether Esau would still carry out his threat to kill him. He became even more terrified when he finally reached the brook Jabbok, which was the border of Esau's territory, and a servant who had gone on ahead reported to him that Esau was coming toward him with four hundred men.

What was Jacob to do? He thought about the matter and decided on this strategy. He called a servant and placed 200 ewes in his charge. He said, "Pass over before me. And when you come to Esau and he shall ask, 'Who are you? And to whom do these ewes belong?' then you shall say, 'They belong to your brother Jacob, and they are a present for you.'" Jacob thought that he might win Esau's favor by this plan. After the 200 ewes he sent 20 rams, and he gave the same charge to the servant who was sent with them. After the 20 rams there were 30 camels. Then there were 40 cows, 10 bulls, 20 asses, and 10 foals, each in a group by itself. Then Jacob sent over all the servants and the handmaids. After that he sent over Leah (who was the least popular wife) with her children. Then he sent over Rachel and her children. Then came the brook Jabbok. And there was Jacob, all alone—and trembling (Gen. 32:13–24).

We are like Jacob. We go to church and sing, "I surrender all . . . the sheep; I surrender all . . . the camels." But we do not give ourselves. That night the angel came and wrestled with Jacob, and brought him to the point of personal submission. Through this experience Jacob became a spiritual man and was used by God to give Israel some of the greatest revelations in the Old Testament about their future and the coming of the Messiah. At what period of Jacob's life are you? Before Jabbok or after Jabbok? If you are still before Jabbok, when is it that the angel is going to come and wrestle with you?

Time with Jesus

The fourth of the eight requirements for a credible witness is a simple one: you must spend time with Jesus. If you do not, then your witness, no matter how brightly it shone forth at one time, will eventually flicker and go out. We are like oil-burning lamps. If we are to shine, two things are prerequisites: (1) we must first be lit by Jesus Christ, and (2) we must be fed by him.

Probably the best illustration of this principle in the entire Bible is the story we looked at previously. Andrew and John became the first witnesses to Jesus Christ, and Andrew became the very first when he went and found his own brother, Simon Peter. What does John the evangelist say of that event? One of the most significant things he says is that it was about four o'clock in the afternoon when he and Andrew stopped and spent the night with Jesus. Four o'clock! What do you suppose they talked about during the hours between then and the fall of night? We can be certain that they did not talk about the weather. They talked about spiritual things. Jesus taught them about God and man and laid groundwork for the first principles of the gospel. After that they went out to be witnesses.

Do you spend time with Jesus? Nothing can be a substitute for that. We know that this is true even in secular terms, for there is not a judge in the country who will accept "hearsay evidence" in his court. Hearsay evidence is secondhand evidence, the kind that begins, "Well, I was not there, but I heard Mr. Smith say that. . . ." No judge in the country will accept such evidence. And neither will the unbeliever, if you are attempting to provide hearsay evidence in place of your own personal witness to Jesus Christ. However, if you have been spending time with Jesus, then you will be able to say, "He has spoken to me. He has ordered my life. He satisfies my longings. Won't you allow him to do the same things for you?" If you can do that, then you will *be* a witness as well as be *giving* one, and the one who is not yet a Christian will know that your witness rings true.

We need to stop at this point, and you need to apply some of the principles that I have been stating. Many years ago I read Dale Carnegie's best seller *How to Win Friends and Influence People.* There is much in that book that I have forgotten; but I will never forget that at one point, about halfway through the book, Carnegie broke into his narrative to tell the reader that he had read enough. Instead of going on he was to put the book down and put some of what he had read into practice. When I came to that point I stopped. I never did read the rest of the book. But I did try to do some of the things he suggested. Let us do that also.

What are the first four principles for a credible witness? They are these: (1) you must know that God's saving work has been done in your life and that it has been done forever; (2) you must know that you are a sinner even after your conversion and that in yourself you do not want God's will; (3) you must be surrendered to God; and (4) you must spend time with Jesus. Let us practice these principles. If we do, we will find that God will bless our ministry and that men and women will come to faith in the Lord Jesus.

20

The Mark of the Christian

John 1:35–51

The next day John was there again with two of his disciples. When he saw Jesus passing by, he said, "Look, the Lamb of God!"

When the two disciples heard him say this, they followed Jesus. Turning around, Jesus saw them following and asked, "What do you want?"

They said, "Rabbi" (which means Teacher), "where are you staying?"

"Come," he replied, "and you will see."

So they went and saw where he was staying, and spent that day with him. It was about the tenth hour.

Andrew, Simon Peter's brother, was one of the two who heard what John had said and who had followed Jesus. The first thing Andrew did was to find his brother Simon and tell him, "We have found the Messiah" (that is, the Christ). And he brought him to Jesus.

Jesus looked at him and said, "You are Simon son of John. You will be called Cephas" (which, when translated, is Peter).

The next day Jesus decided to leave for Galilee. Finding Philip, he said to him, "Follow me."

Philip, like Andrew and Peter, was from the town of Bethsaida. Philip found Nathanael and told him, "We have found the one Moses wrote about in the Law, and about whom the prophets also wrote —Jesus of Nazareth, the son of Joseph."

"Nazareth! Can anything good come from there?" Nathanael asked.

"Come and see," said Philip.

When Jesus saw Nathanael approaching, he said of him, "Here is a true Israelite, in whom there is nothing false."

"How do you know me?" Nathanael asked.

Jesus answered, "I saw you while you were still under the fig tree before Philip called you."

Then Nathanael declared, "Rabbi, you are the Son of God; you are the King of Israel."

Jesus said, "You believe because I told you I saw you under the fig tree. You shall see greater things than that." He then added, "I tell you the truth, you shall see heaven open, and the angels of God ascending and descending on the Son of Man."

Acommon reason many non-Christians give for refusing to become Christians is a lack of credibility in the lives of those who profess to be Christ's followers. This lack of credibility may result from a number of factors. Quite a few years ago a certain Bible teacher was in Chicago for the wedding of a young man in business in that city, and after the ceremony he began to talk to him about his becoming a Christian. The young man replied, "You do not need to waste your time talking to me about that. I work for . . . (here he named a prominent Chicago firm). These men are very prominent in the church, but we know how they carry on their business, since we work for them. I have no desire to be a Christian."

I know, of course, that the misinterpretation of Christianity by some Christians is not sufficient excuse for refusing to believe in the gospel. People should be willing to distinguish between authentic and counterfeit currency. But not everyone makes the distinction. And consequently, what a Christian is and does is necessarily a most important part of his witness for the Lord Jesus Christ.

In the last study, the first of two on the credibility of the Christian's witness, we saw what four of the prerequisites for a credible witness were. At this point we want to pick up our study and consider the next four prerequisites.

Knowledge

The fifth requirement, if you are to maintain a credible witness for the Lord Jesus Christ, is that you must be grounded in the great truths of Scripture. I do not mean by this that you must be a theologian or that you must have mastered the content of the Bible from Genesis to Revelation. If that were required, few Christians could be witnesses. I mean that you must understand the basic content of the gospel as it is contained in Scripture and that you must be able to articulate it in some fashion to others. Of course, the more you know, the better. This is implied in the very nature of a verbal witness.

What does the word "gospel" mean? It means "good news." And what is the good news? The good news is that God has not left us alone in our sin and loneliness to face the certainty of spiritual death and judgment, but that he has come to us in the person of his Son, the Lord Jesus Christ, to die for us and, on the basis of that death, to offer us the gift of eternal life. Moreover, it is the assurance that anyone who will believe these things and receive Christ into his or her life will enter at once into an eternal relationship with God in which God will become his Father and he will enjoy all the privileges of being one of God's sons or daughters. It is this news with all its ramifications that we are to share with other men and women.

Think, too, of the Great Commission. Did you know that this is the main point of the most popular version of the Great Commission? It says,

"Therefore go and make disciples of all nations, baptizing them in the name of the Father and of the Son and of the Holy Spirit, and teaching them to obey everything I have commanded you. And surely I am with you always, to the very end of the age" (Matt. 28:19–20). These verses seem to place the emphasis on *going* into the world to preach the gospel, and many have preached this. Actually, the verb that is translated as the imperative "go" is a participle, not an imperative. So it should be translated "going" or "as you go." The result is that "make disciples" is the only direct command left in the sentence, and the verse should read, "Therefore, going, *make disciples* of all nations." The word "teach" is used in the King James Version and is even repeated twice for emphasis.

Have you tried to fulfill that commandment? Christ was not urging us to go into the world. He expected that we would naturally do that. However, he was urging us to teach, and for that we need a knowledge of the Bible and its doctrinal content. If you do not have that knowledge, I urge you to study the Bible and to put yourself in a position where you can be taught. No one should want to be a "babe" in the Word. We need to go on to maturity.

You Must Be Planted

The sixth requirement for an effective witness is that you must be planted if you are to bear fruit. What must be true of a seed if it is to sprout and be fruitful? Well, first it must be alive. A dead seed will not germinate. Consequently, if you are to bear fruit as a Christian, you must first of all be alive in Christ. But even this is not all that is necessary, for even a living seed will not produce fruit if it is simply left alone on a shelf or in a jar somewhere and is never inserted into the ground. It must be planted. In the same way, you will never bear fruit as a Christian if you merely sit on a pew. You must be planted somewhere in our society.

Another way of saying the same thing is to say that you must know and be with non-Christians. I am afraid that we often find ourselves in the same condition in witnessing as we do in race relations. Many white Christians mean well toward African Americans in our society. The trouble is that they do not know any African Americans. In the same way, few of us know as many non-Christians as we should if we are to be effective evangelists.

How is the situation to be corrected? It will never be corrected by reading a book, although that may help. It will not be corrected by hearing a sermon. It will be corrected only as you roll up your sleeves, get into the world side by side with those who are not yet Christians, get to know them, share their hopes and frustrations, and speak to them. Only then will you be able to point to Christ as the answer to their particular problems. I have often pointed out that when God placed Israel in the world as a witness, he placed her not in the mountains of Tibet or the undiscovered plains of America but in Palestine, at the crossroads of the ancient world. It was there in the midst of the world (but not of it) that she was to bear witness.

Hard Work

The seventh prerequisite is that you must be willing to do hard work. This may seem quite obvious, but it is necessary to say this because not all Christians are noted for their hard work or diligence. In fact, some Christians are quite lazy.

Shortly before his crucifixion Jesus Christ told a story that pointed up the truth of this fact and that encouraged his followers to be diligent. He said that a certain man who was about to take a journey first called his servants and entrusted his wealth to their care. To one servant he gave five talents. The amount was equal to about $5,000, but we must remember that in terms of purchasing power the amount was probably closer to $500,000 as we measure wealth today. To a second servant he gave two talents; to a third, just one. After a time the man came back and demanded a reckoning. The servant to whom he had given five talents had invested it and presented his master with five more talents. The second servant had done the same, producing two more talents. To each of them the master said, "Well done, good and faithful servant. . . . Come and share your master's happiness!"

At last the servant who had been given one talent came forward. His account was a sad one. "'Master,' he said, 'I knew that you are a hard man, harvesting where you have not sown and gathering where you have not scattered seed. So I was afraid and went out and hid your talent in the ground. See, here is what belongs to you.' His master replied, 'You wicked, lazy servant! So you knew that I harvest where I have not sown and gather where I have not scattered seed? Well then, you should have put my money on deposit with the bankers, so that when I returned I would have received it back with interest'" (Matt. 25:24–27). In this reproof the unprofitable servant was condemned for two failings. First, he was condemned for his wickedness, because he unjustly called his lord a hard man. And, second, he was condemned for his sloth or *laziness*. Quite clearly he was even blaming his lord for his own lack of diligence.

Do we do that? I am afraid we do sometimes. The Lord places a great opportunity before us, and instead of considering it an opportunity, we think it a burden. In fact, some Christians seem to consider every opportunity a burden. Watchman Nee, a Chinese Christian who, until his imprisonment in China, was himself a very diligent worker, has written in *The Normal Christian Worker*, "A person who regards everything as a burden cannot be a faithful servant of the Lord; he cannot even be a faithful servant of men. . . . Our characters need to be disciplined till we cease to find work irksome and can delight in spending time and strength and material resources without stint in order to serve others."[1]

Characterized by Love

The final point is that, if we are to win others for Jesus Christ, everything we do must be characterized by love. When E. Stanley Jones was in India on one of his many journeys he met with Mahatma Gandhi. In the course of the visit Jones asked this question: "Mr. Gandhi, what must the Christians do to win India for the Lord Jesus Christ?" Gandhi replied, "There are four things that the Christians must do. First, let Christians live like Jesus Christ. Second, do not compromise your faith. Third, learn all you can about the non-Christian religions. And fourth, let everything you do be characterized by love." I believe that the Indian leader had great insight into the nature of Christianity and that his last point in particular exposed its true priorities.

Is everything you do and I do characterized by love? To have it be so is not optional. It is actually to be what Francis A. Schaeffer in *The Church at the End of the Twentieth Century*, calls "the mark of the Christian," a label to distinguish a Christian "not just in one era or in one locality but at all times and all places until Jesus returns."[2] According to the Bible, others are even to judge the credibility of our life and our witness to Jesus Christ by its presence.

Does this seem extreme to you? It is not, for it is based on the explicit teaching of the Lord Jesus Christ himself. During one of his farewell discourses to his disciples just before his crucifixion, Jesus said, "A new command I give you: Love one another. As I have loved you, so you must love one another. By this all men will know that you are my disciples, if you love one another" (John 13:34, 35). How are the unsaved to know that we are Christ's disciples? By our love! If we love each other! On another occasion Jesus taught that this same love was also to be extended to those we are seeking to win; for he taught that the second most important commandment—after loving God with all our being—is this: "Love your neighbor as yourself."

Do we love like this? Is this our mark? The following two stories measure whether or not this essential mark of the Christian is present in our lives. The first story comes from the years I spent in Basel, Switzerland, doing graduate study. A girl named Sheila, who had come from a bad background in England, had gone to Switzerland when still quite young to make a better life for herself. She was lonely, and having no one to whom to turn, she unfortunately fell in with a young man who did not marry her but who left her with a child. By the time I had met her the child was about four years old, and Sheila herself was on guard with most people and very hostile to the church and Christianity.

In time, through the witness of the English-speaking community, she became a Christian. Some time later my wife and I left to return to America, and she immigrated to Canada. We corresponded with her for about six months after she arrived in Canada, and we had the impression that she was not fitting in with any Christian group in her area. We went to visit her and found that we were right; we began to talk with various Christian people about her. There was interest to a degree, but no real love. We were usually told, "Oh, there is a very good church in our city." And we were given the name. Sometimes it was a Presbyterian church, sometimes Baptist, sometimes independent. But in all our conversations not one person said, "Give me her name and address. I'll stop by and invite her to go with me on Sunday morning."

Finally, being very unhappy, she left that city for another one and (I am afraid) once again fell in with bad company. Eventually, in spite of much effort, we lost touch with her.

The second story is more promising. The Rev. Fernando Vangioni, assistant evangelist with the Billy Graham Evangelistic Association, told it at the Berlin Congress on Evangelism (1966). He said that he was in South America for a series of meetings. After one meeting a woman came up to him and said, "I wonder if you would take time to speak to a girl whom I am bringing to the meeting tomorrow night. She went to New York some years ago full of hope, thinking that America was the land of opportunity. Instead of doing well she went through terrible times in the city. She was used by one man after another. All treated her badly. Now she has returned to this country very bitter, and hostile to all forms of Christianity." The evangelist said he would speak with her.

On the next night the girl was there, but when Mr. Vangioni and she met, there was not the slightest response to his attempts to speak with her. He said he had never looked into eyes that were so hard-looking or listened to a voice so hostile. At last, seeing that he was making no progress, Mr. Vangioni asked, "Do you mind if I pray for you?"

The girl said, "Pray if you like, but don't preach to me. And don't expect me to listen."

He began to pray, and as he prayed he was greatly moved. Something in the tragedy of her life caused tears to run down his face. At last he stopped. There was nothing to add. He said, "All right, you may go now."

But the girl did not go. Instead, touched by this manifestation of love for her, she replied, "No, I won't go. You can preach to me now. No man has ever cried for me before."

I do not know what your reaction to that is. Perhaps the tears came more easily to a man of Latin temperament. But I wonder if you have ever been touched at all for one who is lost and ignorant of Christ's love. Do you merely say, "Oh, we have a wonderful church; she should go there"? Or do you go out of your way to seek and save the lost, crushed, and lonely? We should be able to say, as Paul did, "If we are out of our mind, it is for the sake of God; if we are in our right mind, it is for you. For Christ's love compels us. . . . We are therefore Christ's ambassadors, as though God were making his appeal through us. We implore you on Christ's behalf: Be reconciled to God" (2 Cor. 5:13–14, 20).

21

The Baptism of John

John 1:29–34

The next day John saw Jesus coming toward him and said, "Look, the Lamb of God, who takes away the sin of the world! This is the one I meant when I said, 'A man who comes after me has surpassed me because he was before me.' I myself did not know him, but the reason I came baptizing with water was that he might be revealed to Israel."

Then John gave this testimony: "I saw the Spirit come down from heaven as a dove and remain on him. I would not have known him, except that the one who sent me to baptize with water told me, 'The man on whom you see the Spirit come down and remain is he who will baptize with the Holy Spirit.' I have seen and I testify that this is the Son of God."

Several studies ago, before I began to look at the subject of witnessing in John's Gospel, I noted that after we had completed that study we would be going back to some verses skipped earlier and consider the subject of baptism.

The verses that refer to baptism are verses 29 to 34. These verses refer to John's baptism, the baptism of Jesus by John, and the baptism of the Holy Spirit or Christian baptism. Consequently, they are a proper base on which to discuss the whole subject of baptism and its significance.

I want to say at the outset, however, that almost nothing that follows will be directed toward the traditional differences within the Christian church regarding baptism. Nothing should be construed as a commentary on infant baptism versus adult baptism. Nothing should be applied to the various modes of administering baptism. Instead, it will be directed primarily at

133

understanding the meaning of the identification of believers with Christ, which is what water baptism signifies.

A Difficult Subject

This is an enormous and complicated subject. The truth of this statement can be seen quite easily merely by reflecting on the number of books that have been written about baptism in recent years and on the fact that they do not agree. One of the most influential works on baptism is by Karl Barth, entitled, *The Teaching of the Church Regarding Baptism.* It restates many of the Reformed doctrines about baptism but opposes infant baptism. Shortly after Barth's book appeared, Oscar Cullmann, Barth's colleague at the University of Basel, Switzerland, also wrote a book on baptism, but he disagreed with Barth. His work is called *Baptism in the New Testament.* Joachim Jeremias, a great biblical scholar, wrote a masterful volume entitled *Infant Baptism in the First Four Centuries.* He was contradicted by Kurt Aland *(Did the Early Church Baptize Infants?).* Now we have Jeremias's reply to Aland's contradiction. There are also many other substantial works, such as that by G. R. Beasley-Murray, called, like Cullmann's work, *Baptism in the New Testament.*

Bapto and *Baptizo*

The difficulty of dealing with the subject is compounded further by the fact that there are two very closely related words for "baptism" in the New Testament, instead of one. Although it is a difficulty, recognition of this fact is actually the first step toward solving the difficulty. The first word is *bapto,* which means "to dip" or "to immerse." The second word is *baptizo,* which has quite obviously been transliterated into English to give us our word "baptize."

Whenever a word is transliterated into English, this in itself is quite often an indication of a multiplicity of meanings. If the word *baptizo* had lent itself to an easy translation, an obvious English word would have been used to translate it. Thus, if *baptizo* had meant only "to immerse" (which is what *bapto* means), then "immerse" would be the word used. We would speak of "John the Immerser." Or we would recite, "Go ye, therefore, and teach all nations, immersing them in the name of the Father, and of the Son, and of the Holy Spirit." Actually, this is not the case. Therefore, even the fact of the transliteration is an indication that we must look beyond the purely literal meaning of the word "baptize" to the more important metaphorical meanings.

Here we gain a great deal of help from classical Greek literature, for there is evidence that the Greek classical writers used the word *baptizo* from about 400 B.C. to the second century after Christ. In their writings, *baptizo* always points to a change of identity by any means. Thus, to give a few quite general examples, it can refer to a change having taken place by immersing an object in a liquid, as in dying cloth; by drinking too much wine and getting drunk; by overexertion; and by other causes.

Of all the texts that might be cited from antiquity the one that makes greatest clarity of the distinct use of the two words is a text from the Greek poet and physician Nicander, who lived about 200 B.C. In it he used both the word *bapto*, which we have already seen means "to dip," and the word "baptize" *(baptizo)*. It is a recipe for making a pickle. Nicander says that the vegetable should first be dipped *(bapto)* into boiling water and then baptized *(baptizo)* in the vinegar solution. Quite clearly, both operations had to do with immersing the vegetable in the solution. But the first was temporary while the other, the operation of baptizing the vegetable, produced a permanent change. We could say that the baptizing had identified the vegetable with the brine.

This meaning of the word is also obvious in several texts from the Greek translation of the Old Testament and from the New Testament. Thus, in Isaiah 21:4, we read literally: "Transgression baptizes me; my soul is overcome with fear." This means that the writer was changed from a state of quiet trust in God to fearfulness as a result of his transgressions. Similarly, Galatians 3:27 says, "For all of you who were baptized into Christ have clothed yourselves with Christ"; that is, the Christians in Galatia had been identified with him.

This interpretation of the words *bapto* and *baptizo* is necessary if we are to penetrate to the deepest understanding of the subject. What is more, it is absolutely essential if we are to make sense of the word in some instances.

Identification

Since a firm grasp of the metaphorical meaning of the word "baptize" is essential to this and the studies that follow, let me take a moment to deal with a few verses in which only the understanding of baptism as identification makes any sense at all of the passage.

The first one is Mark 16:16. This verse says: "Whoever believes and is baptized [*baptizo*, not *bapto*] will be saved." There are persons who have read that verse and then drawn the entirely false and indeed foolish conclusion that unless a person is baptized with water he cannot be saved. According to this view, the unbelieving thief crucified with Christ would have been lost. Once we get away from the idea that the verse is talking about water, however, which it is not, and think in terms of the believer's identification with Christ, then the statement becomes clear; and we recognize that Jesus was calling for an intellectual belief in himself plus personal commitment. "He who believes in me and is identified with me shall be saved." In this form the verse is an exact theological parallel to John 1:12 ("Yet to all who received him, to those who *believed* in his name, he gave the right to become children of God") and Revelation 3:20 ("Here I am! I stand at the door and knock. If anyone *hears* my voice and *opens* the door, I will come in and eat with him, and he with me"). All three verses teach that there must be a personal identification with Jesus by the one believing.

The metaphorical meaning of the word "baptize" illuminates another passage—1 Corinthians 10:1–2: "For I do not want you to be ignorant of the fact, brothers, that our forefathers were all under the cloud and that they all passed through the sea. They were all baptized into Moses in the cloud and in the sea." This passage is especially significant, since the people of Israel were quite obviously not covered or immersed in either the sea or the cloud. The cloud was not over them; it was behind them, separating them from the pursuing Egyptians. And if any group was immersed in the sea, it was the Egyptians, who were drowned in it. The only idea that gives any meaning here is a change of identity. Before they crossed the Red Sea the people were in rebellion against Moses. After the Red Sea their original attitude of rebellion was changed into an attitude of obedience and rejoicing, and they were identified with Moses for the remainder of their desert wandering.

My final example of a verse in which the metaphorical meaning of the word "baptize" is required is 1 Corinthians 15:29. It is the most striking of all. This verse says: "Now if there is no resurrection, what will those do who are baptized for the dead?" I guarantee that you will never make sense of that verse by taking it literally unless, like one of the major cults, you are foolish enough to conclude that you can provide salvation for your dead relatives by being immersed in water for them. So far as I know, this is the only group in the world that believes this. Not even the Roman Catholic church would affirm it, in spite of the fact that priests do say masses for the dead and that baptisms for the dead could be lucrative.

If we do not interpret this verse as evidence for the practice of water baptism on behalf of the dead, then, in what sense are we to interpret it? Take it in the sense that I have outlined, and in that sense place it into the context of Paul's argument in this chapter. Paul has been marshaling arguments for the existence of life after death. He has shown that Jesus was raised. He has argued that if there is no resurrection, then the fact of Jesus' resurrection could not have been established. After concluding in verse 20, "But Christ has indeed been raised from the dead, the firstfruits of those who have fallen asleep," he deals with the consequences of the resurrection, speaking of the resurrection of all believers and the eventual victory of Christ over death and evil.

At this point Paul turns to a related subject and begins to talk about the foolishness of living a Christian life, with all its hardships and persecutions, if there is no resurrection. If this life is all there is, then we should get the best out of it and forget trying to live by Christ's standards. On the other hand, if there is a resurrection, then we should be willing to die to sin now in order that we might rejoice with Christ hereafter. That is his argument.

Now let us translate the verse in this context and with the idea of the believer's identification with Christ in place of the word "baptize."

"For what is the sense of being identified as dead men, if the dead rise not at all? Why should they be identified as dead? Why should they be crucified with Christ? And why are we standing in jeopardy every hour? Why are we in danger of persecution by the authorities for our way of life? I protest by your rejoicing which I have in Christ Jesus our Lord, I am identified with Christ in His death every day. That is, I am baptized every day. If after the manner of men I have fought with beasts at Ephesus, what does it get me, if the dead rise not? If there is no resurrection, then let us eat and drink, for tomorrow we shall be dead."[1]

When we understand the passage in this way, 1 Corinthians 15:29–33 becomes a great argument for our separation from the world's standards of conduct. It is an encouragement to put first things first because of our identification with the Lord Jesus Christ.

John and Jesus

We may now apply the full meaning of "baptize" to the baptism of Jesus by John and to John's baptism generally. Certainly we have looked at enough texts to establish the metaphorical meaning.

What was the significance of John's baptism? John explained it himself in Matthew 3:11 by saying, "I baptize you with water for repentance." That is, John came to prepare the way for Jesus by calling men to repentance; and those who repented of their sin he baptized, as a sign that they had repented. We might say that he identified the repenters. Thus, Today's English Version translates the verse, "I baptize you with water to show that you have repented." When Jesus came John also baptized Jesus, but in this case naturally the identification was not for repentance. Jesus had nothing of which to repent. In this case, John was identifying Jesus as the Messiah. Consequently, we are not surprised to find that this is exactly what John himself declares in our text from John's Gospel: "I myself did not know him, but the reason I came baptizing with water was that he might be revealed to Israel" (John 1:31).

Finally we must recognize that when Jesus submitted to John's baptism, he too was undergoing an identification—an identification with mankind. It was not an identification with man's sin, of course; it was a declaration that Jesus was fully man apart from man's sin and that he was not ashamed to be identified with his brethren.

In this, Jesus became the fulfillment of the type of humble and self-effacing character revealed in the Old Testament by Moses. We are told in Hebrews that Moses "when he had grown up, refused to be known as the son of Pharaoh's daughter. He chose to be mistreated along with the people of God rather than to enjoy the pleasures of sin for a short time. He regarded disgrace for the sake of Christ as of greater value than the treasures of Egypt, because he was looking ahead to his reward" (Heb. 11:24–26). That is what the Lord Jesus Christ did for us in an infinitely greater way. He turned his back upon the glories of heaven in order to be identified with us, in order to become one with us; and he did so in love in order that we might become identified with him.

22

The Baptism of the Holy Spirit

John 1:29–34

The next day John saw Jesus coming toward him and said, "Look, the Lamb of God, who takes away the sin of the world! This is the one I meant when I said, 'A man who comes after me has surpassed me because he was before me.' I myself did not know him, but the reason I came baptizing with water was that he might be revealed to Israel."

Then John gave this testimony: "I saw the Spirit come down from heaven as a dove and remain on him. I would not have known him, except that the one who sent me to baptize with water told me, 'The man on whom you see the Spirit come down and remain is he who will baptize with the Holy Spirit.' I have seen and I testify that this is the Son of God."

In the first chapter of John's Gospel, the same verses that tell us that John the Baptist came baptizing with water also tell us that Jesus Christ came to baptize with the Holy Spirit. Thus, we are led to the questions: What is the baptism of the Holy Spirit? How does one receive this baptism? For whom is the baptism of the Holy Spirit intended? The text itself says, "I would not have known him, except that the one who sent me to baptize with water told me, 'The man on whom you see the Spirit come down and remain is he who will baptize with the Holy Spirit.' I have seen and I testify that this is the Son of God" (John 1:33–34).

As we begin to study this subject, we will be guided quite naturally by our previous discussion of the meaning of the word "baptize." Thus, we will not be talking about any particular mode of administering water baptism or about infant versus adult baptism. We will be talking solely about the nature of that "identification," or "transformation," that the Holy Spirit brings.

For All Believers

Here, of course, we are helped by a number of other verses that are found in the New Testament: 1 Corinthians 12:13, Romans 6:3, Ephesians 4:5, and others. These verses are not descriptive of any particular phenomenon associated with the giving of the Holy Spirit in the early church. They are verses that teach us about the meaning of our baptism with the Holy Spirit, and we turn to them because in relation to this doctrine as in relation to all other doctrines the Bible student must be guided by explicit teaching and not phenomena. To give an example, if we were to read in the Bible that someone in need of a great deal of money prayed for it and received it, that would not mean that each of us could invariably make the same prayer and receive the same answer. We would have to be guided in our understanding of prayer by what the Bible says explicitly about it. In the same way, we do not want to be guided in our understanding of the baptism of the Holy Spirit by the fact that some (not all) of the early Christians spoke in tongues as a result of receiving the Spirit, or saw the Spirit descend as small flames of fire. We want to be guided by what the New Testament teaches about the Holy Spirit in general and about his baptism.

One of the most instructive verses about the baptism of the Holy Spirit is 1 Corinthians 12:13. "For we were all baptized by one Spirit into one body —whether Jews or Greeks, slave or free—and we were all given the one Spirit to drink." The context shows us that the body spoken of here is the body of Christ or the true church, and the point of the verse is that all who believe in Christ are baptized by means of the Holy Spirit into his body. Hence, the baptism of the Holy Spirit is for all believers.

As I say this I know there will be some who will question it primarily because of the way in which the phrase "the baptism of the Holy Spirit" is used in our day. It is used to denote an experience generally linked with the gift of speaking in tongues, but this use of the phrase is inaccurate. I am not entering here into a discussion of the gift of tongues. I question much of what passes today for the gift of tongues, but I also believe that God can do anything. If he has chosen to give this gift in a special way today, so be it. I am not questioning that. My point is that the experience of tongues or of any other charismatic gift is not the baptism of the Holy Spirit.

It is also inaccurate to refer to the baptism of the Spirit as a second work of grace, as some have done. I will not question for a moment the need for a second work of grace, so long as the person speaking of it acknowledges the need for a third work of grace, a fourth work of grace, a fifth work of grace, and so on up to infinity. There are many experiences of God's grace in the life of a Christian; the Holy Spirit is the vehicle of them. There is also a need, as the Bible indicates, for a constant filling and refilling with the Spirit. But this filling of the Holy Spirit is not the baptism of the Holy Spirit. That is the point. Therefore, the only accurate usage of the phrase is that which applies it to all true believers as the means by which they become iden-tified with Christ as members of his mystical body.

Another verse is Romans 6:3: "Or don't you know that all of us who were baptized into Christ Jesus were baptized into his death?" This means that all believers are identified with Christ in his death through the Holy Spirit. Ephesians 4:5 says that there is "one Lord, one faith, one baptism." Correctly understood, this verse is a reference to the Trinity. "One Lord" is God the Father, Jehovah. "One faith" is the faith concerning the Lord Jesus Christ. "One baptism" is the baptism of the Holy Spirit. In each case the verses cited speak about an experience common to all who believe on Jesus Christ.

We now see why John the Baptist pointed to Jesus as the One who bap-tizes with the Holy Spirit. To do so was a characteristic of his ministry. "In other words," as John R. W. Stott writes in *The Baptism and Fullness of the Holy Spirit*, "just as John is called 'the Baptist' or 'the baptizer' because it was char-acteristic of his ministry to baptize with water, so Jesus is called 'the Baptist' or 'the baptizer,' because it is characteristic of His ministry to baptize with the Holy Spirit."[1] This happens to all who believe. In this the Lord Jesus Christ fulfilled a long list of prophecies (cf. Ezek. 36:26, 27; Joel 2:28–32) and ushered in the distinctive blessing for all true believers in this age.

Married to Christ

At this point of our study let me introduce an illustration. The illustra-tion is a good one and will not only summarize much of what we have been saying but will also carry us farther along. What is the illustration that the Bible itself uses to describe our identification with Christ? The answer is: marriage (Eph. 5:22–23). In other words, we are identified with Christ in the moment of our belief by means of the Holy Spirit in exactly the same way in which a bride is identified with her husband in the marriage ceremony.

In the first place, the marriage changes the woman's name. She comes into the church as Mary Jones, let us say. She repeats, "I, Mary, take thee, John, to be my wedded husband; and I do promise and covenant, before God and these witnesses, to be thy loving and faithful wife; in plenty and in want, in joy and in sorrow, in sickness and in health; as long as we both shall live." There comes the point in the service where the minister says, "And now by the authority committed unto me as a minister of the Church of Jesus Christ, I declare that John Smith and Mary Jones Smith are now hus-band and wife, according to the ordinance of God and the law of the state." And Mary, who came into the church as Miss Jones, leaves the church as Mrs. Smith. Mary has been identified with her husband by means of the marriage ceremony. In the same way, the name of the believer is changed from Miss Sinner to Mrs. Christian as she is identified with the Lord Jesus Christ. You could even say that it is the Holy Spirit himself who performs the ceremony.

It is not only Mary's name that is changed as a result of the ceremony, however. There is also a legal change. If Mary owned property before the marriage ceremony, she could have sold it as late as that morning with no signature but her own upon the document. After the marriage ceremony she can no longer do that. Instead, she will need her husband's signature also. In addition to the legal change there is a psychological change. Mary knows that she is a married woman and no longer single. She expects to make adjustments. There is also a change socially. Many of her friends from her single days will now gradually be replaced with married friends, and other women will regard her differently as well.

In exactly the same way, there are also many changes that take place in the moment when the Holy Spirit baptizes us into Christ or identifies us with him. We are baptized with the Spirit. We are placed within the body of Christ. We are identified with Christ. We are sealed with the Holy Spirit until the day of the redemption of our bodies. All these changes take place simultaneously and can be summarized by the truths that we are "in Christ" and that it is the Holy Spirit who has placed us there.

"In Christ"

When we were baptized with the Holy Spirit we were baptized "into Christ Jesus" (Rom. 6:3). What does it mean to be baptized "into Christ" or to be "in Christ"? In all there are over a hundred verses in the New Testament that use the word "in" before one of the names of the Lord Jesus, and when these are arranged in order chronologically they show us that we have been placed in Christ before the foundation of the world, that we are identified with him *in* his birth, *in* his circumcision, *in* his death, *in* his resurrection, and that we are to be found *in* Christ forever.

1. The Bible tells us that we were chosen in Christ before the foundation of the world (Eph. 1:4). Donald Grey Barnhouse has written: "Since we have already seen that we enter Christ by the work of the baptism of the Holy Spirit, we must see that the very first work performed by the Holy Spirit in our behalf was our eternal election to be members of His body. In His eternal decrees our God, the Father, the Son, and the Holy Spirit, determined that He should not be solitary forever, and decided that out of the multitude of creatures that would be born as sons of Adam, a vast host should one day become sons of God, and should be made partakers of the divine nature, and should be conformed unto the image of the Lord Jesus Christ. This company, which would become the fullness of Him that filleth all in all, would become sons by the new birth, but members of the body by the baptism of the Holy Spirit."[2] Thus, our first identification with Christ was in our election.

2. We are also identified with the Lord Jesus Christ in his birth. Some will ask, "But how are we identified with Christ in his birth?" The answer is that his birth is a picture of our birth, spiritually speaking. We read in 2 Corinthians

5:17: "If anyone is in Christ, he is a new creation." So we can say that by means of the Holy Spirit we have been identified with Christ in the very life of God.

What happened in the birth of the Lord Jesus? The sinless and divine life of Christ was placed within the sinful and quite human body of the virgin Mary. For a time it appeared that the divine life had been swallowed up, but the life was there and in time revealed itself through the birth of the infant Jesus. In the same way God has announced to us that we shall experience his very own life coming to reside within our hearts. If we reply, as Mary did, "How will this be . . . since I am a virgin?" the answer is that "the Holy Spirit will come upon you, and the power of the Most High will overshadow you. So the holy one to be born will be called the Son of God" (Luke 1:34–35). For those of us who believe, all that is good in us is the result of this planting of the divine nature. We are sons of God solely because of our identification with God's Son.

3. We are identified with Christ in his circumcision, for we read: "For in Christ all the fullness of the Deity lives in bodily form, and you have been given fullness in Christ, who is the head over every power and authority. In him you were also circumcised, in the putting off of the sinful nature, not with a circumcision done by the hands of men but with the circumcision done by Christ" (Col. 2:9–11). Circumcision signifies a separation from the sins of the flesh. Christ was totally separated from such sins. Therefore, we must learn that it is the desire of the Holy Spirit, who has identified us with Christ, to make us like Christ in this separation.

4. We are also identified with Christ in his death, for Romans 6:3 declares: "Or don't you know that all of us who were baptized into Christ Jesus were baptized into his death?" There are two senses in which this is true. First, when Jesus Christ died on the cross I died with him so far as my sin is concerned. God the Father put God the Son to death, and since I was united to him by means of the Holy Spirit from before the foundation of the world, I too was put to death. My sin was punished, and I may now stand boldly in God's presence cleansed forevermore. On the basis of this death I may correctly sing:

> My sin—oh, the bliss of this glorious thought!—
> My sin, not in part, but the whole,
> Is nailed to the cross and I bear it no more,
> Praise the Lord, praise the Lord, O my soul!

Second, there is also a sense in which my identity with Christ in his death refers to my life here and now. In fact, this is the purpose for which the truth is mentioned in Romans 6. The theme is the believer's growth in holiness. The life of sin is in the past. The future is holiness. Consequently, the believer is to count himself dead unto sin but alive unto God through the life of the Lord Jesus (v. 11). We might say that through our identification with Christ in his death, the power of sin over us is broken and we are set free to obey God.

5. Finally, we are also identified with Christ in his resurrection (Rom. 6:5). It is true, of course, that one day even our bodies shall be raised in the likeness of his resurrection, but that is certainly not the present or the primary meaning of our identification with Christ in his resurrection as that doctrine is taught in Scripture. The point is that our identification with Christ in his resurrection gives us the possibility of living out the life of Christ now. Thus we should cry out with Paul, "I want to know Christ and the power of his resurrection and the fellowship of sharing in his sufferings, becoming like him in his death" (Phil. 3:10–11). That is a present experience. The power of his resurrection is the power of the true Christian life.

All this—our identification with Christ in his birth, circumcision, death, and resurrection—is now ours because of our identification with Jesus Christ through the baptism of the Holy Spirit. In a former generation it was the custom often to carve on tombstones the inscription: "Here lies John Smith, who entered into eternal life on the 6th of June, 1854." Do not ever have an inscription like that put on your tombstone. If you have any inscription, let your inscription be to the effect that you were chosen in Christ from before the foundation of the world and that you enjoyed his life within you here as a present possession.

23

Christian Baptism

John 1:29–34

The next day John saw Jesus coming toward him and said, "Look, the Lamb of God, who takes away the sin of the world! This is the one I meant when I said, 'A man who comes after me has surpassed me because he was before me.' I myself did not know him, but the reason I came baptizing with water was that he might be revealed to Israel."

Then John gave this testimony: "I saw the Spirit come down from heaven as a dove and remain on him. I would not have known him, except that the one who sent me to baptize with water told me, 'The man on whom you see the Spirit come down and remain is he who will baptize with the Holy Spirit.' I have seen and I testify that this is the Son of God."

At Tenth Presbyterian Church in Philadelphia, where I serve as the pastor, two steps are usually followed by those who wish to unite with the congregation. First, a person desiring to become a member must meet with the session and give a testimony regarding his own personal faith in Jesus Christ. At this time his name is added to the rolls. Second, he is welcomed publicly before the rest of the congregation on the following Sunday morning. Both steps are normal, but we always tell a new member that his membership does not depend upon the public recognition. On the contrary, he is a member in good standing from the moment of his appearance before the session. He enjoys from

144

that moment all the rights and privileges possessed by any other member of the congregation.

In some ways this is an illustration of the difference between the baptism of the Holy Spirit, which we discussed in our last study, and water baptism, to which study we now come. Both are normal in the natural course of things. But they are two distinct acts, and the second is never essential to enjoying the benefits of being joined to Christ, which is true Christianity.

Rites and Ceremonies

This is the first principle we need to establish in regard to water baptism: *No rite or ceremony ever enters into the essence of Christianity.* In Paul's day, as also in all other ages of the Christian church, there were some who denied this. These persons thought that the blessings of salvation could be enjoyed only by those who adhered to circumcision, that is, who entered into Christianity by the initiatory rite of Judaism. In opposition to their views Paul taught that salvation came purely by grace and was not secured by any act performed by the individual.

In discussing this subject it was normal for Paul to take Abraham as his example, for Abraham was the clearest example in the Old Testament of a man justified before God entirely apart from any ceremonies or from the keeping of the law. Here is his argument in one of its most concise forms: "We have been saying that Abraham's faith was credited to him as righteousness. Under what circumstances was it credited? Was it after he was circumcised, or before? It was not after, but before! And he received the sign of circumcision, a seal of the righteousness that he had by faith while he was still uncircumcised. So then, he is the father of all who believe but have not been circumcised, in order that righteousness might be credited to them. And he is also the father of the circumcised who not only are circumcised but who also walk in the footsteps of the faith that our father Abraham had before he was circumcised" (Rom. 4:9–12).

We learn from this statement, first, that all who believe are saved, whether or not they are circumcised. We learn, second, that God gave Abraham the rite of circumcision, not *before* his justification by faith but *after* it, in order to make clear that the rite was not the means by which Abraham entered into salvation. Therefore, we say again that no rite or ceremony ever enters into the essence of Christianity.

It does not follow from this, however, that all rites and ceremonies are therefore to be cast aside or disregarded by Christ's followers, as some groups have done, who have no sacraments at all. *Some rites or ceremonies have value.* This is the second principle.

According to Paul, this was even true in regard to circumcision. "What value is there in circumcision?" he asks in Romans 3:1. He answered, "Much in every way." Thus, in Romans 4:9–12, the passage we have just read, he points out that circumcision had value to Abraham in being a sign and a seal of God's prior act of justification.

Benjamin B. Warfield, who was one of the greatest Reformed theologians America has produced, writes in his discussion of this subject, "According to this passage circumcision had no function whatever in the procuring or reception of salvation, whether as a means of securing it, or as a condition of its gift, or as a channel of its bestowment. It did not precede salvation as, in one way or another, obtaining it or facilitating its reception; it followed upon it, as presupposing its existence already." However, God in his grace gave Abraham circumcision as a sign and a seal of his righteousness. "The value of circumcision consisted, therefore, just in this: that it marked Abraham out, by a visible sign, as one who had received this righteousness from God and was henceforth to be the Lord's, and it sealed that righteousness to him under a covenant promise."[1]

We may, therefore, make it a third principle that *the rites or ceremonies that do have value have it because they have been established by God as signs of his grace and seals of his covenant promises.*

A Sign

I know there are some who will think that for a message purporting to be about water baptism, I have spent an excessive amount of time discussing circumcision. But I believe the discussion is essential, not only because of the close associations between the two—both are acts initiating a person into the body of God's people—but also because the most detailed New Testament discussion of the place of a rite or ceremony involves circumcision. Clearly this was because circumcision was a problem for the early Christian evangelists and needed discussion, while baptism, in spite of its obvious similarities to circumcision, was not. What is more, the discussion of circumcision has been useful, for it has given us the two terms—"sign" and "seal"—that are most useful in understanding Christian baptism.

The first of these two terms, then, is a "sign." What is a sign? Quite simply, a sign is a visible object designed to point to a reality different from itself and greater. In the case of the sacraments the sign is outward and visible, and the reality to which it points is inward and spiritual. Baptism with water points to our identification with Jesus Christ by means of the Holy Spirit.

Baptism identifies us as being the Lord's. It does not make us the Lord's, but it is the sign that identifies us as belonging to him. Several years ago when I was traveling across the western part of the United States with my family I began to come across signs advising the traveler that he was approaching "Joe's Wigwam." It was a desolate area. The signs were large. So probably for most persons traveling through that area of the country, the signs became the number one source of entertainment for many miles.

The first sign read, "50 miles to Joe's Wigwam"; the next sign: "40 miles to Joe's Wigwam." There was a sign for 30 miles, then 20, 15, 10, 5, 3, and 1. The next sign was an attention getter: "Get Ready! It's Coming!" And then another: "Only 500 Feet." Suddenly, there it was—a large gift shop with a motel and a gas station—and over it the largest sign of all: "Joe's Wigwam." I can almost guarantee that no one who passes through that section of the country ever goes into the gift shop, motel, or gas station and asks, "By the way, who owns this place?" Joe owns it, of course! The signs are there to point to it and indicate this fact.

It is in this sense that Christian baptism is a sign. It does not make a person a Christian any more than Joe's sign gives him title to the gift shop, motel, and gas station. Baptism simply indicates that he is now a Christian.

Moreover, this is not just true in reference to the unbelieving world. Baptism does have a reference to that. It is our way of telling the world that we are not our own, that we have been bought with a price, that we have been identified with Jesus. That is true. But it is also true that it speaks to ourselves. It has been reported of Martin Luther that he had hours when he seemed to be confused about everything, no doubt because of the strain and mental fatigue of being for twenty-eight years in the forefront of the Protestant Reformation in Germany. He questioned the value of the Reformation; he questioned his faith; he even questioned the work of the Lord Jesus Christ himself. But during those hours, we are told, he would write in chalk on his table the two words: *Baptizatus sum!* I have been baptized! Thus he would reassure himself that he really was Christ's and that he had been identified with him in his death and resurrection.

I must interject a word here lest anyone think that because I have referred to Luther in this way, I am assigning some magical property to baptism. That is not the case. Baptism is a sign, not a transaction. In fact, it was actually the failure to see this, coupled with the desire to give the sacrament status as a means of grace entirely on its own that led to the abuse of baptism first in the early Roman Catholic church and then also in the sixteenth century in the various church groupings that resulted from the Protestant Reformation.

The Roman church led the way by ascribing a value to the sacraments in themselves and then elevating them to a position over against preaching and the receiving of biblical knowledge. When this happened, it was the sacrament rather than belief that became necessary for salvation. In the case of baptism there arose the peculiar custom of delaying baptism until the last possible moment before death in order that the greatest number of sins might be washed away by it. In certain sectors of the Protestant church, the same views are expressed through the existence of a sacerdotal priesthood, the elevation of the communion table conceived as an altar, and occasionally even by the language used at either the Lord's Supper or the administration of baptism.

All these practices are inconsistent with the biblical teaching regarding baptism and the Lord's Supper. Thus we lay them aside in order to adhere to the view that sees the sacraments as a sign and a seal of God's covenant.

God's Seal

That brings us to the second point. Baptism is a sign, but it is also a seal. So we ask ourselves, "In what sense is baptism a seal? What is meant by a seal anyway?"

In our day the use of official seals is diminishing, but we still have enough examples to remind us of a seal's significance. If you have ever gone abroad, you will have gone through the experience of procuring a passport, which bears the seal of the United States of America. It is stamped into the paper in such a way that it is impossible to remove or change it, and it validates the passport. Furthermore, if you have ever had to swear to the truth of some statement before a notary public, you would have seen him affix his seal to the document, thereby confirming the oath that you made before him.

In ancient times seals were in much greater use. Since most men, even the very rich or important, could not write, a seal was the equivalent of one's signature. Men carried their seals with them, and they affixed them to letters or documents as a pledge of their work and as a recognition of their responsibility. If we put the two ideas together—the idea of an official seal and a signature—we get some idea of the meaning of a seal in regard to baptism. By receiving baptism we indicate that we are the Lord Jesus Christ's. His name has been affixed to us; his seal on us is evidence that he stands behind his promises.

Once again let me quote from Warfield. "There is nothing in the whole history of the people of God which they value more highly, on which they more deeply felicitate themselves, on which they more securely depend, than that they are called by the name of the Lord. It was to this fact that they appealed when in their affliction they turned to the Hope of Israel, the Savior thereof in time of trouble: 'Thou, O Jehovah, art in the midst of us, and we are called by thy name; leave us not' (Jer. 14:9). It was in this that their jubilation reached its height: 'I am called by thy name, O Jehovah, God of hosts' (Jer. 15:16)."

Thus, says Warfield, "When our Lord commanded his disciples to baptize those whom in their world-wide mission they should draw to Christ 'into the name of the Father and of the Son and of the Holy Spirit,' precisely what he bade them do was to call them by the name of the Triune God, that they might be marked out as his and sealed to him as an eternal possession."[2]

If you are a believer in the Lord Jesus Christ, this is what God has done with you. You have been called to Christ. His name has been affixed to you, and you are now sealed to him as a valued and eternal possession.

Sealed with the Spirit

There is one final point. It is the fact that in the New Testament the word "seal" is actually always applied to the Holy Spirit rather than to the administration of water baptism. This does not mean that water baptism does not have the characteristics of a seal as we have discussed them, but it does mean that the work of the Holy Spirit is so great and so real that the term is reserved quite naturally almost exclusively for his baptism. Thus we are told that when we believed in Christ we "were marked in him with a seal, the promised Holy Spirit" (Eph. 1:13) and that we were "sealed for the day of redemption" (Eph. 4:30).

This is our true security as God's people. In the Book of Ezekiel there is a prophecy that concerns God's dealings with Israel at the end of history. Six men enter Jerusalem to pronounce judgment upon the inhabitants, but before they go in, one man clothed in linen and carrying a writing kit enters to "put a mark on the foreheads of those who grieve and lament over all the detestable things that are done" in Israel (Ezek. 9:4). Afterward the others are told, "Slaughter old men, young men and maidens, women and children, but do not touch anyone who has the mark" (v. 6).

In the same way, you and I and all who believe in the Lord Jesus are identified by the Holy Spirit of God as Christ's men, as Christians. We are made secure in that identification. The Bible says, "God's solid foundation stands firm, sealed with this inscription: 'The Lord knows those who are his'" And it adds, "Everyone who confesses the name of the Lord must turn away from wickedness" (2 Tim. 2:19).

24

You Shall See Angels

John 1:51

He then added, "I tell you the truth, you shall see heaven open, and the angels of God ascending and descending on the Son of Man."

Iwonder if you have ever had a particularly delightful experience and then discovered to your added delight that there was much more of the same to be enjoyed? I remember one experience like that that I had at a very early age. Someone had given me a book that contained one of the adventures of the Hardy boys, two young brothers whose father was a detective, who were always getting mixed up in his adventures. I thought it was one of a kind when I received it, and I loved it. It was a fascinating adventure. But then, imagine my added delight when I discovered that the book I owned was only one of a long series of books with the same characters and that I had only touched the surface of their adventures in my reading.

That kind of experience is one we all have at different periods of our lives. I know you have had it. What I would like to see, however, is that this is also an experience that you can have spiritually. That is, you can learn something particularly wonderful about Jesus, have moments of wonderful fellowship with him, experience his power, and then know that the pleasure can be enjoyed increasingly forever.

What are the words that characterize the Lord Jesus Christ? He is *eternal*. This means that he is without beginning and without ending. He antedates time. He goes beyond it. He is completely independent of it. Length of days does not exhaust him. Jesus Christ is also *immutable,* as God is. That means that he does not change and will never change. He is *omniscient.* There is nothing known or to be known that he does not already know, and all our knowledge is simply our thinking his thoughts after him. Because he is omniscient there will also be no end to our own growth in knowledge as his children. He is perfect and inexhaustible in his *love.* Nothing will mar our experience of his love; nothing will diminish it. His *mercy* and *righteousness* and *holiness* will be a never-ending pleasure for those whom he has redeemed.

What can exhaust the inexhaustible? What finite mind can plumb the infinite? It is impossible. Certainly, at his right hand there will be "eternal pleasures" (Ps. 16:11).

The Problem

In a general way this is quite clearly the point of the very last verse of John 1. The first chapter of John reveals Jesus in a variety of contexts and under an unusual variety of names. He is the Word, the Light, the Lamb, the Son of God, Rabbi, the Messiah, the King of Israel. These titles culminate in the confession of Nathanael who, after some initial skepticism, declares, "Rabbi, you are the Son of God; you are the King of Israel" (v. 49). At this point, however, Jesus answers that all the insight and experience that these confessions embody, wonderful as they are, are only a prelude to an infinite series of such experiences that lie ahead. That is, there is more to come. He therefore declares, "I tell you the truth, you shall see heaven open, and the angels of God ascending and descending on the Son of Man" (v. 51).

In a general way the idea of additional delightful experiences for those who have believed on Jesus lies at the heart of this verse. But when we try to go beyond this, when we hunt for a more precise reference, we run into problems. The verse is a promise, but a promise of what? To be even more explicit, when is heaven opened and when are angels to be seen? Exactly what is this verse talking about?

This is not just a problem for us in our age, of course. It has been a problem for many interpreters down through the years of church history. Why? The difficulty lies not so much in finding an explanation for the verse or a reference for it—many have done that—but in finding an explanation or reference that deals with each of the parts of the puzzle.

There is a puzzle that I am sure many people have seen, made of several pieces of cardboard of various shapes that are to be combined into a square. If you have ever attempted to do this puzzle, you know that it is not difficult to make a square. In fact, you can make several squares of different sizes. The difficulty is that there always seem to be one or more pieces left over. The puzzle is solved only when a square is made in which all the pieces are utilized. It is the same in our handling of John 1:51. This is a puzzle with four pieces, the four major parts of the verse: (1) the reference to the future you *shall* see; (2) the fact that the heavens will open; (3) the reference to angels ascending and descending upon Jesus; and (4) the title given by Jesus to himself, "the Son of Man." Any good explanation of the verse should explain each of these four parts.

There are a number of explanations that refer to just one. Probably the most popular explanation in contemporary books is the one that links the verse to the vision of Jacob in which he saw angels ascending and descending upon a ladder from heaven (Gen. 28:12). The difficulty with this view is in finding a reason why Jesus should allude to Jacob in this context. It is true that Jacob was a type of Christ in one sense. He is the man who left home to find a bride in a foreign country, just as Christ left heaven to redeem his bride, the church. But this is a bit farfetched. And it does not help us much to imagine that Nathanael might have been reading about the Jacob story when Philip called him.

Some explanations refer to a ministry of angels to Jesus during Jesus' lifetime. But the difficulty with this view is that this happened only twice during the lifetime of Jesus, once at the close of his temptation by Satan in the wilderness and once in Gethsemane, and neither Nathanael, Andrew, or Philip was present on these occasions.

In Luther's exposition of these chapters, the father of the Reformation calls attention to the heavens being opened and notes that this also happened twice. It happened at Jesus' baptism (when the dove descended, but not angels), and it happened at his transfiguration. However, as Luther notes, only three of the apostles saw heaven opened at the transfiguration. None saw it at the baptism. Therefore, says Luther, "This story must be interpreted spiritually." Luther refers the story to the church and to the access that all believers have through Christ to heaven.

Is this the explanation? Does this explain the four pieces of the puzzle? I do not think so. On the other hand, I think there is an explanation that does. According to this explanation, when Jesus said, "You shall see heaven open, and the angels of God ascending and descending on the Son of Man," he was not talking about anything that took place during the lifetime of Nathanael. Nor was he talking about anything that took place either in the lifetime of Philip or Andrew or any of the other disciples or even of you and me. He was talking about something that is still future, that is still to come. In other words, although no one has seen the fulfillment of this verse yet, all will one day see it when Jesus Christ returns.

When you take the verse in this sense, all the elements of the verse fall into place. "You shall see" becomes genuinely future, and not just for Nathanael. The heavens are to be opened literally. Angels will accompany Jesus. And the phrase "the Son of Man" receives its true reference as that defined for us in the seventh chapter of the Book of Daniel. "In my vision at night I looked, and there before me was one like a son of man, coming with the clouds of heaven. He was given authority, glory and sovereign power; all peoples, nations and men of every language worshiped him. His dominion is an everlasting dominion that will not pass away, and his kingdom is one that will never be destroyed" (vv. 13–14). This explanation even makes sense of several other verses in the Gospels in which Jesus declared that "the Son of Man is going to come in his Father's glory with his angels, and then he will reward each person according to what he has done" (Matt. 16:27), and again, "In the future you will see the Son of Man sitting at the right hand of the Mighty One and coming on the clouds of heaven" (Matt. 26:64).

Clouds of Glory

If we are to understand this great event, we need to understand first of all that it is a moment of great joy and rejoicing for Christ's followers. Unfortunately, for many Christians today the return of Jesus Christ does not seem to be an event of great joy. They are far from him in fellowship and will be ashamed at his coming.

Revelation 19 portrays this event most graphically, and here all is triumphant. Heaven is astir, and in heaven a great host of persons are shouting hallelujahs. Hallelujah means "praise to Jehovah." First, a great many people shout, "Hallelujah! Salvation and glory and power belong to our God." After this a great multitude shouts again, "Hallelujah." The twenty-four elders and the four cherubim fall down and worship God, crying, "Amen, Hallelujah." Finally a great multitude exclaim, "Hallelujah! For our Lord God Almighty reigns." The picture is one of great joy, for everything is prepared for the Lord's appearing. The Lamb's wife, the glorified church, is ready, clothed in fine linen, clean and white.

Then the chapter proceeds, "I saw heaven opened, and behold, a white horse! He who sat upon it is called Faithful and True, and in righteousness he judges and makes war. His eyes are like a flame of fire, and on his head are many diadems; and he has a name inscribed which no one knows, but himself. He is clad in a robe dipped in blood, and the name by which he is called is The Word of God. And the armies of heaven, arrayed in fine linen, white and pure, followed him on white horses. From his mouth issues a sharp sword with which to smite the nations, and he will rule them with a rod of iron; he will tread the wine press of the fury of the wrath of God the Almighty. On his robe and on his thigh he has a name inscribed, King of kings, and Lord of lords" (Rev. 19:11–16 RSV).

This scene is the fulfillment of the promise Jesus made to Nathanael, and it is one in which you and I shall participate. We shall praise him. We shall glory in his triumphs.

> Thou art coming, O my Savior,
> Thou art coming, O my King,
> In thy beauty all resplendent;

In thy glory all transcendent;
Well may we rejoice and sing:
Coming! in the opening east
Herald brightness slowly swells;
Coming! O my glorious Priest,
Hear we not thy golden bells?

Thou art coming, thou art coming;
We shall meet thee on thy way,
We shall see thee, we shall know thee,
We shall bless thee, we shall show thee
All our hearts could never say:
What an anthem that will be,
Ringing out our love to thee,
Pouring out our rapture sweet
At thine own all-glorious feet.

O the joy to see thee reigning,
Thee, my own beloved Lord!
Ev'ry tongue thy Name confessing,
Worship, honor, glory, blessing
Brought to thee with glad accord;
Thee, my Master and my Friend,
Vindicated and enthroned,
Unto earth's remotest end
Glorified, adored, and owned.

Does that mean anything to you? It should mean a great deal. In this world you and I often find ourselves as a very small minority as Christians, and we are often discouraged. We wonder how we are ever going to get through this year, this week, this day. How will we ever bear a witness? We would find much of our thinking along these lines transformed if we would only learn to see ourselves as servants of this great Jesus, this King of kings and Lord of lords, who is returning one day on the clouds of heaven with his holy angels.

Day of Judgment

We need to see one thing more. It is true that the scene we have been looking at is a scene of glory, but it is also true that it is a scene of judgment for those who have not responded to the preaching of God's grace through the gospel. This is seen in the imagery of the passage. Revelation 19 describes the garments worn by Jesus as having been dipped in blood, and we are told that he has been treading out "the winepress of the fury of the wrath of God Almighty" (v. 15).

Are you prepared to meet this Christ when he returns? The prophet Daniel was one of the Hebrews who was carried into Babylon when Jerusalem was conquered in the sixth century B.C., and he rose to prominence in Babylon, serving as a minister of state under three successive kings. The second of these kings was Belshazzar. One evening Belshazzar threw a party and invited one thousand of his nobles. It was to be a splendid evening. Picture one thousand nobles dressed in the most regal robes, with gold crowns on their heads, lords of a powerful and far-flung empire, heroes of battlefields. Imagine the banquet, the wine, the boastful talk, the abundance of sensual pleasure! Suddenly, in the midst of the revelry, the laughter begins to die away, for a hand has appeared writing on the wall of the palace above the king's table. The words written are, *"Mene, mene, tekel, upharsin."* No one can interpret them. The queen suggests that they find Daniel, who can interpret visions. When Daniel arrives at the banquet hall and sees the writing, he cries, "God has numbered the days of your reign and brought it to an end. . . . You have been weighed on the scales and found wanting. . . . Your kingdom is divided and given to the Medes and Persians." The revelers listen in stunned silence. Some perhaps are skeptical. But that night the city is entered, and Darius the Mede reigns on Belshazzar's former throne.

So it is in our own chaotic century. The world is engaged in its banquet. The laughter grows louder, the food is more and more lavish. Revelers indulge in their sensual pleasure. But the banquet is almost over. The last course is about to be served. Soon the hand will appear, and the words of judgment will be pronounced. Where are you in that picture? Are you in the banquet hall? Or are you among those who wait for the coming of the Lord of lords in glory and yearn for the marriage supper of the Lamb?

25

What's in a Name?

John 1:1–51

Word . . . the light . . . the Lamb of God . . . the Son of God . . . Rabbi . . . Messiah . . . King of Israel . . . Son of Man.

In the title song of the very successful and at times quite beautiful rock opera *Jesus Christ Superstar,* the chorus asks movingly:

> Jesus Christ, Jesus Christ,
> Who are you? What have you
>   sacrificed?
> Jesus Christ Superstar,
> Do you think you're what they
>   say you are?

In one form or another this question has been asked by many thousands of persons down through history, and many different answers have been given. In the last century alone approximately 60,000 books have sought to explain Jesus. Those writing them have differed widely. So, for many who do not know the biblical replies, the question about who Jesus is goes unanswered.

Fortunately, the Bible does answer the question, and nowhere is it answered in more detail and in a shorter space than in the first chapter of John's Gospel.

Commentators have often noticed the number and variety of names or titles given to Jesus in the fifty-one verses of John 1. What has not been noticed is that the titles have been arranged by John to show in chronological sequence who Jesus is, what he has done, and what he is yet to do. Thus they begin with Jesus as the Word, as he was with God from the beginning. They trace him through the years of his incarnation as the Light, the Lamb of God, the Son of God, and Rabbi. And they deal with things yet to come under the names: Messiah, King of Israel, and Son of Man, the last of which refers to Jesus' role in the final judgment. I believe that it is possible to trace the significance of the past, present, and future ministry of Christ in sequence by means of these titles.

Biblical Names

For us names generally do not mean very much. In the East and in the Bible it is otherwise.

Every careful reader of the Bible must often have been struck with the significance of the divine names revealed to various men in the Scriptures. Abraham, the father of our faith, received a progressive revelation of the character of God by means of God's names. Early in his life Abraham had come to know God as *Jehovah,* which means "I am that I am." It was the revelation of God as Jehovah that sent Abraham out of Ur of the Chaldees toward what was later to become the land of Israel. After he had done battle with five kings, Abraham learned to know God as *El Elyon.* This means "the Most High God" and identifies him as the possessor of the heavens and the earth. At the time of the birth of Isaac through a miracle, God was revealed as *El Shaddai,* "God Almighty." Finally, on the mountain God disclosed that he was also *Jehovah Jireh,* which means "the Lord will provide."

Similar revelations were given to Jacob, Moses, David, and the prophets, and all are striking. In fact, they are so striking that many scholars have traced the history of God's revelation of himself to Israel by means of them.

In *The Revelation of the Father,* Anglican Bishop B. F. Westcott has written, "Of God as he is in himself, in his absolute and unapproachable majesty, we can as yet know nothing. But the names by which we are allowed to address him gather up what is shown to us . . . of his working and of his will. The divine names receive and reflect scattered rays of heavenly truth as men can bear their effulgence; and when they have been set in our spiritual firmament they burn for ever. Thus each name authoritatively given to God is, so to speak, a fresh and lasting revelation of his nature. Now in one title and now in another we catch glimpses of his ineffable glory."[1]

We also catch glimpses of the glory of the Lord Jesus Christ by means of such titles. And we may study them, particularly those included by John the evangelist, in order to see the entire sweep of the ministry of the Lord Jesus Christ from the beginning to the end. That this can be done is itself interesting, for it is John's way of saying that Jesus is truly the alpha and the omega, the beginning and the end. It is the purpose of John's Gospel to reveal him.

The Word

The first title is "Word." It occurs three times in verse 1 and is repeated once more in verse 14. We read, "In the beginning was the Word, and the Word was with God, and the Word was God. . . . The Word became flesh and made his dwelling among us."

We have already seen that this title refers to Jesus as the Creator and as the One who, by being God, reveals God. When a thoughtful man of Jewish background would read these verses, he would undoubtedly think of the first chapter of Genesis, in which God speaks and all things come into being. Clearly John is associating Jesus with God the Father in this creative activity. A Greek would read the title and think of his ancient philosophy. To him the *logos* or "word" would refer first of all to the controlling principle of this world. To each of these men, Jew and Greek, John declares that the God who created the world and who previously could only be most imperfectly known is fully revealed in Jesus.

Jesus is not only the first and most complete Word of God, he is also the last Word. No one will find God apart from him.

The Light

The second name for the Lord Jesus Christ is "Light." John says, "In him was life, and that life was the light of men. The light shines in the darkness, but the darkness has not understood it" (vv. 4–5). Later he tells us that John the Baptist came to bear witness to the Light, and he adds, "The true light that gives light to every man was coming into the world" (v. 9).

It is obvious that in one sense "Light" simply reinforces one of the ideas already suggested by referring to Jesus as the "Word." Light is a universal image for the illumination of the understanding through revelation. We express the idea when we say, "Well, the light finally came on," or "he finally saw the light," referring to someone who has just understood something. In this sense, the idea of light reinforces the idea of God's revelation of himself through Jesus.

Yet there is an additional idea in the thought of Jesus' being the Light that makes this title distinct from the former one. It is the contrast of light with darkness. The point is that Jesus is the Light, while men are in darkness because of sin and disobedience. They move out of the darkness only when they come to Jesus.

Many great thinkers have found this. Emile Cailliet, former professor of philosophy at Princeton Theological Seminary, is an example. Dr. Cailliet was highly educated in France in the period before and after the First World War, but his education was naturalistic to the core. He never even saw a Bible until the war was over and he was nearing the end of his studies. These were his years of darkness; his life was described then, as he says, by the title of Eugene O'Neill's play, *Long Day's Journey into Night*. Now, however, his life is a *journey into light,* and he describes it as a discovery of his own sin and Christ's righteousness through finding Jesus himself through the Bible.

He has written of this discovery in his book *Journey into Light:* "A decisive insight flashed through my whole being the following morning as I probed the opening chapters of the Gospel according to John. The very clue to the secret of human life was disclosed right there, not stated in the foreboding language of philosophy, but in the common, everyday language of human circumstances. And, far from moving on their own accord, these circumstances seemed to yield themselves without striving, obedient unto One who inexorably stood out from the gospel narrative—indeed a Person of far more than human nature and stature."[2]

No doubt John was trying to encourage such confessions as he sought to describe the One who leads us all out of darkness into his marvelous light.

The Lamb of God

The most important title is the one that comes next in this chapter, for it is the title that refers to Jesus' work of redemption. It is "the Lamb of God." It occurs in the Baptist's declaration, "Look, the Lamb of God, who takes away the sin of the world" (vv. 29, 36). All the wealth of the Old Testament symbolism in the sacrifices of the patriarchs and of the Mosaic law throws weight on this title, for it shows Jesus to be the sin-bearer, the Passover, the innocent substitute dying in our place. This great truth of substitution—the bearing of the sinner's guilt and penalty by another—is carried over from the Old Testament to the New Testament by means of this metaphor and made an integral part of the gospel message.

This is what Jesus Christ came to do. He came to remove our sin by dying in our place as our substitute. Has he done that for you? Are your sins upon him? Has he borne your reproach? Has he suffered for your iniquity? The Bible says that he will be the Lamb of God for you, if you will confess your sin and trust him to remove it forever.

Son of God

In verse 34 John the Baptist concludes his formal testimony by giving Jesus a fourth title: the "Son of God" (cf. v. 49). There are some critics today, although not as many as there were in the last century, who have sought to lessen this title by denying that Jesus was the Son of God in any unique sense. According to such teachers, Jesus was a son only in the sense that all men are supposed to be "sons" by creation. Actually, this is untenable, and any honest evaluation of the biblical evidences must recognize that Jesus is declared to be God's Son in a way that makes him entirely unique and divine.

At his birth the angel declared, "He will be great and will be called the Son of the Most High" (Luke 1:32); he "will be called the Son of God" (v. 35). God the Father bore witness to him on several occasions declaring, "You are my Son, whom I love; with you I am well pleased" (Mark 1:11; 9:7). The titles "Son of God" and "Son of the Most High God" were used by demons in recognition of his unique authority and divinity (Matt. 4:3, 6; Mark 3:11; 5:7; Luke 4:41). Peter said, "You are the Christ, the Son of the living God" (Matt. 16:16). It is as God's Son that Christ reigns and exercises authority in the lives of those who have come to him.

Rabbi

Jesus is next called "Rabbi," which means "teacher" (John 1:38). Is he your teacher? The greatest mistake you could ever make is to think that he can be your teacher before he has become your Savior.

That was the mistake made by Nicodemus, whose story is told just two chapters later in this Gospel. Nicodemus came to Jesus, saying, "Rabbi, we know you are a teacher who has come from God. For no one could perform the miraculous signs you are doing if God were not with him" (John 3:2). In other words, Nicodemus was very impressed with Jesus and wanted to be instructed by him. But this will not work spiritually. A man must first see Jesus as the Lamb of God and the Son of God before he can have him as Rabbi. Consequently, Jesus replied to Nicodemus, "I tell you the truth, no one can enter the kingdom of God unless he is born of water and the Spirit" (v. 3). If you want the Lord Jesus Christ as your teacher, he will be your teacher. He will show you great and wondrous things out of his Word, so that your heart will burn within you (Luke 24:32). But first, he must be your Savior.

Messiah, King, Son of Man

The last three titles refer to Christ's future actions and may be taken together. They occur toward the end of the chapter. When Andrew calls Simon to Jesus, Andrew declares, "We have found the Messiah" which, John tells us, means "the Christ" (John 1:41). After Nathanael comes to Jesus and recognizes that Philip's claims regarding him are true, Nathanael exclaims, "Rabbi, you are the Son of God; you are the King of Israel" (v. 49). Finally, Jesus replies, "I tell you the truth, you shall see heaven open, and the angels of God ascending and descending on the Son of Man" (v. 51). These three titles—Messiah, King of Israel, and Son of man—refer to two aspects of Jesus' ministry.

The first two titles have to do with his ministry to Judaism. Jesus is Israel's Messiah. He is Israel's king. For this reason I believe that the time will yet come when Jesus will reign over Israel from Jerusalem as the prophets foretold (Isa. 24:23; Zech. 14:9, 16).

The final title is clearly also messianic, but it refers to judgment upon the Gentiles. It is derived from the seventh chapter of Daniel. "In my vision at night I looked, and there before me was one like a son of man, coming with the clouds of heaven. He approached the Ancient of Days and was led into his presence. He was given authority, glory and sovereign power; all peoples, nations and men of every language worshiped him. His dominion is an everlasting dominion that will not pass away, and his kingdom is one that will never be destroyed" (Dan. 7:13–14; cf. Matt. 13:41–43; 24:27, 30; 25:31–46). The scene is one of judgment and of everlasting rule.

Fortunately, the scene of Christ's judgment is still future; and you, if you do not yet know him as the Lamb who takes away your sin, have time to prepare for it. Quite a few years ago, after World War II, an official government study, called the Pearl Harbor Report, demonstrated that no one was prepared for the disaster that struck on the morning of December 7, 1941. The admirals and generals were unprepared; the authorities were unprepared; the nation was unprepared. There was a total lack of preparation, in spite of the ample evidence that existed indicating that a devastating attack would be coming.

Thus will Christ's future judgment as the Son of man appear to the world. We are told it is coming. Men are warned to flee from the wrath of God. Yet the judgment will fall suddenly and unexpectedly upon the many who are sunk in a lethargy of affluence and self-satisfaction. Some will meet the Lord Jesus as their judge. How much better to meet him as the Lamb of God who has taken away sin, as teacher, Savior, and Lord.

26

The First Miracle

John 2:1-11

On the third day a wedding took place at Cana in Galilee. Jesus' mother was there, and Jesus and his disciples had also been invited to the wedding. When the wine was gone, Jesus' mother said to him, "They have no more wine."

"Dear woman, why do you involve me?" Jesus replied. "My time has not yet come."

His mother said to the servants, "Do whatever he tells you."

Nearby stood six stone water jars, the kind used by the Jews for ceremonial washing, each holding from twenty to thirty gallons.

Jesus said to the servants, "Fill the jars with water"; so they filled them to the brim.

Then he told them, "Now draw some out and take it to the master of the banquet."

They did so, and the master of the banquet tasted the water that had been turned into wine. He did not realize where it had come from, though the servants who had drawn the water knew. Then he called the bridegroom aside and said, "Everyone brings out the choice wine first and then the cheaper wine after the guests have had too much to drink; but you have saved the best till now."

This, the first of his miraculous signs, Jesus performed at Cana in Galilee. He thus revealed his glory, and his disciples put their faith in him.

In the fourteenth chapter of the Book of Romans there is a verse that says: "For the kingdom of God is not a matter of eating and drinking, but of righteousness, peace and joy in the Holy Spirit" (v. 17). In our day many Christians have gotten the part about righteousness right. Many even have peace. But as I look about at contemporary Christianity, it seems to me that many are sadly lacking in joy. They have the doctrine right and are even secure in salvation. But there is none of the supernatural joy and exuberance that is to be one of the outward marks of the presence of the Lord Jesus Christ in a Christian.

This is unfortunate, of course, and it is not right. The Bible tells us that one fruit of the Spirit is "joy" (Gal. 5:22). Psalm 32:11 declares: "Rejoice in the LORD and be glad, you righteous; sing, all you who are upright in heart!" In Psalm 16 we read: "You have made known to me the path of life; you will fill me with joy in your presence, with eternal pleasures at your right hand" (v. 11). Jesus declared, "I have told you this so that my joy may be in you and that your joy may be complete" (John 15:11).

According to these verses, the life of the Christian is to be characterized by joy, not by that superficial, raucous joy of which the world is capable, of course, but by that divine and desirable joy that characterized the life of the Lord Jesus Christ. Where do we learn of that joy? I believe that one place is in the verses to which we come now in our study of John's Gospel.

Jesus Was Welcome

These verses tell us a story. "On the third day a wedding took place at Cana in Galilee. Jesus' mother was there, and Jesus and his disciples had also been invited to the wedding" (John 2:1–2). According to the chronology that John gives us for these opening chapters, this was the last of the seven original and eventful days of Christ's ministry. The first was the day on which John the Baptist confronted the Jewish delegation from Jerusalem. The second was the day on which John identified Jesus for the first time as "the Lamb of God." On the third day Andrew and an unnamed disciple (probably John the evangelist) followed Jesus. The fourth day contained the events connected with Andrew's call of his brother Peter. On the fifth day Jesus called Nathanael. The sixth day was spent in traveling. On the seventh day Jesus arrived in Cana and was invited with his disciples to the wedding.

This is also the day on which the public ministry of Jesus began officially. Consequently, the opening verses of chapter 2 are really an introduction to the second main section of the Gospel (chaps. 2–11), which some scholars have called "the book of Christ's signs."

It is an interesting sidelight on these verses that under Jewish law the normal day for a wedding was Wednesday, the day of the week prescribed for the wedding of a virgin. If that is the case here, then we are able to work backward to find that it was the Sabbath when Andrew and the other disciple followed Jesus and spent the day with him. Thus, we have an explanation for their inactivity.

But we must return to this story. Why was Jesus invited to this wedding? We do not know for certain. It is possible that he had been invited to it in advance and had been on his way to it when he called Philip and Nathanael. It may be that the invitation came through Nathanael, for we are told later that Cana of Galilee was Nathanael's hometown (John 21:2). It may be that Jesus was invited because of his mother Mary, who seems to have had a prominent place at the feast. Whatever the case, the point seems to be that Jesus was welcome. And, as I read the story, I seem to sense that the invitation came to him at once as soon as the men and women of Cana learned that he had returned to Galilee from the area of the lower Jordan, where John was baptizing.

I think this point is important, for this is the first of many stories suggesting that Jesus was always welcome among those who were having a good time. Have you ever thought how wonderful it is that Jesus was at home in such company? I am afraid that if some Christians I know were the pattern, there would be very little to expect of true joy and happiness or good times in the Christian life. Some Christians go around with grim looks and long faces. If they ever find themselves in the company of someone else who is having a good time, they immediately suspect that the cause of the fun is either illegal, immoral, or fattening. Jesus was not like that. He did not condemn those who were enjoying themselves, and he was not jealous of them. As a result, he was welcome at their gatherings, and those who had invited him listened to his teachings.

Are you like that? If you are, you may find that people are not only pleased with your company; they may also be willing to listen to your testimony.

Let me tell you a true incident that illustrates this aspect of John's story. A friend of mine, who is now a professor at the University of Pennsylvania, was asked to speak at a banquet that would be attended by the young adult group of a certain church. He had never heard of the church before, or the young adult group, but he went to the banquet and spoke about the call of Christ to the unsaved and about discipleship. After the dinner and his address my friend was ready to go home, but he discovered that this was only the prelude to the evening. The dinner was followed by a wild party at which, as he told me, the noise was so loud that it was almost impossible to talk to anyone. He concluded—and he was right, as it later turned out— that the group was composed mostly of those who were Christian in name only. But what should he do? Should he go home, declaring that Christians do not go to wild parties and that this was a most unfortunate sequel to his talk? Or should he stay, enjoying the good time of the others as much as possible?

My friend decided to stay with the group. During the first few minutes he was there, a girl came up to talk to him. She had been impressed by what he had said at the dinner, but she did not understand it. She asked him to explain again what it means to be a Christian. My friend said that at this point the noise was so loud the two of them had to shout to each other even though their mouths were only inches from each other's ears. But the shouting was worthwhile, for the girl believed and became a Christian. The sequel to the story is that the girl was apparently the key to the whole group. She became a dynamic witness to her friends. Through her witness most of the group believed. She later died of a brain hemorrhage, suddenly, at the age of 25;

but at that time others believed. One young man, who believed, then went on to influence hundreds.

I believe, of course, that there may be environments from which most Christians should stand free. Yet we often apply that thought adversely and forget to be cheerful. Charles Spurgeon once wrote to his students: "Sepulchral tones may fit a man to be an undertaker, but Lazarus is not called out of his grave by hollow moans. . . . I commend cheerfulness to all who would win souls."[1]

They Have No Wine

I do not want anyone to misunderstand me at this point, thinking that I am commending the good times of this world as something superior to the joy of true Christianity. I am not. On the contrary, I believe that, although the Christian should not hold aloof from any genuinely good experiences, it should be the *superior* joy of the Christian that most commends the Lord Jesus Christ to unbelievers.

But this, too, is involved in the story. As the story goes on it is seen that the wine required for the feast is exhausted. This may not mean much to us in a day when practically any lack may be made up by a quick trip to the corner market. But it was a serious thing in those days when a lack could not be easily remedied and when the shortage (if discovered) would certainly prove a great embarrassment to the host. What is more, as we read the various things that the Bible has to say about wine, we soon discover that wine was a symbol of joy. The rabbis said, "Without wine there is no joy." So, to run out of wine would almost have been the equivalent of admitting that neither the guests nor the bride and groom were happy.

We see the symbolism of the wine in Psalm 104:15, which praises the Lord for giving "wine that gladdens the heart of man." In Judges we are told that Jotham recited a parable about the trees of the forest to the men of Shechem in which the vine declined to rule in the forest because, it said, "Should I give up my wine, which cheers both gods and men, to hold sway over the trees?" (Judg. 9:13). In Isaiah we are invited to "Come, buy wine and milk without money and without cost" (Isa. 55:1).

Certainly, John, who always sees the spiritual meaning in the most ordinary events, is suggesting that apart from Jesus the joy of which men are capable is limited and that good times that are nothing more than good times will run out. One young man who had tasted most of what the world has to offer once said to a Christian worker, "My God, is this all there is to life?" It was the worker's privilege to lead him to the source of all life and joy, Jesus.

At this point Mary came to Jesus with the veiled request that he do something. She said, "They have no wine." Jesus, who understood the tone of her statement, replied, "Dear woman, why do you involve me? My time has not yet come" (John 2:4). These words sound harsh to our ears, but they did not have a harsh sound in the original language. "Woman" was a title of respect, much like our word "lady." We remember that Jesus used it again when he was addressing his mother from the cross as he committed her into John's safekeeping. The point of Jesus' reply was that he was not ready to do anything openly because the "hour" of his crucifixion was still years away.

I sense in the story the fact that Mary, who certainly knew her son well, must have detected a change in Jesus' life since his departure from Nazareth; and she could not have failed to notice that he had returned with at least five disciples. Perhaps she was thinking, "Now is the time. Now he should declare himself openly." After all, Mary was only a Jewish mother, and she must have had a mother's ambition for her exceptional son, the rabbi.

Jesus, of course, knew that his times were in the hands of his Father in heaven. He would not be manipulated. And yet—this is a wonderful part of the story—he had no desire to allow the lack of joy or embarrassment either. So he moved quietly. There were six great water jars of stone standing by, containing water used for Jewish purifications. He commanded the servants to fill them with water, which they did—to the brim! When they had done so, he then told them to draw from the pots and carry the water (now made wine) to the master of the banquet, whom we would call the best man or the master of ceremonies. They did so; when the master of the banquet had tasted the wine he said to the bridegroom, "Everyone brings out the choice wine first and then the cheaper wine after the guests have had too much to drink; but you have saved the best till now" (v. 10).

That too is significant. It was *good* wine! It was the *best!* No wonder the Bible tells us that "Every good and perfect gift is from above, coming down from the Father of the heavenly lights, who does not change like shifting shadows" (James 1:17). Jesus himself said, "If you, then, though you are evil, know how to give good gifts to your children, how much more will your Father in heaven give good gifts to those who ask him!" (Matt. 7:11.)

Moreover, have you ever reflected on the quantity of wine Jesus produced? John tells us, probably as an eyewitness, that there were six stone water jars, each containing two or three firkins apiece. That makes twelve to eighteen firkins. Each firkin was the equivalent of nine or ten gallons. Consequently, Jesus must have produced between a hundred eight and a hundred eighty gallons of the very best wine. In his excellent commentary *The Gospel of John*, William Barclay, that impeccable Englishman, is so startled by the amount of wine that he thinks it should not be taken with "crude literalness." He says, "No wedding party on earth could drink one hundred and eighty gallons of wine." But I think the amount is literal and, what is more, that Jesus intentionally produced the wine in abundance.

Do not think, if you come to Jesus, accepting him as your Savior, that the day will come when you will find yourself empty of joy, or disappointed. If that ever happens, it will be because you have drawn away from him, not because he has failed you. Certainly the Christ who produced the abundance of wine, who oversupplied with the loaves and fishes, who said, "He who comes to me will never go hungry, and he who believes in me will never be thirsty" (John 6:35)—certainly such a Christ is able to supply all your need "according to his glorious riches in Christ Jesus" (Phil. 4:19).

Christ or Religion

There is one last point that must also be seen in this story. When John concludes his telling of it, he adds, "This, the first of his miraculous signs, Jesus performed at Cana in Galilee. He thus revealed his glory, and his disciples put their faith in him" (v. 11). Actually, the word that is translated as "miracles" in this verse is the word "signs," and in John a sign is always something that points to a reality greater than itself. Or, to use another word, we could say that the miracles are also, in addition to being literal events, symbolic.

We ask then: Is there something symbolized here that we have not yet covered? I believe there is. We remember, first of all, that throughout the Gospel, John is very sensitive to the fact that Jesus brought to completion and therefore in a sense displaced the religion of the Jews. We notice too that he calls attention to the use of the water jars in the Jewish household; they were for the Jewish purifications. We remember that he has spoken of the blindness of the Jewish people, particularly the leaders, just one chapter before this. In this context, and given John's interests, the empty water jars and the lack of wine speak of the emptiness of religion at Christ's coming. Arthur W. Pink, one of the most complete expositors of this Gospel, has written accurately on this point in his *Gospel of John:* "Judaism still existed as a religious system [there were purifications], but it ministered no comfort to the heart. It had degenerated into a cold, mechanical routine, utterly destitute of joy in God. Israel had lost the joy of their espousals."

What Pink has written of one religion is true, however, of all religion, if Jesus Christ does not stand at its core. Apart from him who is the source of life, who is himself the life, religion is a cold and lifeless thing. Apart from the joy he brings, religion is joyless and hardens personalities. Do you have religion? It will profit you nothing! Or do you have Christ? He alone can quench the hunger and thirst of your heart. He alone can put a song in your mouth that not even the angels can sing. He alone can give you true and everlasting joy.

27

Was Jesus Christ a Revolutionary?

John 2:12-17

After this he went down to Capernaum with his mother and brothers and his disciples. There they stayed for a few days.

When it was almost time for the Jewish Passover, Jesus went up to Jerusalem. In the temple courts he found men selling cattle, sheep and doves, and others sitting at tables exchanging money. So he made a whip out of cords, and drove all from the temple area, both sheep and cattle; he scattered the coins of the money changers and overturned their tables. To those who sold doves he said, "Get these out of here! How dare you turn my Father's house into a market!"

His disciples remembered that it is written: "Zeal for your house will consume me."

Aperson does not need to be an expert in current events to know that we live in an age of impending revolution. The call to revolution has been raised by communism. Radical groups forecast revolution for America. In the student world—whether it be in Los Angeles, New York, Moscow, Paris, Tokyo, Havana, or Djakarta, wherever students gather—there are millions who debate the nature of the revolutionary days in which we live and there are thousands who urge revolution. "We are going to change the world" is the claim of many persons—and, indeed, they may just do it!

But the secular world does not have a monopoly on sounding the call to revolution. It has also echoed from the sanctuaries of the churches. In many of the major denominations, radical clerics have sought to align the prestige of their denominations behind particular sociological and political objec-

168

tives, some of which, according to their advocates, are to be obtained by destroying the present systems of social order and government. This segment of Christendom often points to actions and teachings of Jesus that are thought to support their objectives.

Was Jesus Christ a revolutionary? That question is of crucial importance for Christians who wish guidance for their actions in our time. Was he a revolutionary? The answer to that question, as I hope to show, is "No, he was not." He was not a revolutionary in the way most people understand that word. On the other hand, he was not a defender of the establishment either, and it is correct to say that he actually called men and women to a revolution (although a peaceful one) that was far more radical and long-term than anything that people then would in themselves have dreamed possible.

Pros and Cons

One of the most valuable of the recent books on this subject is a highly condensed monograph by Oscar Cullmann, recently of the universities of Basel and Paris, entitled *Jesus and the Revolutionaries*.[1] In it he points out the complexity of the issues.

On the one hand, notes Cullmann, there are certainly elements in Christ's sayings that allow some radicals to see him as their ally. In Christ's day in Israel there were men known as Zealots (from the Greek word *zelos,* meaning "zeal"). The Zealots were fanatical in their concern for Jewish law and in their expectation of the imminent dawning of the kingdom of God. Many carried swords or daggers that were frequently used in political killings. Hence they were also called Sicarii, which is a Latin term meaning "cut-throats" or "assassins." In time the Zealots produced a politico-religious revolt that led to the Jewish war against the Romans beginning in A.D. 66. As a result of this war Jerusalem was destroyed by the Roman general Titus in A.D. 70. After the fall of Jerusalem one Zealot group continued the resistance until A.D. 74 in the mountain stronghold of Masada, which is a shrine today.

Against this background there are certain elements that have led some scholars to see Christ in this coloring. Jesus, as well as the Zealots, proclaimed that the kingdom of God was at hand. Jesus was critical of Herod, whom he called "that fox" (Luke 13:32). He was executed officially for his alleged Zealot activities (Matt. 27:37). He had among his disciples at least one, Simon the Zealot, who had been a member of a Zealot group before he became Christ's follower. Some of the disciples carried swords (Luke 22:38; John 18:10). And, most striking of all, in the passage that is the basis of our study, we are told that he cleansed the temple in Jerusalem in the midst of the very volatile days of the Passover. Many in his day, as well as in ours, would have considered this the act of an agitator.

On the other hand, as Cullmann also points out, there are elements that reveal Jesus to be the opponent of every act of political resistance and all acts of violence. To begin with, there are the sayings on behalf of nonviolence (Matt. 5:39; 26:52). There are the exhortations to love our enemies (Matt. 5:44). Jesus said, "Blessed are the peacemakers, for they [not the Zealots] will be called sons of God" (Matt. 5:9). On several occasions Jesus repudiated any political elements in his divine mission, principally when he was tempted by the devil (Matt. 4:8–10) and when he was tried before Pilate (John 18:36). Moreover, if some still cite the presence of a Zealot among his disciples, it must be pointed out that this is an argument that cuts both ways. For Jesus also had Matthew, a tax collector, and it is hard to find a greater representative of the establishment than that.

When we put all these texts (not just some) into the picture, we find a Jesus who goes beyond either of these two categories. And we are led to ask: What are his distinctive teachings? And, if it is true in one sense that he does call us to a revolutionary commitment, to what kind of a revolution does he call us?

No Utopias

The first point we need to see then is that whatever the cleansing of the temple may or may not have been about, it was definitely not an attempt to set up an earthly kingdom viewed as a utopia. That was the goal of the revolutionaries, but it was not Christ's goal. In fact, if it was, it was most unsuccessful. A revolt did not come from it; and, what is more, the effects were even of short duration, for the other Gospels tell us that Jesus found it necessary to repeat the same cleansing again three years later near the end of his ministry (Matt. 21:12, 13; Mark 11:15–17; Luke 19:45, 46). Actually, if we are to take his saying about the destruction of the temple with all seriousness (Mark 13:2), it would be most accurate to say that Jesus did not attribute eternal worth to any existing institutions, even the temple and the temple worship. For in his view all belonged to the old order that would one day come under judgment and pass away.

This truth has several important conclusions that flow from it, and we should not miss them. First, it is obviously wrong for us to deify anything human. This applies to democratic institutions as well as to those of socialism or communism. Consequently, we must not make the mistake some Americans make of identifying the American way of life or the American form of government with Christianity. The American way of life may have its good aspects (as well as its bad), some of them derived from Christianity, but America is not in itself God's kingdom.

Second, the followers of Christ are also not to take it into their hands to pronounce judgment upon their rulers. Judgment will be executed, but God alone is capable of such justice. Consequently, in speaking of the turmoil that would take place at the end times, Jesus warned his disciples to flee from Jerusalem rather than to join in insurrections (Matt. 24:15–26). For us this means that Christians are not to take part in movements that are attempting to destroy the system.

The third conclusion is that, in the time prior to the final judgment, the state even in the hands of corrupt rulers will have a proper role. Jesus illustrated this most clearly in the story of the tribute money. One of the political parties of the day, the Herodians, had come to Jesus with a question meant to trap him into a fatal admission. They asked, "Is it right to pay taxes to Caesar or not?" (Matt. 22:17). In other words, should a loyal Jew pay taxes? If Jesus said yes, he would be despised by a large section of the people, particularly the Zealots, for whom this was a point of patriotic zeal and religious honor. He would cease to be a leader. On the other hand, if he said no, then he could be denounced to the Roman authorities as an insurrectionist. What did he do? Jesus took a coin, and after pointing out that Caesar's image was on one side, he replied, "Give to Caesar what is Caesar's, and to God what is God's" (v. 21).

There were some, no doubt, who took this reply as a compromise. There were some who accused him because of it, for it was brought up against him at his trial before Pilate: "We have found this man subverting our nation. He opposes payment of taxes to Caesar and claims to be Christ, a king" (Luke 23:2). Nevertheless, this was not Christ's teaching, Jesus acknowledged the absolute authority of God. He taught that all human institutions would one day be brought under judgment and pass away. Nevertheless, there was still a proper role for the state and a proper duty toward it. One of these duties was to pay taxes.

We may apply this point by saying that withholding taxes on the grounds that much of the tax money goes for the military is not a justifiably Christian form of social protest.

No Complacency

But we need to stop here to be sure that no one is taking this as an endorsement of the present world order or, which is also wrong, an endorsement of all the acts of our government. It is true that Jesus had no room for utopias— except, of course, for the one that he himself was going to bring. But neither did he have room for complacency. On the contrary, he constantly called men to the most radical involvement with himself and in spiritual terms to the most revolutionary outlook possible.

In the spring in which Jesus Christ was crucified, the Roman authorities in Jerusalem had arrested a Zealot for his revolutionary activities. His name was Barabbas. The Bible tells us that the charge was for insurrection and murder, which means that Barabbas had been among the bands who were seeking to drive the Romans from Palestine by means of guerrilla tactics and political assassinations. He would have argued that life under Rome was oppressive. He was fighting the racism, the injustices, the militarism of the oppressors. Perhaps he was even a heroic, noble figure as men measure heroes. But he was arrested, and they locked him up.

Then there was Jesus, another man also charged with being a revolutionary. The Bible never suggests that they met. But if they had met, I imagine that Jesus would have agreed with much of what Barabbas was saying. He would have said, "Barabbas, your diagnosis of the system is right. The Romans boast of their justice; they are all for law and order. Herod was elected on that platform. But the administration of the law is corrupt, and they will prove it in a few hours by executing me. Moreover, you are also right about the Pharisees. They too are far more interested in preserving their own necks than they are about justice. Caiaphas himself said, 'You know nothing at all. . . . It is better for you that one man die for the people than that the whole nation perish.' You are right. There is oppression. There is racism.

"Nevertheless, you are making one big mistake. Your diagnosis is correct, but your treatment is faulty. You are being revolutionary in your attitude to the Roman and Jewish authorities. But you are not being at all revolutionary with yourself. In fact, you are being complacent. What makes you think that the system you will set up will be any less corrupt than the system you are involved in overthrowing? What makes you think that you are any more moral than the Romans or that you would act with any less self-interest than Caiaphas? I am here to tell you that you are all corrupt. The Jew is as corrupt as the Roman. The poor man is as corrupt as the rich man. The black man is as corrupt as the white man. The slave is as corrupt as his master. Consequently, you can only change things by changing people.

"Barabbas, I have come to change people. And when I change people, these people are going to revolutionize society. They will not overthrow society, but wherever they can they will attempt to set the systems of this world right."

This, of course, is where the cleansing of the temple comes in. John tells us, "When it was almost time for the Jewish Passover, Jesus went up to Jerusalem. In the temple courts he found men selling cattle, sheep and doves, and others sitting at tables exchanging money. So he made a whip out of cords, and drove all from the temple area, both sheep and cattle; he scattered the coins of the money changers and overturned their tables. To those who sold doves he said, 'Get these out of here! How dare you turn my Father's house into a market!' His disciples remembered that it is written: 'Zeal for your house will consume me'" (John 2:13–17). Jesus did not seek to eliminate temple worship. He sought to reform it. In other words, within the sphere of his influence he worked to transform what was into what it always should have been.

Such people are dangerous. They will either be loved or hated. In Christ's day most of the world turned from this all-demanding, revolutionary type of commitment. Pilate addressed them and asked, "Whom should I release to you? Jesus or Barabbas?" They answered, "Barabbas." Why should they have asked for Barabbas—Barabbas, the man who was going to burn their houses down and destroy the system? Tom Skinner, who tells this story in his book *Words of Revolution,* says: "It's very simple. If you let Barabbas go, and he starts another disturbance or another riot, you can always call out the National Guard, the Federal troops or the Marines to put his thing down. All you have to do is push a few tanks into his neighborhood and you can squash whatever he's up to. You can find out where he's keeping his guns and raid his apartment. You can always stop Barabbas. But the question is: *how do you stop Jesus?* How do you stop a Man who has no guns, no tanks, no ammunition, but still is shaking the whole Roman empire? How do you stop a Man, who—without firing a shot—is getting revolutionary results? They figured there's only one answer—get rid of Him. . . .

"Barabbas would never really ask to run your life. Barabbas would exploit you, but he wouldn't ask to run your life. Jesus would ask to run your life. Jesus would ask for the right to rule over you! And that's the problem. Men would rather be enslaved to tyranny than let Jesus rule their lives. They would rather be exploited than let Christ determine their lives. So they said, 'Give us Barabbas.'"[2]

The Call

It is the same today. Is Jesus Christ a revolutionary? No, he is not. He was executed wrongly on that count. And yet, like all revolutionary leaders, he demands the utmost of involvement, love, and self-sacrifice from his followers. Jesus did not offer a life of ease. Like Churchill, he offered men blood, tears, toil, and sweat. He told his disciples, "If anyone would come after me, he must deny himself and take up his cross and follow me" (Matt. 16:24). He demanded their all! There were few to follow him.

Will you dare to follow him? It is worth reflecting on who it was who first responded to his teaching. There were establishment figures as well as Zealots—that did not seem to matter—but there were few of the soft, well-heeled figures of southern Palestine. There were not many priests, not many rulers. The ones who followed him were the vigorous, rough-speaking fishermen types from Galilee. For they had the courage, and they were not afraid to be despised for being different. Have you that courage? Jesus will not ask you either to defend the status quo or to overthrow it. But he will give a new perspective. He will make you a new man or woman, capable of radical obedience within the bounds of true Christianity.

28

He Gave Them a Sign

John 2:18–22

Then the Jews demanded of him, "What miraculous sign can you show us to prove your authority to do all this?"

Jesus answered them, "Destroy this temple, and I will raise it again in three days."

The Jews replied, "It has taken forty-six years to build this temple, and you are going to raise it in three days?" But the temple he had spoken of was his body. After he was raised from the dead, his disciples recalled what he had said. Then they believed the Scripture and the words that Jesus had spoken.

Someone once asked a well-known Bible teacher what he considered to be his greatest spiritual need. The teacher replied that he was conscious of very many lacks in his life, but he believed that his greatest lack was knowing more of the Word of God so that he might know God better. When the person responded that he found this surprising, since the Bible teacher quite obviously spent most of his time studying the Bible, he was told in reply, "I know enough of the Bible to know how much more there is to know. And I know that all knowledge of God depends upon such knowledge. Sometimes I feel like a man who has been running for a long distance—chest heaving, lungs pulling for more oxygen."

This reply was perceptive, of course, for it was an acknowledgment of one of the great underlying principles of Christianity. It is the principle that no one ever understands spiritual truths apart from the Bible and that, as a result, no one can come to know God by any other means.

174

Some persons think they can know God by means of their own human reason. But reason is a blind alley spiritually. It has always been the great minds exercising their powers apart from the Word of God who have produced the great heresies. Some think they can discover God by listening to a so-called "inner voice," but the voice is often nothing more than an expression of their own inner desires, as psychologists repeatedly point out. Quite a few think that spiritual truths can be verified by supernatural events or miracles. But the Bible everywhere teaches that even miracles will not lead men and women to understand and receive God's truth unless they themselves are illuminated by the Bible. Thus, Jesus said, "If they do not listen to Moses and the Prophets, they will not be convinced even if someone rises from the dead" (Luke 16:31). I believe that we can state categorically that there is no knowledge of God apart from Jesus Christ and that there is no knowledge of Jesus Christ apart from a knowledge of the Bible.

Natural Wisdom

This truth is illustrated for us in the story to which we now come in our verse-by-verse study. Jesus had just performed a great sign by driving out of the temple in Jerusalem all those who were selling and bartering in the outer court of the Gentiles. This was a fulfillment of Psalm 69:9: "For zeal for your house consumes me." Nevertheless, in spite of the text and its fulfillment, those who were threatened by Christ's action were not thinking scripturally and consequently did not see the hand of God in Christ's action. They had already had one very dramatic sign. There was also a variety of unspecified miracles to be considered (John 2:23). But they rejected these things and instead demanded something more. The Bible says the Jews demanded: "What miraculous sign can you show us to prove your authority to do all this?" (v. 18).

What further sign could Christ give? There was only one, even though (because of their willingness to evaluate his ministry in the light of the Scriptures) they would eventually reject it also. Jesus therefore referred to his death and the resurrection that was to follow it, saying, "Destroy this temple and I will raise it again in three days" (v. 19). At this time no one understood Christ's saying. The rulers never understood it, and the disciples only began to understand it after the event and in the light of biblical revelation.

The reaction of the leaders of the Jews on this occasion is a great example of the attempts of men to understand spiritual things when they have not had their minds illuminated by Scripture. And the point is that such an attempt will always result in our seeing things only on the physical level.

Let me illustrate by this comparison. Several months ago on a trip that I was taking to the West Coast with my family I passed through one of the gambling towns in Nevada. If you have ever been to one of these towns yourself, you know that the most common sights in the gambling cities (with the exception of the neon lights) are the slot machines. They seem to be everywhere.

The person playing the machine puts in his money, a quarter or a dollar coin—whatever it might be—and then pulls down a lever that is attached to the side. When he does this the wheels begin to spin with a whirring sound, and then they begin to stop one after the other and show various pictures. There is a standard and easily recognizable sound, first the whirring and then three clunks as the wheels stop turning. If certain combinations of pictures come up, the person playing the machine gets some money back. Most of the time nothing happens. Then, if the person is a gambler and a fool, he puts in more money. After the same sounds—whirr, clunk, clunk, clunk— nothing happens again.

This is exactly what took place when Jesus spoke words of spiritual truth. Take the third chapter of John. Nicodemus was a ruler of the Jews, and he came to Jesus by night. He said, "Rabbi, we know you are a teacher who has come from God." Jesus answered, "I tell you the truth, no one can see the kingdom of God unless he is born again." That was a coin of spiritual truth being dropped into Nicodemus's slot. We take a breath, and we can almost hear the wheels begin to whirr as Nicodemus digests Christ's teaching. He answers, "How can a man be born when he is old? Surely he cannot enter a second time into his mother's womb to be born!" In other words, Jesus was speaking about the new life that a person receives by faith; and Nicodemus was saying to himself, "Human birth? Human birth? That means a father and a mother, conception, wombs, nine months of growth, babies, mother's milk." He came up with a blank.

We find the same thing repeated just one chapter later. In John 4 there is the account of Christ's meeting with the woman of Samaria. The two of them met at a well, so Jesus referred to wells and water in order to explain that he was offering to satisfy her spiritual thirst. The woman was unable to think on these terms. So the wheels went round, and she began to think, "Water? Water? Wells? The well is deep, water is heavy, it's a long way up the hill, this is a hot country, buckets, water jars—wouldn't it be nice if I didn't have to do this every day?" So she said out loud, "Sir, give me this water so that I won't get thirsty and have to keep coming here to draw water." As in the case of Nicodemus, there was a great whirring, but nothing clicked.

We must not think that this is the case only with the unchurched either, for at the end of the story in the same chapter we find that the same thing happened in a conversation between Christ and his disciples. During the time that Jesus had been talking to the woman, the disciples had been in the city buying food to eat. When they had returned and had urged him to take some of it, saying, "Rabbi, eat," Jesus referred to his previous conversation with its blessing in the life of the woman, answering, "I have food to eat that you know nothing about." What did the disciples do? They pulled down the lever and then asked one another, "Who brought him lunch?"

That is what happens when men and women confront spiritual truths with their own human ability. And it is exactly what happened in our story. Jesus referred to his resurrection, saying, "Destroy this temple, and in three days I will raise it up," and they did not have the wisdom to ask, "What are you referring to?" Instead, they assumed his remark to be an idiotic reference to the temple of Herod, and they therefore asked, "It has taken forty-six years to build this temple, and you are going to raise it in three days?" (v. 20).

Roots of Unbelief

The first point I have made, then, is that no one understood what Jesus was saying when he first said it, because no one tried to understand it on the basis of biblical revelation. The second point is that the Jewish rulers (in spite of further miracles and signs) never did understand it. Why was this so? The answer to this question takes us a bit deeper into their attitude and into the reasons for disbelief generally.

We have already seen that the rulers had not been listening to the Bible, and because they had not been listening to the Bible they were not ready to listen to Jesus Christ either. In the Bible God speaks to men. But because they did not hear him there, neither did they hear him when he spoke to them face-to-face. The rulers were not really asking Jesus Christ for a sign. I know they asked, "What sign do you show us that you do these things?" But what they were really expressing was their anger at Christ's actions. They wanted to know what possible justification Jesus could give for having driven the money changers out of their temple, particularly when they had said that the money changers had a right to be there.

Men and women are like that with God today, even in our own world and in our churches. God speaks, but many do not really listen. One reason why they do not listen is that they are so wrapped up in their own outlook and their own way of doing things that they are privately angry with God for not conforming to their plans. Is that your attitude? If it is, then you must learn to forget your anger and instead learn to see things from God's point of view. God's point of view—the only valid one—is revealed to us in Scripture.

Another reason why the rulers did not believe in Christ and did not approach things scripturally was that they did not want to hear what Jesus had to say. Why did Jesus refer to the temple being destroyed? Well, on one level he did so to provide a fresh illustration of his death and resurrection. But that is only one level. Isn't it also true that this illustration was meant to suggest the passing of the temple and the worship that was conducted there and to suggest that it would be replaced with a spiritual worship after his death and resurrection? Whatever the case, this is certainly what happened. The temple had been begun by Herod in about 20 B.C. It was now about A.D. 26, which meant that the temple had been in construction for forty-six years. It would be another thirty-seven years before the entire construction was finished—that is, about the year A.D. 63—and then seven years later the whole magnificent edifice would be destroyed by the Romans. The history of the temple is a great lesson in the futility of identifying buildings with true worship, and Christ's reference to it was a warning of the passing of traditional Judaism.

If there was anything these rulers did not want to hear, it was that. And since they were not ready to hear what Christ first had to say to them, they were not ready to listen to anything. Perhaps this is true of you also. When we listen to God he always begins by pointing out our need of himself. He shows us our sin and allows us to see a bit of our own rebellious heart. Perhaps you sense that he is doing that, or will do it; so you refuse to listen. You will not read the Bible or study it. If that is the case in your life, then you must learn that all good cures begin with an accurate diagnosis. And you must allow God to lead you from a recognition of your need to that which will satisfy it completely.

Do not think that this is something that only certain persons must experience. It is true for all, even theologians. One theologian, Professor John Baillie of the University of Edinburgh, Scotland, has written of his own experience with God: "What I now realize very clearly, and am ready to confess, is that much of the trouble in the days when I could not hear God's voice was that I was not really listening. I was partly listening perhaps—giving, as it were, one ear to His commandments; but no promise is made in the Bible to those who partly listen, but only to those who hearken *diligently*. And why did I not thus hearken? It was that there were certain things I did not want to hear. We sometimes speak of people being 'conveniently deaf' to human communications, but there is such a thing also as being conveniently deaf towards God. . . . There are certain things we just do not want to be told. They would be too inconvenient, too upsetting, too exacting. The readjustment they would involve would be too painful."[1]

Finally, people will not believe in Christ because their minds are filled with the wrong ideas that we have all received from this world. Nearly all the ideas of this world are antithetical to those revealed in the Bible. So if we have our minds filled with the ideas of the world, as the Jewish rulers in this story did, we will not hear Jesus, and spiritual truths will seem foolish or incomprehensible to us. Instead of this we must allow God to transform us to "demolish arguments and every pretension that sets itself up against the knowledge of God, and take captive every thought to make it obedient to Christ" (2 Cor. 10:5).

The Disciples

Let me suggest a final contrast before we end this study. Most of the story revolves around the rulers who did not want to hear and who did not approach the things of God scripturally. But they are not the only ones in the story. There are also the disciples. They were just a small group, mostly fishermen, men who were unlearned by the standards of that day. They had no reputation in the eyes of the world. They had no fame in Jerusalem. But they knew the Scriptures a little bit, and they had begun to interpret the things that were happening to them in the light of it.

Did you ever notice that this passage begins and ends with a reference to the Scriptures? The verses are 17 and 22, and they tell us that one of the acts of Christ they understood then as a result of knowing the Scripture and that another of Christ's acts they understood later as a result of knowing the Scripture. It was all through the Scripture. We are told that after Jesus had cleansed the temple, his disciples thought about the Scriptures and "remembered that it was written, 'Zeal for your house has consumed me'" (v. 17). In other words, they were remembering Psalm 69:9 and were saying to themselves. "Yes, Jesus really is the Messiah, and he is fulfilling this Scripture." Later Jesus talked about destroying the temple and raising it up in three days. None of them understood it then; but we are told that as they learned to live in the Scriptures, as Jesus did, the time came when they looked back on the resurrection and understood it in terms of the Old Testament prophecies.

How does it stand with you? Do you approach things scripturally as God wants you to? Or are you still trying to puzzle out God's truth with your own weak faculties of reasoning? The Bible tells us that we will only advance spiritually and that we will only hear God's voice as we approach him through the pages of his book.

29

Christ and the Heart of Man

John 2:23–25

Now while he was in Jerusalem at the Passover Feast, many people saw the miraculous signs he was doing and believed in his name. But Jesus would not entrust himself to them, for he knew all men. He did not need man's testimony about man, for he knew what was in a man.

There is an old law of physics called Newton's Law that says that every action produces a reaction. It is always true in the physical realm and perhaps most always true in all of life. A person does something, and others react. A person says something, and something else happens.

This was true in the time of the Lord Jesus Christ. For instance, in the second chapter of John's Gospel there are three sets of actions by Jesus, each of which produced a distinct reaction. At the beginning of the chapter Jesus had turned water into wine at the marriage feast at Cana. Not many knew of this miracle, but we are told that the disciples who did know of it believed on him. This was the first reaction. A few days later Jesus drove the money changers from the temple in Jerusalem. This was a sign too. Nevertheless, the rulers of the people reacted to him in anger, demanding, "What miraculous sign can you show us to prove your authority to do all this?" Finally, we are told that when he was at the feast he did further miracles with the result that many more "believed in his name."

Here were three levels of response to Jesus and his actions, ranging from the total disbelief of the leaders to the partially informed faith of the first disciples. We would say, "Well, some of the reactions were bad; some were better; some were quite good. Let's emulate the apostles." It is therefore somewhat of a shock to come to the end of the chapter and find, in spite of the obvious differences between these various groups of people that seem so significant to us, that the Lord Jesus Christ did not trust anyone. The text tells us, "But Jesus would not entrust himself to them, for he knew all men. He did not need man's testimony about man, for he knew what was in a man" (vv. 24–25). The Greek tells us quite literally that although many trusted in him, he did not trust in them; and the reason why he did not trust in them was that he knew what was in them.

The Heart of Man

What does God see when he looks into the heart of man? If we are to answer this question accurately, we must recognize first that only God can see into our hearts. Consequently, the picture he paints will naturally be different from what we might expect to find there.

We should not be surprised at our own inability to see into man's true nature, for this is demonstrated for us almost every day. Not so long ago I read about a man who had suddenly fled from this country with a large amount of money that was not his. It was from company funds. Up to that point he had been a trusted member of the firm. He had gained a certain amount of recognition for his work. He was well thought of by most of his coworkers and friends. He had a respected family. Yet he was a thief, and none of his family, friends, coworkers, or acquaintances had really known him.

The story could be repeated many times over, probably at least once or twice from your own experience. People cannot see into the minds of other people. Only God can do that. He "searches our hearts" (Rom. 8:27) and "knows the heart" (Acts 15:8). Consequently, we must not be surprised if his view of the hearts and minds of men differs from our own.

One of our great American short stories tells in a humorous way about a student taking a biology course in his first year at a university. The course was all right, but the student had a serious problem with the laboratory part of it. As part of his laboratory work he was supposed to draw the bacteria he saw through a microscope. Unfortunately, he was never able to see anything through his microscope. All he could ever see, the story tells us, was a white blur that looked like milk. In the same way, when we look into the human heart, apart from the magnification of the heart provided by the Word of God, all we see is the milk of human kindness, with perhaps a few small smudges of what the Bible calls sin. God has the heart of man in focus, with the result that he is never fooled by human goodness.

What, then, *does* God see when he looks into the heart of man? The answer is shocking to those who are not steeped in Scripture. The Bible tells us that according to God the heart is filled with madness, mischief, and evil. It is impenitent, darkened, gross, hard, proud, blind, filled with lust. It is far from God. God says, "The heart is deceitful above all things and beyond cure. Who can understand it?" (Jer. 17:9). It is a grim picture, but it is only as we begin to see the heart as God sees it that we can begin to appreciate the greatness of God's love.

The Heart in History

At this point, however, we need to stop to look at the matter historically. Let me ask this question: What is the first great event in the Bible put there to reveal the heart of man to us? The answer is: the fall of Adam and Eve. What does it show? The answer is: It shows man in his state of rebellion against God, a rebellion in which he refuses to go God's way even if his own way kills him.

It is popular in our day to blame the fall of the race on the woman, just as Adam did when God came to him in the Garden. Adam said, "The woman you put here with me—she gave me some fruit from the tree, and I ate it" (Gen. 3:12). We blame the woman, but this is not the way in which the Bible talks about it. The Bible tells us that Eve was deceived by the devil and so fell through error. But it also declares that when Adam sinned he did so, not through deceit or weakness but in willful rebellion against God. First Timothy 2:14 teaches this beyond any doubt, for it says "Adam was not the one deceived; it was the woman who was deceived and became a sinner."

Let me explain that a bit further. Suppose for a moment that Adam had sinned first and then the woman. And suppose that God had come to the couple in the Garden, saying, "What have you done?" If that had been the case, the women could have answered, "I have just been doing what you told me to do. You gave me the man to be the head of our home. So when he ate of the tree, I obeyed him and did it also." That is what the woman could have said if Adam had sinned first, and the fall of the race would have been incomplete. However, Adam did not sin first. The woman sinned first, and so, "the woman . . . became a sinner."

But now, if the woman was deceived, this was obviously not so with the man. Adam knew what he was doing. Consequently, his guilt was greater. God had placed Adam in the Garden as lord under himself of all creation. There were trees in the Garden; and God had said to Adam, "I want you to feel free to eat of all the trees north of here, south of here, east of here, and west of here. But as a symbol of your dependence upon me I am marking this one tree—the tree of the knowledge of good and evil—as a tree from which you shall not eat. Moreover, so you will know that I mean business, I am warning you that in the day in which you eat of it you will surely die." Adam looked at the tree and then said, in effect, "I do not care if you have given me all the trees north of here, south of here, east of here, and west of here. So long as that tree remains in the Garden as a symbol of my dependence upon you I will hate it." So he ate of the tree and died—first, spiritually and then, later, in soul and body also.

The fall of man is what would be called in theology a *de novo* act, an act that was entirely new, that had no connection with anything that had gone before it. It was essentially a rebellion. Man had said, "I am the captain of my soul; I am the master of my fate; I hate anything that opposes me, even God." So man sinned, and his rebellion passed upon the race.[1]

We are like Adam, and our children are also. Suppose your child is sitting at the table in a bad mood and you say to him, "Come on now, Johnny, sit up and eat your dinner." Instead, Johnny folds his arms and sort of spits to show his feelings about what you are trying to get him to do. You say it a second time, "Come on, Johnny, you have to eat if you're going to grow up to be a big, strong boy." He reaches his hand toward his dish, grabs a spoon, and then begins to wave the spoon around. Finally he knocks his milk over. In other words, he does anything but what you want him to do and thereby illustrates how Adam's rebellion has passed through us to our children.

Spiritual wisdom comes at the point at which we will accept God's description of our nature and ask him to lead us into ways that can please him.

Sinai

Let me take you to another biblical event that reveals the hearts of men as God sees them. Much later, after God had begun to establish a race through whom he was going to send the Redeemer, God delivered the race from Egypt, bringing them into the desert to the foot of Mount Sinai. God had delivered Israel through what is probably the greatest collection of miracles in all history. He had brought them to Sinai in order that he might give them the law. The Bible says that God descended upon the mountain in the midst of a cloud of smoke and fire. So awe-inspiring was the sight that even Moses said, "I am trembling with fear" (Heb. 12:21).

As the hours turned to days and the days to weeks, however, the people who were left in the valley gradually overcame their fear of the mountain and began to forget the power of God and the miracles. They grew cynical and impatient. They said, "Where is Moses, who brought us up out of Egypt? We don't know what has become of him." Before long they began to remember the worship of Apis the bull and Hathor the cow that they had known in Egypt, and they approached Moses' brother Aaron to ask him to make an image of Apis or Hathor for them. Aaron should have refused immediately and indignantly. But Aaron was weak, like many Christians. He reminded himself that politics is the art of the possible. So he took their gold, melted it in the fire, and when he was done he had enough of the metal to make a little calf. That satisfied the people. So they began to sing and dance and worship the calf, saying, "These are your gods, O Israel, who brought you up out of Egypt" (Exod. 32:4).

Meanwhile, up on the mountain God was still speaking to Moses, giving him the law. How ironic it was, the contrast between the law and the behavior of the people! God was saying, "I am the LORD your God, who brought you out of Egypt, out of the land of slavery. You shall have no other gods before me. You shall not make for yourself an idol in the form of anything in heaven above or on the earth beneath or in the waters below. You shall not bow down to them or worship them; for I, the LORD your God, am a jealous God, punishing the children for the sin of the fathers to the third and fourth generation of those who hate me, but showing love to a thousand generations of those who love me and keep my commandments" (Exod. 20:2–6). But while God was saying this the people turned their backs on the One who had delivered them from Egypt.[2]

Look to the Cross

Pass over the centuries to the time of Jesus Christ and then try to find an excuse for man's behavior. Someone might argue that the doctrine of man's sinfulness is abstract and that we only understand the concrete. He might say, "If only we had an example of what true goodness and obedience are, then we would all acknowledge the right and follow it." But would we? Not at all! Jesus came. He was the perfect example. He said to his enemies on one occasion, "Which of you convicts me of sin?" There was absolute silence. No one had anything with which to charge him. Yet it was these same men who mocked him, taunted him, and finally delivered him over to the Romans to be crucified.

That is the heart of man. That is what Jesus saw. It is how God sees you and me today. And yet—this is the wonderful thing—God loves you in spite of your sin and has proved it by letting Christ die for you.

It is not hard to love someone who is lovely. We all do that. It is often possible to love someone who is unlovely. Some do that occasionally. But to love someone who is rebellious, proud, arrogant, corrupt, ruthlessly independent, and who will crucify the very one who most loves him—that is real love! Of that sort of love only God is capable.

If you really desire to know the extent of God's love, look to the cross. You see Christ hanging there. You watch the hours of darkness descend on the land, the hours in which Christ was made sin for you and bore your punishment. You hear his cry, wrung from him in the moments in which he was separated from God as your sin-bearer: "My God, my God, why have you forsaken me?" That is how much God loves you. "But God demonstrates his own love for us in this: While we were still sinners, Christ died for us" (Rom. 5:8).

We live in a miserable, vascillating age. It is almost impossible for me to relate how many people I have heard say to me in one form or another: "Nobody loves me." It is often true. It may be true for you. It may be true that no one really understands you, that you are unloved by your parents, your children, your acquaintances. Yet there is One who does understand you—Jesus Christ. He knows everything about you. He sees your heart, and he loves you anyway.

30

The Man Who Came by Night

John 3:1

Now there was a man of the Pharisees named Nicodemus, a member of the Jewish ruling council.

Quite a few years ago Governor Neff, of the state of Texas, received an invitation to speak at one of the penitentiaries in that state. He spoke to the assembled prisoners, and afterward said that he would be around for a while to listen to anything any of the convicts might wish to tell him. He would take as much time as they wanted, and anything they would tell him would be kept in confidence. The convicts began to come, one at a time. One after another told him a story of how they had been unjustly sentenced, were innocent, and wished to get out. Finally one man came through who said to him, "Governor Neff, I don't want to take much of your time. I only want to say that I really did what they convicted me for. But I have been here a number of years. I believe I have paid my debt to society and that, if I were to be released, I would be able to live an upright life and show myself worthy of your mercy." This was the man whom Governor Neff pardoned.

I know, of course, that there are imperfections in that illustration. For one thing, some of the men who claimed to be innocent might actually have been innocent. For another, the man who was pardoned might have been deceiving the governor and might have led a much more disreputable life after his release. Still, the point of the story stands: the first step in the reha-

185

bilitation of any man lies in his admission of guilt. To benefit from a doctor, the patient must admit that he is sick.

Just as this is true in medicine, business, and criminal rehabilitation, so is it true spiritually. Therefore, much of the Word of God is given over to revealing man's need so that a person might acknowledge his need and turn to God for pardon.

A Representative Man

This pattern of the biblical revelation is found in John's Gospel. Our studies of the Gospel thus far have taken us through the first two chapters of the book, with the result that we come now to the record of the two-thousand-year-old conversation between Nicodemus and Jesus, contained in chapter 3. This chapter stresses the need for the new birth and for faith in the Lord Jesus Christ, but before it does this it first of all stresses man's *need* for these. Therefore, we must first see Nicodemus as a representative of all men standing as sinners before God.

The first two chapters of the Gospel have been concerned with the person of Jesus primarily, but it is also true that they have been concerned with man. In the first chapter, John pointed out that when the true Light shone in the world, men as a whole did not respond to him (vv. 10–11). In chapter 2, John tells us that although many seemed to believe in Jesus as a result of his miracles, nevertheless "Jesus would not entrust himself to them, for he knew all men" (v. 24). The failure of men in spiritual things is now John's theme, and Nicodemus is to be seen as his first concrete example.

This is much more apparent in the Greek text of the Gospel than it is in the English. Still, it can also be seen in the English so long as we remember that the chapter and verse divisions of our Bibles were not in the original text. With these eliminated we can easily see that when John begins to say in 3:1, "Now there was a man of the Pharisees named Nicodemus, a member of the Jewish ruling council." He is deliberately repeating the word "man" which occurs in the previous chapter. There we are told that Jesus knew what was in *man* and therefore did not commit himself to *man*. Nicodemus is a man. Consequently, we must begin with the recognition that he is introduced above all as a representative of the human race.

A Pharisee

He is a good representative too, at least from a human point of view. For if we had lived in Christ's day and had been forced for some reason to choose a man to represent us, a man who would embody the best of our culture, education, ethics, and piety, Nicodemus would have been a good choice. We would not have chosen the emperor or many of the rulers of Rome, for these men were demonstrably corrupt. We would not have chosen the philosophers of Greece, for they had little knowledge of religion. We would not have chosen a common, ignorant person. But we would have chosen Nicodemus. Nicodemus had everything. And yet—this is the point of John's account—he was a failure spiritually because he had never found God.

Notice his achievements. First of all, Nicodemus was a *Pharisee*. In our day we have a bad picture of the Pharisees, primarily because of the harsh words Jesus spoke about them. In our minds the word "Pharisee" is almost a synonym for hypocrite. It suggests ritualistic religion. In Jesus' time the religion of Judaism was largely an ethical cult, and the Pharisees were the chief exponents of the ethical way of life. All this is true. Yet in other ways the Pharisees were probably the best people in the whole country. To begin with, there were never really very many of them. William Barclay notes that there were never more than six thousand Pharisees, and that because of their limited number they actually formed a kind of select brotherhood. Moreover, they were serious about the law. The Pharisees were the theological conservatives of their day. They believed that the Old Testament was the revealed Word of God and that the first five books of the Old Testament, the Pentateuch, contained an inspired code of ethics to be believed and practiced literally. In some ways the greatest glory of the Pharisaic religion lay in the fact that it applied the law literally. It was the goal of the scribes to work out the exact meaning of the law; it was the determined purpose of the Pharisees to keep it.

As a Pharisee, Nicodemus represented those of his day and ours who seek the meaning of life in religion but do not find it. He belonged to the church, but he knew nothing of that personal, life-transforming relationship to Jesus Christ upon whom the true church is founded.

Second, Nicodemus was a *scholar*. This is perfectly evident from the fact that he was a Pharisee, for the Pharisees were great students of the law. Yet it is evident in another way also.

Have you ever noticed the fact that although Nicodemus was a Jew he nevertheless had a Greek name? Nicodemus is Greek for "one who conquers the people." This might not mean much in America where we have a great mixture of races and cultures, where a man might as well be called Karl, James, Joseph, or Pierre and have it mean little concerning him. But in Palestine, in the first Christian century, it was significant. For the most part those who lived in Judea had Hebrew or Aramaic names. However, those in the upper classes, who were exposed to Greek as well as Jewish culture, often gave their children two names, a Greek name as well as a Hebrew one. Evidently this had been true of Nicodemus, which indicates that he had a Greek education. Moreover, since he apparently preferred to be known by his Greek rather than his Hebrew name, Nicodemus probably had a preference for Greek over Hebrew culture and may actually have been a Hellenist, that is, one who read the Old Testament in Greek and who looked at it in the light of the categories of Greek philosophy. It was therefore a highly educated man as well as a highly moral and ethical man who came to Jesus in the warmth of that Judean night.

Isn't it true that he is a representative of many highly educated people in our day? We have been told by many in our century that education is the means to solve the world's problems. As a result we have the most highly educated mass of people in our country and in the world that this race has ever seen. It seems that a man needs a high school education just to wash dishes. Still the problems are not solved, and the unrest that characterizes our day is as evident on the campuses as in the ghettos. If the example of Nicodemus is to teach anything, it is to teach that education is not the answer to man's spiritual unrest and longing.

Third, Nicodemus was a *politician.* John says in writing about him that he was "a member of the Jewish ruling council." That means that he was a member of the Sanhedrin. The Sanhedrin was the highest legislative body in Judaism, combining in itself all the powers that we generally divide up among the legislative, administrative, and judicial branches of our governments. Naturally, under Roman rule the powers of the Sanhedrin were more restricted than they had once been. There were times when the members of the Sanhedrin were unable to inflict the death penalty, as for instance, at the trial of Jesus. Still the Sanhedrin was the chief authority in Israel. It conducted trials, investigated heresies, wrote laws, and carried on most of the official dealings between the people of Judea and the Roman authorities. Nicodemus was a member of this exclusive, governing body.

It is part of the same picture that Nicodemus may also have been among one of the most distinguished families in Judea, even when measured by the standards of this elite body of politicians. The basis for this supposition lies in the fact that Josephus, in his *Antiquities,* twice mentions a high-ranking Jewish family in which the name Nicodemus is prominent. He tells us that nearly one hundred years before the conversation recorded here, when Aristobulus, the Jewish ruler, needed an ambassador to the court of Pompey, the Roman emperor, he chose a man named Nicodemus to bear his message. He also writes that after this time, during the Jewish war of A.D. 66–70, a man named Gorion was given the responsibility of negotiating the surrender of the garrison at Jerusalem and that he was the son of a certain Nicodemus (or Nicomedus) who would therefore have lived in Christ's generation. If these facts are significant, it may mean not only that Nicodemus was an extremely pious person, not only highly educated, not only a politician, but also that he came from one of the most distinguished and best-known families in the entire nation.

He would have been even more important than a Rockefeller, Astor, Stevenson, Einstein, or Eisenhower. For in one sense he was all these things in one.

Isn't this the kind of man you would choose to represent you? Or the kind of man you might like to be? Of course, he is. Yet the point of his story, the reason why John records Nicodemus's conversation with Jesus, is that in spite of his achievements, in spite of his prominence in education, politics, culture, and religion, Nicodemus had a great need. He needed to know God. Because he did not know God he was psychologically ill at ease, unhappy, lost, and spiritually blind.

Rebirth

A person might ask quite rightly how these things can be so. How can a man who has achieved everything from a human point of view still be unhappy? How can the achievers of this world be lost? The answer comes out in the story. For the first point that Jesus made in speaking with Nicodemus is that all men need a new birth. Jesus said, "Of course you don't have the solutions to life, Nicodemus; for the solutions to life are spiritual and no man can see them unless he has come to life spiritually." His actual words were: "I tell you the truth, no one can see the kingdom of God unless he is born again" (v. 3).

According to Jesus, the starting point in the Christian life is rebirth. Before his new birth a man is a child of wrath. He is alienated from God, as Nicodemus was, and he has no real understanding of spiritual things. God comes to him to plant saving faith within his heart, for we are told that even faith does not come from ourselves; it is the gift of God (Eph. 2:8). Then God brings the words of Scripture to our attention. Finally, the Holy Spirit takes the words of Scripture and plants them within the womb of our heart with the result that life is conceived. Hereafter the man can declare, "If any one is in Christ, he is a new creation" (2 Cor. 5:17 RSV). It is true that the man still retains much of his old nature, but now he begins to see things differently and the life within begins to grow.

The full meaning of the new birth will become more evident as the chapter goes on, but this study should not end without providing an example of the kind of change the new birth can produce. Nicodemus will not do for an example, for we are never told how he responded to this teaching by Jesus. So far as we know he never understood it and never believed. Still there is another excellent example of a man who did.

This man was a rabbi, just like Nicodemus. He came from a good family and was versed in Greek as well as Hebrew culture, just like Nicodemus. This man had studied with the best men of his day. He was a Pharisee, like Nicodemus. He was even (in one sense) a politician, for he was associated with the Sanhedrin. He put down sectarian groups that threatened his brand of Judaism. Still there came a time, as this learned rabbi was on the way to Damascus with an assignment to ferret out and imprison the Christians of that city, when he met Jesus Christ and received new life from him.

Afterward he wrote about it, saying that all his achievements, like those of Nicodemus, had really proved worthless. In fact, they were worse than worthless—they were actually harmful—for they had kept him from true saving faith in God's Son. He wrote: "If anyone thinks to base his claims on externals, I could make a stronger case for myself: circumcised on my eighth day, Israelite by race, of the tribe of Benjamin, a Hebrew born and bred; in my attitude to the law, a Pharisee; in pious zeal, a persecutor of the church; in legal rectitude, faultless. But all such assets I have written off because of Christ. I would say more: I count everything sheer loss, because all is far outweighed by the gain of knowing Christ Jesus my Lord, for whose sake I did in fact lose everything" (Phil. 3:4–8 NEB).

This was the experience of the apostle Paul. It is recorded in the Book of Philippians. Is this your experience? Is this your life? Or are you still trying to discover a life of contentment and blessing through your own limited achievements and human understanding? It will not come through your own efforts. It will only come through the new birth found and expressed by faith in the Lord Jesus.

31

Intellectuals or New Men?

John 3:2

He came to Jesus at night and said, "Rabbi, we know you are a teacher who has come from God. For no one could perform the miraculous signs you are doing if God were not with him."

The longer I live the more convinced I become that the natural man will do almost anything to dodge the full implications of the gospel. The gospel declares that Jesus Christ died to save men, but when this is proclaimed the non-Christian immediately begins to think of all the other meanings Christ's death might have, and so avoid the right one. The gospel states that Jesus Christ is the sole way to God. The one who has not yet come to Christ begins to advance other ways of salvation and to argue in defense of the many non-Christian religions. In the same way, whenever the Bible speaks of man's total inability to please God, many will immediately reject that and seek for exceptions.

This aspect of human nature is known to God, of course. Thus, much of the Bible is given over to declaring the full scope of man's need. In fact, this is one of the two greatest themes of the Bible. The first is the utter inability of man to save himself. The second is the way of salvation provided by God through the death and resurrection of Jesus Christ.

In an indirect way, the extent of man's need is seen in the conversation between Nicodemus and Jesus that is recorded in John 3. The first verse has shown man's need in reference to the many external accomplishments of which a talented man is capable. Nicodemus was a well-educated, earnest, even a pious politician, but none of these achievements could save him. He was lost and lonely. He needed to be born again. It is possible, however, that some might read the account and agree—up to this point. "And yet," they might say, "what about the extent of man's knowledge? Man's greatest strength is in his mind. Can't a man find true happiness and peace with God through his intellect?" It is in answer to this type of argument that the story now goes on to show that even man's intellect is inadequate when applied to spiritual things.

The Fall

To understand why man's mind is an inadequate tool for coming to know God, we need to go back to the story of the fall of man as recorded in the Book of Genesis.

To begin with, the Bible says that when God created man he created him in his own image. This means many things, but among them is the fact that since God is a trinity, man became a trinity also. God exists in three persons: Father, Son, and Holy Spirit. Man also became a trinity when God created him with a body, soul, and spirit. Everyone knows what the body is: that part of man that we can see. Man shares with the plant world the fact that he has a body. In addition to a body, man also possesses a soul. A soul is that part of man that gives him his identity. It is with the soul that man thinks, feels, reacts, and aspires. A man is linked to the animal world by his soul, for the animals also have a sense of identity. That is why Jesus said, "The foxes have holes, and the birds of the air have nests." That is, they know who they are, and they return to that which is theirs.

In addition to a body and a soul, however, a man also possesses a spirit, or (as we should probably say for all men since the fall) he possesses the capacity for one. It is this capacity that sets man apart from the animal world. The spirit is that part of man that has consciousness of God. Consequently, man worships, while the animals do not.

This was the man that God placed in the Garden, a man with a body, soul, and spirit. God said to him, "The whole earth is for your enjoyment. You can eat of all the trees in the garden, but as a symbol of your dependence upon me I am marking out one tree, the fruit of which you shall not eat. This is the tree of the knowledge of good and evil, and the day that you eat of this tree you will die." Adam looked at the tree. Then, after a suitable pause, he ate of it, thereby saying to God, "I do not care for all the trees north of here, east of here, south of here, or west of here. As long as this tree stands in the middle of the Garden it reminds me of my dependence upon you, and I hate it. I will therefore eat of it and die."

What happened when Adam ate of the forbidden fruit? He died, of course. But how did he die? Well, he did not die physically at first. That came later. First, his spirit died. That was the part of his being that had communion with

God. Consequently, the communion was broken, and man proved that it was broken by running away from God when God came to him in the Garden.

Second, man began to die in his soul. Since the soul is the seat of man's intellect, feelings, and identity, man therefore began to lose his identity, give vent to bad feelings, and suffer the decay of his intellect. This is the type of intellectual and spiritual decay portrayed in the first chapter of Romans where we are told that having given up the worship of the true God, people's "thinking became futile and their foolish hearts were darkened. Although they claimed to be wise, they became fools and exchanged the glory of the immortal God for images made to look like mortal man and birds and animals and reptiles" (Rom. 1:21–23).

We must not take this to mean that man lost his ability to reason. That is not true. It simply means that man lost his ability to reason his way to God. An illustration may help us here. There is a condition in the human body, known to doctors as *myasthenia gravis,* in which the muscles of the body cannot respond to the signals being sent from the brain. In the human body the brain normally originates the signal for a muscle to expand or contract. The signal is sent to the muscle through a nerve and is received in the muscle by an apparatus known as the motor-end-plate. In the condition I mentioned, the motor-end-plates are missing. Consequently, the signal is sent to the muscle through the nerves, but it is never received by the muscle. Because it is not received, the muscle does not respond, and because the muscle does not respond it eventually withers away and dies.

That is exactly what happened in man when his spirit died through the fall. In the human system the spirit was meant to play the part of the motor-end-plate. It was meant to receive God's signals. When Adam and Eve sinned, the motor-end-plate died. Thus, although the signals are still there, although God is speaking, people do not hear him and their spiritual life withers. Eventually, of course, even the human body dies. So it is written, "Dust you are and to dust you will return" (Gen. 3:19).[1]

It is possible to describe salvation completely in reference to these three parts of man's being. Man sinned, and man died—body, soul, and spirit. So when God begins to save a man he begins to work with his body, soul, and spirit, only in reverse order. The salvation of the spirit comes first. This is justification; by it man receives a new spirit. The salvation of the soul is second. This is sanctification; in sanctification man receives a new soul (for God does not merely patch up the old one). The salvation of the body comes last. This is the resurrection in which man receives a new body.

Running from God

In our studies we are going to deal with this great plan of salvation. But first we need to see two major results of what I have been saying.

The first result is that man no longer seeks God. In fact, man runs from God. He does this in religious ways as well as in secular ones. God is good.

Man is sinful. If man's intellect were functioning properly, the intellect should tell him that all truth, joy, growth, and happiness is to be found in fellowship with his Creator. But when man fell his mind began to be warped in regard to spiritual things so that now he thinks happiness is to be found in independence. God comes with the offer of salvation and renewed fellowship, and man says, "No, not that. Anything but that." And he runs away.

I know that someone will ask, "What do you mean when you say that man runs away from God? I *sought* God. In fact, I am still seeking him. I sought God in the Presbyterian church, and when I couldn't find God in the Presbyterian church I left it and became a Baptist. When I couldn't find God in the Baptist church I left that church and became a Methodist. Now I am a Pentecostal, and if I don't find God in the Pentecostal church I am going to leave the church and become a Mormon." You have not been seeking God; you have been running away from him! When God got close to you in the Presbyterian church and said, "My child, this is the truth about your condition and your need for a Savior," you turned from him, saying, "I don't like that way of talking about religion; I'm going to go elsewhere." You went to the Baptist church. But when God got close to you in the Baptist church you became a Methodist. Now you are a Pentecostal. The truth is that you are not seeking God; you are running away from him.

Some time ago a minister told me a story that illustrates this truth. He had come in the early days of his ministry to a very liberal church. His prayer in those days—because he knew that many would be offended with the true gospel—was, "Lord, just let them leave quietly." And, of course, many did—before the church began to grow to its present size. The day came when one woman, who had been his greatest supporter at the beginning, walked out very much offended. As she did, she stopped to tell him, "Sir, I am leaving this church and I will not be back. No man is going to call me a miserable sinner!" Such is the heart of our fallen race.

The second result of the fall, as it affects man's reason, is that he now needs revelation if he is to know anything at all about God. In other words, not only does he not come to God by reason; it is also true that he is incapable of coming. Thus, we find Paul writing: "No eye has seen, no ear has heard, no mind has conceived what God has prepared for those who love him—but God has revealed it to us by his Spirit" (1 Cor. 2:9–10). This means that a person will never understand spiritual truth unless God first takes the initiative in saving him.

Nicodemus

All that goes before is really a theological introduction to the second verse of John 3. So I now want to illustrate it by John's story.

Nicodemus came to Jesus by night and said, "Rabbi, we know you are a teacher who has come from God. For no one could perform the miraculous signs you are doing if God were not with him" (v. 2). Apart from the word

"Rabbi," which was his direct form of address, the first words that Nicodemus uttered were his claim to considerable intellectual knowledge. He said, "We know." He then began to rehearse three things that he knew: (1) that Jesus was continuing to do many miracles; (2) that the miracles were intended to authenticate him as a teacher sent from God; and, therefore, (3) that Jesus was a teacher sent from God to whom Nicodemus should listen. Unfortunately for Nicodemus, the point of the story is that Nicodemus's whole conception of Jesus Christ was wrong in spite of his knowledge. His intellect had deceived him. That is why Jesus rebuked him by saying, "I tell you the truth, no one can see the kingdom of God unless he is born again" (v. 3). There had been hundreds of teachers sent from God during the long course of Jewish history. Many of them had been authenticated by miracles. But Jesus was not one of these teachers. They were men. Jesus Christ was God. They had come to teach about God. He was God come to teach, die, and reveal himself to men.

The second way in which Nicodemus illustrates the results of the fall on the human intellect is that he reacted to Christ's words in purely natural terms. We referred to this when considering John 2:18–22. Jesus replied to Nicodemus's words by saying that a man must be born again before he can understand things spiritually. This was simple spiritual teaching, but it was a mystery to Nicodemus. Jesus was speaking of the need for new, spiritual life. But all Nicodemus could think of was obstetrics. Jesus had said, "You must be born again." Nicodemus began to think of all the concepts that could possibly be associated with the only kind of birth he knew—physical birth. Then when that didn't make sense he asked, "How can a man be born when he is old? Surely he cannot enter a second time into his mother's womb to be born!" (v. 4).

Jesus answered, in effect. "No, Nicodemus, I don't mean obstetrics. I am speaking of the kind of birth that takes place by means of God's Spirit."

A Comprehensive Cure

That brings us to the cure that God has for man's intellect. The cure begins with man's spirit, for it is there that the communion with God was broken. The new birth means that God has restored communication. Before the new birth the motor-end-plates were missing. Now they are restored, and man begins to receive and understand what God is saying.

We must not think, however, that the salvation of man stops there. For since the fall affected man's mind, so does salvation affect it. Only salvation affects it positively. Think how many verses speak of the transformation that God wills for man's mind after his conversion. In some ways Romans 12:1–2 is the touchstone: "Therefore, I urge you, brothers, in view of God's mercy, to offer your bodies as living sacrifices, holy and pleasing to God—this is your spiritual act of worship. Do not conform any longer to the pattern of this world, but be transformed by the renewing of your mind. Then you will be able to test and approve what God's will is—his good, pleasing and per-

fect will." Isaiah speaks of the mind also, for he writes: "You will keep in perfect peace him whose mind is steadfast" (Isa. 26:3). Peter wrote: "Prepare
your minds for action" (1 Peter 1:13). Finally, perhaps the greatest verse in
the New Testament about the task of reordering our minds is the place where
Paul writes, "We demolish arguments and every pretension that sets itself up
against the knowledge of God, and we take captive every thought to make it
obedient to Christ" (2 Cor. 10:5).

    This is the task that is set before you in this life, if you are a Christian. This
is why you must study the Bible and expose yourself to sound teaching. It
must always stand as a great biblical principle that God does not save men
by means of the human intellect. He wants new men. But let it also be said
that he wishes to train the thoughts and order the intellect of the new men.

32

Becoming New Men

John 3:3–5

In reply Jesus declared, "I tell you the truth, no one can see the kingdom of God unless he is born again."

"How can a man be born when he is old?" Nicodemus asked. "Surely he cannot enter a second time into his mother's womb to be born!"

Jesus answered, "I tell you the truth, no one can enter the kingdom of God unless he is born of water and the Spirit."

A young Arab was proceeding down the road on a donkey when he came upon a small bird, a sparrow, lying upon his back in the road. There he was, a small scrawny object with two thin legs pointed skyward. At first the Arab thought the sparrow was dead. When he found that the bird was alive, however, the Arab got down from his donkey and went forward to speak to him. "Are you all right?" he asked.

"Yes," the sparrow answered.

"Then what are you doing lying on your back with your legs pointed up at the sky?"

"Haven't you heard the rumor?" the sparrow asked in return. "They say that heaven is going to fall."

"If it does," said the Arab, "surely you don't think you're going to hold it up with those two scrawny legs?"

The bird looked at him with a solemn face for a moment and then retorted, "One does the best one can."

197

We laugh at the story, of course, but the folly of the sparrow is only an illustration of the folly of human beings who think they can hold off the wrath of divine judgment by the scrawny legs of human achievements. According to the Bible, this cannot be done. Thus, the first few verses of John 3 have been showing that no man can please God either by his own achievements or by his intellect. Instead a man must be born again. At this point, however, Nicodemus asks the question that anyone might quite properly ask, "All right, you say that a man must be born again. How, then, is it possible? How *can* a man be born again?" To this question—perhaps the most important question that anyone can ask—the third chapter of John gives two answers.

Birth from Above

The first answer to Nicodemus's question is the answer Jesus gave even before he asked it. Jesus said, "No one can see the kingdom of God unless he is born again" (v. 3). Later he said the same thing by repeating, "You must be born again" (v. 7). The answer involved in this statement lies in the meaning of the Greek word translated "again." It is one of two Greek words that are often translated "again" in our Bibles. One is *palin,* which refers quite simply to the repetition of an act. The other word, the one used here, is *anōthen,* which also refers to the repetition of an act but which implies more.

In the first place, *anōthen* can also be translated "from above." This is the meaning of the word in John 3:31 that says, "The one who comes from above is above all; the one who is from the earth belongs to the earth, and speaks as one from the earth. The one who comes from heaven is above all." "Above" points to heaven. So when the Bible uses *anōthen* instead of *palin* in the first part of the chapter, it is suggesting that the new birth is supernatural and has its origin in God.

Then, too, there is an even finer distinction that also bears this out. *Palin,* as I have said, refers to the repetition of an act. *Anōthen* also refers to the repetition of an act, but it involves one additional detail, the fact that the repetition of the act has the same source as the first act. Suppose that the pianist Van Cliburn and I are in a room and that Van Cliburn has just completed playing the piano parts of Tchaikovsky's great piano concerto. People want to hear it again. Now if they were Greek and should say, "Play it again *(palin),*" that would mean that I could sit down at the piano and try and do it. It would only mean that they wanted to hear the music repeated. However, if they should say, "Play it again *(anōthen),*" it would mean that the repetition of the music would have to have the same source as the first playing. In other words, Van Cliburn would have to play the concerto. Thus, when Jesus said, "Unless he is born again," he was suggesting that the new birth would have to have the same source as the original birth. That is, Nicodemus would have to be brought to life spiritually by God.

This distinction takes us back to the early chapters of Genesis, before the fall, where we are told that "The LORD God formed the man from the dust of the ground and breathed into his nostrils the breath of life" (Gen. 2:7). When Adam sinned he lost God's life, first spiritually and then physically. Thus, Jesus told Nicodemus that he needed to be born again as Adam was born. God was the source. Therefore, Nicodemus needed to have a fresh impartation of spiritual life; there had to be a new creation.

Water and Wind

The second answer to Nicodemus's question—"How can a man be born again?"—is the answer given in verse 5. Jesus answered, "Truly, truly, I say to you, unless one is born of water and the Spirit, he cannot enter the kingdom of God" (RSV). This verse carries Jesus' explanation of the new birth a bit further, for having explained it in reference to its source he now begins to explain in a more technical way how the new birth takes place. It takes place literally by "water" and "breath" or, as most translations say, "of water and of the Spirit." In other words, Jesus first spoke of the source of the new birth. He now speaks of the means by which it occurs.

At this point we must acknowledge that several interpretations of the phrase "of water and of the Spirit" have been given. One of these interpretations takes the word "water" as referring to physical birth. I heard this explanation first during my years in college. It is based on the fact that physical birth is accompanied by the release of the embryonic fluid from the womb of the mother. If this were the proper explanation, Jesus would be saying that in order for a person to be saved he must first be born physically and then his physical birth must be followed by a spiritual birth.

True as this may be, it does not seem to be the proper interpretation of the statement. For one thing, the word "water" is never used in this way elsewhere in Scripture. For another, a reference to the necessity of physical birth is so self-evident that the question arises whether Jesus would waste words in this fashion. The third and decisive problem with this view is that since Jesus was probably claiming that a person is born again by water as well as by the Spirit, if water refers to physical birth, this is simply not true. Physical birth is not part of the answer.

The second interpretation of the phrase is that which sees water as referring to water baptism. Unfortunately, this is not substantiated either by the text or by biblical theology. The text says nothing at all about baptism, and the Bible elsewhere teaches that no one is saved by any external rite of religion (1 Sam. 16:7; Rom. 2:28–29; Gal. 2:15, 16; 5:1–6). Baptism is a sign of what has already taken place, but it is not the agent by which it takes place.

Some years ago a young woman came to me wanting to be married to a young man whom I had not yet met. I arranged for us to get together and in the course of the resulting conversation discovered that neither the young woman nor the young man were Christians. The man was quite open about

200 it and regarded

it and regarded the church service as merely a public ceremony. The young woman thought she was a Christian, largely because she had come from a family of churchgoers and had been baptized in her infancy by a bishop. When I pointed out that baptism never made anyone a Christian this woman was greatly offended. She was even more offended when later I declined to perform the ceremony.

Someone will object to this on the grounds that John the Baptist supposedly baptized people for new life, but this is wrong teaching. John called for repentance, and when men or women repented he baptized them as a sign to others that this had happened. The proof of this is seen in the fact that John actually refused to baptize certain of the Pharisees and Sadducees because they did not show evidence of any genuine change in their lives.

The third interpretation of the phrase "of water and of the Spirit" is one that takes both parts of the phrase symbolically. "Water," the argument goes, refers to cleansing; "Spirit" refers to power. Therefore, one must be both cleansed and filled with power. William Barclay is one who holds this view. It is true, of course, that the sinner must be cleansed from his sin and that it is the Christian's privilege to be endued with power from on high, but it is questionable whether this is the primary meaning of this passage. Strictly speaking, both cleansing and power accompany the new birth, while these verses are dealing with the way in which the new birth itself comes about. Moreover, neither of the ideas is related at all to the birth metaphor as the context seems to require.

One of the great students of the Greek New Testament, Kenneth S. Wuest, proposed a fourth explanation. It is based upon the use of the word "water" as a metaphor in other New Testament texts. Wuest points out that "water" often is used in Scripture to refer to the Holy Spirit. He thinks that this is the case in John 4, for instance, where Jesus tells the woman of Samaria that he will give her "a spring of water welling up to eternal life" (John 4:14). Another case is John 7:37–38, where almost the identical language is used. After this statement John himself adds, as if in parentheses, "By this he meant the Spirit, whom those who believed in him were later to receive" (v. 39). Wuest also refers to Isaiah 44:3 and 55:1, both of which should have been known to Nicodemus. If this is the correct interpretation of the phrase "of water and of the Spirit," then we have a repetition of ideas, and the word "and" should be taken in its emphatic sense. We would normally indicate this by translating the word as "even." Thus, Jesus would be saying, "I tell you the truth, no one can enter the kingdom of God unless he is born of water, even the Spirit."

The explanation given by Wuest is a good explanation. Nevertheless, it seems to me that another must be preferred. Wuest begins by pointing out that the word "water" is often a metaphor for the Holy Spirit. This is true, but it is not the only spiritual reality that is suggested by that metaphor.

Water is also a metaphor for the written Word of God, the Bible. Thus, Ephesians 5:26 says that Christ gave himself for the church "to make her holy, cleansing her by the washing with water through the word." In 1 John the same author who composed the fourth Gospel distinguishes between the witnesses to Christ on earth of "the Spirit, the water and the blood" (1 John 5:8). Since he then goes on to speak of God's written witness to the fact that salvation is in Christ, in this context the Spirit must refer to God's witness within the individual, the blood to the historical witness of Christ's death, and the water to the Scriptures. Psalm 119:9 declares, "How can a young man keep his way pure? By living according to your word." Jesus said, "You are already clean because of the word I have spoken to you" (John 15:3).

A related text is James 1:18, which actually cites the Scriptures as the channel through which the new birth takes place, although without using water as the metaphor. "He chose to give us birth through the word of truth, that we might be a kind of firstfruits of all he created."

When we see Christ's words in this light, we see that God is here pictured as the Divine Begetter, the Father of his spiritual children, and we learn that the written Word of God together with the working of his Holy Spirit is the means by which the new birth is accomplished. That is why the Bible tells us that it pleased God to save people by the foolishness of preaching, for people are reborn through the efforts of others who proclaim God's Word (Rom. 10:14–15; 1 Cor. 1:21).

Spiritual Conception

One more verse makes this even clearer: 1 Peter 1:23. It says, "For you have been born again, not of perishable seed, but of imperishable, through the living and enduring word of God."

There are many symbols for the Word of God in the Bible. We are told that the Bible is "a lamp" to our feet and "a light" to our path (Ps. 119:105). The Word is like "a fire . . . and like a hammer that breaks a rock in pieces" (Jer. 23:29). It is "milk" to the spiritual infant and "strong meat" to those of a more mature age (1 Peter 2:2; Heb. 5:11–14). It is a sword (Heb. 4:12; Eph. 6:17), a "mirror" (1 Cor. 13:12; 2 Cor. 3:18; James 1:23), a "schoolmaster to bring us to Christ" (Gal. 3:24). It is a branch grafted into our bodies (James 1:21). These are great images, but none is so bold as the one used by Peter in this passage.

In the first chapter of 1 Peter, Peter has been talking about the means by which a person enters the family of God. First, he has discussed his theme *objectively* in terms of Christ's death, writing that "it was not with perishable things such as silver or gold that you were redeemed . . . but with the precious blood of Christ, a lamb without blemish or defect" (vv. 18, 19). Second, he has discussed the basis of the new birth *subjectively*, pointing out that it occurs through faith: "Through him you believe in God, who raised him from the dead and glorified him, and so your faith and hope are in God"

(v. 21). Finally, having mentioned these truths, Peter goes on to discuss the new birth in terms of God's sovereign grace in *election*. This time, however, he emphasizes that God is the Father of his children and that we are born again spiritually by means of the Word of God, which Peter likens to the male life germ. The Latin Vulgate makes this image of Peter's even clearer than our English versions, for the word used there is *semen*.

When we take these passages together and then add to them all that the Bible has to say about faith and about the work of the Holy Spirit in salvation, we find that we are able to grasp the essential nature of the new birth in terms of human conception. What happens when a man or a woman is born again? The answer is that God first of all plants within the heart of the person what we might call the ovum of saving faith, for we are told that even faith is not of ourselves, it is the gift of God (Eph. 2:8). Second, God sends forth the seed of his Word so that the seed of the Word, which contains the divine life within it, pierces the ovum of faith that God has already placed within our hearts. The result is conception. By this means, a new spiritual life comes into being, a life that has its origin in God and that therefore has no connection whatever with the sinful life that surrounds it.

God did not use anything of Abram when he made Abraham. He did not use anything of Simon when he created the new Peter. He did not use anything of Saul when he made Paul. He does not use anything of your old sinful and Adamic nature when he produces the new life of Christ within you. That is why we can now say, "Therefore, if anyone is in Christ, he is a new creation; the old has gone, the new has come" (2 Cor. 5:17). Thus did Jesus speak to Nicodemus.

Thus does Jesus speak to you, whoever you may be. If you are one who has never believed on the Lord Jesus Christ as your Savior, you must realize that you will never be able to enter God's family by any achievements of your own. The work is God's alone, and it was accomplished objectively through the death and resurrection of Christ. If you are a believer, you should find encouragement in the fact that all the people of God, from Abel on down to the last believer who will ever live, are born again by the same process and are therefore in the family of God through God's activity. This should be your confidence, if you are a Christian. "For God's gifts and his call are irrevocable" (Rom. 11:29). Moreover, we know that what God has promised "[he has] power to do" (Rom. 4:21).

33

Flesh and Spirit

John 3:6

"Flesh gives birth to flesh, but the Spirit gives birth to spirit."

T he first great principle of the new birth is that God does not avail himself of anything found in the natural man when he begets a Christian. Man is fallen and totally depraved from God's point of view. He is fallen in body, soul, and spirit, and God does not begin to patch these up when he saves him. Instead of the old spirit, now dead, God implants a new spirit, having its source in himself. Instead of the old soul, God begins to construct a new soul so that the man comes to desire new things. Instead of the old body, which will one day die and decompose, God will eventually give a new body patterned after the resurrection body of the Lord Jesus Christ. Thus, the Christian becomes a fresh beginning by God and can be called "a new creation" (2 Cor. 5:17).

The verse to which we come now, John 3:6, gives us a reason why this state of affairs is as God declares it to be. Moreover, it carries us beyond the mere facts of the new birth to the principles by which the new life is to be lived out in the Christian. The verse says, "Flesh gives birth to flesh, but the Spirit gives birth to spirit."

The reason this verse gives for the way in which God operates should be especially understandable to us who know something about genetics. Likes produce likes. A male dog and a female dog produce puppies rather than kittens. Cats produce cats. Horses produce horses. Plants produce plants.

People produce people. In the same way, God tells us, that which comes out of the natural man can produce only that which is natural to man and which is sinful as a result. Man can produce nothing spiritual. On the other hand, that which comes forth from God produces only that which is characteristic of God and which is therefore sinless and eternal.

The Natural Man

If we are to understand this statement by the Lord Jesus Christ, we need to understand the terms involved. This is true of any verse of the Bible, of course, but it is particularly true of this verse due to the fact that the most important term in it is used in different ways in the Bible and in current speech.

The term that is turned about in today's speech is the term "flesh." What is flesh? In current English usage the word "flesh" refers almost entirely to the fleshly parts of the body, at times being almost synonymous with the word "skin." Yet this is not at all what the term means biblically. In the Bible the word "flesh" refers to the entire individual—body, soul, and spirit. Since the fall of man it refers to the individual as he is motivated by his sinful nature.

For instance, at the beginning of Genesis we are told that when God brought the first woman to the first man in Eden, Adam said, "This is now bone of my bones and flesh of my flesh; she shall be called 'woman,' for she was taken out of man. For this reason a man will leave his father and mother and be united to his wife, and they will become one flesh" (Gen. 2:23–24). When Adam said, "They will become one flesh," he was not talking about a sexual or bodily union alone, although that was part of it. He was saying that the man and woman were to be united body, soul, and spirit, and that they were thereafter to become what you and I might call one organism. Consequently, at the very beginning of the Bible the word "flesh" is used to denote the whole of man's being.

After the fall of man the word "flesh" conveys a slightly different meaning, still involving all of man's being but also denoting man as he is moved by his depraved human nature. The term now points to man as he is motivated by that nature rather than as moved by the Spirit.

We can be helped in our understanding by the following illustration. All of us have seen a tug-of-war in which two individuals or two groups struggle to pull a marker on a piece of rope across a line. So long as the struggle is even the marker more or less stays in the middle. When one person weakens or falls down, the marker moves over to the other side, and the stronger team wins. In some ways this is what human nature was like before the fall. The center of the human person, the soul, was like the marker. On one side was a person's body with its appetites. On the other was the spirit with its consciousness of God. God made people so that the spirit would dominate. The spirit was to determine the course of human beings' path and development. However, when Adam and Eve sinned, the human spirit died. Thereafter, people were led about by the appetites of the body or flesh with the result that even the proper functions of the body were debased and true human nature was distorted.

We could illustrate the same point by comparing the human spirit to the motor in an airplane cruising at 35,000 feet. The human body is the fuselage. The soul is the pilot. When the motor is running, the body of the plane is an asset, for the wings keep the plane up and the other parts assist in flying it. However, when the motor stops, the fuselage is a distinct liability, for it is too heavy and the plane will crash. That is what it means to be "fleshly." It means to be dominated by the body without the ongoing thrust of the spirit.

At this point we must stop to consider several terms that are synonymous with the word "flesh," for much of what is said about the flesh in the Bible is said by means of these other terms. Sometimes the reference is to our "old man" or our "old nature." At times it is the "heart." We are said to be "carnal," "fleshly," "soulish." The flesh is sometimes called "the natural man." Whatever the term used, however, the teaching is that the fleshly or natural man cannot please, obey, or even understand God.

This is the plain teaching of many passages of Scripture. For instance, David says, "Surely I was sinful at birth, sinful from the time my mother conceived me" (Ps. 51:5). Paul exhorts: "Put off your old self, which is being corrupted by its deceitful desires" (Eph. 4:22). Jeremiah tells us that "the heart is deceitful above all things and beyond cure" (Jer. 17:9). Jesus said, "For from within, out of men's hearts, come evil thoughts, sexual immorality, theft, murder, adultery, greed, malice, deceit, lewdness, envy, slander, arrogance and folly. All these evils come from inside and make a man 'unclean'" (Mark 7:21–23). Paul wrote: "Those controlled by the sinful nature cannot please God" (Rom. 8:8). First Corinthians 2:14 declares: "The man without the Spirit does not accept the things that come from the Spirit of God, for they are foolishness to him, and he cannot understand them, because they are spiritually discerned."

Whatever you do, therefore, do not make the mistake of thinking when you come to these verses that they describe people other than yourself, the criminals, derelicts, hypocrites, thieves, or perverts of our society. This is not the way God intends them. These words describe every man as he is since the fall apart from a miraculous intervention of God to save him. They describe you. Thus, according to the teaching of the Bible it is correct to say that neither you nor I are able to please God. The Bible says: "All have turned away, they have together become worthless; there is no one who does good, not even one" (Rom. 3:12).

Painting the Pump

With this background in the biblical terminology, we now need to get back to our text. For the text teaches that the reason why God does not save people on the basis of anything in them is simply that a sinful human nature will never be able to produce anything other than sinful human nature. It is possible to polish it up a bit and put it in a good light so that it does not look quite so bad as it is, but it will still be sinful.

The natural man does not like this, of course, for most people spend much of their lives trying to improve the old nature. This may make life a little more bearable for other people, even for the individual himself, but from God's point of view it is a bit like painting a pump that is over a well of bad water. It is true that a painted pump looks better than an old rusty pump. It is true that the pump can be elevated. It can be given a gold handle. A person can write poems about it, even construct a monument to it. But nothing that is done to the pump will change the fact that it is over bad water. No embellishment will change the fact that bad water comes from it.

Kenneth S. Wuest has written, "The teaching here is that man in his totally depraved condition cannot be improved. Reformation will not change him into a fit subject for the kingdom of God. The flesh is incurably wicked, and cannot by any process be changed so as to produce a righteous life. What that person needs, Jesus says, is a new nature, a spiritual nature which will produce a life pleasing to God, and which will be a life fit for the kingdom of God. This is what Jesus teaches in the following words: 'And that which has been born of the Spirit is as a result spirit, and is spiritual in nature, and stays spirit.' That is, the new birth is a permanent thing, produces a permanent change in the life of the individual, and makes him a fit subject for the kingdom of God."[1]

Let me ask you Christ's question: Are you born again? Do you have the life of God within you? Is there a new spring of water within or are you still painting the pump over the spring of your old human nature? You must face this question honestly, for the Bible teaches that there is no good in you that can satisfy God's righteousness. In order to please God, you must have the life of God inside.

Life in the Spirit

If you have been following the progression of Jesus' conversation with Nicodemus as we have unfolded it, you will have noticed that our exposition of John 3:6 has already brought us to the heart of Christ's argument. A man cannot be saved by any human effort because human efforts can only produce human results. Human results are sinful. Therefore, a person must be born again. At this point, however, I want to take you one step beyond the argument of Christ with Nicodemus to that teaching about the Christian life that is developed later in Christ's discourses and in the rest of the New Testament.

Let us start with this important question. What happens to the old or fleshly nature when a person is born again? The person receives a new nature, of course. He has a new spirit. The new spirit is the offspring of the Holy Spirit, the offspring of God. But what happens to his old nature? What happens to the flesh?

There are some who teach that the flesh is "eradicated" or, if you prefer this terminology, that the flesh is "transformed" so that it is no longer sinful. But this is not true, and our text refutes it. That which is born of the flesh remains flesh. Paul had a new nature, but he was the first to declare that he also had an old nature that was entirely bad. He wrote: "I know that nothing good lives in me, that is, in my sinful nature. For I have the desire to do what is good, but I cannot carry it out" (Rom. 7:18). Paul's old nature struggled against his new nature causing him to cry out for that victory that only the Lord Jesus Christ can provide. The apostle John knew that he retained his old nature also (as is the case with all Christians) for he wrote to Christians saying, "If we claim to be without sin, we deceive ourselves and the truth is not in us" (1 John 1:8).

The real answer to the question I asked is therefore that the flesh remains with us and, what is more, that it struggles against the new nature. The new nature can do nothing bad. The old nature can do nothing good. So there will always be a conflict, a struggle, a warfare.

When you become a Christian you may think that all your struggles are over, and you may be disappointed and even discouraged to learn that in one sense the struggle is only beginning. Before, you were unhappy but not schizophrenic. Now you are struggling. If this has been your experience, you must not despair. Nor must you think that because the old nature is apparent you are therefore to go on sinning freely every day with the old nature predominating. On the contrary, you have been given a new spirit precisely so that the flesh will not dominate.

How, then, are you to achieve such a victory? There are three ways. First, the Bible says that we are to think of the old nature as dead. In one sense, of course, this is not true, for the old nature is still with us, as I have indicated. Yet in another sense it is true; for God tells us that he has broken its power at the cross of Christ and therefore considers it a dead issue in the life of the Christian. On this basis Paul writes in his letter to the Romans: "In the same way, count yourselves dead to sin but alive to God in Christ Jesus" (Rom. 6:11). He exhorts the Colossians: "Put to death, therefore, whatever belongs to your earthly nature: sexual immorality, impurity, lust, evil desires and greed, which is idolatry. Because of these, the wrath of God is coming" (Col. 3:5–6).

When we are tempted to sin we are to pray, "Lord, I know that my old, fleshly nature has been crucified with Christ so that its power to overcome me is broken. I ask you to keep it broken and give me the victory." God will do this if we ask him.

Second, the Bible tells us that we are to feed the new nature while starving the old. This is what Peter meant when he wrote to the Christians of his day, "Therefore, rid yourselves of all malice and all deceit, hypocrisy, envy, and slander of every kind. Like newborn babies, crave pure spiritual milk, so that by it you may grow up in your salvation" (1 Peter 2:1–2). It is as though the old nature were a lion capable of tearing our Christian life in pieces. God says that he has placed the lion within a cage where he is dead so far as any overt activity in the believer's life is concerned. What then are we to do? Are we to feed the old nature with the world's way of thinking and acting so that the lion within grows stronger and can eventually break out of his cage? Of course not! We are to starve the fleshly nature and indulge the spirit. This can be done only through Bible study. It is only through a knowledge of God's truth that the Christian can become strong.

Finally, the Bible tells us that we are to "live by the Spirit," for then we "will not gratify the desires of the sinful nature" (Gal. 5:16). What does it mean to walk in the Spirit? It is primarily a matter of our inmost determination. God tells us that for a Christian, he has restored that will toward spiritual things that was lost in the fall. Then, let us use it. Let us place ourselves in circles where the life of the Spirit may grow. Let us read the Bible. Let us pray. Let us make Christian decisions. When we do this, we will find ourselves increasingly victorious, and the fruit of the Spirit—love, joy, peace, patience, gentleness, goodness, faithfulness, kindness, self-control—will grow in us.

34

The Breath of God

John 3:7–8

"You should not be surprised at my saying, 'You must be born again.' The wind blows wherever it pleases. You hear its sound, but you cannot tell where it comes from or where it is going. So it is with everyone born of the Spirit."

We come now to a third reference to the Holy Spirit. There has already been a reference to the him in 3:5, where Jesus told Nicodemus that the new birth takes place "of water and the Spirit." This means that spiritual life is generated whenever the Spirit implants the seed of God's Word within the human heart. Another reference occurred in verse 6: "Flesh gives birth to flesh, but the Spirit gives birth to spirit." In discussing this verse we spent most of our time on the meaning of the word "flesh," asking how the Christian's fleshly nature is to be overcome.

The next verses deal almost entirely with the Spirit, so we need to focus exclusively on him in this study. To explain it, we must consider who the Spirit is, what is said about his activity, and finally what this should mean to us personally.

The Meaning of Spirit

In the first place, we need to define the word "spirit." Because of the nature of the English language, we suffer in our day from an unfortunate confusion over the words "ghost" and "spirit," which we constantly use in the phrases "the Holy Ghost" or "the Holy Spirit." The confusion arises from the fact that English, unlike most of the European languages, is a fusion of two lan-

209

guage groups, one Germanic in origin and the other Latinate. Before 1066, the year William the Norman conquered England, the language spoken in England was Anglo-Saxon. It existed in a variety of dialects, but all were Germanic in origin. Consequently, although there were various pronunciations of a word, generally speaking the same word was used for any given object. An ox was an ox, a brother was a brother, and so on. After the Norman Conquest a whole new vocabulary entered England because the Normans, who were now the ruling class, spoke French. Now there were two words for most objects. As the languages fused to give us English, in many cases both words were preserved. Thus, we still have the Anglo-Saxon word "ox," but we also have the word "beef," which is based on a French word, *boeuf,* originally identical to "ox" in meaning. In the same way, "brother" is Germanic in origin—the word is *Bruder*—but we also have the words "fraternize," "fraternal," and "fraternity," which are based on the equivalent French term *frère.*

This doubling of words has also taken place for many biblical or theological terms. It is true of the words "saint" and "holy," for example. These words are identical in their root meanings. Thus, if you should go to Germany today and pick up a German Bible, you would find the words *Die heilige Schrift* on the cover, while within you would find the Gospels of Holy Matthew, Holy Mark, Holy Luke, and Holy John. The French call their Bible *La Sainte Bible,* and their Gospels are by Saint Matthew, Saint Mark, Saint Luke, and Saint John. We have kept the word "Saint" for the authors but not for the Bible, and the word "Holy" for the Bible but not for the authors. Yet the two words are essentially identical.

It is precisely the same with the words "spirit" and "ghost," in spite of the fact that these two words have taken on distinct colorings of their own as the result of nine hundred years of English usage. Today we use the word "ghost" to refer to the spirit of a dead person supposedly returning to haunt a place or a living human being. Hamlet used the word in this way when he referred to his father's ghost. Nevertheless, this is not the sense in which the word "ghost" is used in the phrase "the Holy Ghost." In this case "ghost" is identical with the word "spirit." Actually, it is because of the tendency in our day to identify the word "ghost" with the spirits of the dead that many ministers, including myself, abandon the phrase "the Holy Ghost" entirely and instead use the phrase "the Holy Spirit," except when singing the doxology or reciting the Apostles' Creed.

God's Breath

If the words "spirit" and "ghost" are identical, and if they do not refer to the returning spirits of the dead, then what do the words mean? This question leads us to consider the root meaning of the word "spirit."

What is the Spirit? Quite obviously, the basic reference is to the Third Person of the Trinity, to God, and on the human level to that part of man that has God-consciousness. Beyond this, however, we find that the word has some fascinating and stimulating overtones. In the Latin language from which we get our word "spirit," the word is *spiritus,* which means "breath." We recognize this truth every time we use one of the English words derived from it. For instance, in English the word *spiritus* has given us the words "aspire," "conspire," "inspire," "perspire," and "expire." They all refer to different ways of using one's breath. When men aspire, they take a deep breath and try harder. When men conspire, they put their heads together and breathe in and out with one another. A man is inspired when another man (or God) blows some of his breath into him. A person perspires by breathing out through the skin. When we expire, we breathe out for the last time; we die.

At this point we can see why Jesus referred to the wind in trying to teach Nicodemus about the Holy Spirit, for the wind is quite evidently an excellent symbol of God's breath. Jesus referred to it to teach that God allows his breath to go where he wishes and to produce effects of his choosing.

In the Greek language, the language in which the New Testament is written, the corresponding word is *pneuma.* It too refers to breath. This word is harder for English-speaking people to pronounce than the Latin word *spiritus* because of the initial two consonants, *pn.* So we do not have so many words based on it. Yet, we still have the words "pneumatic" and "pneumonia." The first word refers to any tool that is air operated, as a pneumatic drill. The second word refers to a disease of the breath box or lungs.

Finally, just as the Latin and Greek words for "spirit" all refer to breath, wind, or air, so also does the Hebrew word. This word is *ruach,* which you cannot even say properly without exhaling. *Ruach!* It is the sound of a breath. When we understand this we have some sense of the poetry of the opening verses of the Bible in which the creative Spirit of God blows over the water like a troubling wind. No one English version can capture both ideas—wind and spirit—but the New English Bible at least suggests the idea of the wind, with a reference to God's Spirit preserved in a footnote. The New English Bible declares: "In the beginning of creation, when God made heaven and earth, the earth was without form and void, with darkness over the face of the abyss, and a mighty wind that swept over the surface of the waters" (Gen. 1:1–2).

Our Gracious God

What happens when we take this basic sense of the word "spirit" and apply it to our text? Quite simply it means that a person can be born again only as the result of God's breathing new life into him. What is more, it is teaching us that this never happens merely at man's volition but solely according to the good pleasure of God.

So it has been throughout all history. Take the case of Abraham. He was the man through whom God established the Jewish nation and from whose descendants Jesus was born. Was he a follower of God before God called him? Not according to Scripture. Joshua, in a spiritual charge to the people of Israel shortly before his death, wants them to remain true to Jehovah, so he begins by reminding them of their pagan past as that out of which their gracious God has brought them: "This is what the LORD, the God of Israel, says: 'Long ago your forefathers, including Terah the father of Abraham and Nahor, lived beyond the River and worshiped other gods. But I took your father Abraham from the land beyond the River and led him throughout Canaan and gave him many descendants. I gave him Isaac. . . . Now fear the LORD and serve him with all faithfulness. Throw away the gods your forefathers worshiped beyond the River and in Egypt, and serve the LORD" (Josh. 24:2–3, 14). According to these verses, Abraham had been a worshiper of idols like all the people about him. Thus, the movement of God's Spirit in calling him was a movement of pure grace.

We pass over the years to the time of Jesus Christ, and once again the unexpected occurs. A Jewish person who believed in Jesus might have felt that with the coming of the Messiah the culmination of God's blessing had occurred. Here is the fulfillment of Israel's hope! Here he is! But God, who knows all things and orders all things for his own purposes, ordered them in such a way that Jesus would not be received by Israel generally and that instead the doors of salvation would be opened to the Gentiles. Who would have thought that God was going to call to himself millions from the nations of the Gentiles? No one. Yet the Spirit of God moved, and the result was a new revelation of God's grace.

One more example will bring this aspect of the Spirit's moving down to our own time. For years now the impact of the organized churches in America has been declining. Here and there are significant exceptions, particularly in those churches where the gospel is still preached and full authority is given to God's Word. But, by and large, membership is down and attendance is decreasing. Seventy-five percent of all Americans feel that religion is losing its influence in this country, as opposed to 14 percent who held that opinion in 1957, and this is true in spite of large expenditures of money and unprecedented efforts to revive organizational Christianity. However, just as many are beginning to say that the trend is irreversible and some are even calling it beneficial, God breathes upon America and thousands of the so-called "hippies" or "street people" begin to turn to him.

The following case history epitomizes it all. Many will remember the late Episcopal Bishop James Pike, who rose to national fame through his controversial opinions and frequent denials of church doctrines. He began as a lawyer, was ordained a bishop in 1958, then together with the man who was then Stated Clerk of the United Presbyterian Church, Eugene Carson Blake, launched the proposal for a gigantic merger of Protestant denominations (later known as the Consultation on Church Union). Unfortunately, Pike's ecclesiastical rise was accompanied with an increasing decline of his commitment to biblical doctrines, which embarrassed the Episcopal church and led to several charges of heresy, although there were no heresy trials. On the personal level, there were numerous tragedies. He had a drinking

problem, which led to his joining Alcoholics Anonymous. He had three mar-
riages, the first being annulled, the second ending in divorce after producing four children. One son committed suicide. After he died, Pike claimed
he contacted him through a Philadelphia medium named Arthur Ford. Pike
left the church and finally died in the Judean desert in 1969 while research-
ing a book on the historical Jesus, which he had reportedly told friends would
be the most sensational of his writings yet.

This is a most tragic story and one that to me at least seems to epitomize
all the weaknesses of organizational Christianity. One can read it and think,
"If there was ever a place where God could never be expected to work it
would be with James Pike and his family." Yet one of the leaders of the Jesus
movement in the 70s was Christopher Pike, another of James Pike's sons.

His story is told by Edward E. Plowman in *The Jesus Movement in America*.[1] In
his early youth Christopher Pike was a troubled youngster. When he was fifteen a friend introduced him to marijuana. A year later, in 1967, the year in
which his mother and father were divorced and his father began to experi-
ment with psychic phenomena, another friend gave him LSD. He turned to
yoga. At times he felt that he was confronting an evil force that wanted his soul.

One day, on a visit to the University of California campus at Berkeley,
Christopher Pike heard converted hippie Ted Wise testify to Christ from the
steps of Sproul Hall. This set Chris wondering. In 1970, in his rooming house
at Berkeley, he began to read the New Testament. Here he found what his
father with his critical approach to the Bible had apparently missed. He found
a real Jesus. Chris felt drawn toward him. In time he got down on his knees
and poured out all the loneliness, frustration, and disappointment that had
been packed up inside him for years, and he received Jesus as his Savior.

What was it that changed Abraham from a worshiper of idols with no
knowledge at all of the true God and that got him moving out across the
desert to a country he had never seen before? Why did he fix his eyes on "the
city with foundations, whose architect and builder is God" (Heb. 11:10)?
What was it that captivated the attention of the Gentiles who were the numer-
ical strength of the growing Christian church and that brought new life to
them and their communities? What was it that reached Christopher Pike,
lifting him out of the despair of his past life and present lifestyle to a fresh,
transforming encounter with Jesus Christ? What is it that reaches, stirs, convicts, regenerates and changes men and women today?

It is not the eloquence of human reasoning, though God uses faithful,
reasoned presentations of Bible truth? It is not evangelistic techniques or
impressive testimonies or miraculous signs and wonders. It is the breath of
the living God, the Holy Spirit, who speaks through the Scriptures to create
new life in spiritually dead people. It is what has saved you, if you are a follower of Jesus Christ. The Spirit "moves wherever [he] pleases," and God
alone must have credit for it all.

35

Christ Speaks to Skeptics

John 3:9-13

"How can this be?" Nicodemus asked.

"You are Israel's teacher," said Jesus, "and do you not understand these things? I tell you the truth, we speak of what we know, and we testify to what we have seen, but still you people do not accept our testimony. I have spoken to you of earthly things and you do not believe; how then will you believe if I speak of heavenly things? No one has ever gone into heaven except the one who came from heaven—the Son of Man."

Almost everyone knows the difference between a believer and a skeptic, but I am not sure that everyone knows the difference between an honest skeptic and a dishonest skeptic. An honest skeptic is one who may have doubts about certain truths or doctrines but who will face up to them when he is presented with evidence; and he will alter his life as a result. A dishonest skeptic is one who has doubts about truths or doctrines but who will not face up to the evidence. Thus, when he is blasted out of one foxhole of disbelief, he will immediately take refuge in a second. If he is blasted out of that foxhole, he will begin to look around for a third.

Unfortunately, I am afraid that there are aspects to the conversation between Nicodemus and Jesus, recorded in the third chapter of John, to make us suspect that Nicodemus was a dishonest skeptic, like many people today. He had come with real problems. There was much in Christ's teaching that he genuinely could not understand. Yet Jesus seemed to end his conversation with him, not by stressing those things that were beyond the rabbi's knowledge but by faulting him for not believing in those things that were within it. "How can this be?" Nicodemus asked. "You are Israel's teacher," said Jesus, "and do you not understand these things? I tell you the truth, we speak of what we know, and we testify to what we have seen, but still you people do not accept our testimony. I have spoken to you of earthly things and you do not believe; how then will you believe if I speak of heavenly things? No one has ever gone into heaven except the one who came from heaven—the Son of Man" (John 3:9–13).

Apparently Nicodemus had been refusing to accept that which he could know and was rebuked by Christ for that refusal.

A Difficult Text

If we are to understand these verses, we must first make some effort to determine precisely what they are saying. This is true of all Scripture, of course, but it is particularly necessary in this case simply because so few who read these verses have any real awareness of their meaning.

Isn't it true that most people, perhaps yourself included, have always understood these verses to be referring merely to the fact of the new birth? In one sense, of course, they do refer to it (as I shall show later). But most people take them as referring merely to the fact of the new birth itself and therefore see Christ as rebuking Nicodemus for failing to know about the new birth and about the roles of the Holy Spirit and the Scripture in producing it in men. At the same time, I am convinced that most of those who think this way about the passage are also just a bit puzzled about certain elements in it that do not seem to fit this picture.

For instance, it can hardly escape our notice that in verse 11 Jesus stops speaking in the singular voice and begins to speak in the plural. He says, "We speak of what we know, and we testify to what we have seen, but still you people do not accept our testimony." If this is a testimony about the new birth, who are the others with whom Jesus associates himself? Could the "we" be the Trinity? This is not characteristic of Jesus' speech or of the language of the fourth Gospel. Could the "we" be the Old Testament prophets, culminating in John the Baptist? Could it be the disciples? These explanations are possible. Actually, I believe they are correct. But still we must wonder why Jesus would include a reference to the prophets or to the disciples in the context of his own very distinct teaching about regeneration.

Another problem that this passage raises concerns the contrast between "earthly things" and "heavenly things." Nicodemus seems to be chided for his failure to believe in things that pertain to the earth; but if this is a reference to the new birth, it seems highly inappropriate, particularly since Jesus has been stressing that the new birth originates with God in heaven. I must admit that none of these problems is insurmountable; the problems are just great enough to make the careful student of the chapter unhappy with the traditional explanations of Christ's teaching.

Is there a better explanation? I believe that the best explanation, and the true solution, lies in the realization that in these verses Jesus was not speaking about the new birth itself but about the results of the new birth and that he was chastising Nicodemus, not for his failure to understand about the new birth (who can understand it?) but for his failure to believe in it on the basis of its observable effects. In other words, Christ's words refer to the verse immediately preceding—the verse that says, "The wind blows wherever it pleases. You hear its sound, but you cannot tell where it comes from or where it is going. So it is with everyone born of the Spirit" (v. 8)—and not to the earlier parts of the discourse. In this case, the "earthly things" refer to those results of the new birth that can be observed by anyone through earthly senses. "Heavenly things" refers to that which can be known only through revelation; for example, the nature of the new birth itself, and the atonement, which is mentioned immediately afterward. The "we" refers to all who have observed these things and are thereby convinced of the power of God to change lives.

If I were to paraphrase this passage, then, I believe I would do it something like this: "Nicodemus answered Jesus, saying, 'I have never observed the new birth. I can't believe it is possible.' Jesus answered, 'Do you mean to tell me that you have risen to the point of being a teacher in Israel and yet have never observed the transformed life of a person who has been touched by my Spirit? I am telling you the truth when I say that all of us are speaking about things that we know personally and are testifying to things that we have often observed in others. You don't believe us. If I have testified to transformations in others that can be observed and you do not believe, how could you believe if I were to tell you about things that can be known only by revelation?' "

Changed Lives

Quite obviously this is a text that has two applications, one to those like Nicodemus, who are not yet Christians, and the other to those who are. Let us take the application to non-Christians first. Perhaps you are one who has not yet believed. You say there is much in the Christian gospel that you cannot understand. I agree with you; there is much that I also cannot understand. You say that most of what you do understand seems contradictory to everything that you have thought previously. I am not surprised. For God's thoughts are not our thoughts, neither are his ways our ways (Isa. 55:8). You say that you cannot be sure of the Bible. That may be quite honest, for not all persons have been exposed to the overwhelming evidence of its inspiration and total reliability. These may be partially valid, even adequate excuses. But have you never faced the evidence of the power of the gospel to transform the lives of Christians?

Let me dramatize this question by a story from the life of Harry A. Ironside, a story that he tells in *Random Reminiscences*. Early in his ministry the great evangelist and Bible teacher was living in the area of San Francisco Bay, working with a group of believers called "Brethren." One Sunday as he was walking through the city, he came upon a group of Salvation Army workers who were holding a meeting on the corner of Market and Grant Avenues. There were probably sixty of them. When they recognized Dr. Ironside, they immediately asked him if he would not like to give his testimony. He did, giving a word about how God had saved him through faith in the bodily death and literal resurrection of the Lord Jesus Christ.

As he was speaking Ironside noticed that on the edge of the crowd there was a well-dressed man who had taken a card from his pocket and had written something on it. As Ironside finished his talk this man came forward, lifted his hat, and very politely handed him the card. On one side was his name, which Ironside immediately recognized. The man was one of the early socialists who had made a name for himself lecturing, not only for socialism but also against Christianity. As Ironside turned the card over, he read, "Sir, I challenge you to debate with me the question, 'Agnosticism versus Christianity' in the Academy of Science Hall next Sunday afternoon at four o'clock. I will pay all expenses."

Ironside reread the card aloud and then replied somewhat like this. "I am very much interested in this challenge. Frankly, I am already scheduled for another meeting next Lord's Day afternoon at three o'clock, but I think it will be possible for me to get through with that in time to reach the Academy of Science Hall by four, or if necessary I could arrange to have another speaker substitute for me at the meeting already advertised. Therefore I will be glad to agree to this debate on the following conditions; namely, that in order to prove that Mr. _____ has something worth fighting for and worth debating about, he will promise to bring with him to the hall next Sunday two people, whose qualifications I will give in a moment, as proof that agnosticism is of real value in changing human lives and building true character.

"First, he must promise to bring with him one man who was for years what we commonly call a 'down-and-outer.' I am not particular as to the exact nature of the sins that had wrecked his life and made him an outcast from society—whether a drunkard, or a criminal of some kind, or a victim of his sensual appetite—but a man who for years was under the power of evil habits from which he could not deliver himself, but who on some occasion entered one of Mr. _____'s meetings and heard his glorification of agnosticism and his denunciations of the Bible and Christianity, and whose heart and mind as he listened to such an address were so deeply stirred that he went away from that meeting saying, 'Hence-forth, I too am an agnostic!' and as a result of imbibing that particular philosophy found that a new power had come into his life. The sins he once loved, he now hates, and righteousness and goodness are now the ideals of his life. He is entirely a new man, a credit to himself and an asset to society—all because he is an agnostic.

"Secondly, I would like Mr. _____ to promise to bring with him one woman—and I think he may have more difficulty in finding the woman than the man—who was once a poor, wrecked, characterless outcast, the slave of evil passions, and the victim of man's corrupt living . . . perhaps one who had lived for years in some evil resort, . . . utterly lost, ruined, and wretched because of her life of sin. But this woman also entered a hall where Mr. _____ was loudly proclaiming his agnosticism and ridiculing the message of the Holy Scriptures. As she listened, hope was born in her heart, and she said, 'This is just what I need to deliver me from the slavery of sin!' She followed the teaching and became an intelligent agnostic or infidel. As a result her whole being revolted against the degradation of the life she had been living. She fled from the den of iniquity where she had been held captive so long; and today, rehabilitated, she has won her way back to an honored position in society and is living a clean, virtuous, happy life—all because she is an agnostic.

"Now," he said addressing the gentleman who had presented him with his card and the challenge, "if you will promise to bring these two people with you as examples of what agnosticism can do, I will promise to meet you at the Hall at the hour appointed next Sunday, and I will bring with me at the very least 100 men and women who for years lived in just such sinful degradation as I have tried to depict, but who have been gloriously saved through believing the gospel which you ridicule. I will have these men and women with me on the platform as witnesses to the miraculous saving power of Jesus Christ and as present-day proof of the truth of the Bible."

Ironside then turned to the Salvation Army captain, a girl, and said, "Captain, have you any who could go with me to such a meeting?"

She exclaimed with enthusiasm, "We can give you forty at least just from this one corps, and we will give you a brass band to lead the procession!"

"Fine. Now, Mr. _____, I will have no difficulty in picking up sixty others from the various missions, gospel halls, and evangelical churches of the city; and if you will promise faithfully to bring two such exhibits as I have described, I will come marching in at the head of such a procession, with the band playing 'Onward, Christian Soldiers,' and I will be ready for the debate."

Apparently the man who had made the challenge must have had some sense of humor, for he smiled wryly and waved his hand in a deprecating kind of way as if to say, "Nothing doing!" and then edged out of the crowd while the bystanders clapped for Dr. Ironside and the others.[1]

Christ changes lives. He has done this down through the centuries; he is continuing to do so in our century, in our time. I can give examples from my own experience. There are examples from my own congregation. If you are not a Christian, can you honestly say that you have never observed any examples of the genuine transformation that can come about in a person as a result of his hearing and responding to the Christian gospel? I doubt it. Therefore, if you are not yet a Christian, I invite you to face the reality of these things and yield your life to the One who is also able to make you a new creature through Christ Jesus.

Are You Changed?

I said earlier that there are two applications of these important verses from John 3. One application is to non-Christians, as I have shown. The second application is to Christians. Are you a Christian? What about your life? Unfortunately it is possible for a Christian to live a life that is so much like the life of the world that he will never be able on the basis of his life to point anyone to the Lord Jesus Christ as the Savior. Does that describe you? Ask yourself, "Has my life been changed? Can I point to anything that will hold up as tangible evidence for myself and others of the power of God through Jesus to transform my thinking and my lifestyle?"

I know that there are different causes for unbelief among the unsaved. It is quite often sin, for sin keeps a person from God. Sometimes it is a false sense of priorities. Still it is often true that persons are kept from Christ by a low standard of living among those who are called by his name. Your life should be different. It should reflect the reality of Christ's life within you.

36

The Serpent in the Wilderness

John 3:14–15

"Just as Moses lifted up the snake in the desert, so the Son of Man must be lifted up, that everyone who believes in him may have eternal life."

There are many things that separate true Christianity from the other religions of this world, but the most important is that Christianity is not a "works" religion. All the other religions or systems of religion known to us through history or through anthropology have at their base some system of good works by which the follower of the religion earns merit. Christianity insists, on the contrary, that we cannot earn anything, that all that could possibly be done has already been done for us by the Lord Jesus Christ and that salvation is therefore entered, not by doing anything but by receiving God's gift. Even the Christian life grows out of that initial and complete accomplishment by the Lord Jesus.

This truth is taught many places in Scripture. Paul wrote, "For it is by grace you have been saved, through faith—and this not from yourselves, it is the gift of God—not by works, so that no one can boast" (Eph. 2:8–9). To Titus he wrote, "He saved us not because of righteous things we had done, but because of his mercy" (Titus 3:5). It is not surprising, therefore, as we come to the end of Christ's words to Nicodemus about the new birth, to find another clear and forceful statement of this principle. Nicodemus had not understood about the new birth. He had not even been willing to acknowledge its effects in the lives of God's children. Christ had chided him for that.

Nevertheless, Jesus apparently seemed unwilling to terminate the conversation without pointing in some fashion to the basis of the salvation he was to bring. He therefore spoke of his death and the necessity for belief in himself by saying, "Just as Moses lifted up the snake in the desert, so the Son of Man must be lifted up, that everyone who believes in him may have eternal life" (vv. 14–15).

This is the first instance in John's Gospel in which Jesus picked up an incident or practice of the Old Testament as foreshadowing some aspect of his earthly work.

Serpents of Death

If we are to understand what Jesus was saying, we need to go back to the strange story in the Old Testament to which he was referring. The story is told in Numbers 21:4–9.

The people of Israel had been traveling in the desert under the leadership of Moses, and they had recently traveled from the neighborhood of Mount Hor near the Red Sea to the borders of Edom. This is the area of the Near East in which Petra is located; it is some of the most inhospitable territory on earth, as I found out during a visit to Edom in 1961. The Bible tells us that "the people became impatient on the way" (Num. 21:4). As a result of their difficulties the people began to murmur against God and Moses, as they had done many times before, claiming that they had been led into the wilderness to die there and complaining of God's treatment of them. Because of these complaints God sent fiery serpents among them. These bit the people, and many of the people died. The people came to Moses asking him to intercede between them and the Lord. When Moses did this, God commanded him to make a serpent out of bronze and to erect it on a pole in the midst of the Israelite camp. The heart of the story lies in God's promise that everyone who had been bitten by the fiery serpents needed only to look to the brazen serpent on the pole to be cured.

It goes almost without saying that in itself the remedy proposed by God and enacted faithfully by Moses was absurd. In our day especially, with our knowledge of illness and of the cures effected by the various drugs and antibiotics available to us, we are aware that there was not the least bit of therapeutic value in the bronze serpent. At the best it could have been a warning to avoid the serpents. In such a situation we only begin to understand the story when we see it as a way of pointing the people's faith back to God. We only understand it fully when we see it as intended to prefigure the raising up of the Lord Jesus Christ on the cross, by which sacrifice we are saved from sin.

Not of Works

The force of the story lies not merely in the obvious parallel to Christ's death, as I have stated it, but in the implied comparison between what God commanded the people to do and all other methods that might have been imagined by the people to have had some value.

Think what those methods might have been. First, the people might have imagined that they could have made some medicines to offset the poison. Donald Grey Barnhouse, in *God's Remedy,* has written well on this passage. "The brewing of potions and the making of salves would have given them all something to do and would have satisfied every natural instinct of the heart to work on behalf of its own cure. [But] there was nothing of the kind mentioned. They were to cease from human remedies and turn to a divine remedy. The fact that they were not told to make a human remedy is indicative of the greater fact that there is no human remedy for sin. Men have been bitten by the serpent of sin. How are they going to be cured of its bite? There is nothing but death awaiting them as a result of their wound unless God Himself shall furnish a remedy. Men rush around in the fury of human religions seeking a palliative for sin. They perform all sorts of rites, chastising the flesh, humbling the spirit. They undertake fasts and pilgrimages. Like the man in Israel's camp who refused to look at the brazen serpent, but spent his time brewing concoctions for ameliorating his own conditions, they are carried off to spiritual death through the poison that is in their being. The man who trusts in religion instead of looking to Christ will be eternally lost."[1]

In the second place, the people who had been bitten by the serpents were not encouraged to follow any path of self-reformation. We might imagine them acknowledging to themselves that they had certainly gotten into a bad area of the country and had been exceptionally foolish in giving the serpents an opportunity to bite them. "Henceforth," they might have said, "we shall be more careful. We shall see that this will never happen again." Quite obviously, even if they had been able to do this there would still have been no cure. For the poison was in them, and those who had been bitten, died.

There is a verse in the Book of Ecclesiastes that tells us "God will call the past to account" (Eccl. 3:15). This means that even if you were to turn over a new leaf today and hereafter live in a way that was totally acceptable to God—which is, however, impossible—God would still be forced to require full payment for those violations of his law that you committed before your reformation.

You yourself think that way, you know. Suppose for a minute that you operate a small store. You have a customer who has not been paying his bill for some months and who comes to you saying, "Mr. So-and-So, I realize that I have been making a very grave mistake in the way I have been dealing with you. I have been buying on credit, and I have fallen quite head over heels in debt. I am reforming. Henceforth, I am going to pay cash for everything I buy."

You are very glad to hear that, of course, and you say so. "I am very glad to hear that you are turning over a new leaf. When will you be able to make full payment on your old bill?"

"Oh, you don't understand," your customer answers. "I am going to pay cash from now on. Certainly you won't hold that old unpaid account against me? I am turning over a new leaf."

If that happened to you, no doubt you would reply and be correct in saying, "I am sorry, but I am unable to do business that way. If you pay your account, I shall be glad to continue doing business with you. But if you do not, there can be no sales. Business requires me to demand that which is past." In the same way, God requires what is past. So no one will ever be cured from the effects of sin's poison by any form of moral reformation.

In the third place, the people who were dying in the desert were not told to band together and fight the deadly serpents. Barnhouse again writes: "If the incident had been met after the fashion of our day, there would have been a rush to incorporate the Society for the Extermination of the Fiery Serpents, popularly known as SEFS; and there would have been badges for the coat lapel, cards for district workers, secretaries for organization branches, pledge cards, and mass rallies. There would have been a publication office and a weekly journal to tell of the progress of the work. There would have been photographs of heaps of serpents that had been killed by the faithful workers. The fact that the serpents had already infected their victims would have been played down, and the membership lists would have been pushed to the utmost.

"Let us accompany one of the zealous workers as he might take a pledge card into the tent of a stricken victim. The man had been bitten and the poison had already affected his limbs. He lies in feverish agony [for the phrase "fiery serpents" refers to the effects produced in the ones bitten, not in the color of the snakes], the glaze of death already coming to his eyes. The zealous member of the Society for the Extermination of Fiery Serpents tells him of all that has been done to combat the serpents, and urges the man to join— as a life member if possible (fee $10,000), a sustaining member (fee $1,000), contributing member (fee $25), or annual member (anything the organizer can get). The dying victim fumbles in his pocketbook for money and then takes a pen in hand. His fingers are held by the worker who helps him form his signature on the pledge and membership card, and the man signs in full—and dies."[2]

There are some who will think this fanciful and even a possible slander on worthwhile social work projects, but I am convinced that this is an accurate picture of much that passes for so-called humanitarian endeavors. I am not against works of social welfare. Today's great social work programs sprang from Christian principles and in many cases were launched by committed believers. Nevertheless, the point of the parallel stands. Sin is not cured by social organization. By all means let us mop the fevered brow. Let us comfort the stricken patient. But let us also recognize that the cure of sin's sting lies only in the death of the Lord Jesus Christ and in the promises of God that accompany it.

Fourth, the people who had been bitten by the deadly serpents were not told to pray to the serpent on the pole. You must not misunderstand me here. Prayer is a good thing, but prayer is for believers only. Man cannot pray for his own salvation. Christ died for sinners. This salvation is to be believed. The Bible says, "If you confess with your mouth, 'Jesus is Lord,' and believe in your heart that God raised him from the dead, you will be saved. For it is with your heart that you believe and are justified, and it is with your mouth that you confess and are saved" (Rom. 10:9–10).

Finally, the people who had been bitten were not commanded to buy some relic of the serpent or possess some fragment of the pole upon which the serpent of bronze had been erected. The notion that salvation can come by relics is perhaps the most absurd and totally pagan idea ever associated with Christianity, and yet today there are millions who believe that they can come closer to heaven by adoring a piece of the cross or the bones of a saint. History should illuminate such folly. During the Middle Ages, those who traveled to the Holy Land were asked to bring back souvenirs of Christianity, just as a visitor to Europe or the Far East might be asked to bring back souvenirs today. The Arabs, who were good businessmen, quickly supplied the demand and did so well that it is said that the Middle Ages possessed enough particles of the true cross to build several cathedrals. Unfortunately the possession of such relics eventually gave way to worship and to the belief that a person could be saved by touching or possessing them.

It is interesting to note that the same thing happened with the bronze serpent erected by Moses until God had Hezekiah step in to destroy it. Someone apparently preserved the serpent, and it remained in Israel for hundreds of years, gaining more and more worshipers. At last, when he became king, Hezekiah "broke into pieces the bronze snake Moses had made, for up to that time the Israelites had been burning incense to it. (It was called Nehushtan.)" (2 Kings 18:4). The last word, as Barnhouse observes, is a sneer; for it might be translated correctly as "merely a piece of brass." Thus does God speak of the supposed virtues of the relics of a ritualistic religion: piece of bone . . . dirty linen . . . rusty metal . . . stinking candles.

Resting on Christ

By this time, of course, you will have understood that the only thing required of the dying Israelites was that they should have believed God's word about the serpent and have looked to it as he commanded them. In the same way, we are to look to Christ's cross. We have been bitten by sin, as they were bitten. We are dying of sin, as they were dying. God sent his Son in the likeness of sinful flesh and for sin that we might believe on him and not perish.

What does it mean to believe? Many years ago now, when John G. Paton first went out as a pioneer missionary to the New Hebrides islands, he found that the natives among whom he began to work had no way of writing their language. He began to learn it and in time began to work on a translation of the Bible for them. Soon he discovered that they had no word for "faith." This was serious, of course, for a person can hardly translate the Bible without it. One day he went on a hunt with one of the natives. They shot a large deer in the course of the hunt, and tying its legs together and supporting it on a pole, laboriously trekked back down the mountain path to Paton's home near the seashore. As they reached the veranda both men threw the deer down, and the native immediately flopped into one of the deck chairs that stood on the porch, exclaiming, "My, it is good to stretch yourself out here and rest." Paton immediately jumped to his feet and recorded the phrase. In his final translation of the New Testament this was the word used to convey the idea of trust, faith, and belief.

"Stretch yourself out on the Lord Jesus Christ, and you will be saved" (Acts 16:31). "For God so loved the world that he gave his one and only Son, that whosoever stretches himself out on him shall not perish but have eternal life" (John 3:16). "Just as Moses lifted up the snake in the desert, so the Son of man must be lifted up, that everyone who stretches himself out on him may have eternal life" (John 3:14, 15). Have you done that? Will you do it? If you will do it, turning away from any faith in yourself, your own good works, religion, your efforts at self-reformation, your prayers and relics, looking to the cross of Christ on which God dealt with sin and on the basis of which he promises new life to the sinner, then God will heal you. This is the heart of Christianity. God has provided salvation for you in Jesus Christ. Say, "I believe that, Lord. I trust the work of Jesus Christ for my salvation."

37

The Love of God

John 3:16

For God so loved the world that he gave his one and only Son, that whoever believes in him shall not perish but have eternal life.

There are many passages in the Bible that have been chosen by some great person or other as a favorite text. John Wesley often said that his favorite verse was Zechariah 3:2: "Is not this man a burning stick snatched from the fire?" David Livingstone preferred the last words of Matthew 28:20: "Surely I am with you always, to the very end of the age." John Newton said that his favorite verse was Romans 5:20: "But where sin increased, grace increased all the more." Luther had Romans 1:17 as his life text: "The righteous will live by faith." Each of these verses has spoken to some man in his own particular condition and has become for him the greatest text in the Bible. But the verse we come to now is everyone's text.

There is hardly a place in the world to which the gospel of Jesus Christ has gone that this verse has not become almost instantly known. It is the first verse that translators put into another language. Millions of people have been taught to recite it. It is inscribed on books and buildings. It is reflected in songs. John 3:16! "For God so loved the world that he gave his one and only Son, that whoever believes in him shall not perish but have eternal life." This great verse with its emphasis upon God's love and the gift of his love in Jesus Christ is stupendous.[1]

226

In the early 1960s, the great Swiss theologian Karl Barth was in this country for a series of lectures, speaking in Chicago and in Princeton, New Jersey. There were discussion periods occasionally, connected with these addresses, and at one of the discussion periods an American asked a typically American question: "Dr. Barth, what is the greatest thought that has ever passed through your mind?" Barth paused for quite a long time as he obviously thought about his answer. Then he raised his head and said with grace and childlike simplicity:

> Jesus loves me! This I know,
> For the Bible tells me so.

This is a truth that Christians in all ages have acknowledged, and the more that they have discovered the person of Jesus Christ in the Bible, the more they have realized it.

I want to look at God's love in this study, our first study of John 3:16, and I want to begin by reviewing some of the verses that speak about it.

A Great Love

The first verses are Ephesians 2:4–5. These are verses in which the apostle Paul speaks of God's love, saying, "But because of his great love for us, God, who is rich in mercy, made us alive with Christ even when we were dead in transgressions—it is by grace you have been saved." These verses tell us that God's love is *great*.

In preparation for this study I began to think about the term "great" in ways that I had never done before, and I came to the conclusion that we have lessened the force of what God means by the way we use the word. During the week before I wrote this chapter, I had attended a "Current Events Week" at a Christian school. While there I said that some of the points made by the speakers were "great." After the meetings were over I told the president of the school that I felt that the points made would have a "great" effect on the students in the weeks and months ahead. Later in the week I attended a Young Life banquet in Philadelphia, and I said in that context that the evening was "great," that the speakers were "great," that the program of Young Life was "great." I used the term honestly. Yet none of these things even begins to measure up to what the Bible means when it says that the love of God is great. God is the master of the understatement. Consequently, when he tells us that his love is great, he is telling us that it is so great that it goes beyond our own ideas of greatness or our own understanding.

John 3:16 was the verse through which D. L. Moody learned to appreciate the greatness of God's love. Moody had been to Britain in the early days of his ministry and there had met a young English preacher named Henry

Moorhouse. One day Moorhouse said to Moody, "I am thinking of going to America."

"Well," said Moody, "if you should ever get to Chicago, come down to my church and I will give you a chance to preach."

Moody did not mean to be hypocritical when he said this, of course. He was merely being polite. Nevertheless, he was saying to himself that he hoped Moorhouse would not come, for Moody had not heard him preach and had no idea of what he would say should he come to Chicago. Sometime later, after Moody had returned home, the evangelist received a telegram that said, "Have just arrived in New York. Will be in Chicago on Sunday. Moorhouse." Moody was perplexed about what he should do, and to complicate matters he was just about to leave for a series of meetings elsewhere. "Oh, my," he thought, "here I am about to be gone on Sunday, Moorhouse is coming, and I have promised to let him preach." Finally he said to his wife and to the leaders of the church, "I think that I should let him preach once. So let him preach once; then if the people enjoy him, put him on again."

Moody was gone for a week. When he returned he said to his wife, "How did the young preacher do?"

"Oh, he is a better preacher than you are," his wife said. "He is telling sinners that God loves them."

"That is not right," said Moody. "God does not love sinners."

"Well," she said, "you go and hear him."

"What?" said Moody. "Do you mean to tell me that he is still preaching?"

"Yes, he has been preaching all week, and he has only had one verse for a text. It is John 3:16."

Moody went to the meeting. Moorhouse got up and began by saying, "I have been hunting for a text all week, and I have not been able to find a better text than John 3:16. So I think we will just talk about it once more." He did. Afterward Moody said it was on that night that he first clearly understood the greatness of God's love.

Infinite Love

The Bible not only says that the love of God is great; it also says that it is *infinite*. This is what Paul means when he writes in the third chapter of Ephesians that his prayer for Christians is that they "may have power, together with all the saints, to grasp how wide and long and high and deep is the love of Christ, and to know this love that surpasses knowledge—that you may be filled to the measure of all the fullness of God" (Eph. 3:18–19). How can we comprehend the infinite love of God? We can know it, but only in part. We have been touched by his love and bathed in part of it; yet the fullness of such love lies forever beyond us as the vastness of the universe lies beyond the finite, probing eye of man. God's love is boundless and unfathomable.

One of our seldom sung hymns puts this aspect of God's love in memorable language. It was written by Frederick M. Lehman; but the final stanza

was added to the song afterward, when it was found written on the wall of a
room of an asylum by a man who, before he died, had obviously come to
know the immeasurable extent of God's love.

> The love of God is greater far
> > Than tongue or pen can ever tell,
> It goes beyond the highest star
> > And reaches to the lowest hell.
> The guilty pair, bowed down with care,
> > God gave His Son to win:
> His erring child He reconciled,
> > And pardoned from his sin.

> Could we with ink the ocean fill
> > And were the skies of parchment made;
> Were every stalk on earth a quill
> > And every man a scribe by trade,
> To write the love of God above
> > Would drain the ocean dry,
> Nor could the scroll contain the whole
> > Though stretched from sky to sky.

> *Chorus*
> O love of God, how rich and pure!
> > How measureless and strong!
> It shall for evermore endure—
> > The saints' and angels' song.

This is our song, if we have come to know in part that great and immeasurable love of God toward us through Christ Jesus.

A Love That Gives

Third, God not only tells us that his love is great and is infinite, he also
tells us that his love is a *giving* love. This is the heart of John 3:16. How much
does God love you? God loves you so much "that he gave his one and only
Son."

We are going to be considering the gift of God in the next study, but we
do not want to miss even here the great lesson there is in that statement.
Once in the early days of my ministry, when I was still working in Washington,
D.C., I became interested in the subject of God's love and discovered as I
studied the Bible that there is hardly a verse in the New Testament, in speaking of God's love, that does not also speak in the immediate context (and
sometimes within a space of a few words) of the cross. How do we know that
God loves us? Because we are able to love one another a little bit? Because
the world is beautiful? Because we value love? Not at all! We know that God

---

loves us because he has given us his only-begotten, his unique, Son. It is in the face of the selfless, self-sacrificing Jesus Christ that we learn of God's character.

God loves you! Do you know that? God *loves* you! He has demonstrated that love for you in Jesus Christ!

Unchangeable Love

Finally, God not only tells us that his love is great, infinite, and giving; he also tells us that his love is *unchangeable*. This is perhaps the most wonderful aspect of all. The heart of the matter is that God loves in such a way that nothing you or I have done or will ever do will alter it.

This is a point made by one of the greatest stories in the Bible, the story of Hosea and his unfaithful wife, Gomer. Hosea was a preacher. One day the Lord came to him and said, "Hosea, I want you to marry a woman who is going to prove unfaithful to you. You are going to love her, but she is going to turn from your love. Nevertheless, the more faithless she becomes, the more faithful and loving you will be. I want you to do this because I want to give Israel an illustration of how I love them. Your marriage will be a pageant. You will play God. The woman will play the part of Israel. For I love Israel with an unchangeable love, and she runs from me and takes other gods for lovers."

Hosea did as God had told him to do. So the Book of Hosea tells us, "When the Lord began to speak through Hosea, the Lord said to him, 'Go, take to yourself an adulterous wife and children of unfaithfulness, because the land is guilty of the vilest adultery in departing from the Lord.' So he married Gomer daughter of Diblaim, and she conceived and bore him a son" (Hosea 1:2–3).

At this point of the story God intervened, for he had said that he was going to order each stage of the relationship between Hosea and Gomer. God intervened to give a name to this son. "Call his name Jezreel," God said. Jezreel means "scattered," for God was going to scatter the people of Israel all over the face of the earth. After a time Gomer conceived again and bore a daughter. "Call her Lo-Ruhamah," God said. Lo-Ruhamah means "not pitied." God was saying that the time would come when he would "no longer show love to the house of Israel" (v. 6). Finally, another son was born and Hosea was told to call him Lo-Ammi. Lo-Ammi means "not my people." "For," said God, "you are not my people, and I am not your God."

If the story stopped at this point the ending would be exceedingly dismal, and the pageant would be illustrating the opposite of the unchangeable love of God. But it does not stop here, and God intervenes again to tell how the story will end. "I am going to change the names of those children one day," God promised. "I am going to change Jezreel to Jezreel." It is the same word but with a second meaning, a change from "scattered" to "planted," because in the ancient world the same gesture by which a man would throw something away was that by which he would plant grain. God was promising to plant the people once again in their own land, as he has done in our own generation. "Moreover," said God, "I am going to change Lo-Ruhamah to Ruhamah and Lo-Ammi to Ammi because the time is coming when I will again have pity upon those who will have again become my children." The Bible says, "Yet the Israelites will be like the sand on the seashore, which cannot be measured or counted. In the place where it was said to them, 'You are not my people,' they will be called 'sons of the living God'" (v. 10).

The time came in the marriage when the events that God had foretold happened. Gomer looked around and caught the eye of a stranger. Before long she had left with him, and Hosea was alone.

The life of a woman like that goes downhill. For if she had left Hosea for the company of a man who could give her a Cadillac and a fur coat this year, it is equally certain that the year following, when the first lover had grown tired of her, she would be found with a man who could only give her a fur-lined collar and an Oldsmobile. The year after that she would be in fake fur and a Volkswagen, and the year after that she would be pulling something out of the garbage heap. So it was with Hosea's wife. The time came when she was living with a man who did not have the means to take care of her, and she was hungry.

"Now," said God to Hosea, "I want you to go and see that she gets the things she needs, because I take care of the people of Israel even when they are running away from me." Hosea went and bought the groceries. He gave them to the man who was living with his wife, but he said that Gomer did not even know he had bought them. The story tells us, "Their mother has been unfaithful and has conceived them in disgrace. She said, 'I will go after my lovers, who give me my food and my water, my wool and my linen, my oil and my drink.' . . . She has not acknowledged that I was the one who gave her the grain, the new wine and oil, who lavished on her the silver and gold" (Hosea. 2:5, 8).

Does God love like that? Yes, he does! Have you ever run away from God? Of course, you have! What happened? God paid your bills! If you have been running away from God, do you realize that it is God who gives you the strength to run? Here is a girl who says, "I don't care if God is calling me into Christian work. I'm going to turn away and marry this young man." God says, "Who gave you the good looks that made the young man interested?" Another person says, "I want to be famous." So he goes to New York and writes a book that later becomes a movie. He makes lots of money. But God says, "Who gave you the talent to write the book in the first place? Did not I, the Lord?" You cannot run away from God's love successfully. You can run, but God pursues you. He steps before you and says, "My child, I am the One who has been providing for you all this time. Won't you stop running and allow me to take you to myself?"

The final act of the drama was approaching. The time came when Gomer sank so low that she was sold as a slave in the city of Jerusalem, and God told Hosea to go and buy her. Slaves were always sold naked. Thus, when a beautiful girl was on sale, the men bid freely and the bidding always went high. Here was Gomer. Her clothes were taken off. The bidding began. One man bid three pieces of silver. Another said five . . . ten . . . twelve . . . thirteen. The low bidders had dropped out when Hosea said, "Fifteen pieces of silver." A voice from the back of the crowd said, "Fifteen pieces of silver and a bushel of barley." "Fifteen pieces of silver and a bushel and a half of barley," said Hosea. The auctioneer looked around for a higher bid. Seeing none he declared, "This slave is sold to Hosea for fifteen pieces of silver and a bushel and a half of barley." So Hosea took his wife (whom he now owned), put her clothes on her, and led her away into the anonymity of the crowd.

You say, "Is that a true picture of God's love?" Yes, it is! That is how God loves you. Listen to what the Bible says about it: "The LORD said to me, 'Go, show your love to your wife again, though she is loved by another and is an adulteress. Love her *as the LORD loves the Israelites,* though they turn to other gods and love the sacred raisin cakes.' So I bought her for fifteen shekels of silver and about a homer and a lethek of barley. Then I told her, 'You are to live with me many days; you must not be a prostitute or be intimate with any man, and *I will live with you*'" (Hosea 3:1–3).

Oh, the greatness of the unchangeable love of almighty God! God loves you and me like that! We are the slave sold under the bondage of sin. We are the one placed upon the world's auction block. The bidding of the world goes higher and higher. "What am I bid for this person's soul?" At this point Jesus Christ, the faithful bridegroom, enters the slave market of sin and bids the price of his blood. "Sold to Jesus Christ for the price of his blood," says Almighty God. So he bought you. He clothed you in his righteousness. And he led you away with himself, saying, "You are to live with me many days; you must not be a prostitute or be intimate with any man, and I will live with you."[2]

God's Love, Our Pattern

You say "What does that have to do with me?" It has everything to do with you. Are you one who has never known that love, never realized that Jesus Christ loved you like that, that he still loves you? To be touched with such love is to throw yourself at his feet in adoration and marvel that you could ever have violated such a great and unalterable compassion. The Bible tells us that God "commends" such great love toward us (Rom. 5:8). Won't you allow the hardness of your heart to melt before God's love and allow Jesus Christ to be your great Savior and bridegroom?

Perhaps you are one who has already done that. You have believed in Christ, but the reality of that love has become distant for you and you have never fully realized that the love of Christ is to become the pattern of your love. He is to be your model. You need to ask whether your love has been great, whether it has the character of that love which is infinite, whether it is a giving love, whether it is unchangeable. Ask it now. Does your love change when the person whom you love does not respond quickly? Or does it hold firm? Do you continue to love when your wife, husband, child, or friend does not seem to see things the way you do and contradicts you? Do you love as Christ loves? You are called to show forth that love; for as others see it they will be drawn to the Lord Jesus.

38

God's Greatest Gift

John 3:16

For God so loved the world that he gave his one and only Son, that whoever believes in him shall not perish but have eternal life.

It is commonplace in our day to say that God loves men. But many who say this fail to recognize that we know this is so only because of Jesus Christ. How do we know that God loves us? Not because of creation certainly, for the evidence of creation is ambiguous. There are tidal waves and hurricanes as well as gorgeous sunsets. Not because we tend to value love, for not all of us do. Not because love is "wonderful" or "grand" or because it "makes the world go round." We know that God loves us because he has given his Son to be crucified for us and thereby to bring us back into fellowship with himself. Thus, if the love of God is one of God's greatest attributes (as we saw in our last study), the gift of Christ is most certainly his greatest gift. For it is through Christ that we come to know God's love and love God.

Sometime ago I came across a little card upon which someone had printed John 3:16. The verse was arranged almost word by word down one side of the card, and on the other side of the card across from the words of the verse was a list of descriptive phrases, one for each part. The person looking at the card would read: "God (the greatest Lover) so loved (the greatest degree) the world (the greatest company), that he gave (the greatest act) his only begotten Son (the greatest gift), that whosoever (the greatest opportunity) believeth (the greatest simplicity) in him (the greatest attraction) should not perish (the greatest promise), but (the greatest difference) have (the greatest certainty) everlasting life (the greatest possession)." And then over it all, revealing a spiritual perception that was most accurate, there was the title "Christ—the Greatest Gift."

Have you ever come to appreciate God's greatest gift to you, the gift of the Lord Jesus Christ? We are going to look at some of the reasons why he is a great gift and why you should believe on him.

God So Loved

The first reason why Jesus Christ is the greatest of God's gifts is that Jesus is the *best* God had to give. God so loved the world that he gave the very best.

This truth is seen in several ways in John 3:16. First, it is obvious from the word "only-begotten," which is used of Jesus. To our way of thinking, this word (it is one word in Greek) refers mainly to physical generation, but it means more than that in the original language. A great deal of theological controversy in the church was once caused by those who took it as simply physical generation; they argued that since the Bible says Jesus was the "only-begotten" Son, there must have been a time before he came into being. In other words, he did not exist from eternity but rather was the first being God created. This was foolish, of course, because the Bible does not teach this and the word does not have this meaning primarily. Primarily the word means "unique." Jesus is the unique Son of God; there is no one like him, no one who is his equal. Therefore, because Jesus Christ is the very image of God and because there is no one like him, when God gave Jesus, he gave the best gift in the universe.

God also gave the best in another sense. For Jesus Christ is not at all a creature made in the image of God, as man is; he is God incarnate. Consequently, when God gave Jesus he gave himself. To give oneself is the greatest gift anyone can give. Sometime ago I read a story of a minister who was talking to a married couple who were having marital difficulties. There was much hardness and bitterness, coupled with a lack of understanding. At one point the husband spoke up in obvious exasperation. "I've given you everything," he said to the wife. "I've given you a new home. I've given you a new fur coat. I've given you a new car. I've given you . . ." The list went on. But when he had ended the wife said quietly. "That much is true, John. You have given me everything . . . but yourself."

We hear that story and we recognize the truth of the principle: the greatest gift that anyone can give is himself. Then we look at Jesus, who is God incarnate, and we recognize that God gave the very best—himself—for us.

An Eternal Plan

The second reason why Jesus Christ is God's greatest gift is that Jesus was a gift planned from before the foundation of the world. God had always intended to give Jesus. This is why so many of the verses in the Bible speak of God having put Jesus to death. Isaiah 53:10 speaks of the crucifixion eight centuries before it took place, saying, "Yet it was the LORD's will to crush him and cause him to suffer." Peter knew this truth. On the day of Pentecost he spoke of Jesus who "was handed over to you by God's set purpose and foreknowledge; and you, with the help of wicked men, put him to death by nailing him to the cross" (Acts 2:23). For the same reason the Book of Revelation speaks of Jesus as "the Lamb that was slain from the creation of the world" (Rev. 13:8).

We must not think that the entrance of sin into the world through Adam and Eve was an event that somehow caught God by surprise or that it caused God to begin to ponder what he should do to correct it. God knew all from the beginning. Consequently, before he even set the universe in motion, before he created us, he had determined to send Jesus Christ to die for the salvation of our race.

Perhaps the greatest declaration of this principle lies in a poignant story from the life of Abraham, the story of the call of God to Abraham to offer up his son Isaac on Mount Moriah. It is told in the twenty-second chapter of Genesis. I believe that Jesus was referring to this event when he told the Jews of his day, "Your father Abraham rejoiced at the thought of seeing my day; he saw it and was glad" (John 8:56), and that through it Abraham learned that God was to give Jesus Christ to be our Savior.

To see the story in its proper perspective we must begin with the fact that Abraham was an old man by our standards when God came to him to ask him to offer up Isaac. He had been eighty-six years old when his first son, Ishmael, had been born to Hagar, Sarah's slave girl. He was one hundred years old when Sarah at last gave birth to Isaac. Now Isaac had become a young man, perhaps fifteen years of age or more, and Abraham was more than one hundred fifteen. Moreover, Abraham had loved his son from birth, as any father would, and he now loved him deeply with a love that had grown stronger over the years in which he had seen him grow to young manhood. He loved him doubly, not only because he was the son of his old age, the result of a miracle, but also because he was the son of promise.

At this point God came to Abraham again—as he had many times before—and said to him, "Abraham."

"Yes, Lord."

"I am going to ask you to do something."

"Yes, Lord."

"I want you to take Isaac, the son of promise, the one through whom you are going to have a great posterity and through whom I am going to send the Messiah—I want you to take this Isaac to a mountain that I will show you and there offer him for a burnt offering. I want you to kill him."

I do not know the extent of the trial this must have been to Abraham's faith or how much of the night he wrestled with this great problem. But whatever the struggle was, and however deep, it was all over by the following morning, for the Abraham that emerged in the morning was an Abraham committed to obedience. The story says, "Early the next morning Abraham got up and saddled his donkey. He took with him two of his servants and his son Isaac. When he had cut enough wood for the burnt offering, he set out for the place God had told him about" (Gen. 22:3).

There are many lessons in this story, of course, but there is one in particular that we should see before we go on. On one level at least, the test of Abraham was a test of his devotion to God. Was God going to be everything to Abraham? Or was something else, even God's gift, going to share and cloud that vision? It was Abraham's triumph that he did not put the gifts before the Giver.

Isaac can stand for many things that have become quite precious to you. The Chinese evangelist Watchman Nee once wrote, "He represents many gifts of God's grace. Before God gives them, our hands are empty. Afterwards they are full. Sometimes God reaches out his hands to take ours in fellowship. Then we need an empty hand to put into his. But when we have received his gifts and are nursing them to ourselves, *our* hands are full, and when God puts out his hand we have no empty hand for him." When that happens we need to let go of the gift and take hold of God himself. Nee adds, "Isaac can be done without, but God is eternal."[1]

God Will Provide

Yes, the testing of Abraham was certainly a test of his devotion to God, but it was something else also. It was a spiritual test or, as we could also say, a test of his spiritual perception.

Think of the things Abraham had learned in the years before Isaac's birth. He had been tempted to think that God would not keep his promises and that a household servant would be his legal heir. God had taught him that the blessing would not come through the household servant. Abraham had once wanted to substitute Ishmael, the son of Hagar, for Isaac—before Isaac was born. But God had told him that the blessing would not come through the son of the Egyptian slave girl. God had shown Abraham through a miracle that the blessing was to come through Isaac, and now God had asked Abraham to kill him.

We must imagine the reasoning that passed through the mind of Abraham in the dark hours of that desert evening. He must have said something like this: "I know that Isaac is the son of God's promise, and God has shown me time and again that he will not send the blessing through another. Yet, this same God tells me to sacrifice him, to put him to death. How can this be? If I put him to death, as God has demanded, how can God fulfill his promise? How can God do it?" The puzzle was real. But then, as Abraham wrestled with this supreme test of God's logic, it must have come to him that the God who performed a miracle in bringing about Isaac's birth was also capable of working a miracle to bring him back from the dead. This was the solution he discovered during the long desert night. Thus, as Abraham started for the mountain in the morning he must have been saying mentally to Isaac, "Come on, boy, we are going to see a miracle. God has asked me to sacrifice you on Mount

Moriah. But if God is going to be faithful to his promise, he is going to have to raise you up again from the dead. We are going to see a resurrection."

Someone may think that I have merely made up this part of the story, but this is the way it happened. The proof of it occurs in at least two parts of the Bible. The first is in the story itself. Abraham had come to the foot of the mountain with the boy, and he was ready to go on without the young men who were with him. As he takes the kindling and he and Isaac prepare to climb the mountain, Abraham says to the others: "Stay here with the donkey while I and the boy go over there. We will worship and then we will come back to you" (Gen. 22:5). Think of that: *we will come back to you.* Who would come? Abraham and Isaac! What does that mean? It means that although Abraham believed that he was going to offer the sacrifice, he also believed that God was going to perform a resurrection and that he would be able to come back down the mountain with his boy.

The second proof is Hebrews 11:17–19, which is the full New Testament commentary on the incident. "By faith Abraham, when God tested him, offered Isaac as a sacrifice. He who had received the promises was about to sacrifice his one and only son, even though God had said to him, 'It is through Isaac that your offspring will be reckoned.' Abraham reasoned that God could raise the dead, and figuratively speaking, he did receive Isaac back from death." That means that Abraham looked for a resurrection.

Thus far the story has already been great in itself, but the point I wish to make is the point that is found in the sequel. Abraham *did* go up the mountain, as God had commanded him, and there bound Isaac to the altar. He raised his hand ready to plunge a knife into his son. He would have killed him. But just as the knife was ready to fall, God intervened. God provided a substitute, a ram caught in the bushes. And he said (in effect), "Abraham, you don't need to sacrifice your son. I never intended that you should go through with it. I only wanted to test your willingness to obey me and to show you in this way what I will do one day for your salvation and for the salvation of all who will believe in my Son, the Messiah." This, I believe, was the moment in which Abraham saw the day of Jesus Christ and, seeing it, was made glad.

God revealed his ways to Abraham. The Bible says, "Surely the Sovereign LORD does nothing without revealing his plan to his servants the prophets" (Amos 3:7). So the time came when the events God had planned from before creation and had revealed to Abraham two thousand years beforehand took place. Abraham was only called upon to offer his son. But when the time came for God to offer his Son, the hand that was poised above Christ fell. God put his Son to death, and God's greatest gift had been given.

The Need of Man

The third reason why Jesus Christ is the greatest of God's gifts to fallen man is that he is perfectly suited to the needs of fallen man. Nothing else is! What are the needs of man? What are your needs?

Your first need is for a sure word from God, for *knowledge* of God. Jesus is the answer to that need, for it is Jesus alone who brings us the knowledge of who God is, what he is like, and what he desires for mankind. This is why Jesus is called *the* Word so many times in John's writings. Do you want to know what God is like? If so, do not spend your time reading the books of men. Do not think that you will find out by meditating. Look to Jesus Christ. Where will you find him? You will find him in the pages of the Bible. There you will find the strength, mercy, wisdom, and compassion that are the essence of God's character.

Your second great need is for a *Savior*. We do not merely have a need for sure knowledge. We have knowledge of many things, but we are unable to live up to our knowledge. We are sinners. Consequently, we not only need a sure word from God, we need a Savior. Jesus is the Savior. He died to save you from sin and from yourself. Do you know him as Savior?

Finally, we have those needs that are part and parcel of living a finite sinful life. What are those needs? One way of looking at them is the way popularized by the American psychiatrist Erich Fromm. Fromm suggests that man is confronted with three existential dilemmas. The first is the dilemma of life versus death. We want to live, but we all die. Jesus is the answer to that problem, for he gives eternal life to all who believe on him. Jesus said, "I am the resurrection and the life. He who believes in me will live, even though he dies; and whoever lives and believes in me will never die" (John 11:25, 26). The second of Fromm's dilemmas is the dilemma of the individual and the group. Jesus is the answer to that problem too, for he has come to break down all walls and to make of his followers one new man which is his mystical body (Eph. 2:14–16). The last of Fromm's dilemmas is that arising from the conflict between our aspirations and our actual achievements. We all fall short of what we would like to be and believe ourselves intended to be. Jesus is the answer to that problem also, for he promises to make us all that God created us to be in the first place. We are to be conformed to Christ's image (Rom. 8:29). One of our hymns looks forward to that day when our salvation shall be complete, and declares:

> Then we shall be where we would be,
> Then we shall be what we should be;
> Things that are not now, nor could be,
> Soon shall be our own.

The Lord Jesus Christ is the greatest gift that God has ever offered or could ever offer to the human race. Are you indifferent? Or do you respond to the offer, joining the millions of others who have believed in Christ with all their heart and mind and who now say, "Thanks be to God for his indescribable gift" (2 Cor. 9:15)?

39

To All Who Believe

John 3:16–17

For God so loved the world that he gave his one and only Son, that whoever believes in him shall not perish but have eternal life. For God did not send his Son into the world to condemn the world, but to save the world through him.

Early in my ministry I talked to a young man about Christianity. He told me that he firmly believed he was a Christian. As we talked further, however, I discovered that although he believed he was a Christian, he did not believe in the divinity of Jesus Christ. For him Jesus was only a man. He did not believe in his atoning death or in the essential or complete reliability of the New Testament documents concerning him. He had not even read most of them. He did not believe in the resurrection of Christ. He did not acknowledge Christ as Lord of his life. I pointed out that all these matters are involved in a person's being a Christian, but he simply answered that in spite of what I said he still firmly believed in his heart he was a Christian. Such faith was merely acute subjectivity.

What is real faith? This question is important, for although in one sense the gospel of salvation through Jesus Christ is as wide as humanity—the Bible tells us that "God so loved *the world* that he gave his one and only Son"—on the other hand, it is also as narrow as the company of those who have faith in him, for the same verse goes on to tell us that only those who believe on Christ will be saved. "For God so loved the world that he gave his one and only Son, that whoever believes in him shall not perish but have eternal life"

(John 3:16). Faith is the indispensable channel of God's saving grace, according to these and many other verses. Consequently, our understanding of John 3:16 will be incomplete until we deal with the nature of saving faith and seek to apply the truths of this verse personally.

An attempt to deal with the true nature of faith is made necessary merely by the nature of Christianity, for we are told that "without faith it is impossible to please God" (Heb. 11:6) and "by grace you have been saved, through faith" (Eph. 2:8). Besides this, however, the study is made particularly necessary for us simply because of the extraordinary emphasis upon faith in the fourth Gospel.

It is true, of course, that if one looks up the word "faith" in an English concordance he will not find the word listed under any book written by the apostle John, except for a single case in 1 John 5:4. But this is merely because John prefers the verb form of the same Greek word *(pisteuō* rather than *pistis)*, which is generally translated by the word "believe" in our English New Testament. "To believe" in someone and "to have faith" in someone are exactly the same thing. Consequently, it is only when one looks up the word "believe" that he finds out what John says about faith and notices John's particular emphasis. Actually, we have encountered the word "faith" or "believe" eight times in this Gospel already. It occurred three times in the first chapter and three times more in chapter two. In our present chapter it is used no less than seven times, twice already. All together there are ninety-eight uses of the word in the Gospel's twenty-one brief chapters. This compares with a combined usage of the words "faith" and "believe" just eighteen times in Mark and only fifty-five times in Romans.

With an emphasis such as this, we need to see precisely what faith is. Moreover, since the blessings of salvation are said to become ours only through faith, and since John claims that the Gospel was written to lead us to faith (John 20:30–31), we are wise to ask how we can exercise faith personally. How does faith operate to make this wonderful salvation mine?

The Nature of Faith

Unfortunately, there is much confusion about the meaning of faith in our day simply because we apply it to people, and people are untrustworthy. Every so often we read detailed reports of some negotiations between labor and management in which the partners are encouraged to work out their demands in good faith. This means that each side is to bargain honestly, believing that the other party is doing likewise. However, when the agreement is reached the first act is to draw up a detailed written agreement each of the parties must sign. Why? Obviously because, although each side wants to believe in the good faith of the other, each also knows that people are untrustworthy and must therefore be bound by written guarantees. The same recognition lies behind the formalities of the marriage ceremony, penalty clauses in building contracts, and many other things.

With this background to the use of the word, it is no wonder that faith has often taken on overtones of wishful thinking and then has been applied to God and to spiritual things with that meaning. The unsaved world thinks of faith as a "pie-in-the-sky" philosophy and prefers only what it can "see" or "hear" or can be assured of "now."

Similar thinking lies behind any definition of faith that tries to turn it into subjectivity. Actually, this view is probably the most common misunderstanding of faith in our own century due to the impact of existentialism in the church through such thinkers as Rudolph Bultmann, Paul Tillich, Bishop John A. T. Robinson, and others. In such formulations faith becomes merely that which I wish to hold and not something that is related to truth or evidence.

Against these distortions of the meaning of faith, because nothing about men is ever entirely reliable, the Christian must insist that biblical faith is of a different order entirely and that faith in the biblical sense, simply because it is faith in God, is reliable. That is why faith can be "sure of what we hope for and certain of what we do not see" for the Christian (Heb. 11:1). Some have used this verse in support of a "pie-in-the-sky" type of religion but, actually, it teaches the reverse. The word "substance" does not mean "substitute," as though faith were a substitute for evidence. It means "a title deed to a piece of property." That is what faith is. God tells us that although none of us has entered fully into the inheritance that is ours through faith, nevertheless, faith is our title to it. Faith is itself the evidence of things not yet fully seen.

I admit that if this were a human title deed, there would still be some room for doubt. In human terms there would still be the possibility that some office clerk could have mixed up the deeds or that he might have sent them to the wrong person. It would be possible for a deed to be issued when there was still a prior claim on the property or a lien against it. However, in dealing with God such errors are impossible. God is omnipotent and infallible. The infallible God gives the deed. The all-powerful God stands behind it. When God calls upon people to believe what he tells them he calls upon them to do the most sensible thing they will ever do in their lives; that is, believe in the only being in the universe who is entirely reliable. That is what John means in his first epistle when he writes: "We accept man's testimony, but God's testimony is greater" (1 John 5:9).

Faith's Content

What precisely does God call upon us to believe? The answer is that he tells us many things and expects us to believe them all. The Bible is full of them. However, if we want to simplify the matter of salvation to its most basic points we may say that God wants us to *believe* two things primarily and that he then calls upon us to *do* a third.

First of all, God asks us to believe that we are less perfect than he is and, therefore, deserve to be separated from his presence forever. Another way of saying the same thing is to say that we are sinners and that God must punish sin. The Bible says that this is precisely why we need a Savior. In fact, John 3:16 says it, for it speaks of the possibility of perishing. If we could somehow get by, if we could somehow rate with God either by being a little less sinful than we are now or by trying harder ("we're still number 2"), then there would be no need for a Savior. But this is not the case. We are sinful. God is perfect. Consequently, since God cannot tolerate sin, we must admit that we deserve to be separated from him.

Sometimes people object to this teaching because they think that it makes them the same as the worst criminals. In one sense, it does. Both equally need a Savior. Yet that confuses the point. The main point is that God is perfection. Thus, no matter how far short of his perfection we come, we still come short and, coming short, we miss it all.

Several years ago in America a bit of deadly botulism poison was found in a particular brand of vichyssoise soup. This is one of the most deadly poisons known to man, and one person at least died and another was paralyzed before the source of the poison was discovered and the contaminated soup destroyed. Let me ask this question: How much botulism poison was needed to make the soup unsuitable for human consumption? A whole canful? Of course not! Several milligrams? No! The smallest amount of poison would ruin the can. In the same way, God asks you to take his word that you are a sinner, whether small or great, and to believe that sin has ruined you.

The second truth that God asks you to believe is that he loves you in spite of your sin and that he has acted in Jesus Christ to remove that sin and to begin to make you perfect once more by conforming you to Christ's image. This is the heart of John 3:16 and 17. We are sinners. We deserve to perish. In fact, we are already under God's condemnation. But John tells us: "For God so loved the world that he gave his one and only Son, that whoever believes in him shall not perish but have eternal life. For God did not send his Son into the world to condemn the world, but to save the world through him." God loves you. Christ died for you. There may be much about this that you cannot now understand. There is much about it that I do not understand. But God wants you to believe that he did this in order that you might not perish but rather enter into his eternal life.

Do you believe these things? Do you believe that you are a sinner? Do you believe God when he tells you that you deserve to perish ultimately? Do you believe that God sent Jesus to die for you and by his death to bring you salvation? If you do, then he calls upon you to do something. He asks you to bring your faith out of the realm of mere intellectual conviction into the area of action, saying, "Yes, Lord, I do believe these things. Thank you for dying for me. I commit my life to you and promise to go in the way you lead me whatever that may involve." If you will make that commitment, God has already given you eternal life and has begun the transformation that will one day make you like the Lord Jesus Christ forever.

Strong in Faith

I do not want to leave the matter of faith there, important as the point may be. For we have only been talking about the initial moment of saving faith, when faith first seizes upon Jesus Christ as Savior. Faith does not stop there. When the Christian is called to faith in Jesus Christ, he is called to a life of living by faith, a life in which his belief in God is meant to grow stronger as he comes to know God better and to trust him more completely.

Someone is going to say, "But that is what scares me. I know that my faith is not strong, and I am afraid that if I begin to follow Jesus I will faint at some point and want to draw back. My faith is weak." Praise God that you recognize that! What you must learn, however, is that one of God's purposes in saving you is to make your faith strong, and for that he will continue to work with you and lead you in every aspect and moment of your earthly life.

Take the faith of Abraham as an example. Abraham is cited many times in the Bible as an illustration of a man who had great faith, but Abraham's faith did not begin great. The eleventh chapter of Hebrews gives us the progression of this faith as God sees it. Abraham is praised for his faith four times. The first verse on Abraham says, "By faith Abraham, when called to go to a place he would later receive as his inheritance, obeyed and went, even though he did not know where he was going" (v. 8). That was faith, but such faith did not need to be strong. It was only faith in God's ability to lead the Hebrew patriarch out of Mesopotamia and into Palestine.

Actually, the fact that Abraham's faith was weak at this point is dramatized by a very interesting detail from his story. When God came to Abraham in Ur of the Chaldees, Abraham was called upon to leave that place, journey up the Mesopotamian river valley, cross over the northern end of the great Arabian desert, and then travel down through the areas that are now modern-day Syria and Lebanon to what is now Israel. The entire journey measured over a thousand miles. Abraham began in the best of faith. Yet when we come to the end of the first chapter of his story, as told in Genesis (Genesis 11), we find that Abraham had stopped at Haran, a little town in Syria. Haran was a long way from Ur, it is true, but it was also a long way from Palestine. Unfortunately, Abraham stayed in Haran until his father died, and it took another call of God to him to get him moving again, this time when he was seventy-five years old. At this point in the story Abraham's faith was weak, but God's promises to him were not withdrawn because of it.

Abraham's faith was not allowed to rest at this initial level. The next verse of Hebrews 11 goes on to say: "By faith [Abraham] made his home in the promised land like a stranger in a foreign country; he lived in tents, as did Isaac and Jacob, who were heirs with him of the same promise" (v. 9). This level of faith was stronger, for it was faith exercised in the face of many dangers and difficulties. During these years, Abraham's faith grew remarkably.

In verse 11, the author of Hebrews goes on to speak of the faith that both Abraham and Sarah exercised in believing that God would give them a son when both were past the age of being able to have children. Here faith had become strong, for it was a faith based on the assurance that God was able to perform miracles. The fourth and final reference to Abraham's faith refers to that complete trust in God which he had when God asked him to offer up his son. This was a faith that led Abraham to believe that God was going to perform a resurrection. Hebrews says: "By faith Abraham, when God tested him, offered Isaac as a sacrifice. He who had received the promises was about to sacrifice his one and only son, even though God had said to him, 'It is through Isaac that your offspring will be reckoned.' Abraham reasoned that God could raise the dead, and figuratively speaking, he did receive Isaac back from death" (vv. 17–19).

I do not know where you are along this pathway of faith. Perhaps you are one who has not even taken the initial step of believing what God has to say about your sinful condition and about his offer of complete salvation through Jesus Christ. If so, this is where you should begin. God says, "How can you believe in my ability to do miracles in your life, if you cannot even believe the truths that I have to teach about Jesus?"

Perhaps you have begun to walk by faith, but you have found difficulties. That is not strange. God sends storms as well as calm. The difficulties are intended to help you grow strong. Learn to trust him. The God of Abraham is the same today; he can help you as he helped the patriarchs.

Finally, you may be one whom God is asking to believe in miracles. I do not know what the particular miracle may be in your life. It may be a personality trait that God is promising to change. It may be a difficult situation at work or at home. It may involve finances. Whatever it is, you grow strong in faith by learning to trust him. In some of these experiences you may learn something about God's plans and nature that you would learn in no other way. What is your attitude? Doubtful? Rebellious? Do not let it be. Instead, say, "Yes, Lord, I believe all you are saying. Help me to believe and grow strong."

40

Condemned!

John 3:18–21

Whoever believes in him is not condemned, but whoever does not believe stands condemned already because he has not believed in the name of God's one and only Son. This is the verdict: Light has come into the world, but men loved darkness instead of light because their deeds were evil. Everyone who does evil hates the light, and will not come into the light for fear that his deeds will be exposed. But whoever lives by the truth comes into the light, so that it may be seen plainly that what he has done has been done through God.

Wе come now to verses that are a necessary addition to the great and wonderful truths of John 3:16–17. Those verses tell us that "For God so loved the world that he gave his one and only Son, that whoever believes in him shall not perish but have eternal life. For God did not send his Son into the world to condemn the world, but to save the world through him." When this is said, however, the question immediately arises, "Yes, but what of those who do not believe?" The verses to which we now come deal with that question, telling us that those who have not believed are even now under God's condemnation: "Whoever believes in him is not condemned, but whoever does not believe stands condemned already because he has not believed in the name of God's one and only Son" (John 3:18).

Crime and Punishment

Most men and women do not like this teaching. Yet it is a fact that sin has consequences and that one of these is alienation from God and God's judgment.

On one level at least we recognize this in purely human affairs. Some years ago I developed an interest in Russian literature and began to read the great Russian novels. Among them were the works of Fyodor Dostoevsky. Most of Dostoevsky's novels are great by almost any standard, but the one that has remained uppermost in my mind over the years is *Crime and Punishment.* This is the story of a young student in Russia who commits a serious crime. His name is Raskolnikov. Raskolnikov is poor and needs money; therefore he murders an elderly pawnbroker who, he argues to himself, is of use to no one and whose life really doesn't matter. As the result of his crime Raskolnikov is launched upon what he thinks is going to be a prosperous life. Yet in the novel there is a relentless outworking of judgment for Raskolnikov's act. Punishment follows crime. The novel's point is that the young man stood condemned from the moment in which he performed the act.

Most who read the novel recognize the justice of its plot, but the far more serious fact is that the same principles apply spiritually. We must not think, if we are to take the witness of Scripture seriously, that when the gospel is preached to a man or woman the person involved is standing upon what we may call neutral ground. It is not that he can either choose his own way with a corresponding wrath and condemnation from God or that he can go God's way with its corresponding joy and blessing. According to Scripture, man has already made his choice. People have already chosen their own way. Thus, as Isaiah writes, "We all, like sheep, have gone astray, each of us has turned to his own way; and the LORD has laid on him the iniquity of us all" (Isa. 53:6). Paul declares, "There is no one righteous, not even one; there is no one who understands, no one who seeks God" (Rom. 3:10–11; cf. Ps. 14:1–3).

We may not like it, but whether we like it or not, these things are true from God's perspective. We have gone our own way. We have already committed the crime. Therefore, every one of us already stands under God's judgment.

The Case for the Prosecution

At this point, however, we come to a second question. We have already asked, "But what of those who have not believed or will not believe?" We have seen that these are under God's wrath. But now we ask for what reasons. Why is man condemned in his present state? The answer to this question is really the case for the prosecution against man and leads us to the second half of the verse I read earlier and to those that follow it.

The first answer to why people are condemned is that they have "not believed in the name of God's one and only Son" (John 3:18). What is the name? The name is: Jesus. And what does "Jesus" mean? The answer to that question is to be found in the words of the angel to Joseph when the name was originally given to his parents before Jesus' birth. The angel said, "You are to give him the name Jesus, because he will save his people from their sins" (Matt. 1:21). The first two letters of the name are the first two letters of the great Old Testament name for God, Jehovah. The remaining letters are from the word for "save" or "salvation." Thus, the whole name means "Jehovah saves" or "Jehovah will save." It follows then that when John says men are condemned because they have not believed on the name of the one and only Son of God, he means they are condemned because they will not have the Lord Jesus Christ as their Savior.

This is the hardest thing for people to do. If you have witnessed to other people about the gospel, you know that there is much in the gospel that they do not have trouble accepting. Most people do not have difficulty believing in the existence of God. The Bible recognizes this indirectly when it says that only fools deny it (Ps. 14:1; 53:1). Most people do not have difficulty accepting the fact of God's love or God's power. Many people will believe that the same God of Love, who created them, also has a purpose for their lives. If they are not cynical because of circumstances, many will even listen to you talk about Jesus Christ so long as you talk about him as a man who came to teach a high system of morality and to set an example for us to follow. However, if you talk about the Lord Jesus Christ as the Savior, as the One who died to save sinners, there you will find hostility and vigorous rejection.

I know of one young woman whose life is an illustration of this principle. She was a student at the University of Pennsylvania. While there she attended a series of Bible studies on the life of Christ. She agreed with many of the truths that were brought out. But when it came to the point at which Christ was held up as the Savior of a fallen, sinful race as the only way in which a man or a woman can come to God, this young woman rebelled. She said, "I can accept the rest, but I cannot accept this business about Jesus Christ. I will not admit my need of him to be my Savior."

The second reason given by John for God's condemnation of men who have not believed in Christ occurs in verse 19. He says, "Light has come into the world, but men loved darkness instead of light because their deeds were evil." This means that people are condemned not merely because they have not accepted the Lord Jesus Christ as their Savior—this could be attributed to a lack of understanding—but also because they actually prefer sin. The light has come, but they have turned from it. They have done so because their deeds are evil.

From the account of the reaction of the rulers of the Jewish people to Jesus during his lifetime, we can understand how this works. These men were the acknowledged high-achievers of the people before Christ's coming. The law had been given. They were the ones who supposedly had kept it. But when Jesus Christ came, he was so much better than they were that next to him their goodness looked tarnished, like Christmas tinsel does in February. So they hated him. The result was that they preferred to have him killed, removed from sight, rather than allow him to expose the corruption that was in their own hearts and cure them of it.

The condemnation is not merely that we fall short of God's standards of perfection. The condemnation is there because we do not even aim in the right direction. We do not really want God's goodness.

The following illustration will help to make this clear. Imagine a child who is learning to throw a ball. He is to throw it, and his father is to catch it. The child is given the ball. He throws it. But instead of the ball going directly to the father it goes off about thirty degrees to the right. The father says, "You'll have to do better than that; I can't be running after the ball all afternoon."

The child replies, "But you're too far away. Come in closer." So the father moves in about ten feet. The child throws again, and this time the ball goes off about thirty degrees to the left. "You're still too far away," the child says. The father comes closer, but once more the ball goes off at an angle. Finally, the father is standing right in front of the child; the child throws, but the ball goes in the other direction entirely. What is the trouble? The trouble is not entirely with the distance between the child and the father, although that is part of it. The problem is with the child's aim.

In the same way, the problem with sinners is not merely with the great distance between our own level of conduct and God's standards. The trouble is also that we do not go in the right direction even when we aim at those standards.

Finally, John lists one more reason for God's condemnation of the human race. It is because men hate the light. The light has come and men hate it. Does that describe you? Or are you one who is allowing God to draw you to the light that shines in the face of Jesus Christ?

There is an emphasis upon light in this passage. John mentions light five times. "*Light* has come into the world, but men loved darkness instead of *light* because their deeds were evil. Everyone who does evil hates the *light*, and will not come into the *light* for fear that his deeds will be exposed. But whoever lives by the truth comes into the *light*, so that it may be seen plainly that what he has done has been done through God." According to these verses, people do not like the light; instead, they prefer darkness. If you ever come to the point where you do love the light, it must be because God has already begun a new work in you.

Not Condemned

That leads to our final point. Condemned? Yes! But also not condemned. For the gospel is the good news that although you and I and all men are born under the judgment of God, it is never necessary for anyone to remain there. Today there is a way of escape. What has made the difference? Jesus! Jesus has died. He has taken your sin upon himself and borne its punishment. He was condemned in your place. Thus we can read, "Therefore, there is now no condemnation for those who are in Christ Jesus" (Rom. 8:1).

Let me tell you of one young man who learned this. His name is David Hoyt; his story, like that of Christopher Pike (see the chapter on John 3:7–8), is told in Edward E. Plowman's book *The Jesus Movement in America*. David was a member of a hippie community in California when he met Kent Philpott, a Golden Gate Baptist Seminary student. David was already into one of the eastern religions, but through Kent's ministry he began to attend a series of Bible studies that met in the basement of the Krishna temple during the guru's absence. The studies spoke to him. He began to see himself as he really was. His own testimony is that while, on the one hand, it looked as though he were seeking the light through the mysticism of the eastern religions, actually he was preferring the darkness of his own soul to God's truth. Dissension among members of the temple bothered him. He could not seem to find inner peace. He prayed, asking God to show him the truth.

The next morning while everyone was at certain rites, the universal altar, which contained representations of the world's religions, caught fire in the basement. David and the others rushed down in time to salvage the only article that had escaped the flames—a Bible. David received it as an answer to his prayer. He opened it and stumbled upon the very passage we have been studying. There he saw his own heart. He was one who had been preferring the darkness to the light. He saw God's great love, a love that had sent Jesus Christ to bear his judgment. David said, "I was set free from an evil spirit that had kept me from the truth; I felt clean and whole for the first time in my life."

After that David Hoyt was used of God to reach many young people with the gospel.[1]

Now Is the Time

Does the story of David Hoyt's conversion describe you? Have you believed in Jesus or are you still in the category of those who stand condemned? There are only two roads, two destinies. If you have not already put your trust in Jesus and in what he has done for you, will you do it today? Will you believe on him?

Someone says, "Well, I have been thinking about it." Thinking about it will not do. That great Baptist preacher Charles Haddon Spurgeon once wrote that if you continue to think about it, "you will think yourself into hell." "I am praying about it," says another. The Bible does not ask you to pray about it either. If you are not a believer in the Lord Jesus Christ, the Bible calls upon you to believe on him. That is all. That is the only useful response. Immediate faith is what I, as a minister of the gospel, demand of you in the name of Jesus who died for you and rose again. Today God sends you this message, "The times of your ignorance I have winked at, but now I command all men everywhere to repent." I cannot promise you that if you refuse to believe you will ever have another chance to commit your life to Jesus. "Now is the accepted time," God says, "behold, now is the day of salvation."

During the early days of the ministry of Dwight L. Moody, the great evangelist launched a series of meetings in Chicago, with promise of the largest crowds that he had addressed up to that time. He was speaking on the life of Christ, and on the first Sunday night, October 8, 1871, he took as his topic the trial before Pilate. As he came to the end of his message he turned to Matthew 27:22, "What shall I do, then, with Jesus who is called Christ?" He concluded, "I wish you would take this text home with you and turn it over in your minds during the week, and next Sabbath we will come to Calvary and the cross, and we will decide what to do with Jesus of Nazareth."

It may have been an artistic device. But speaking of it in later years, Moody called that conclusion to his morning's address the greatest mistake of his life. For even while Mr. Sankey was singing the final hymn—

> Today the Savior calls;
> For refuge fly;
> The storm of justice falls,
> And death is nigh—

the fire engines began to sound on the street on their way to their first contact with the great Chicago fire in which Moody's hall was laid in ashes and in which it is estimated that over a thousand persons lost their lives. Moody never saw that congregation again, and some of those he spoke to that night undoubtedly died in that fire.

Make no mistake. The gospel is not for another time, another age, a more convenient moment. My business is not with tomorrows. Today is the day of God's grace. Look up and live! The Bible says, "Whoever believes in him is not condemned, but whoever does not believe stands condemned already because he has not believed in the name of God's one and only Son" (John 3:18).

41

Last Words of a Humble Man

John 3:22–30

After this, Jesus and his disciples went out into the Judean countryside, where he spent some time with them, and baptized. Now John also was baptizing at Aenon near Salim, because there was plenty of water, and people were constantly coming to be baptized. (This was before John was put in prison.) An argument developed between some of John's disciples and a certain Jew over the matter of ceremonial washing. They came to John and said to him, "Rabbi, that man who was with you on the other side of the Jordan—the one you testified about—well, he is baptizing, and everyone is going to him."

To this John replied, "A man can receive only what is given him from heaven. You yourselves can testify that I said, 'I am not the Christ but am sent ahead of him.' The bride belongs to the bridegroom. The friend who attends the bridegroom waits and listens for him, and is full of joy when he hears the bridegroom's voice. That joy is mine, and it is now complete. He must become greater; I must become less."

H umility is a virtue all men preach, none practice, and yet everybody is content to hear." So wrote an English jurist named John Selden, about the middle of the seventeenth century. These words are not universally true, of course, as we shall see in a moment, but they are true for many people and they characterize much of human nature. Although people praise humility, most persons think of themselves much as a character in the Gilbert and Sullivan comic opera *Ruddigore*, who said, "You've no idea what a poor opinion I have of myself . . . and how little I deserve it."

252

We all recognize that humility is important and desirable. It is one of the great Christian virtues, the opposite of pride. But where does it come from if it is so difficult to attain? And does anyone, in fact, possess it? Part of the answer is to be found in the last words of John the Baptist recorded in John's Gospel, for John the Baptist was a very humble man.

John's Last Days

To understand the setting for these words, we must recognize the fact that the Baptist had achieved a great deal of popularity as the result of his preaching. Luke tells us that "multitudes" went out to hear John. Matthew tells us that people came to him from "Jerusalem and all Judea and the whole region of the Jordan" (Matt. 3:5). Apparently the multitudes included all segments of the population—Pharisees, Sadducees, tax collectors, soldiers, the rich, and the poor. John speaks of an official delegation from Jerusalem. We are told that on some occasions, John was praised as a reincarnation of either Elijah or another of the prophets.

In time John's popularity came to the palace of Herod, the tetrarch of Galilee. Herod called for John and listened to him preach. Mark tells us that at the beginning Herod heard John gladly and did many good things as the result of John's preaching (Mark 6:20). Unfortunately, Herod enjoyed John's preaching only so long as John preached in generalities. When he was specific enough to speak out against the fact that Herod was then living with his brother Philip's wife, Herodias, Herod's enthusiasm cooled.

John had said, "It is not lawful for you to have your brother's wife." This so angered Herodias that eventually she succeeded in having John arrested and later killed.

At the time of which the author of the fourth Gospel is writing, however, John's imprisonment had not yet occurred, and John was still in the midst of his ministry. Yet another thing had happened. It turned out that the crowds around Jesus had begun to grow, and many who had been following John now detached themselves from him and began to follow Jesus. It seems that John's disciples were the ones most worried about it, for they did not like to see their teacher taking second place to anyone else.

Finally, in the context of a discussion about the proper procedure for the various Jewish rites of purification, someone expressed his concern. "Rabbi, that man who was with you on the other side of the Jordan—the one you testified about—well, he is baptizing, and everyone is going to him" (John 3:26). This was the same as saying, "John, your star is sinking. What shall we do?" It was an invitation to John to feel injured and neglected. To the disciples, John's witness to Jesus had been a very generous thing, and it was intolerable to think that Jesus should now be detracting from the Baptist's ministry. "Rebuke him," they were asking. "Say something to stop him." Instead John's reply is an immediate justification of Jesus' success. Instead of feeling sorry for himself, John actually rejoiced in the popularity of the newcomer.

God's Sovereignty

What did John say? The exact words are important, for they do not merely reveal the state of John's thinking about himself and Jesus' ministry, they also show us the necessary ingredients for achieving this same level of humility in our own lives.

First, John said, "A man can receive only what is given him from heaven" (v. 27). This was an awareness by John of God's sovereignty in all things. It was the first of several things that kept John humble. If the newcomer was attracting and winning more followers than John himself, this was not because he was stealing them away from John or acting dishonestly in presenting his claims. It was because God was giving them to Christ to be his followers.

I wonder if you have a proper sense of God's sovereignty in such matters? To have it will not mean that you are free to be lazy in your Christian life and then blame your lack of achievement on God. John did not do this, for we read that even after Jesus had begun his ministry John went right on preaching and baptizing (v. 23). He continued doing what God had given him to do. No, believing in the sovereignty of God does not mean that we can be lazy, but it does mean that whatever the results of our efforts, we will see God's hand in them and will not be jealous of another through whom God apparently achieves more.

Moreover, we will not be proud of our imagined spiritual insight or be jealous of another's understanding if we are aware that even this comes only from above. Jesus taught this in response to the unbelief of certain of the cities of his day in which great works were done. He said, "I praise you, Father, Lord of heaven and earth, because you have hidden these things from the wise and learned, and revealed them to little children" (Matt. 11:25). To Peter he said, "Blessed are you, Simon son of Jonah, for this was not revealed to you by man, but by my Father in heaven" (Matt. 16:17). It is written of Lydia, a woman to whom Paul preached on his second missionary journey, "One of those listening was a woman named Lydia, a dealer in purple cloth from the city of Thyatira, who was a worshiper of God. The Lord opened her heart to respond to Paul's message" (Acts 16:14). Paul wrote, "For who makes you different from anyone else? What do you have that you did not receive? And if you did receive it, why do you boast as though you did not?" (1 Cor. 4:7).

To recognize that all spiritual insight and advance comes from God is to be freed from jealous efforts at comparison. It is to recognize that all Christ-centered and totally committed service, whatever the results, ranks equally with God. Any task done for God is necessarily a great work.

Self-Awareness

A second factor in John's humility was his own self-awareness. John knew who he was and what it was to which God had called him. He continues, "You yourselves can testify that I said, 'I am not the Christ but am sent ahead of him'" (John 3:28).

Do you and I have the same self-awareness? If we do, it will mean that on one level at least we will recognize ourselves to be nothing. This is God's own appraisal of us as conveyed in Christ's famous sentence: "Apart from me you can do nothing" (John 15:5). On the other hand, it will mean that when we do accept that statement we can go on to recognize the importance of what we are given to do by God. If a person will accept God's verdict, he can become something for God. If he rejects that verdict of nothingness, he is, of all men, the most nothing! If a man will believe what God says about him, he will admit to what he really is and will enter by faith into what he should be in Christ.

In the twelfth chapter of Romans the apostle Paul writes this about humility: "For by the grace given me I say to every one of you: Do not think of yourself more highly than you ought, but rather think of yourself with sober judgment, in accordance with the measure of faith God has given you" (v. 3). In this verse, although it is hidden in the English translation, one Greek word, *phroneo*, occurs four times. This word describes a man who is in his right mind. It is, for instance, the word that would have been used by a man making a will. He would have begun it by saying, "Being *sane* and *in my right mind*, I . . . do hereby bequeath," and so on. The word is preserved in English in the words phrenetic, phrenitis, and phrenology, all of which have to do with the brain.

With that definition in mind let us now translate the verse, using the idea of sanity. "For I say, through the grace given unto me, to every Christian among you, do not indulge in an insane estimate of yourself, but rather be sane about it so that your estimate of yourself is sound." This John did when he fixed his mind on the fact that God had called him merely to be the forerunner of the Lord Jesus Christ and a witness to him.

Christ above All

The third factor in John's humility was that he had his eyes fixed on Christ. He was the friend of the bridegroom, John said (John 3:29). It was not his wedding. His function was to serve the groom. This too applies to all Christians. If we have our minds on other people, even a little bit, we will always find room for pride; for no matter how bad we are or how poorly we are doing, we will always be able to find someone who does things worse and be proud that we are better. On the other hand, if we have our eyes fixed on Jesus, we will have our attention riveted on one who is so infinitely above us that we will consider ourselves at best only his unprofitable servants.

Arthur W. Pink has expressed it in this way: "Humility is not the product of direct cultivation, rather it is a by-product. The more I try to be humble, the less shall I attain unto humility. But if I am truly occupied with that One who was 'meek and lowly in heart,' if I am constantly beholding *His* glory in the mirror of God's Word, then shall I be 'changed into *the same image* from glory to glory, even as by the Spirit of the Lord' (2 Cor. 3:18)."[1]

I wonder if we do that? Do we live our lives looking unto Jesus, caring what he thinks and not worried about the critical judgments of those of this world? Or are we constantly thrown off balance by the world and its values?

One summer when I was just a boy, I took a trip to California with my family. It was one of the *Eternity* magazine tours, and there was a great crowd of people along, including Donald Grey Barnhouse. One day a number of us went to Monterey where there was an amusement park. In one building we saw a very large barrel, about seven or eight feet in diameter and about thirty or forty feet long. It lay on its side and revolved, the challenge being to walk through it without being upset.

For some reason this was a particular challenge to Donald Barnhouse, so he started through it. Unfortunately, he was only into the barrel about two or three yards when his feet got higher than his center of gravity and down he went. The first thing everyone knew was that he was rolling around on the bottom. The man who ran the amusement stopped the barrel from turning, and Barnhouse came out. He said, "Start it up. I'm going to do it again."

The man who controlled the barrel said, "Wait a minute. First, you should know that there is a secret for walking through the barrel. Do you see that mirror at the other end?"

Barnhouse said, "Yes."

"What do you see in the mirror?"

"I see you," answered Barnhouse.

"That's right," the man replied. "You see me. Now this time when you walk through the barrel forget about the fact that it is turning. Don't even look at the barrel. Instead look at me in the mirror. That way you will have a true sense of the vertical, and you will be able to adjust the speed of your steps to keep from falling." This time, when the barrel was started, Barnhouse walked through it triumphantly.

The secret of walking through the barrel was to keep one's eyes on the man who runs it. It is the same spiritually. Who is it who runs the affairs of this life with all its ups and downs, all its crises, joys, and disappointments? The answer is: God! Who has it all under control? God! How, then, is the Christian to walk through this life without losing his balance spiritually? The answer is: By keeping his eyes upon God! Moreover, we can extend the illustration to point out that in this life we do not even see God directly but are permitted to see him as he is reflected in the pages of his written Word. The Bible is a mirror that shows us God. "Now we see but a poor reflection as in a mirror; then we shall see face to face" (1 Cor. 13:12).

Joy for Others

Finally, there were two more factors in John's life that kept John humble before God. They are the fourth and fifth reasons for his humility. The fourth is that John found joy in leading others to Jesus. This is implied in the bride and bridegroom imagery, for it was the function of the friend of the bridegroom to conduct the bride to the man she was about to marry. John said, "This is my joy."

Do you know that joy? Some persons think that there is great joy in material possessions, but things in themselves do not satisfy. Others think that there is joy in worldly fame, achievement, or pleasure, but these goals are relatively unrewarding. They satisfy at best for a short time. Real joy comes in being able to say to Jesus Christ, "Here I am, Lord, use me," and then finding that out of his grace he is able to use you to bring others into a saving relationship to himself.

He Must Increase

The final factor in John's humility was his knowledge of the fact that whatever might happen in this world, whatever glory the world might or might not give him, the ultimate outcome would be increase of the glory given to Jesus Christ and the bowing of every human knee before him. "He must become greater; I must become less," said John in conclusion.

Do you know that truth? When William Carey, one of the great pioneer missionaries to India, lay dying he turned to a friend and said, "When I am gone, don't talk about William Carey; talk about William Carey's Savior. I desire that Christ alone might be magnified."

I know as I teach these things that some will be thinking: "Oh, but if I am humble, doesn't that mean that I will never be able to achieve anything in this world? Won't I become a Caspar Milquetoast type of person? Won't I be stepped on constantly?" No! You misunderstand humility if you think that is the result of it. Actually, to humble oneself before God in this way gives one great boldness before men. The Bible tells us that Moses was the meekest man who ever lived (Num. 12:3). Yet the man who had humbled himself before God, who had taken off his shoes before the burning bush, was the same man who was able to march into the court of the most powerful monarch of his day, the ruler of Egypt, and thunder out God's warning: "Thus says the Lord GOD of Israel, Let my people go."

And so can we! The story is told of John Knox, the great Scottish reformer, that one day, as he was approaching the court of Bloody Mary in his office of chaplain to her majesty, he was warned to postpone the visit since she was in one of her angriest moods and might be dangerous. Knox continued on his way, replying, "Why should I be afraid of a queen when I have just spent four hours on my knees before God?" Here was genuine humility. Knox had bowed so low before God that he did not fear to stand high before an earthly monarch.

42

The Bride and the Bridegroom

John 3:29

"The bride belongs to the bridegroom. The friend who attends the bridegroom waits and listens for him, and is full of joy when he hears the bridegroom's voice. That joy is mine, and it is now complete."

These words are intended to illuminate John the Baptist's important role in the great drama of salvation. He is the *shoshben* who, according to Jewish custom, arranged the marriage ceremonies and conducted the bride to her husband. Even more importantly, however, they also teach us about Jesus Christ in the role of the bridegroom and about what believers in Christ have become because of their engagement to him.

In the annals of the Persian kings there is a story about the wife of one of the generals of Cyrus, the king mentioned in Isaiah who ruled several hundred years before the birth of Christ. The wife, the story says, was charged with treason and after a trial was condemned to die. At first her husband did not realize what had taken place, but he was told about it and at once went bursting into the throne room. He threw himself on the floor before the king and cried, "Oh, Lord, take my life instead of hers. Let me die in her place." Cyrus, who by all historical accounts was a humane and fairly sensitive man, was touched by this offer. He said, "Love like that must not be spoiled by death." Then he gave the husband and wife back to each other and let the wife go free. As they walked away happily the husband said to his wife, "Did you notice how kindly the king looked upon us when he gave you the pardon?" The wife replied, "I had no eyes for the king. I saw only the man who was willing to die in my place."

I believe that if we can enter into the spirit of that story, we can also understand what the Bible means when it shows us that Jesus Christ is the great lover, bridegroom, husband, and provider of his church. He is the One who not only offered himself in our place but who actually died for us in order that he might present us to himself "radiant . . . without stain or blemish" (Eph. 5:27). As his bride our eyes, hearts, minds, and souls should be fixed upon him.

Jesus Is God

Before we begin to apply this theme to ourselves, however, we need to see what it teaches about Jesus Christ. This is important, for John was teaching that Jesus is God. This is seen in the fact that when John the Baptist applied the image of the bridegroom to Jesus he was certainly not just making the comparison up. John was applying an Old Testament image to Christ, and the point is that in the Old Testament Jehovah, the God of Israel, is the bridegroom.

The earliest suggestion of the image in the Old Testament, so far as I can tell, is in the Book of Exodus. Here, in the context of the giving of the law, God tells Israel, "Do not worship any other god, for the LORD, whose name is Jealous, is a jealous God. Be careful not to make a treaty with those who live in the land; for when they prostitute themselves to their gods and sacrifice to them, they will invite you and you will eat their sacrifices. And when you choose some of their daughters as wives for your sons and those daughters prostitute themselves to their gods, they will lead your sons to do the same. Do not make cast idols" (Exod. 34:14–17). In these verses the fact that Jehovah is the bridegroom or husband of Israel is not spelled out explicitly, but it is implied in the argument that for Israel to worship other gods is harlotry. These verses are the seed of the later imagery.

By the time we get to the Book of Deuteronomy, the warning against committing spiritual adultery, which is found in Exodus, is changed to a prophecy that this is precisely what will happen. Thus we find God saying to Moses, "You are going to rest with your fathers, and these people will soon prostitute themselves to the foreign gods of the land they are entering. They will forsake me and break the covenant I made with them" (Deut. 31:16).

In the prophetic books we find that Israel has already done this, departing from the Lord. Here the language becomes explicit. Isaiah writes, "For your Maker is your husband—the LORD Almighty is his name" (Isa. 54:5). Several chapters later Isaiah again says, "As a bridegroom rejoices over his bride, so will your God rejoice over you" (Isa. 62:5). From this point on the comparison occurs more frequently, several times in the books of Jeremiah and Ezekiel, for instance. Finally, the entire personal story of Hosea and the opening chapters of his prophecy are based on this theme. In all of these books God is the faithful lover and husband. Israel is the unfaithful wife and bride.

When we put this imagery into the context of John the Baptist's preaching, we find that John was identifying the Lord Jesus Christ with God. John preached on the basis of Old Testament themes. He knew that Israel was the bride and Jehovah was the bridegroom. Now Jesus appears, and John immediately casts him in God's role. In mathematics, whenever you have two equations like "A equals B" and "B equals C," it is always possible to make a third equation which says that "A equals C." The rule is that things equal to the same thing are equal to each other. In the same way, if Jehovah is the bridegroom and Jesus Christ is the bridegroom, it follows that Jesus is Jehovah.

Is he your God? Is he your bridegroom?

The Church

The second major teaching of the bride and bridegroom imagery is of the high calling of the church. She is the one for whom Christ died. She is married to him. Consequently, she is called to be faithful.

This is the sense in which the imagery is developed several times in Paul's writing. For instance, in the eleventh chapter of 2 Corinthians Paul writes of his concern lest the church he had established in Corinth prove unfaithful to the Lord Jesus. "I am jealous for you with a godly jealousy. I promised you to one husband, to Christ, so that I might present you as a pure virgin to him. But I am afraid that just as Eve was deceived by the serpent's cunning, your minds may somehow be led astray from your sincere and pure devotion to Christ" (vv. 2–3). In the following verse he shows that unfaithfulness occurs whenever the church, which is called by his name, adopts "another Jesus," "another spirit," or "another gospel" as its message.

Do you see what this means? It means that the church of Jesus Christ can be faithful, but she can also be unfaithful. She can commit spiritual adultery. She commits adultery whenever she departs from the Jesus of the Bible, the spirit of Jesus that witnesses to him through Scripture, or the gospel of salvation by faith in Christ alone.

Has the church done this? This is a question that must be asked afresh in each age. Have we another Jesus, another spirit, or another gospel in our churches? I am not speaking of faithful churches when I say this, of course, but I believe that (with the exception of such churches) honesty forces us to admit that this has indeed happened in our age. The quest of another Jesus is called often laudably "The Quest of the Historical Jesus." The trend to another spirit occurs whenever people follow private leadings or visions rather than the clear statements of Scripture. Another gospel emerges whenever works are mixed with faith in salvation. This has occurred, but it is all apostasy. We must counter such trends with the insistence that membership in the church of Jesus Christ involves great ethical and doctrinal responsibility as well as high privileges.

Sex and Marriage

In an appendix on the theme of the bride and the bridegroom in *The Church at the End of the Twentieth Century*, Francis A. Schaeffer also notes that the bride and bridegroom theme speaks to the issue of sexual morality and the standards for Christian marriage. This is important also, particularly in our day when the old sexual norms are threatened and when faithfulness in marriage seems to be losing its appeal for many persons.

Why is it that promiscuous sexual relations and unfaithfulness in marriage are wrong? There are three major reasons, Schaeffer notes. First, these things are wrong simply because God says so. That which is right is right and that which is wrong is wrong, not because men judge it to be right or wrong, but because good is related to God's character. His character is the morality of the universe. Hence, if he tells us that something is wrong, it *is* wrong, however we may feel about it personally.

The second reason why promiscuity or unfaithfulness is wrong is that these things are not good for us as God made us. It is true that right is right and wrong is wrong because God says so, but it is equally true that morality is related to the way in which we are made. Thus, we find ourselves entering into a fuller realization of the happiness we are made for as we obey God's laws. And conversely, we find ourselves upon an increasingly destructive path when we flout them.

The final, and best, reason why promiscuous sexual relations and marital unfaithfulness are wrong is that these things break the picture of what God intends marriage to be. Schaeffer states, "Marriage is set forth to be the illustration of the relationship of God and his people, and of Christ and his church. . . . The relationship of God with his people rests upon his character, and sexual relationship outside of marriage breaks this parallel which the Bible draws between marriage and the relationship of God with his people." Women are to love as the church loves Christ. Men are to love as Christ loves. "If we break God's illustration by such a relationship, it is a serious thing."[1]

How do we apply this personally? It depends upon who we are and where we are on the graded spectrum of love, marriage, and sex. Some are not yet married but will be thinking about it. If you are in this category, you must determine to hold up the highest possible standards of marriage and then evaluate the one you are thinking of marrying in terms of them. Young woman, you must look at your young man and ask, "Can he be as Jesus Christ to me?" If he cannot be, look elsewhere. Young man, you should ask, "Do I love this young woman enough to give myself for her? Am I willing to cover up her faults and be patient with her, as God instructs me to do? Am I willing to die for her?" If you are not willing to do these things, it is not right for you to marry her.

Others will be beyond thinking about marriage. They are already married, and there are difficulties. If you are in this category, you must not give up because of the difficulties. To do so would be to suggest that God gives up on us, and this is untrue. Instead you must love with a love that overcomes difficulties—first, by changing yourself and then by winning over the other person. If you will yield to Christ and his standards, he will begin by making of you a new creation and then end by making all things new.

The Lord's Return

Finally, there is this great lesson in the image. Not only does the theme of the bride and the bridegroom teach us of the deity of Jesus Christ, not only does it set the highest standards for the conduct of the church and for individual conduct in the areas of sex and marriage—it also teaches us about the return of Jesus Christ. We see this when we apply the image in time, for in a temporal sense we are presently only engaged to Jesus Christ awaiting that final consummation of the engagement at the future marriage supper of the Lamb.

Does an engaged woman look forward to her wedding day? Of course she does! So should we also look forward to our Lord's return and act accordingly.

How do you live as you wait for the Lord's return? Let me illustrate how you should live by these two contrasting stories from the book *God's Methods for Holy Living* by Donald Grey Barnhouse. At the time of the First World War there was a young aristocrat in England who married and then went off to the trenches on the continent. The young bride wrote that she was preoccupied with war work and was nursing in a certain hospital. She apologized for not writing often, saying that she was spending long hours every day tending the war wounded. Some time later, when her husband was coming home on leave, a friend, who knew what was actually going on, said to him, "If I were you, I would not write in advance that I am coming. I would simply slip over quietly." The husband did so. He went to the hospital where his wife was supposed to be working and found that those working there had never heard of her. She was not at her apartment either. Someone said, "Oh, she will probably be at a tea dance at the Ritz today." The husband went there and found his wife in the company of another man. In time, he found out a good deal more and was granted a divorce by British authorities.

The other story is this. At the beginning of the same war, in the western part of America, there was a young couple who had made plans to be married. Everything was in readiness. They had a small cottage. They had furnished it. The date was set for the marriage. Suddenly war was declared, and the young man, who was in the reserve, was called up to active duty. He was to be sent to the Mexican border to train before being shipped off to France. On the day before he was to be sent off for training, the young woman said to him, "I know that it is not quite the date for our wedding, but you might be ordered overseas immediately; you might be killed, and I would much rather go through life bearing your name than go through life always explaining that the man I loved had been killed in the war. So let's be married now." On the next day they were married; and for their honeymoon the husband went with the troops, and the bride went alone to the little cottage.

She was very lonely, of course, as you can imagine, and she longed for the day when she would again see her lover-husband. Day after day he wrote to her. He sent her gifts—a Navajo rug, some Mexican lace, some Indian pottery. Months passed, and the day came when she was so lonely that she sat down on some pillows in front of the fireplace, spread out the rug, put the other gifts on a piece of furniture, and then began to read through all the accumulated letters while having herself a good cry. Suddenly, as she was reading the letters, there was a step on the porch, the door opened, and there he was! He had sent a telegram, but it was delayed, as telegrams often were in those days. He had arrived before it. When she saw him and realized that he was home, the young bride jumped to her feet, scattered the letters about, and even knocked over the pottery. A few of the letters fell into the fire, but she did not care at all. He had returned to her, and having him she had all.

The one who tells those stories then wrote, "Dear friends, our Lord Jesus is coming back and He is going to find you and . . . me in one of those two attitudes. Will you be flirting with the world, or will you be occupied with His love letters, His gifts, His work, thinking of Him?"[2] Jesus *is* coming. The Bible says that "Everyone who has this hope in him purifies himself, just as he is pure" (1 John 3:3).

43

The Revealer Has Come

John 3:31–36

"The one who comes from above is above all; the one who is from the earth belongs to the earth, and speaks as one from the earth. The one who comes from heaven is above all. He testifies to what he has seen and heard, but no one accepts his testimony. The man who has accepted it has certified that God is truthful. For the one whom God has sent speaks the words of God, for God gives the Spirit without limit. The Father loves the Son and has placed everything in his hands. Whoever believes in the Son has eternal life, but whoever rejects the Son will not see life, for God's wrath remains on him."

In a small but very excellent book written by A. W. Tozer, there is an illuminating paragraph that refers to the inferential character of the average man's faith in God. This means that for most people God is the end result of a chain of reasoning rather than a reality. According to such people there may be much to suggest God's existence. There is the beauty of nature, the immensity of space, the order of matter. "He must be," they say. "Because these things are, he is." Other people argue in the same way from the experience of a parent or friend. "God was real to my mother," they say, "so he must be real. I believe in him because others believe in him." Still others find their belief in God linked to their belief in such things as truth, goodness, beauty, or ethical ideals.

Quite obviously, each of these chains of reasoning is unique. Still, as Tozer notes, those who hold them have one thing in common. "They do not know God in personal experience. The possibility of intimate acquaintance with

264

Him has not entered their minds. While admitting His existence they do not think of Him as knowable in the sense that we know things or people."[1]

Unfortunately, although this is primarily true of non-Christians, there is also a sense in which it is at least partially true of some believers. For although they believe in Christ and trust him in one sense, still for them God is unreal and they go through life attempting to love an ideal or be loyal to an abstract doctrine or principle.

If you are at any point of this wide spectrum of those for whom God is unreal, then the verses to which we come now are for you especially. They are about Jesus Christ, and they speak of him as the great witness to God, the great revealer of him. They say, "The one who comes from above is above all; the one who is from the earth belongs to the earth, and speaks as one from the earth. The one who comes from heaven is above all. He testifies to what he has seen and heard, but no one accepts his testimony. The man who has accepted it has certified that God is truthful. For the one whom God has sent speaks the words of God, for God gives the Spirit without limit. The Father loves the Son and has placed everything in his hands. Whoever believes in the Son has eternal life, but whoever rejects the Son will not see life, for God's wrath remains on him" (John 3:31–36).

The Perfect Witness

What is it that makes a person a good witness? We know something of the answer to this question because of our knowledge of the procedures in courts of law. The first thing that is required if a man is to be a good witness is that he must have firsthand information. He must have seen or heard that about which he is testifying. For this reason, no judge in the land will accept hearsay evidence.

Second, a good witness must be willing to testify. He must be willing to speak up, to get involved.

Third, the witness must be reliable. That is, his witness must be substantial and possess enough self-consistency to be believed. These three requirements make for a perfect witness. By this standard—and this is John's point—Jesus Christ is the perfect witness concerning God. Thus, in verse 31 John stresses the fact that Jesus has firsthand information concerning God because of his origins. In verse 32 he points out that Jesus did bear witness to this knowledge. Finally, in verse 34 he shows that the witness is reliable "for God gives the Spirit without limit."

Firsthand Information

The first point is that Jesus Christ possessed accurate knowledge of God the Father. This is linked to his supremacy over all other teachers and prophets. These may have possessed part of the truth, but even at the best their insights were secondary. They reported only what God had revealed to them. Jesus was God incarnate. His origins were heavenly. Consequently, he has revealed the truth perfectly out of the fullness of his knowledge.

On this point William Barclay writes, "If we want information, we have to go to the person who possesses that information. If we want information about a family, we will only get it at firsthand from a member of that family. If we want information about a town, we will only get it at firsthand from someone who comes from that town. So, then, if we want information about God, we will get it only from the Son of God; and if we want information about heaven and heaven's life, we will only get it from Him who comes from heaven. When Jesus speaks about God and about the heavenly things, says John, it is no carried story, no secondhand tale, no information from a secondary source. He tells us that which he himself has seen and heard. To put it very simply, because Jesus alone knows God, he alone can give us the facts about God, and these facts are the gospel."[2]

In his Gospel, John has a special way of emphasizing the fact that Jesus alone possesses such knowledge. It is not present, or at least is not present in the same degree, in the other Gospels. John stresses the fact that Jesus is the perfect witness because he alone has been *sent* into the world by God.

Here a few statistics will be helpful. In John's Gospel the phrase "he (or 'the Father') who sent me" is found on the lips of Jesus twenty-three times. The Greek verb in that phrase *(apostellein)* occurs seventeen times in phrases that speak of God's commissioning of the Son, and there are other phrases that speak from man's perspective of the fact that Jesus Christ has "come." Jesus is the One who "came down from heaven." He "has come into the world." He "came from the Father," or God. In the final discourses, as the time of Jesus' death draws near, the emphasis shifts quite naturally from the fact that Jesus came into the world to the fact that he is now to return to the Father. In John 16:28, the themes of the coming and the return are bound together. "I came from the Father and entered the world; now I am leaving the world and going back to the Father." These phrases have little or no reference to the identification of Jesus as the Messiah as similar phrases do in the other Gospels. Instead, they refer to Jesus' ability both to impart heavenly gifts and to speak the words of God to men. Jesus is the perfect witness because he is able perfectly to reveal God. "No one has ever seen God, but God the One and Only, who is at the Father's side, has made him known" (John 1:18).

Moreover, according to the Bible and to the Gospel of John particularly, the sending of Jesus Christ into the world involves much more than the sending of a prophet, as in Old Testament times, or the sending of the apostles into the world as evangelists in the New Testament era. These men were messengers. They were sent by God. But Jesus is not *a* messenger. He is *the* messenger. It is true that John the Baptist is also said to have been sent by God (1:6, 33; 3:28) and that the disciples later are sent in their turn into the world (17:18; 20:21). But neither the Baptist nor the disciples exert a claim to any independent revelation. They are only sent to bear witness to Jesus Christ. He alone speaks and acts out of the fullness of his knowledge of his Father.

In John 9 there is a story that illustrates all that I have been saying. It is a story of how a blind man came to know God through Jesus. The man has no knowledge of God at the beginning of the story. His physical blindness is a symbol of his spiritual blindness. Jesus heals him. As he does so he says, "While I am in the world, I am the light of the world" (v. 5; cf. 8:12). Through this contact the man begins to understand something of who Jesus is, and he increases in spiritual sight until he eventually comes to argue pointedly for the truth of Christ's heavenly origin. The high point of the story is reached in the contrast between the testimony of the man who had been born blind and the denial of Christ by the Jewish rulers. The Jews argue from the basis of their knowledge of the law and Moses. They say, "We know that God has spoken to Moses, but as for this man, we do not know where he comes from" (v. 29 RSV). The man who had been born blind replies, "Why, this is a marvel! You do not know where he comes from, and yet he opened my eyes. . . . If this man were not from God, he could do nothing" (vv. 30, 33 RSV).

The man who was blind had been led by the healing of his eyes to the spiritual perception that Jesus had come from God and therefore spoke and acted out of a true knowledge of God. Thus, while his understanding of Jesus began with the confession that he was merely a "man" (v. 11), it soon progressed to the fact that he was "a prophet" (v. 17) "of God" (v. 33) and then to a worship of him (v. 38). By contrast, the failure of the leaders to recognize the truth of Christ's coming from God actually intensified their spiritual blindness and led to their rejection of Christ's testimony entirely.

Where do you stand in this picture? Are you one for whom God is only an inference? Or have you come to "the light of the knowledge of the glory of God in the face of Jesus Christ" (2 Cor. 4:6)?

A Willing Witness

There is also, as I have indicated, a second requirement for a perfect witness. Not only must a witness have firsthand information about that which is to be testified; the witness must also be *willing* to testify. Was Jesus willing? Of course, he was. He got involved. Therefore, John writes, "He testifies to what he has seen and heard" (v. 32).

It is interesting to me that John puts the verb "testify" in the present tense here, as indeed he does with all the other verbs that speak of Christ's witness. We would tend to use the past tense, for we would reason that Jesus came, bore his testimony, and then returned to heaven. This is not what John does. For John, Jesus is still testifying. Well then, we ask, where do we hear his testimony? The answer is: in the Bible. Is the Bible something that is dead, irrelevant, or dated, then? Not for John! And not for any who have come to know Christ and to have experienced the living power of the Bible to speak on his behalf. The Bible is living. Christ is living. Moreover, it is through the Bible that he continues to speak and bear his witness to heavenly things in our days.

Reliable Testimony

Jesus also fulfilled the third requirement for the perfect witness. His witness was consistent. It was complete and therefore totally reliable. John indicates this when he writes, "For the one whom God has sent speaks the words of God, for God gives the Spirit without limit. The Father loves the Son and has placed everything in his hands" (vv. 34–35).

I must admit that because of the way this phrase is written in the Greek, several different interpretations of it are possible. It could mean three things. First, it could mean that Jesus Christ gives the Spirit to believers without measure. The verse has often been taken in that light, but this view is faulty. Certainly Jesus does not withhold the Spirit from his own. But whatever the case, none of us possesses the Spirit in the measure that he is possessed by Jesus; and it is far more true to say of ourselves, as is said elsewhere, that "to each one of us grace has been given as Christ apportioned it" (Eph. 4:7).

The verse could also mean that the Spirit does not give by measure; that is, that the Spirit himself gives liberally. That is true in one sense, but it does not seem to fit the context of these verses and is at best only a barely possible reading of the Greek text.

The third view, the one that is to be preferred, is that the Father has not withheld any measure of the Spirit from the Son. This is John's way of saying that there is perfect communion and communication between the Son and the Father, with the result that the Father guarantees the truth and total reliability of Christ's words. This is not true of any other religious teacher; in fact, no other teacher (except a madman) would claim it. In all the teaching of all the other religious teachers of this world, truth is always mixed with falsehood. Therefore, those who teach, if they are wise, always point beyond themselves to that which is higher. This was never done by Jesus. Others pointed down the road to a far destination. Jesus claimed that he was that destination. Others taught that they had aspects of the truth. Jesus said that the truth had come in his person. Others offered to show the way to God. Jesus said that he is the way to God. "I am the way and the truth and the life. No one comes to the Father except through me" (John 14:6).

Are these things true? If they are, Jesus is the only truly reliable witness to who God is and to what he requires. Since he requires your life and total allegiance, you ought (as the man who had been born blind) to worship him.

Running Away

At the end of his book, *Runaway World*, Michael Green, the principal of London Divinity School, deals with the means men and women use to escape an honest investigation of Christ's claims. Sex is one obvious means of escape, according to Green. So are drugs, mysticism, conformity to our culture, the rat race, vice, even (for some persons) social involvement. Perhaps you are involved in one or more of these pursuits as a means of escape from the claims of Jesus.

But what of him? Is he the One he says he is? If he is, none of these means of escape will do. In fact, in order that no one might miss this, John ends his whole presentation of Christ's claims with a forthright statement of the issues, "Whoever believes in the Son has eternal life, but whoever rejects the Son will not see life, for God's wrath remains on him" (v. 36).

What will you say when you meet him? What possible excuse can you offer? Green writes: "'I didn't believe you ever existed?' What utter nonsense; what culpable ignorance of the evidence! 'I didn't think your life was attractive enough, noble enough'? What manifest hypocrisy: it was rather that the standards of the man of Nazareth were too high, too costly, was it not? Or shall the excuse be simply 'I did not bother'? How do you think that will look to the Son of God, who became man for you, loved and died for you, rose again in order to take over your life and make a new man of you? No, all excuses will wither and wilt before the truth, the love, the self-sacrifice of Jesus. Final truth about the world, mankind and God has been disclosed by the Other who came into our very midst, the one who declared 'I am the truth.' By our relation to him we shall be judged."[3]

It is my profound prayer, as we close our studies of this great third chapter of John's Gospel, that you will not ignore Christ's witness but instead will enter into eternal life through believing in and committing yourself to him who died for you and rose again.

44

Christ at Sychar's Well

John 4:1–6

The Pharisees heard that Jesus was gaining and baptizing more disciples than John, although in fact it was not Jesus who baptized, but his disciples. When the Lord learned of this, he left Judea and went back once more to Galilee.

Now he had to go through Samaria. So he came to a town in Samaria called Sychar, near the plot of ground Jacob had given to his son Joseph. Jacob's well was there, and Jesus, tired as he was from the journey, sat down by the well. It was about the sixth hour.

During the years that I spent in Europe studying for the Christian ministry, I had opportunities to witness the universality of the gospel call that is generally lacking to one who spends his whole life in America.

I remember particularly a combination of such opportunities that occurred toward the end of my three-year residency in Switzerland. Within a week of having completed my doctoral examinations at the University of Basel, I left Basel for Berlin for the first great World Congress on Evangelism sponsored on that occasion by Billy Graham and the evangelical Protestant magazine *Christianity Today.* As I boarded one flight after another on the way to Berlin—for the routing required several changes—I noticed that others, obviously also bound for the meetings, began to board the planes. At first there were workers from Switzerland—Germans, Americans, and Swiss. Then there were those from other parts of Europe—Frenchmen, British citizens, Italians. Eventually there were some from the nations of Africa and Asia. By the time we had arrived in Berlin and the other delegates had also assembled, more than 1,200 had gathered from a total of more than one hundred nations, and the four official languages of the assembly—French, English, German, and Spanish—were supplemented by dozens of others spoken in the corridors of the *Kongresshalle,* where the meetings were held, and in the hotels. Socially, the delegates spanned the gap from Emperor Haile Selassie I of Ethiopia to recent converts from the pagan tribes of Ecuador, Indonesia, and rural Africa.

The day after the Congress closed, I returned to Basel to my duties as pastor of the small church that had grown up there during the years I had spent in Switzerland. I remember that as I stood up to preach the next Sunday, I thought of the correspondingly wide breadth of backgrounds and experiences that were represented even in this one small congregation. It was a world congress in miniature. Here were Swiss, German, American, British, Japanese, and Filipino Christians, and they too represented extremes of intellect, education, wealth, and social position.

In America, where there is not so great an extreme of nationalities and where the churches are often unfortunately socially oriented, the fact that the gospel of Jesus Christ speaks to all men is not always so apparent. Still this is true, and we correctly sing:

> In Christ there is no East or West,
> In him no South or North,
> But one great fellowship of love
> Throughout the whole wide earth.

According to God's Word, there is no child of Adam who may not come freely and boldly to the Lord Jesus Christ and in him find a glorious salvation.

This is the true universalism of the Christian faith, not that all men *will* be saved but that all men *may* be saved. It is the teaching of Scripture that no one will ever be barred from Christ because of his sex, intellect, education, race, nationality, wealth, or social position. This simplicity is the glory of God's grace.

A Second Example

Today we come to a dramatization of this principle from the fourth chapter of John's Gospel. If you can remember back to the first of our studies in the third chapter, you will recall that Nicodemus, who appears in that chapter, is the first person introduced by John to show the need of men and women for the gospel of Jesus Christ and to provide a context in which Jesus explains what it is he offers them. At the end of chapter 2, John wrote of the initial response of some men to Jesus: "But Jesus would not entrust himself to them, for he knew all *men.* He did not need *man's* testimony about *man,* for he knew what was in a *man*" (John 2:24–25). The next verse, 3:1, then begins "Now there was a man of the Pharisees named Nicodemus . . ." Quite obviously Nicodemus is brought forward as John's first great example of the human race.

We must not think, however, that Nicodemus was the only one who needed the gospel. There were others; in fact, all men and women need it. Thus, to learn this truth we are brought to the second of John's examples, the unnamed woman whom Jesus met in Samaria in the vicinity of Sychar's well.

According to John, the woman of Samaria was an immoral woman; and she apparently had a bad reputation, if we are to judge by the fact that she came to draw water in the heat of the day when no one else, particularly the other women, would be present at Jacob's well. She came for water only. But instead she met Jesus. He spoke to her and gave her the water of life, a gift that she had never dreamed of but that satisfied her most important thirst— her thirst for God—completely. The story closes with the witness of this woman to others from her town, with the result that many of them also believed on Jesus, confessing that he was the Messiah and their Savior.

It is difficult to imagine a greater contrast between two persons than the contrast between the important and sophisticated Nicodemus, this ruler of the Jews, and the simple Samaritan woman. He was a Jew; she a Samaritan. He was a Pharisee; she belonged to no religious party. He was a politician; she had no status whatever. He was a scholar; she was uneducated. He was highly moral; she was immoral. He had a name; she is nameless. He was a man; she was a woman. He came at night, to protect his reputation; she, who had no reputation, came at noon. Nicodemus came seeking; the woman was sought by Jesus.

A great contrast. Yet the point of the stories is that both the man and the woman needed the gospel and were welcome to it. If Nicodemus is an example of the truth that no one can rise so high as to be above salvation, the woman is an example of the truth that none can sink too low. Thus, it is by no means an accident that John has placed these two wonderful stories together at the beginning of his Gospel and that they end in 4:42, with the Samaritans' statement that "This man really is the Savior of the *world.*"

Do you know the Lord Jesus Christ as your Savior? If you do not, you should learn that the gospel is as much for you as it is for anyone and that you need it as much as did the respected Nicodemus or the immoral woman of Samaria.

A Race without God

The fact that Nicodemus and the woman were different is important. It makes the point I have just elaborated. Yet if we are to proceed further with the story, we need to abandon the differences between the man and the woman at this point and instead concentrate on their similarities. Surprisingly, as we do this we find that the similarities are even more important than the differences and that it is on this basis alone that our study really can go forward.

What is it that Nicodemus and the woman at Sychar's well had in common? One answer is that they both thought that they were all right spiritually. There was an inner hunger, to be sure. This appears in the stories, and I will mention it later. But in their minds, and perhaps also in their entire outlook on life, each thought that he or she was all right. Nicodemus thought so because of his religious and intellectual achievements, the woman because of her superstitions and the religious traditions of the Samaritans. It is noteworthy that in their conviction that all was well when all was not well, Nicodemus and the woman have a great deal in common with the majority of those who live in our own very self-satisfied era.

Second, both Nicodemus and the woman were crudely literal, or materialistic, in their reaction to Jesus' spiritual teaching. In each case Jesus taught about the need for receiving new life from him. But when he spoke of it to Nicodemus, using the image of the new birth, Nicodemus thought that he was talking about obstetrics. And when Jesus spoke to the woman of the possibility of receiving "living water," she thought only in terms of the great distance between her home and Sychar's well and of the joy of not having to carry the heavy waterpots. These reactions were an illustration of the teaching of the apostle Paul given later to the Corinthians; for Paul was speaking of such spiritual blindness when he wrote, "The man without the Spirit does not accept the things that come from the Spirit of God, for they are foolishness to him, and he cannot understand them, because they are spiritually discerned" (1 Cor. 2:14).

Unfortunately, in their naturalistic reaction to Christ's teaching Nicodemus and the woman are also one with men and women of all ages, perhaps, above all, those of our own very materialistic age. Today we are asked, "Hasn't science shown beyond all doubt that we are living within a closed materialistic system and therefore are without and have no need of God?" We are asked, "Aren't the aspects of human behavior that used to be called religious really only a projection of family relationships and therefore entirely explicable in terms of present-day psychology? In fact, isn't religion itself merely a primitive attempt to give meaning to the data of human experience, a task which has now been achieved much more completely and satisfactorily through scientific investigation and discovery?" To persons asking such questions reality is limited to that which the five senses can grasp, and the most important terms of Christianity are meaningless. It follows from this that the twentieth-century materialist, just as certainly as the first-century materialist, needs to meet the Christ of Christianity and come to know the supernatural basis and reality of the Christian faith.

John R. W. Stott of All Souls' Church in London has written that what such people need is to be confronted with what he calls "authentic" Christianity. "Authentic Christianity—the Christianity of Christ and His apostles—is supernatural Christianity. It is not a tame and harmless ethic, consisting of a few moral platitudes, spiced with a dash of religion. It is rather a resurrection religion, a life by the power of God."[1]

Third, Nicodemus and the woman of Samaria had in common the fact that they, like all men and women, were empty spiritually and thus sensed a need for God even though their outlook on life and their intellectual convictions denied it.

Do you sense this need? Many have known and spoken of it even though they may not have known precisely what it was they needed or longed for. One commentator calls attention to an expression of this from the pen of Sinclair Lewis. In one of his books, Lewis writes of a respectable business man who has kicked over the traces and gone off with a girl he thinks he loves. She says to him, "On the surface we seem quite different; but deep down we are fundamentally the same. We are both desperately unhappy about something—and we don't know what it is."[2] The woman at the well could have said this to Nicodemus. Many women could say it to their husbands, many men to their wives. What is this longing? Augustine probably talked about it best when he confessed to God, "Thou hast made us for Thyself, and our hearts are restless until they find their rest in Thee."

Finally, Nicodemus and the woman had in common the fact that they were lost spiritually; that is, in the words of the apostle Paul, they had "sinned and [had fallen] short of the glory of God" (Rom. 3:23). This was the root of all their other problems and was their most significant similarity.

What does it mean to be lost? The dictionary defines "lost" as "ruined, destroyed, having wandered from the way, absorbed, wasted, hardened beyond sensibility or recovery, insensible." If to these definitions we add the thoughts of deliberate waywardness and rebellion, the resulting definition is not far from the biblical teaching about man as he is apart from God. Romans 3:12 tells us that "all have turned away," that we have "together become worthless." In this verse the word that is translated "turned away" means lost as the result of an active, willful departure from God's way. The Greek translation of the Old Testament, the Septuagint, uses the same word 139 times to paint a horrible picture of our rebellious race.

According to God, mankind has willfully abandoned the way to him. "We all, like sheep, have gone astray, each of us has turned to his own way; and the LORD has laid on him the iniquity of us all" (Isa. 53:6). One commentator has written on this point, "We have rejected the law of God, spurned his calls of love, refused his counsel and laughed at his reproof. We have become worse than beasts in our relationship with our Creator. In our language, we speak of 'animal characteristics' in man and call the obstinate ones mulish, dogged, or pigheaded. But God tells us that this is to insult the animal creation, for we read: 'For the LORD hath spoken: I have nourished and brought up children, and they have rebelled against me. The ox knoweth his owner, and the ass, his master's crib; but [my people] know nothing, my people have no intelligence' (Isa. 1:2, 3). And our Lord laments over us, 'Woe to the sinful nation, to the people laden with iniquities, to the race of evil ones, to the rotten children. They have abandoned the Lord. They have despised the Holy One of Israel. They have drawn themselves backwards' (v. 4).

"From Genesis, where we find sinning man hiding among the trees, to Malachi, where God declares 'ye are turned aside out of the way' (Mal. 2:8) there is one long history of sin against love and rejection of grace. The position of man is even worse than that of the Devil, the fallen angels, and the demons. There is no record that there was ever made to them an offer of salvation, but of the human race there is the record that the greatest love of the universe was offered to them and that they wilfully rejected it. The Lord Jesus Christ stands weeping, 'O Jerusalem, Jerusalem, thou that killest the prophets, and stonest them which are sent unto thee, how often would I have gathered thy children together, even as a hen gathered her chickens under her wings, and ye would not' (Matt. 23:37)."[3]

The Way

Let me ask this simple question. What do you need to do when you are lost? You need to find the way back. And what do you need if you are unable to find it? You need a Savior. Imagine yourself without a sure direction, without the necessities of life, without any confidence in the future. What do you do? You look for one who can save you and show you the way home.

That is what Jesus came to do. He came to show a fallen, rebellious race, a race composed of people like Nicodemus, the woman of Samaria, you and me, the way home to God our heavenly Father. Of course, there is one great difference between the salvation that Jesus brought and the salvation that might be brought to someone merely lost in the woods. In the second case, the way need only be shown. In Jesus' case, the way had to be made, as it was, by his death. Jesus died for you in order that he might bear all the judgment and wrath of God that should have fallen on you because of your sin.

Will you come to him? There is no other way. The Bible says that God's righteousness, which is by faith in Jesus, is offered "to all"—that is the true universalism of the Christian faith—but that it comes only "to all who believe" (Rom. 3:22).

45

Living Water

John 4:7-14

When a Samaritan woman came to draw water, Jesus said to her, "Will you give me a drink?" (His disciples had gone into the town to buy food.)

The Samaritan woman said to him, "You are a Jew and I am a Samaritan woman. How can you ask me for a drink?" (For Jews do not associate with Samaritans.)

Jesus answered her, "If you knew the gift of God and who it is that asks you for a drink, you would have asked him and he would have given you living water."

"Sir," the woman said, "you have nothing to draw with and the well is deep. Where can you get this living water? Are you greater than our father Jacob, who gave us the well and drank from it himself, as did also his sons and his flocks and herds?"

Jesus answered, "Everyone who drinks this water will be thirsty again, but whoever drinks the water I give him will never thirst. Indeed, the water I give him will become in him a spring of water welling up to eternal life."

In the city of Philadelphia, where I live, there is a beautiful drive that leads out of the city along the eastern bank of the Schuylkill River. Along the drive there is a section of the riverbank lined with boathouses, called Boathouse Row; and across from Boathouse Row there is a statue of a pilgrim with a Bible under his arm. Many who pass the statue by car never see more than the pilgrim. But if a person is on foot and is exploring the riverbank, he soon finds a stream that empties into the Schuylkill near the pilgrim, as well as a trail that winds along it. If he follows this trail up over Sedgley Hill toward Brewery Town, he comes upon the source of the spring. There, over the spring's source, he sees an inscription

276

once placed by the city government—"Whosoever drinketh of this water shall thirst again."

The quotation over the source of Sedgley spring is true, so far as it goes. No one would think of denying it. But it is only half a quotation. For the other half of the quotation one must turn to Christ's words to the woman of Samaria when she came to Jacob's well to draw water.

As Jesus spoke to the woman about water he made the obvious statement—"Everyone who drinks this water will be thirsty again." But then he also made a second statement, and in this statement there is a great promise. He offered a new kind of water, saying, "Whoever drinks the water I give him will never thirst. Indeed, the water I give him will become in him a spring of water welling up to eternal life" (John 4:14). This promise is the basis for our study in this chapter.

A Weary Christ

It is not often that I have been really thirsty—certainly not in this country—but of one thing about thirst I am convinced: most people understand very little about it until they spend time in a tropical land, particularly an arid and extremely warm land such as the Middle East. Several times when I have been traveling in the Middle East I have found myself in places where a traveler dared not drink the water. I remember vividly how uncomfortable and at times almost desperate one becomes until a place is reached where the water is drinkable and intense thirst can be quenched. People seldom experience this in America and other English-speaking lands. So in our literature water appears often as a symbol of beauty or perhaps (in great quantities) even of destruction but seldom as a symbol for life. It is entirely different in a culture where water is a symbol of that without which a person will surely die.

We must see this as we turn to Jesus' conversation with the woman of Samaria, for the point there is that Jesus is as necessary for spiritual life as water is for physical life.

Jesus had been traveling with his disciples from the area of the lower Jordan to Galilee and had to go through Samaria, as the story tells us (v. 4). This was not entirely true in a purely geographical sense. From the area of the lower Jordan to Galilee there were two routes. One led through Perea on the eastern side of the Jordan to the northern end of the valley where it crossed over into Galilee. The other, the way Jesus took, went through Samaria, the country west of the Jordan. Normally, orthodox Jews would take the eastern route; it was longer but it avoided Samaria. They did this because of their hostility toward the Samaritans. When John tells us, then, that Jesus "must needs" go through Samaria, he obviously means Jesus had to go that way to meet the Samaritan woman.

So Jesus went through Samaria. About noon on the second day of travel he came to the vicinity of the Samaritan town of Sychar. Being tired from his journey, he sat at the foot of the hill leading up to Sychar, on the edge of Jacob's well. The disciples were sent off to the city to buy something to eat while Jesus rested.

What a picture of Jesus! Here was a Jesus who was not wearied merely by the heat. He could have stayed in the cooler area of the Jordan. Here was a Jesus who was wearied in his search for sinners and who had become thirsty seeking those to whom he was to offer the water of life. On the same errand he would one day experience an even greater thirst on the cross. One of the great devotional writers of our time, Geoffrey T. Bull, a missionary the Chinese imprisoned on the Tibetan border from 1950 to 1953 but later released, remarks on this aspect of Jesus' encounter with the woman: "If she could have seen just then what Jesus saw, she would have glimpsed another noonday when the sun would mourn in blackness and this same Stranger cry out from a Roman cross, 'I thirst!' She would have seen in him the shadow of a great rock in a weary land, the smitten Christ from whom the living waters flow. . . . He was thirstier than she knew. He was speaking for the very heart of God. He was moving in the travail of his soul and looked for satisfaction in the restoration of this sin scarred woman."[1]

Jesus became man and experienced all that we experience, but the point of the incarnation is that he did this to redeem men. So if he was weary, thirsty, hot, and on the road to even greater suffering, he was weary and hot for your sake and mine. Jesus suffered for the Nicodemuses, the women of Samaria, and the others whom this world holds. If you are already a believer, perhaps you should ask yourself whether you have ever wearied yourself in the pursuit of other men and women. Have you ever become hot or uncomfortable trying to communicate the gospel to others?

A Thirsty Woman

There is another picture in the first verses of John 4. The one picture is of a wearied Christ. The second is of the woman. She was a Samaritan, and she undoubtedly had had many opportunities to return the hatred of the Jews for the Samaritans by hating the Jews in return. Perhaps she had even had a taste of their hostility a few minutes before meeting Jesus, for she was coming down the hill at the same time that Peter and the other disciples had gone up, and we can be certain that at this stage of their lives, Peter and the others would never have moved off the path for any woman, much less a Samaritan and one with loose morals at that. Perhaps she had been pushed aside or made to wait while the body of Galileans marched by.

Probably she came to the bottom of the hill with this fresh reminder of the hatred of the Jews in her mind, and as soon as she got to the well the first thing that she discovered was another Jew. She could tell he was a Jew by his dress. She was silent. She wasn't about to speak to him! While she was getting ready to lower her bucket into the well, however, Jesus made a request. He asked for a drink. When she remarked at the fact that he, a Jew, should do something as unheard of as to ask water of a Samaritan woman, he aroused her curiosity even further by offering her a new kind of water, "living water," that would be a spring of water within her "welling up to eternal life."

This is always the way it is in the spiritual realm. Jesus comes to us first. If we were left to ourselves, we would leave him sitting on the edge of the well forever. But he does not leave us to ourselves. Instead he comes to us. He asks the first question. He initiates the conversation. He uses all devices to break through to our hearts. Sometimes it is a question, sometimes a command, sometimes a chance remark made by someone else, but it is always from him.

Jesus offered the woman "living water." But what does that mean? What does it mean when he offers it to us? The woman, of course, at first understood the words with crude literalness, just as Nicodemus had understood the words about being "born again" literally. In Jewish speech the phrase "living water" meant water that was flowing, like water in a river or stream, as opposed to water that was stagnant, as in a cistern or well. Living water was considered to be better. Therefore, when Jesus said that he could give her "living water" the woman quite naturally thought of a stream. She wanted to know where Jesus had found it. From the tone of her remarks it is evident that she even thought his claim a bit blasphemous, for it was a claim to have done something greater than her ancestor Jacob had been able to do. Had Jacob been able to find a stream he would certainly not have taken the trouble to dig a well that was roughly a hundred feet deep. This was the level on which the woman was thinking.

Still the phrase should have meant more than this to anyone who was accustomed to thinking biblically. It should have meant more than this to the woman. Many times in the Old Testament God is pictured as the One who alone can supply living water to satisfy the thirst for God that exists in man's soul.

Isaiah wrote, "With joy you will draw water from the wells of salvation" (Isa. 12:3). David said, "As the deer pants for streams of water, so my soul pants for you, O God" (Ps. 42:1). God declared through Jeremiah, "My people have committed two sins: They have forsaken me, the spring of living water, and have dug their own cisterns, broken cisterns that cannot hold water" (Jer. 2:13). In Isaiah 44 God makes the promise, "For I will pour water on the thirsty land" (Isa. 44:3). In chapter 55 he declares, "Come, all you who are thirsty, come to the waters; and you who have no money, come, buy and eat!" (v. 1). Several times in the writings of Ezekiel and Zechariah there is a picture of a river of life flowing out from God's presence in Jerusalem (Ezek. 47:1–12; Zech. 13:1; 14:8). In the New Testament, in the Book of Revelation, there is a reference to these themes in the promises for the end time, "For the Lamb at the center of the throne will be their shepherd; he will lead them to springs of living water. And God will wipe away every tear from their eyes" (Rev. 7:17).

Much of the Old Testament is filled with this pictorial religious language revealing the thirst of the soul, a thirst that can be satisfied only by God. However, the woman chose to misunderstand Christ's words by taking them literally. She was blind because she would not see.

Jesus was claiming to be the One who alone can satisfy human longing. Have you tested his claim? You may try to fill your life with the things of this world—money, fame, power, activity—but though these will satisfy for a time, they will not do so permanently. I have often said that they are like a Chinese dinner. They will fill you up well, but two or three hours later you will be hungry again. Only Jesus Christ is able to satisfy you fully.

A Springing Fountain

There is one more point that is of great importance to this study. Up to now we have been thinking mostly about the phrase "living water" from verse 10. Jesus said, "If you knew the gift of God and who it is that asks you for a drink, you would have asked him and he would have given you living water." This verse is important, but we must not overlook the point that four verses further on, in verse 14, Jesus repeats his offer with a significant variation. In verse 14 he says, "But whoever drinks the water I give him will never thirst. Indeed, the water I give him will become in him a spring of water welling up to eternal life."

No one has ever seen a well of water springing up. Only the water in a spring springs up. The water in a well just lies there. So Jesus is not talking about a well. The woman had come to a well. Jesus has invited her to a spring. Now he adds that if she allows him to place this spring within her, the spring will never cease but will continue to bubble away forever.

Imagine, if you will, that you have just purchased a piece of property upon which you are going to build a house. There is water on the property. If the water is in a well, the water will give you no trouble. If you are there with your bulldozers to clear the ground for your house, all you have to do is push some dirt into the hole and the well will be gone forever so far as you are concerned. It is entirely different, however, if the source of the water on your property is a spring. Try to do the same as you did with the well. You push some dirt over a spring, and it seems to be gone. Five o'clock comes. The workmen go home. But the next morning, when the workmen come back, the stream will be there again, having simply pushed its way through the ground. A well can be covered. A spring seeps through anything you may place over it.

This is what the Lord Jesus Christ is saying. He is promising to place a spring within the life of anyone who will come to him. This spring will be eternal, free, joyous, and self-dependent. But he is also warning you that you will never be able to bulldoze anything over it!

We try, of course. I have done it myself. I know of many who have believed in Christ but who have come to a place in their lives where his way seems inconvenient and who have tried to stifle his presence by piling some foreign substance over the spring. Some have said, "I'm glad that I'm saved, but I'm going to go my way while I'm young. I paid too much attention to religion in my youth. Now I'm just going to cover it up." So they try. But instead of succeeding they discover that God just comes bubbling through.

Let me ask another question: What happens when a spring comes bubbling through dirt? The answer is: It produces muddy water. Is it the spring's fault? No! The fault lies in the dirt that has been pushed on top of it. Does this describe your life? Are you a Christian who has run from God, trying to cover over his presence, but instead only had your life filled with muddy water? If this does describe you, why don't you allow the Lord Jesus Christ to remove the dirt and purify the spring of his life within you?

Let me warn you that you cannot go your own way indefinitely. You will never get away with that. God must be true to his character, and God says that in his holiness he is determined to perfect the image of his Son, the Lord Jesus Christ, within you. If God were to allow you to go any way you want and make a success of it, then he would be a liar when he says that Jesus Christ is the only way, the only truth, and the only life. God is no liar. So he will make a mess of your life, a ruin of your life, if he has to, until you come to the point where you will let him perfect that work in you he began when you first tasted of the Lord Jesus.

Will you yield to him? If you do, he will satisfy any longing that you may ever have had. He put it there in the first place. And he will do with you that which is pleasing in his sight and which will bless others.

46

Facing the Truth

John 4:15–18

The woman said to him, "Sir, give me this water so that I won't get thirsty and have to keep coming here to draw water."

He told her, "Go, call your husband and come back."

"I have no husband," she replied.

Jesus said to her, "You are right when you say you have no husband. The fact is, you have had five husbands, and the man you now have is not your husband. What you have just said is quite true."

Several years ago I heard of a person who had become a nominal Christian because, as he said, he was looking for an "easy" or "comfortable" religion. I was amused when I heard this, but also a bit saddened, for I knew that the person had never understood the first thing about himself or about true Christianity.

Millions of volumes have been written about Christianity, of course. But this should not obscure the fact that at the heart of the faith there is a great simplicity. Christianity presents a twofold revelation. There is the revelation of God, primarily in Jesus Christ; and there is the revelation of ourselves. The two are related. Thus, no one has ever seen God unless at the same time he has seen himself to be a sinner. This has been the experience of all who have seen him—Moses, Isaiah, David, Peter, who, when they saw God, immediately confessed their sin. Conversely, no one has ever really seen himself unless God has been present to reveal the true state of his heart to him.

Another way of saying the same thing is this. Christianity begins by bringing people to the truth about their own depraved condition, but it does so to convince them of their need of Jesus Christ and to prepare them for understanding who he is and what he has accomplished for them by his death and resurrection.

Jesus said, "It is not the healthy who need a doctor, but the sick. I have not come to call the righteous, but sinners" (Mark 2:17). It is only when you and I have recognized the nature of sin and its gravity that we will come to the One who is our soul's physician.

Guilt Exposed

The fact that we all need to recognize our sin and its gravity does not only lie at the heart of some abstract presentation of Christianity, however. It also lies at the heart of some of the most concrete of the biblical stories. In fact, in the story of the encounter of Jesus Christ with the woman of Samaria, which we are now studying, it is both the heart and turning point of the narrative.

Up to verse 15 of the fourth chapter, in which the story is told, much had been said both by the woman and by Jesus, but we cannot feel that any of it has really touched the woman deeply. It is true that Jesus, a Jew, had spoken to her first and so surprised one who had never known anything but scorn from her Jewish neighbors. Still her reaction was not much more than surprise. It is also true that Jesus had aroused her curiosity by offering her a new type of water, "living water," which would be a spring of water within her "welling up to eternal life." But even this offer must have been received lightheartedly and perhaps even humorously by the woman. It was an amusing game, this verbal byplay with the interesting Jew, but it was not serious. Presumably the woman even continued to go about preparing to lower her bucket into the well to draw water.

Suddenly Jesus jolted her to her senses with a single sentence. It was not unkind; everything he said to the woman *was* kind. Still it was a sentence that must have hit the poor woman like a sudden slap in the face and at once have exposed her most serious failing and deep guilt. Jesus said, "Go, call your husband and come back" (v. 16).

At once the woman was recalled to her failure. "I have no husband," she said. She wanted to end that line of discussion as soon as possible.

Jesus said to her, "You are right when you say you have no husband. The fact is, you have had five husbands, and the man you now have is not your husband. What you have just said is quite true" (vv. 17–18). At this point all the woman's pretentions vanished completely, and, although she tried twice thereafter to change the subject (vv. 20 and 25), she knew that all her thoughts and actions were exposed before this man who was able to tell her all that she had ever done.

Not Allegory

It has been held quite widely by a number of New Testament scholars— perhaps in some cases to avoid the implications of Christ's supernatural insight and divinity—that the reference to the five husbands may be allegory; in fact, that the entire story may be allegorical. The basis for this theory lies in the fact that according to 2 Kings 17:29–31, when the original inhabitants of Samaria were exiled by the Assyrians in 721 B.C., people from five different places (each with their own gods) were brought in to replace them. According to this view, the woman would stand for Samaria. The five husbands would stand for the five false gods to whom, it could be said, the Samaritans had married themselves. The sixth man, to whom they were not legally married, would stand for Jehovah whom the Samaritans worshiped, but ignorantly.

This ingenious theory does not bear scrutiny. Thus, the teaching of the story about Christ's supernatural insight and the sinfulness of men and women stands.

In the first place, although it is true that people from five different cities are mentioned in 2 Kings 17:29–31, the fact is that when the gods of these people are mentioned in the same verses, it is not five that are listed but seven. The allegory breaks down at its most significant point. Second, as Leon Morris points out in his commentary, the false gods that are mentioned in 2 Kings were not introduced one after another, as the husbands would be, but were worshiped simultaneously. Third, it is inconceivable that John the evangelist would picture Jesus as speaking of the five false gods as legitimate husbands, while referring to Jehovah as the One with whom the people were living in adultery. The whole of the biblical tradition, which John knew, would reverse that.

No, the situation was real, and Jesus actually saw into the heart of the Samaritan woman. Do you realize that he also sees into your heart? It does not matter what your sin is—whether it is the sin of this woman, that of Moses, David, Peter, or merely the disobedience and rebellion that lurks in each of us. The Bible tells us that "nothing in all creation is hidden from God's sight. Everything is uncovered and laid bare before the eyes of him to whom we must give account" (Heb. 4:13). He sees your heart. He knows all that you have done. Will you accept this? Will you acknowledge your sin before him? If you will, then God has already taken the first step necessary to bring you to him.

All Have Sinned

I know, as I say this, that for many the thought of sin is distasteful. Sin is unpopular, and Christians are often criticized for dwelling too much upon it. This is not because Christians love sin, however. It is simply because Christians are realists. They recognize that sin is an everyday experience and the number one problem of mankind. What is more, they recognize that the Bible everywhere insists upon this.

"The Scripture declares that the whole world is a prisoner of sin," writes Paul (Gal. 3:22). In 1 Kings 8, the chapter that contains King Solomon's great prayer at the dedication of the temple, Solomon declares, "There is no one who does not sin" (v. 46). David wrote, "They are corrupt, their deeds are vile; there is no one who does good" (Ps. 14:1). Psalm 143:2 declares, "No one living is righteous before you." Isaiah observed, "We all, like sheep, have gone astray, each of us has turned to his own way; and the LORD has laid on him the iniquity of us all" (Isa. 53:6). In the New Testament, in the first letter of the apostle John, we are admonished, "If we claim we have not sinned, we make him out to be a liar and his word has no place in our lives" (1 John 1:10).

This is also the burden of the first chapters of Paul's letter to the Romans. It is here, in fact, that we find the doctrine of the universality of man's sin stated in its most comprehensive form. Like a doctor's diagnosis these chapters probe man's spiritual illness; they conclude by declaring that all are incurably sick and that there is no hope for anyone apart from faith in the Lord Jesus Christ and in his atonement.

According to these chapters there are three types of men. The first type is what we would today call a hedonist, the man whose basis for life is materialism. Paul discusses him in Romans 1:18–32. The hedonist does not acknowledge any standard other than those of his own making. Consequently, he has determined to live for his own enjoyment and for whatever extraordinary pleasures he can find. "Why is this man a sinner?" Paul asks. "He is a sinner because he is on a path that is leading him away from God and therefore away from any real beauty, truth, or inner satisfaction." As Paul describes it, this path is marked by empty imaginings, darkened intellects, a profession of wisdom by one who is actually foolish, and finally a perversion of the worship of God that leads to a final abasement of man (vv. 21–23). In finding contemporary examples we do not have to look very far into the world around us.

What should a person do if he has been driving down a road to some destination but has taken a wrong turn? If he knows the country thoroughly, he could try to cut over to where he should be. But if he knew the country that well, he would not have been lost in the first place. Normally the only thing to do is to turn around and go back. It is the same spiritually. Some persons go very carefully down the path I have just been describing and never get far. Others abandon all caution and get quite far along, like the Samaritan woman. But the cure for each is the same. Each must first stop. This is known as repentance. Then he or she must turn around. This is conversion. And the person must go back. The hedonist is a sinner because the way he is taking leads him from God.

The second type of person, the type discussed in Romans 2:1–16, is what we would call a moral man. In Paul's day this was the Greek philosopher or professor of ethics. In our day it would be anyone who has high ethical standards but who does not believe in the Lord Jesus Christ as his Savior. Most people think of themselves in this category.

Why does God consider this person a sinner? The answer has two parts. First, he is a sinner because he has come short of perfection, which is God's standard of righteousness. It is the standard of the life of the Lord Jesus Christ, the only perfect human being who ever lived. Second, he is a sinner because he falls short of his own standards, no matter how high or low they may be.

Let me ask you this question. You probably do not consider yourself a hedonist. You consider yourself a moral person. Well, what is your standard of morality? You may say, "My standard is the Sermon on the Mount. Isn't that a good standard?" Yes, that is a good standard, but the question is not whether or not the Sermon on the Mount is a good standard. The question is: Do you live up to it? In the Sermon on the Mount Jesus said, "Be perfect, therefore, as your heavenly Father is perfect" (Matt. 5:48). Are you perfect? Of course not! In that case, you are condemned by the standard of your own choosing.

You may not like that conclusion, of course. So you may say, "Well, I'll just lower my standard, if that is what the Sermon on the Mount involves. I'll make my standard the Golden Rule—'Do unto others as you would have others do unto you.'" Well, do you keep that standard? Do you always do to other people all that you would like done by them to yourself? Once again, the answer is no! So even the Golden Rule condemns you.

The point is that all of us are condemned by whatever standard we may erect, for none of us is able to live up to even the lowest standards of morality completely and consistently. We are all sinners, and deep within we know it. It is interesting and quite relevant that it was a recognition of these facts—that there are standards and that all men break them—that led as a first step to the conversion of C. S. Lewis, who began as an atheist and agnostic but became the most brilliant Christian apologist of our century.

There is one more type of person, however. Paul describes him in Romans 2:17–29. This is the man who would admit most if not all of what I have been saying and yet who would attempt to escape the conclusions by maintaining his faith in religion. "I have been baptized," he would say. "I am confirmed. I have given large sums of money to the church's support and served on its committees." "Well, good for you," Paul answers, "but you are still a sinner."

"Me, a sinner? Why?"

"Because God requires a complete perfection, including a change of the heart," Paul answers, "and none of the outward accouterments of religion—church membership, the sacraments, service, or stewardship—can do anything about it."

In the city of Basel, Switzerland, where I lived for three years, there is a carnival each year called *Fashnacht*. It is much like the Mardi Gras that is celebrated in predominantly Catholic countries or Catholic areas of a country, but it is held during the first week of Lent instead of before it, presumably to show that Basel is Protestant. Whatever the case, *Fashnacht* certainly does not show the city to be Christian in the biblical sense, for the carnival is always a time of riotous behavior in which the normally restrained and stolid Baselers let themselves go morally. Everyone knows what goes on. There are even jokes about it. But no one knows precisely who is doing what because the revelers wear masks. Each year during *Fashnacht,* however, the Salvation Army makes an attempt to challenge people to a higher standard of conduct by placing large posters around the city bearing the German inscription *"Gott sieht hinter deine Maske. "* This means, "God sees behind your mask." The point is that God knows what is going on within and who is doing it.

The Lord Jesus Christ is looking into your heart and mind. What does he see? Does he see all that you have done and are doing, unconfessed and demanding his judgment? Must he say of you, "There is no one righteous, not even one; there is no one who understands, no one who seeks God. All have turned away, they have together become worthless; there is no one who does good, not even one" (Rom. 3:10–12)? And is there no more to say? Or can he look at you as one who is indeed a sinner, but whose sin has been judged in his death and who now stands before him clothed in God's own righteousness?

This is the gospel. All have indeed "sinned and fall short of the glory of God" (Rom. 3:23). But "there is now no condemnation for those who are in Christ Jesus" (Rom. 8:1).

The Invitation

I know that, as a result of this study, there may be some who have seen something of their own sinfulness, and I know that the first reaction upon seeing one's sin is to back off in despair. "If I am really so sinful," a person asks, "how can God love me? How can he have anything to do with me?" If you are saying that, I must not close without showing you one more phrase in Christ's words to the Samaritan woman. What did Jesus say to the woman? He said, "Go, call your husband"—that is true; it was an attempt to establish her sinfulness—but he finished the sentence by saying, "But when you have done that come back again."

"Go, call your husband." That was a word for her conscience. "Come back again." That was a word for her heart.

In the same way he speaks to you. You must see your need. You need to face the truth about your own condition. Yet you must also hear his warm invitation. "Come to me" (Matt. 11:28). The way is open. Say, "Yes, I am coming, Lord Jesus."

47

Salvation Is of the Jews

John 4:19-22

"Sir," the woman said, "I can see that you are a prophet. Our fathers worshiped on this mountain, but you Jews claim that the place where we must worship is in Jerusalem."

Jesus declared, "Believe me, woman, a time is coming when you will worship the Father neither on this mountain nor in Jerusalem. You Samaritans worship what you do not know; we worship what we do know, for salvation is from the Jews."

I do not know what Emily Post, Amy Vanderbilt, or Miss Manners would have thought of the Lord Jesus Christ if they had been living in the first Christian century and had heard him teaching the people and speaking to them. But I am sure that if they had overheard his conversation with the woman of Samaria, which we have been studying, at one point at least they would all have pronounced him bigoted and intolerable. Jesus had spoken to the woman of Samaria about her sin, reminding her that she was living with a man to whom she was not married, and this would be bad enough to one who thinks first of all of etiquette. But then, after the woman had obviously and politely tried to change the subject by asking the Lord's opinion on the rival Jewish and Samaritan claims about God and the forms of proper worship, Jesus actually claimed that in his day at least the Jewish way of worship was the only valid one and that the Samaritans knew nothing spiritually.

288

"Sir," the woman said, "I can see that you are a prophet. Our fathers worshiped on this mountain, but you Jews claim that the place where we must worship is in Jerusalem" (vv. 19–20). She was about to go on by asking which way was correct but Jesus anticipated her, interrupting. He said, "Believe me, woman, a time is coming when you will worship the Father neither on this mountain nor in Jerusalem. You Samaritans worship what you do not know; we worship what we do know, for salvation is from the Jews" (vv. 21–22).

If the question of the woman were asked in our day, no doubt many would attempt to sidestep it. Many preachers and even many theologians would answer by some vague appeal to ecumenicity or to the general areas of agreement among most of the world's religions. Some would be embarrassed. Jesus took none of these approaches. Instead of dodging the question or merely attempting to be polite, Jesus spoke forcefully, acknowledging that the Jews had filled a unique place in the history of salvation—in fact, that there was no salvation apart from them—but then pointing to the day when all national distinctions would pass away and when men and women would worship God in spirit and in truth on the basis of faith in his death and resurrection.

Why did he say this? To understand why Jesus answered as he did is to understand the way of salvation more perfectly and to move away from all forms of human religion—whether of Jew or Gentile—toward a true religion based on God's grace.

Rival Religions

Before we can come to this point, however, we need to understand something of the rivalry that existed between the Jews and the Samaritans. About 750 years before Christ's conversation with the woman, when the northern half of the Jewish nation, the nation of Israel, had been carried off into captivity by the Assyrians, the conquering people had moved other people back into the area to resettle it. This move is described in the Old Testament in 2 Kings 17, where we are also told that the settlers were sent out from the five city-kingdoms of Babylon, Cuth, Hamath, Ava, and Sepharah.

It is not possible to transport an entire population, of course. So the result was that some Jewish people remained. Perhaps they had hidden in caves, bribed their captors, or escaped captivity. Almost at once these Jews began to intermarry with the newcomers, thereby producing a race that was partially Jewish and partially Assyrian. For the orthodox Jew this was an almost unforgivable sin. It was, in fact, forbidden in the Old Testament. Therefore, in the eyes of the pure-blooded Jews who remained in the southern kingdom of Judah, those who remained in the north actually lost their right to be considered Jews at all and forfeited their heritage.

In time the same type of defeat that had resulted in the captivity of the northern kingdom also befell the south. The southern Jews did not lose their identity, however. For seventy years they were held in captivity by the

Babylonians. Nevertheless, when the exiles returned from Babylon at the end of that period and began to rebuild their city and its temple, they were still Jewish and were proud of their heritage. Perhaps for this reason and perhaps also because of the teaching of the law, the southern Jews refused help in rebuilding the temple when such help was offered to them by the Samaritans in about 450 B.C. In anger the Samaritans then built their own temple on Mount Gerizim in Samaria, contrary to the law. This was the temple to which the Samaritan woman referred. Eventually this became a rival temple, and the religion of the Samaritans became a rival religion.

What was the status of this temple? What was the status of the Samaritan faith? These were the questions at issue, and it was these that Jesus was answering.

In answering them it is interesting that Jesus did not stress racial superiority. There could be no question of racial pride simply because Jesus was in Samaria to win the Samaritans. Nevertheless, the Samaritan religion was a man-made religion, and Jesus would not allow the Samaritan woman to believe that any religion of human origin, a religion based on human ideas, is acceptable to Jehovah. Human religion was not acceptable then, and it is not acceptable today. Accordingly, salvation was of the Jews alone because only the Jews possessed a religion that had its origin in God. Moreover, it was only in Judaism, with its system of sacrifices and temple worship that there was any true sense of the holiness of God and of the necessity of a substitutionary sacrifice as the grounds of forgiveness and of an acceptable approach to him.

Since this is a difficult point, let me say it again in other terms. Salvation is always of God's grace, not of human merit; and since grace was offered to the sinner on the grounds of the death of an atoning sacrifice and since in Christ's time that sacrifice could only be offered at Jerusalem by a legitimate priest, a descendant of Aaron, it is obvious that there could be no salvation for anyone except through the Jewish priesthood which in turn was available only to a circumcised member of one of the tribes of Israel. Jesus was impressing this upon the woman, thereby reasserting the right of God to establish the means of approach to him and encouraging her to turn from any trust in human religions.

Gentile Salvation

I do not know whether the record of the conversation between Jesus and the woman of Samaria that we have in John 4 is the whole of the conversation. It may be only an attenuated version. But I do know that if Jesus had gone on to explain these truths to the woman, he could have drawn on three great examples from the Old Testament.

The first example he could have drawn upon was Ruth. Ruth was a Moabitess, a foreigner who had been married to the son of a Jewish woman named Naomi. She had met her husband in Moab, where Naomi and her sons had gone during a period of famine in Israel. The sons had died, and when Naomi decided to return to her own land Ruth, her daughter-in-law, determined to go with her. Ruth had apparently learned from Naomi during the years they were together, and she had come to worship Naomi's God. At first Naomi tried to persuade Ruth to remain in Moab, but Ruth would have none of it. Ruth replied, "Don't urge me to leave you or to turn back from you. Where you go I will go, and where you stay I will stay. Your people will be my people and your God my God" (Ruth 1:16). These are beautiful words, but I am afraid that the beauty of the words has kept many persons from noticing the far more important ordering of the thought. Ruth wanted to join Naomi in the true worship of Jehovah. But notice, she could not say "Your God will be my God" until she had first said "Your people will be my people." In her statement Ruth confessed her need for a change in nationality before there could be a change in her God.

A second example of this truth can be seen in the account of Naaman, the Syrian. He was a general of the most powerful state of his day. He was strong and respected. There is no reason to think that he was any less ruthless than any other military commander. He was feared. Yet he was also pitied, for somewhere along the way he had contracted leprosy, and there was no known cure.

Through a young Jewish slave girl, who had doubtlessly been captured during one of his raids, Naaman learned of the existence in Israel of Elisha who (he had been told) could cure him. He went to Palestine. But when Elisha refused even to come out to meet him and instead merely sent him word that he was to wash himself seven times in the Jordan, all the national pride of the general rose to the surface, and he expressed his scorn of the muddy river that could not even begin to compare, he said, with the beautiful rivers of his country. As he cooled down, however, a servant helped him to change his mind. "It's worth a try," the servant argued. "If Elisha had asked for a ton of gold, you would have given him that. Why not dip in the river? Try it. You've come a long way. It will cost you nothing." Naaman did and was cured.

Now, however, there follows the significant part of the story. Naaman did something strange. He asked for several sacks of dirt. Naaman explained, "Please let me, your servant, be given as much earth as a pair of mules can carry, for your servant will never again make burnt offerings and sacrifices to any other god but the LORD" (2 Kings 5:17).

Think what that means! We must imagine that the work is done and the caravan of horses with their riders, followed by the mules with their burden of dirt, returns to Syria. Word runs ahead that Naaman is returning and that he is cured of leprosy. There is a joyous reception when the travelers arrive. But then, before the night comes and Naaman retires, the dirt that has been brought from Israel is poured into a frame made to receive it, and Naaman takes his place upon the earth of Palestine to pray to Jehovah—a Gentile who is willing to come as a Jew, relying on the same grace that was shown by the Jews' God when he healed him.

The final story comes from Esther. It reveals the same truth. In Esther's day there had been a dirty little bit of anti-Semitism that arose because Haman, a high Persian official, hated a Jew named Mordecai. Esther, the adopted daughter of Mordecai, intervened, and the gallows built for Mordecai by Haman bore Haman's body instead. The people were saved. It was a great day, and there was much rejoicing. It was also a great demonstration of the power of the Jews' God to preserve them, and this fact caused many of the Persians to believe on him: "And many people of other nationalities became Jews because fear of the Jews had seized them" (Esther 8:17). What does that mean? It is simply the Old Testament's way of saying that many of the Persians were saved. They became Jews, being admitted to one of the Jewish tribes, and then were permitted to bring their sacrifices to a Jewish priest and to receive God's forgiveness on the ground of the death of the substitute.

Salvation for All

These three examples are enough to show that Jesus was entirely in line with the Old Testament tradition when he declared that before his time the Gentiles had to become Jews in order to be saved. But we must not overlook the fact that at the same time that he was reaffirming these truths, Jesus also predicted a change that was to come shortly. It is true that salvation was of the Jews, but soon the offer of salvation was to be broadened to include all persons—Jews and Gentiles—and the way of approach was to be revealed as faith in the only complete and perfect sacrifice that he alone would provide by dying for sinners.

God did not nullify his promises to Israel. He fulfilled them in Christ. Thus, the day came when the long period of preparation with its sacrifices and temple worship came to an end. At the very moment when Christ died there was an earthquake. The veil of the temple, which had divided the holy place of the temple from the Holy of Holies, through which only the high priest could pass—and that only once a year on the Day of Atonement—was torn in two from top to bottom. Thus God signified that henceforth he was done with sacrifices. The final sacrifice, Jesus of Nazareth, had been offered. The priesthood, too, was ended. Now only Christ was high priest. Even the temple was superceded, for now the only way to God was through Jesus.

Do you believe these things? If you do, you are today among those who can come boldly to the throne of grace through Jesus Christ and can find grace to help in your need. You do not have to make a pilgrimage to present your sacrifice. You do not need to change your race. All that you have to do is abandon your own efforts to obtain salvation and come to God by faith in him who declared himself to be the way, the truth, and the life (John

14:6). If you do, you will find him to be all that the Scriptures declared him to be. He is the Son of God—the Savior.

To Jew and Gentile

The Christian belief that Jesus of Nazareth is the Messiah who fulfilled all to which the sacrifices pointed cannot be entirely acceptable to those who are steeped in the Jewish religion and who wish to retain their Judaism. Nothing but a sellout to a watered-down doctrine of universalism will make the Christian religion universally popular. But at the same time Jewish people must recognize that apart from Jesus Christ and under the Old Testament laws, there is no way in this day for me, a Gentile, to approach the Holy One of Israel. To do that I would have to abandon my own nationality and then be initiated into one of the twelve tribes of Israel (which is impossible because their identity has been lost). I would then have to bring a lamb as an atonement for my sin to the high priest (who no longer exists) and have it sacrificed by him on the altar of a temple in Jerusalem at a site now occupied by a Mohammedan mosque.

There is no other way of salvation for a Gentile under the teaching of the Old Testament. Salvation is of the Jews. So if Jesus is not the Messiah, the one through whom the blessing of Abraham is to come upon the nations, the *goyim,* then today all who cannot bring their sacrifices are lost. The veil still hangs before the holy presence of Jehovah; the wall of partition between the Jew and Gentile still stands. It is only through Jesus' shed blood, the blood of the perfect sacrifice, to which all the Old Testament sacrifices point, that I stand cleansed and spotless before God. It is only through him that I share with the believing Jew a vital and transforming access to God's presence.

At the same time the Gentiles must be reminded that the fact that Jesus was a Jew is itself a great and definitive blow against all anti-Jewish prejudice. Moreover, the fact that he endorsed the Old Testament must draw me toward it. To love the Lord Jesus Christ more is to love the Jew more. It is to rejoice in God's continued and evident blessing upon the Jews, to pray for the peace of Jerusalem, and to look for the time when (according to the prophetic books of the Bible) God will again use the Jews to bring new and added blessing upon the nations.

48

How to Worship God

John 4:23-24

"Yet a time is coming and has now come when the true worshipers will worship the Father in spirit and truth, for they are the kind of worshipers the Father seeks. God is spirit, and his worshipers must worship in spirit and in truth."

Christian worship is the most momentous, the most urgent, the most glorious action that can take place in human life."

These words by the noted Swiss theologian Karl Barth undoubtedly find an echo in the hearts of all who truly know God and earnestly desire to serve him, regardless of their opinion of Barth's theology. But in spite of the obvious truth that the worship of God is an important and even urgent imperative for Christians, it is a sad fact that in our day much that passes for worship is not worship at all, and many who sincerely desire to worship do not always know how to go about it or where to begin. "What is worship anyway?" some ask. "Who can worship? Where can one worship? How does one worship?" ask others.

One Bible student has written: "Thanks to our splendid Bible societies and to other effective agencies for the dissemination of the Word, there are today many millions of people who hold 'right opinions,' probably more than ever before in the history of the church. Yet I wonder if there was ever a time when true spiritual worship was at a lower ebb. To great sections of the church the art of worship has been lost entirely, and in its place has come

294

that strange and foreign thing called the 'program.' This word has been borrowed from the stage and applied with sad wisdom to the type of public service which now passes for worship among us."[1]

Are these words true, even in part? Are the questions I have just repeated genuine? If so, there is an answer for them all in the words of Jesus. Jesus said, "Yet a time is coming and has now come when the true worshipers will worship the Father in spirit and truth, for they are the kind of worshipers the Father seeks. God is spirit, and his worshipers must worship in spirit and in truth" (John 4:23–24).

Worship Is Essential

Before we begin to look at these words in detail, however, we must first of all see that worship itself is an important subject and that these are important verses for dealing with it.

There are several ways of showing this. For instance, in Philippians 3:3 the apostle Paul speaks of worship as one of the three great marks that reveal the presence of the new nature within the Christian. He writes: "For it is we who are the circumcision, we who worship by the Spirit of God, who glory in Christ Jesus, and who put no confidence in the flesh." Most Christians would quickly acknowledge the last of these points. It is a question of holding to the true gospel. Many would also think highly of the second point, for joy is important. It is a mark of the Spirit, according to the fifth chapter of Galatians. I strongly suspect, however, that not many think of the worship of God as a mark of the presence of the new nature within. Yet in this verse it is included along with the other essentials.

Another way of making this point is to note that there are three great "musts" in John's Gospel. The first "must" occurs in 3:7, where Jesus says, "you *must* be born again." The second "must" is in verse 14 of the same chapter. There Jesus says, "The Son of Man *must* be lifted up." The verses we are studying give us the third "must," for they tell us that all who worship God "*must* worship in spirit and in truth." These three great doctrines—the necessity for the new birth, the necessity of Christ's death, and the necessity of true worship—belong together.

Perhaps it is not even irrelevant to point out that this is the major passage in which John deals with the nature and necessity of worship, for of the thirteen uses of the words "worship" or "worshiper" in John's Gospel, ten of them occur in this section, and it is only here that worship is actually discussed and defined.

Spiritual Worship

What is worship? Part of the answer is to be seen in the fact that if you and I had been living in England during the days of the early formation of the English language, between the period of Geoffrey Chaucer and William

Shakespeare, we would not have used the word "worship" at all. We would have said "worth-ship," and we would have meant that in worshiping God we were assigning to God his true worth. Philologically speaking, this is the same thing as "praising" God or "glorifying" his name.

If someone should ask the two most important questions that follow from that definition, however—namely, "What is God's true worth?" and "How do we become aware of it?"—we are immediately brought to the heart of Christ's words to the Samaritan woman. For Jesus said that those who acknowledge God's true worth must do so "in spirit and in truth." In other words, they must do so "in truth" because truth has to do with what his nature is, and they must do so "in spirit" because they can only apprehend it spiritually.

Let me explain that a bit further. Many persons have been led astray in thinking that when Jesus spoke of "spirit" in this verse he was speaking of the Holy Spirit. I do not believe that this is the case. There is a sense, of course, in which we only come to worship God after the Holy Spirit has been at work in our hearts moving us to do so. But in this verse Jesus is not speaking of that. He is speaking of spirit generally (without the definite article), not *the* Holy Spirit, and he is teaching that in the age he was inaugurating by his death and resurrection the place of worship would not matter, for a man or a woman would not worship merely by being in the right place and doing certain right things. He would worship in his spirit, which could be anywhere.

I can make this even clearer by placing it in the context of the three parts of man's nature. Man is a trinity. He has a body, soul, and spirit. Jesus is saying that nothing is true worship of God except what takes place in man's spirit.

Many people worship with the body. This means that they consider themselves to have worshiped if they have been in the right place doing the right things at the right time. In Christ's day the woman thought this meant being either in Jerusalem, at the temple there, or on Mount Gerezim at the Samaritans' temple. In our day this would refer to people who think they have worshiped God simply because they have occupied a seat in a church on Sunday morning, or sung a hymn, or lit a candle, or crossed themselves, or knelt in the aisle. Jesus says this is not worship. These customs may be vehicles for worship. In some cases they may also hinder it. But they are not worship in themselves. Therefore, we must not confuse worship with the particular things we do on Sunday morning.

In addition, however, we must not confuse worship with feeling, for worship does not originate with the soul any more than it originates with the body. The soul is the seat of our emotions. It may be the case, and often is, that the emotions are stirred in real worship. At times tears fill the eyes or joy floods the heart. But, unfortunately, it is possible for these things to happen and still no worship to be there. It is possible to be moved by a song or by oratory and yet not come to a genuine awareness of God and a fuller praise of his ways and nature.

True worship occurs only when that part of man, his spirit, which is akin to the divine nature (for God is spirit), actually meets with God and finds itself praising him for his love, wisdom, beauty, truth, holiness, compassion, mercy, grace, power, and all his other attributes. William Barclay has written on this point, "The true, the genuine worship is when man, through his spirit, attains to friendship and intimacy with God. True and genuine worship is not to come to a certain place; it is not to go through a certain ritual or liturgy; it is not even to bring certain gifts. True worship is when the spirit, the immortal and invisible part of man, speaks to and meets with God, who is immortal and invisible."[2]

Liturgy

Incidentally, the truth that we are to worship God in spirit also has bearing upon the question of the various types of liturgy used in Christian churches, for it means that, with the exception of liturgical elements that suggest wrong doctrine, there is no liturgy that in itself is either inherently better or worse than another. For any given congregation, one type of service will presumably be more valuable than another. But the decision regarding what that type of service will be ought to be arrived at—not by asking whether one likes emotional or nonemotional hymns, extemporaneous or read prayers, congregational responses or silence—in short, whether one prefers Anglican, Lutheran, Presbyterian, Methodist, Baptist, Congregational, or Quaker services—but by asking how effective the service is in turning the attention of the worshiper away from the service itself to God. In this respect an order of worship is to be evaluated on the same basis that we use to evaluate the preacher.

In thinking through this particular issue I have been helped by the concepts of C. S. Lewis. Lewis was a member of the Church of England and was accustomed to various forms of what we generally call a "liturgical" service. Nevertheless, Lewis did not plead for liturgy. He asked merely for what he called "uniformity," on the grounds that "novelty" in the worship service at best turns our attention to the novelty but may actually turn it to the one who is enacting the liturgy.

Lewis wrote, "As long as you notice, and have to count the steps, you are not yet dancing but only learning to dance. A good shoe is a shoe you don't notice. Good reading becomes possible when you need not consciously think about eyes, or light, or print, or spelling. The perfect church service would be one we were almost unaware of; our attention would have been on God."[3] We should pray that God will use any form of church service in which we happen to be participating to that great and essential end.

Worship in Truth

Finally, we need to notice that the true worship of God is a worship not only in spirit but in truth. What does that mean? What does it mean to worship God "in truth"?

First, it means that we must approach God *truthfully,* that is, honestly or wholeheartedly. That is what Jesus was referring to in a negative way when he said of the people of his day, "These people honor me with their lips, but their hearts are far from me. . . . they worship me in vain" (Matt. 15:8–9). According to Jesus, no worship is true worship unless there is an honesty of heart on the part of the worshiper. We must not pretend to worship. We must worship truthfully, knowing that our hearts are open books before God.

Second, we must worship on the basis of the *biblical revelation.* This is also implied in the verses I have just quoted. For the verse that begins "They worship me in vain" immediately goes on to condemn those who have substituted "rules taught by men" for the doctrines of Scripture. "Your word is truth," says the Scripture (John 17:17). So if we are to worship "in truth," as God commands us to do, our worship must be in accord with the principles and admonitions of this book.

When the Protestant Reformation first took place under Martin Luther in the early sixteenth century and the doctrines and principles of the Word of God, long covered over by the traditions and encrustations of ceremony of the medieval church, again came forth into prominence, there was an immediate elevation of the Word of God in Protestant services. Calvin particularly carried this out with thoroughness, ordering that the altars (long the center of the Latin mass) be removed from the churches and that a pulpit with a Bible upon it be placed in the center of the building. This was not to be on one side of the room, but in the very center, where every line of the architecture would carry the gaze of the worshiper to the Book that alone contains the way of salvation and outlines the principles upon which the church of the living God is to be governed.

Finally, to approach God "in truth" also means that we must approach God Christocentrically. This means "in Christ," for this is God's way of approach to him. Jesus himself signified this when he said to his disciples, "I am the way and the truth and the life. No one comes to the Father except through me" (John 14:6). This is a difficult point for many to accept, of course. But it is precisely because of the difficulty that God has taken such pains to teach that this is the way of approach to him. We see this even in the Old Testament in the instructions given to Moses for the design of the Jewish temple.

What was the original tabernacle? It was not an edifice of great beauty or permanence. It had no stained-glass windows, no great arches. It was made of pieces of wood and animal skins. Nevertheless every part of it was significant. The tabernacle taught the way to God. Take that tabernacle with its altar for sacrifice, its laver for cleansing, its Holy Place, and its Holy of Holies, and you have a perfect illustration of how a person must approach God. The altar, which is the first thing we come to, is the cross of Christ. It was given to teach that without the shedding of blood there is no remission of sins and to direct attention to the Lamb of God who should come to take away the sins of the world. The laver, which comes next, is a picture of cleansing, which Christ also provides when we confess our sins and enter into fellowship with him. The table of shewbread, which was within the Holy Place, speaks of Christ as the bread of life. The altar of incense is a picture of prayer, for we grow by prayer as well as by feeding on Christ in Bible study. Behind the altar of incense was the great veil, dividing the Holy Place from the Holy of Holies. This was the veil torn in two at the moment of Christ's death to demonstrate that his death was the fulfillment of all these figures and the basis of the fullness of approach to the Almighty. Finally, within the Holy of Holies was the ark of the covenant with its mercy seat upon which the high priest placed the blood of the lamb once a year on the Day of Atonement. There, symbolized by the space above the mercy seat, was the presence of God into whose presence we can now come because of the great mercy of God revealed in the death of Christ for us.

There is no other way to come to God. To come through Christ—the Christ of the altar, laver, shewbread, incense, veil, and mercy seat—is to come in truth. He is the truth. You must come in God's way and not in any way of human devising.

An Inexhaustible God

The wonder of Christian worship is that when we come to God in the way which he has established, we find him inexhaustible and discover that our desire to know and worship him further is increased. Bernard of Clairvaux was one who knew this. He wrote toward the middle of the twelfth century:

> Jesus, thou Joy of loving hearts,
>   Thou Fount of life, thou Light of men,
> From the best bliss that earth imparts
>   We turn unfilled to thee again.
> We taste thee, O thou living Bread,
>   And long to feast upon thee still;
> We drink of thee, the Fountainhead,
>   And thirst our souls from thee to fill.

When we so come, when we worship in that way, we find ourselves approaching what the compilers of the Westminster Shorter Catechism rightly described as the chief end of man. The catechism asks, "What is the chief end of man?" It answers, "Man's chief end is to glorify God, and to enjoy him *forever*."

49

"I Am He"

John 4:25-26

The woman said, "I know that Messiah" (called Christ) "is coming. When he comes, he will explain everything to us."

Then Jesus declared, "I who speak to you am he."

Did you ever stop to think that the character and accomplishments of a person can be summarized by the various names that are given to him during the course of his life? Or did you ever realize that it is sometimes possible to give a whole biography of a person through names alone?

Let me do this for the life of Julius Caesar, the great Roman general and emperor. The earliest name of Julius Caesar was Julius or Jules. As he grew older it would have been Julius Gaius, involving the family name. Titles were added that were earned throughout his career: soldier, general, quaestor, consul. He was elected Pontifex Maximus, Tribune, and Caesar. Finally, as the feeling of his contemporaries turned against him, Julius became an "ambitious ruler" and finally an "enemy of the people." A person who knows these titles as well as the details of how they were given to Caesar could easily sum up the whole career of the Roman emperor by means of them.

The same thing is true of the names of Jesus Christ. Only here the names are much more important. The names of Caesar are names given by men in recognition of his work. The names of Jesus are names given by God in order to reveal Christ's divine nature and the significance of his ministry. Thus, we know Jesus as the Word of God; the Lamb of God, who takes away the sin of the world; the Son of God; the Son of man; the Savior; the Light of the world; the Lord; the Beloved; our great High Priest; the Conqueror; the King. Some of these titles have already been studied briefly in our survey of the first chapter of John's Gospel, where they occur. These are great names. No wonder Isaac Watts wrote in one of his hymns:

> Join all the glorious names
>   Of wisdom, love and power,
> That ever mortals knew,
>   That angels ever bore:
> All are too mean to speak his worth,
>   Too mean to set my Savior forth.

We come now to a name that is in some respects greater than them all.

"I AM THAT I AM"

We must remember at this point that Jesus had been talking to the woman of Samaria about her sin and of her need for "living water." She had tried to change the course of the conversation on several occasions, first by asking Jesus where it was that men and women ought to worship—in Jerusalem or in Samaria—and then by attempting to postpone any final commitments until the Messiah should come. The woman said, "I know that Messiah is coming. When he comes, he will explain everything to us." Jesus answered her briefly in one great sentence, "I who speak to you am he" (John 4:25–26). Apparently, this truth finally broke through to the woman's consciousness, and she left her water jar to go back to the city, calling, "Come, see a man who told me everything I ever did. Could this be the Christ?" (v. 29). The words of Jesus were undoubtedly the turning point in the woman's conversion.

Unfortunately, the full import of Christ's claim is obscured by the English translation. As we read the words, they seem to express no more than the claim: "Yes, I am the Messiah." That is important in itself, of course, and we shall come back to it. Nevertheless it is less than the words imply. Actually, the words are a title. To be precise, Jesus did not really say, "I am *he*." The "he" has been added by the English translators. He simply said, "I am." The point of his claim is that the title "I am" was similar to, if not identical with, the great Old Testament name for God: Jehovah.

At this point we can understand why it is possible to call this title—"I am"—the greatest of all names for the Lord Jesus Christ. It is possible to understand why Paul wrote of him: "Therefore God exalted him to the highest place and gave him the name that is above every name, that at the name of Jesus every knee should bow, in heaven and on earth and under the earth" (Phil. 2:9–10). The name which is above all other names is "Lord," which means "Jehovah." This is in its turn an exact equivalent of the words "I am."

This is God's own name. Thus, the name is above all earthly names, and it is at this name—Jehovah, Lord, "I am"—that all beings in heaven and earth shall bow.

How much of this registered with the woman of Samaria we do not know. We do know that several other times during his ministry Jesus used the words "I am" to refer to his deity. He once said to the Jews, "If you do not believe that I am the one I claim to be, you will indeed die in your sins" (John 8:24). That meant that they would not be saved unless they recognized that he was God. We also know that even the Jews themselves once took the word in this sense, for later in the same conversation, after Jesus had explained more clearly who he was and had said, "Before Abraham was born, *I am*" (v. 58), we read that those listening to Jesus attempted to stone him for blasphemy.

In all, the claim of Christ to be the great "I am" occurs seven times in John's Gospel (in 4:26; 6:20; 8:24, 28, 58; 13:19; 18:5), always as an expression of his claim to be God. And there are seven other very important instances in which the words are coupled with a noun describing him as the source of all good and the answer to all man's needs. Jesus said, "I am the bread of life" (6:35) . . . "the light of the world" (8:12, 9:5) . . . "the gate" (10:7, 9) . . . "the good shepherd" (10:11, 14) . . . "the resurrection and the life" (11:25) . . . "the way and the truth and the life" (14:6) . . . and "the true vine" (15:1, 5).

Obviously, not all of this was known to the woman or even could be known to her. Yet, the use of God's name—Jehovah—could not fail to be striking. "Can this be the Messiah?" she must have asked. "Is he a spokesman for God? Is he one who is so close to God that he can use God's name of himself?" No doubt she was pondering these questions as she went off to call others to the One "who told me everything I ever did."

The Messiah

Whatever may have been the woman's understanding of Christ's claim to be God—and she may have understood much more than we think—there can be no doubt that the woman fully understood that he was at the very least claiming to be the Messiah. The Samaritans were expecting the Messiah, as were the Jews. When the woman exclaimed, "When he comes, he will explain everything to us," she was probably thinking of the prophecy of the coming of the Messiah that is found in Deuteronomy 18:18. In that verse God told Moses of a coming prophet who should tell the people "all things."

Actually, in some ways the Samaritan expectation of the Messiah was purer than that of the Jews themselves, for it did not have the political overtones that the idea had in Judaism. Jesus was always careful not to admit to being the Messiah in the sense the Jews gave it. Although the Samaritan view was imperfect, it was not false. They looked for a prophet. Thus, Jesus did accept the title when they gave it to him.

In Hebrew the word *mashiach*, which gives us the word "Messiah," means "the anointed one," as does the Greek word "Christ." This in turn refers to the fact that during certain periods of Old Testament history a man chosen by God for a special ministry was consecrated to that ministry by a ceremony in which his head was anointed with oil. That was the way in which kings were set apart for their royal office, for instance. To give one example, it was the way in which Samuel signified God's choice of the young shepherd boy, David, to be the future king, replacing the disobedient King Saul (1 Sam. 16:13; cf. 10:1). This was the way the high priests were installed in their offices (cf. Exod. 28:41). It was even true that on some occasions at least prophets were also anointed, for Elijah anointed his successor Elisha with oil before he himself was taken up into heaven (1 Kings 19:16). The anointed one—whether prophet, priest, or king—was a person set apart by God for a special task.

In time this general meaning of "messiah" acquired a more specific one, for God had promised to send a deliverer who would embody everything that the previous anointing could only faintly symbolize. He would be a great prophet, for he would fulfill God's words to Moses: "I will raise up for them a prophet like you from among their brothers; I will put my words in his mouth, and he will tell them everything I command him" (Deut. 18:18). He would be a great priest, for he would present the perfect sacrifice for man's sin. Finally, he would be a great king, for he would reign forever on the throne of King David (2 Sam. 7:11–16).

A prophet! A priest! A king! This was what Jesus claimed in his conversation with the woman of Samaria. He claimed that all the promises concerning a deliverer of Israel and of the nations were fulfilled in him. He was the One for whom the human race had been waiting.

Two Genealogies

Either Jesus of Nazareth is God's Messiah, as he claimed to be, or else there will never be a Messiah. The evidence is in the two genealogies of Jesus found in Matthew and Luke, for according to these accounts, Jesus exhausts all messianic lines of descent from King David.

This proof of Jesus' messiahship has been set forth by many scholars, especially in the early centuries of church history. It has been stated since by James Orr of Scotland. Let me quote from a more recent and particularly lively statement by Donald Grey Barnhouse. "First . . . there [are] two genealogies. The lines [of descent] run parallel from Abraham to David, but then Matthew comes down to Jesus by way of Solomon, the son of David, while Luke comes down to Jesus by way of Nathan, the son of David. In other words, the two genealogies are the lines of two brothers and the children become cousins. . . . The whole point of the difference lies in the fact that Solomon's line was the royal line and Nathan's line was the legal line.

"For example, the former king of England had an older brother, now the Duke of Windsor, who had a prior claim to the throne of Britain. Suppose that Windsor had been the father of a son by a real queen before he abdicated. It can readily be seen that such a child might be a strong pretender to the throne in case there was no other heir apparent. George VI is in the royal line for he has reigned; any child of Windsor might claim to be in a legal line. Nathan was the older brother of Solomon, but the younger brother took the throne. Nathan's line ran on through the years, and ultimately produced the virgin Mary. Solomon's line ran on through the years and ultimately produced Joseph. Matthew does not say that Joseph begat Jesus, but that he was the husband of Mary of whom was born Jesus (Matt. 1:16). And Luke uses a word for son that includes what we should call a son-in-law.

"But the greatest proof of all lies in one of the names in the account of Matthew: the name Jechonias. It is that name that furnishes the reason for the inclusion of the genealogy of Jesus' step-father, for it proves that Joseph could not have been the father of Jesus, or if he had been, that Jesus could not have been the Messiah. In the use of that name there is conclusive evidence that Jesus is the son of Mary and not the son of Joseph. Jechonias was accursed of God with a curse that took the throne away from any of his descendants. 'Thus saith the Lord,' we read in Jeremiah 22:30, 'write ye this man childless, a man that shall not prosper in his days: for no man of his seed shall prosper, sitting upon the throne of David, and ruling anymore in Judah.' Not one of the seven sons (1 Chron. 3:17–18) of this man ever possessed the throne. No carnal son of this man could have been king because of the curse of God. If Jesus had been the son of Joseph, he would have been accursed and could never have been the Messiah.

"On the other hand, the line of Nathan was not the royal line. A son of Heli would have faced the fact that there was a regal line that would have possessed the crown and would have contested any claim that came from the line of Nathan. How was the dilemma solved? It was solved in a manner that is so simple that it is the utter confusion of the agnostics who seek to tear the Bible to pieces. The answer is this: the line that had no curse upon it produced Heli and his daughter the virgin Mary and her son Jesus Christ. He is therefore eligible by the line of Nathan and exhausts that line. The line that had a curse on it produced Joseph and exhausts the line of Solomon, for Joseph's other children now have an elder brother who, legally, by adoption, is the royal heir. How can the title be free in any case? A curse on one line and the lack of reigning royalty in the other.

"But when God the Holy Spirit begat the Lord Jesus in the womb of the virgin without any use of a human father, the child that was born was the seed of David according to the flesh. And when Joseph married Mary and took the unborn child under his protecting care, giving him the title that had come down to him through his ancestor Solomon, the Lord Jesus became the legal Messiah, the royal Messiah, the uncursed Messiah, the true Messiah, the only possible Messiah. The lines are exhausted." Barnhouse concludes by observing that "any man that ever comes into this world professing to fulfill the conditions will be a liar and the child of the devil."[1]

Is Jesus your Messiah? He is the only Messiah you will ever have. Come to him. Come to him now! If you do, you will find that he is able to give you new life and satisfy you fully.

A Lesson in Patience

Let me make one more point in closing: the name "Messiah" includes a lesson in patience. For it is a name that is linked to the expectations of those with whom God had been dealing for the thousands of years of Jewish history. When Adam and Eve sinned God came to them in grace, clothing them with skins and promising a deliverer who would come from the seed of the woman. They looked for the Messiah. God appeared to Abraham, promising that out of his loins would come one that should bring blessing to Israel and the nations. Abraham looked for the Messiah. God appeared to the prophets and through them repeated the promise to the Jewish people. They looked for the Messiah. In Christ's day people were still looking: Simeon, Anna, Elizabeth, and others. For all these long years there had been no fulfillment. It was only at the end of this period of waiting that God's Messiah actually came and fulfilled the promises given.

The great New Testament scholar B. F. Westcott has written: "It cannot have been for nothing that God was pleased to disclose his counsels, fragment by fragment, through long intervals of silence and disappointment and disaster. In that slow preparation for the perfect revelation of himself to men which was most inadequately apprehended till it was finally given, we discern the pattern of his ways. As it was in the case of the first advent, even so now he is guiding the course of the world to the second advent. We can see enough in the past, to find a vantage ground for faith; and, when the night is deepest and all sight fails, shall we not still *endure*, like the men of old time, *as seeing the invisible?* . . .

"By that title 'Christ' God teaches us to wait. . . . By that title 'Christ' God teaches us to watch. . . . By that title 'Christ' God teaches us to hope. It is the pledge of his personal love shown through all the ages. It is the pledge of the final establishment of his kingdom of which the sure foundations are already laid. False hopes, selfish fancies, earthly ambitions were scattered by Christ's first coming. But he brought that into the world which gives their only reality to all the emblems of power. *Thy throne, O God, is for ever and ever: a sceptre of righteousness is the sceptre of thy kingdom.* Life if we look at it in Christ is transfigured: Death if we look at it in Christ is conquered. When we interpret what he has done through the church in preparation for his second coming by the light of what he did through Israel in preparation for his first coming, we can wait and watch and hope, certain of this in all checks and storms and griefs that he shall *reign till all enemies are put under his feet.*"[2]

If you will trust the Lord Jesus Christ as your Messiah and Savior, he will save you and will transform you into one who shows no anguish about an unknown future but instead shows forth a quiet confidence in God.

50

The Cry of New Life

John 4:27–30

Just then his disciples returned and were surprised to find him talking with a woman. But no one asked, "What do you want?" or "Why are you talking with her?"

Then, leaving her water jar, the woman went back to the town and said to the people, "Come, see a man who told me everything I ever did. Could this be the Christ?" They came out of the town and made their way toward him.

I t is not at all surprising that the disciples were amazed and bewildered when they returned from the city of Sychar to Jacob's well and found the Lord Jesus Christ talking with the Samaritan woman. According to their standards of conduct, this was highly irregular. It was bad enough that she was a woman. The rabbis had said, "Let no one talk with a woman in the street, no, not with his own wife." They had argued, "Each time that a man prolongs conversation with a woman he causes evil to himself, desists from the law, and in the end inherits Gehinnom." But beyond this, in addition to being a woman, the person to whom Jesus was talking was a loose-living Samaritan, a sinner. And the disciples knew, as did everybody, that "Jews do not associate with Samaritans."

This was more than ample ground for the surprise and bewilderment that John tells us overtook the disciples. But the amusing part of the story is in the fact that the disciples would have been far more surprised and bewildered if they had been able to see what had taken place in the life of the woman as a result of the Lord's conversation with her.

Rebirth

What had happened was that the woman had been born again. She is the first clear example in the Gospel. She had come down the hill a child of Adam's race, thinking only of the life she had known and of her very mundane need for more water. Instead she had met the second Adam, Jesus, who had filled her with a desire for a quality of life that she had never dreamed of and who had revealed himself to her as the One through whom that life is imparted to men and women. As a result of Christ's words the woman believed on him and became his witness.

How do we know that the woman of Samaria had been born again? We know it because of the changes that took place in her. Sometime ago I was reading a book on childbirth that included within it a partial listing of the changes that take place in a baby's life during the first few seconds after its birth. I am told that there are dozens of these changes. To begin with, eyes that have previously been accustomed to darkness must adjust themselves to the light. A body that was used to temperatures of nearly 100 degrees Fahrenheit within the mother must adapt to temperatures approximately 20 degrees lower. The circulation of the infant's blood changes, no longer flowing through the umbilical cord, as it did when the child was in the womb, but instead flowing through the lungs. A valve in the heart, which had been open until birth, must close permanently so that the used blood and fresh blood circulating through the heart will not mingle. Lungs must fill with air and begin their lifelong function. These and many other changes involving the nose, throat, digestive tract, and skin, must all take place within a few seconds of birth if the baby is to live its new life and be healthy.

In the same way, there are certain changes that must take place within the life of the one who has been born again spiritually. These took place in the life of the Samaritan woman, and since they took place we know that she was converted. These changes must also occur in the life of those who are born again in our day. If they do not take place, there are grounds for questioning whether the birth from above has occurred.

Confession of Christ

The first thing that the doctor or nurses attending upon the birth of the baby want to hear is a cry. The cry of the child is evidence to the doctors that air has entered the lungs and that the baby has begun to breathe. This is the same spiritually. When a man or a woman is born again, the first thing that any Christian should desire to hear is the cry of new life, evidence that the breath of God has come into the person.

This is why the Bible speaks in many places about the need for a public confession of faith in Jesus Christ. It is not true that the birth of the child of God depends upon the outward confession, as if a person needs to confess Christ before God will receive him into his family. It is rather the other way around. We confess because we have been born again. At the same time it is equally untrue that a confession of Jesus Christ is optional. Some persons think that they can be secret believers, but the Word of God never considers this a possibility. What does the Word of God say? "Whoever acknowledges me before men, I will also acknowledge him before my Father in heaven. But whoever disowns me before men, I will disown him before my Father in heaven" (Matt. 10:32–33). "If you confess with your mouth, 'Jesus is Lord,' and believe in your heart that God raised him from the dead, you will be saved. For it is with your heart that you believe and are justified, and it is with your mouth that you confess and are saved" (Rom. 10:9–10).

It is at this point that we find the greatest contrast between Nicodemus, whose story is told in John 3, and the woman of Samaria, whose story is told here in chapter 4. So far as any human being could judge, Nicodemus was, of the two persons, the one who was most interested in spiritual things. He came to Jesus, after all; the woman did not come. Christ *sought* the woman. Nicodemus asked Christ the first question; the woman was approached by Jesus. Nicodemus actually asked how one could be saved, while the woman apparently tried to avoid the same point when it was involved in Christ's questions. To all appearances Nicodemus was the more sincere and spiritually oriented person. Yet there is not the slightest evidence that he actually believed, while the woman showed her faith in every aspect of her speech and conduct.

Nicodemus had heard a great sermon on the new birth, but there was no personalized confession. We see him twice more in John's Gospel, but again the same statement is true. In chapter 7 we are told how the Jewish leaders were plotting to take Christ's life. Nicodemus intervened, "Does our law condemn anyone without first hearing him to find out what he is doing?" (John 7:51). This was a good point. It was an argument for civil liberties. We can applaud it. But it was not confession by Nicodemus of faith in the Lord Jesus Christ as his Savior, and that alone is what would evidence the new birth. Similarly, after Christ's death Nicodemus came with Joseph of Arimathaea to embalm the dead body (John 19:39), but many unbelievers would do as much out of guilt or sentimentality.

Nicodemus may have believed—*may* have believed, I say—but once again we have no evidence for it. We fail to hear the cry that is the evidence of the breath of God within the human being.

It is so different with the woman of Samaria. She had not wanted to be saved. She did not even want to talk with Jesus on a personal level. Still she was born again, and she proved it immediately by departing for the city of Sychar with the personal invitation and testimony, "Come, see a man who told me everything I ever did. Could this be the Christ?" (John 4:29). Jesus had revealed himself to her as the Messiah. She believed his testimony, and the claim that the Messiah had come quite naturally became the core of *her* testimony. "The Messiah is here," she was saying.

Changes of Values

The story of the conversion of the woman of Samaria also gives us a second evidence of the fact that she had been born again. She had a change of values, a change in her interests. John indicates it beautifully when he tells us, "Then, leaving her water jar, the woman went back to the town and said to the people . . ." (v. 28).

I like this personal touch by John who recounts the story. The fact that John tells us that the woman left her water jar is important on one level, at least, as evidence that the story is being told by an eyewitness. This is the sort of thing John often notices and reports—as in the first chapter, in which he reports the hours of the day at which the two disciples stopped to spend the night with Jesus, or that it was night when Judas left the upper room to betray his master, or the fact that the disciples caught 153 fish after Jesus had told them where to cast their nets when he met with them in Galilee after his resurrection. Such details are the mark of the eyewitness; yet the observation by John that the woman left her water jar behind has more significance than its merely being further evidence of John's reliability.

Think how well this fits the story. From one point of view the story is all about water. The woman had come for literal water. There had been a discussion of wells and water. Christ had offered her living water. Now having found the water that alone satisfies the soul, the woman thinks no more of her water jar.

I wonder if you have experienced a change in your life and values as a result of pondering the truths of the gospel. I do not mean, "Have you been totally transformed overnight?" That does not often happen, although it can. Generally, the Christian life is one of growth, just as a baby must grow through childhood, adolescence, and into adult life. I do not mean, "Have you been totally transformed?" I mean, has there been at least a partial transformation of your values? Are you different now since you have believed? Are you being changed?

This is one of the great themes of John's Gospel. It is true that John is very much concerned that there be a vigorous verbal witness to the Lord Jesus Christ. But at the same time he is equally aware that the believer's life must back up the verbal witness. This theme emerges quite strongly in the final discourses of Jesus just before his crucifixion. In those discourses Jesus says that the disciples are to be one among themselves, just as he and the Father are one (John 14:20; 17:11, 21–22). They are to be committed to their task "in truth" (John 17:19). They are to *do* the truth (John 3:21; 1 John 1:6–7). They are to love one another (John 15:17). They are to keep his commandments (John 14:15). At every point the reality of the new life is to show itself in the life of the believer.

If this is not true of you, perhaps you need to leave the water jars of your old desires and interests in order to bear a vigorous and believable witness to the Lord Jesus.

Concern for the Lost

The final proof of a genuine change in the woman of Samaria is a new concern on her part for others. She had a verbal *confession* followed by a *change* in values. Now she had also a *concern* for the lost. Previously she had known many of the people of Samaria. Some of them she had known too well. But she had never been concerned for them. Probably they had often used her, at least some of them had. She had used them. Now for the first time she was concerned for their salvation. On the basis of the things she had learned she was now overflowing with a desire for them to meet Jesus. We are told: "Then, leaving her water jar, the woman went back to the town and said to the people, 'Come, see a man who told me everything I ever did. Could this be the Christ?' They came out of the town and made their way toward him" (John 4:28–30).

What is it that actually gave this woman a concern for those who had been close to her? Someone might answer, "Gratitude, gratitude for what Jesus had done for her." But gratitude would have kept her near Jesus at the well. It would not have sent her to the city. Someone else might answer, "A new awareness of who Jesus was." But certainly this alone would only have encouraged her to discover more about him. Someone might argue that it was "satisfaction at the way he had answered her questions." But again this would hardly have made her a soul winner. All these reactions, good as they were, would only have kept the woman of Samaria near Jesus.

What made her want to share her discovery? There is only one answer. It was love, the love of the Lord Jesus already beginning to spring up within her. She had learned of this love from Christ. He had loved her, a sinful woman. Now she was to love as he loved. Before, she had loved in one sense only. It was an imperfect, human love. Perhaps it was even largely sexual. Now she was able to love with a measure of the love with which Christ had loved her. This was a divine love, and it changed her completely.

Let me tell you how the gospel first came to Korea, the only Far Eastern country where today there is a substantial Christian population (in excess of 25 percent). Robert J. Thomas, a Welshman, was a colporteur working in China for the Scottish Bible Society. In the course of his work he learned that the Korean language is based on Chinese and that, as a result, the Korean intellectuals could read it. His main responsibility was toward the millions in China, of course. But the love of Christ for the Koreans constrained him, and he determined to push on to that country. An American ship called the *General Sherman* was sailing to Pyongyang, a large city in the north. He boarded it. As the ship drew near Pyongyang a sharp fight broke out between the officers of the American ship and the Korean coast guard. The ship was burned in the conflict, and all the passengers were killed. The death of Thomas was unusual. As the ship and the passengers were sinking, he struggled to reach the shore and staggered up out of the water, his arms filled with books. They were Bibles. He thrust these into the hands of the

Koreans who clubbed him to death. It was through such love that the gospel first came to Korea in the year 1866.

The Bible sets this pattern for us when it declares, "For Christ's love compels us, because we are convinced that one died for all, and therefore all died. And he died for all, that those who live should no longer live for themselves but for him who died for them and was raised again" (2 Cor. 5:14–15). Do you love because Christ first loved you? Are you burdened to share the gospel with others who have not yet believed on our Savior?

The Invitation Repeated

Finally, I wonder if you have ever thought about the specific invitation to the men of the city offered by the Samaritan woman. We have already been thinking of three great words each beginning with the letter *C*. They are the evidences of the fact that she had been born again—a *confession* of faith in Christ, a *change* of values, a *concern* for the lost. Three great words beginning with *C!* But here is a fourth, the word "come." This was the heart of her invitation, and she had learned it (as she had learned everything else) from Jesus. What had Jesus said to her? Jesus had said, "Go, call your husband, and come back" (v. 16). Now she, who had come, repeated the invitation, "Come, see a man who told me everything I ever did. Could this be the Christ?" (v. 29).

Come! This is a great word of the Christian gospel. It has brought peace to millions of restless hearts and satisfaction to many that were empty and lonely.

Think of the great verses that contain it. It was God's word to Abraham, "*Come* into the land which I shall show thee" (Acts 7:3 KJV). It was God's call to Moses to be Israel's deliverer, "*Come,* I will send you to Egypt" (Acts 7:34). David wrote, "*Come* and see the works of the LORD, the desolations he has brought on the earth" (Ps. 46:8). God spoke through Isaiah, saying, "*Come* now, let us reason together . . . though your sins are like scarlet, they shall be as white as snow; though they are red as crimson, they shall be like wool" (Isa. 1:18). The angels spoke the word to all skeptics as they pointed the disciples to the empty tomb, "*Come* and see the place where he lay" (Matt. 28:6). It was Christ's invitation, "*Come,* follow me" (Mark 10:21). "*Come* to me, all you who are weary and burdened, and I will give you rest" (Matt. 11:28). Finally, it will be the song of the angels as they invite the redeemed to the marriage supper of the Lamb (Rev. 19:17) and of Jesus himself as he says to his own, "Come, you who are blessed by my Father; take your inheritance, the kingdom prepared for you since the creation of the world" (Matt. 25:34).

If you have heard that invitation from the lips of the Lord, it is your privilege and duty to pass that word on. As in the case of the woman of Samaria, God's "Come!" must become our "Come!" Come! It is the greatest invitation in the universe. Won't you come? If you have already come, won't you share the invitation with another?

51

Christ, the Soul Winner

John 4:30

They came out of the town and made their way toward him.

When Jesus Christ told his disciples that they were to "Go and make disciples of all nations, baptizing them in the name of the Father and of the Son and of the Holy Spirit" (Matt. 28:19), the Lord was giving them marching orders for the church. They were to be his witnesses. They were to carry the gospel everywhere. When this is said the questions immediately arise: But what *constitutes* the Christian's witness? And *how* can a Christian witness? The first of these questions was answered when we considered the witness of John the Baptist, recorded in the first chapter of John's Gospel. The second question can be answered in the context of Christ's dealings with the woman of Samaria recorded in chapter 4.

Previously we noted that a genuine Christian witness consists of three things (see the chapters on John 1:19–51). First, the witness must realize that he has no independent importance in himself. He must know that he is not the answer to man's problems. Second, he must know that Jesus *is* the answer and must point men and women to him. Third, the witness must point others to Christ with the express intention of having them believe on him. John the Baptist did each of these things well, and this made him the first great example of a witness to Jesus Christ in John's Gospel.

It is entirely possible that a person might understand these truths and even want to witness to Jesus Christ, however, and yet not know how. He might say: I know what I should do, but how do I do it? How do I show that Jesus is the answer to the kid next door who is on drugs? How do I get my sophisticated roommate to admit her need for Jesus Christ? How do I get the mechanic who works on my car to listen to my testimony? How do I over-come the built-in hostility toward the gospel by those who work with me every day? What words do I use to talk about Christ to my wife, my husband, my children, or my friends? If you have ever asked these questions or are still asking them, then a study of the way in which Jesus related to the woman of Samaria should be of help to you and should allow you to build upon the truths we have already considered.

As I look at Christ's dealings with the woman of Samaria, I see five great principles emerging. We can learn from these principles. Moreover, if we do, we will experience results similar to those recorded by John. We are told that many of the Samaritans "came out of the town and made their way toward him" (John 4:30).

The Sinner's Friend

The first great principle is this: *Be a friend* to those you are trying to win. Jesus showed himself a friend to those who were lost. He is described as hav-ing been a friend of publicans and sinners; this (although intended criti-cally) was good reporting. Jesus could have kept aloof from mankind, just as we can keep aloof. But he would have won no one that way. Instead, Jesus went to the sick, lost, lonely, distressed, and perishing, and moved among them as a friend. In this story we find him in the woman's country, at the woman's city, sitting on the woman's well (vv. 5–6).

There is an illustration of this basic fact about the Lord Jesus in one of the books by Watchman Nee, the Chinese evangelist. Nee had been talking to another Christian in his home. They were downstairs, as was his friend's son. The friend's wife and mother were in an upstairs room. All at once the little boy wanted something and called out to his mother for it.

"It's up here," she said. "Come up and get it."

He cried out to her, "I can't, Mummy; it's such a long way. Please bring it down to me."

He was very small. So the mother picked up what he wanted and brought it down to him. It is just that way with salvation. No one is able to meet his own need spiritually, but the Lord Jesus Christ came down to us so our need could be met. Nee writes, "Had He not come, sinners could not have approached Him; but He came down in order to lift them up."[1]

I wonder if you are like that in your witnessing? Do you keep aloof or do you go to others? Another way of asking the same thing is to ask whether or not you have contact with non-Christians socially. Do you go to their homes, sit in their kitchens, ask them their interests?

A great deal of our difficulty in this area comes from the fact that Christians have often looked at the world as if it would inevitably get them dirty if they should get into it. They have taken verses like 2 Corinthians 6:17—"Therefore come out from them and be separate"—as meaning that Christians are to have no dealings with the world, rather than seeing that the words only have to do with avoiding conformity to the world, not isolation from it. Jesus did not teach isolation, and he did not practice it. He said in his great prayer for us recorded in John 17, "My prayer is not that you take them out of the world, but that you protect them from the evil one" (v. 15). When he departed for heaven he left his disciples in the world to evangelize it.

I am convinced that we need very practical ways of displaying friendship with the unbelievers we contact—the friendship that was so evident in the life of Jesus. For a start you might invite a number of non-Christian friends into your home for dinner. You might go to a concert with them. You might take in a sports show. Why not befriend your coworkers? Join a club, a choral society, a civic organization. It is not even a loss to go shopping together or invite your friends in for coffee. These are only beginning suggestions. If you are serious about taking the gospel to the lost, the Lord will show you other fruitful avenues of getting to know non-Christians. Just remember: Take the initiative and be friendly.

Ask Questions

Second, *ask questions*. It is never a bad move to ask questions. As we read the story of Jesus' encounter with the Samaritan woman, we discover that this is precisely what he did, and that he did it at the beginning of the conversation. He asked for a drink (v. 7). Looking at the conversation from the outside, as we do look at it, this is almost amusing. The woman was the one with the needs; she had the real questions. Jesus was the One with the answers. Nevertheless, Jesus humbled himself by asking her for a favor and so established an immediate and genuine point of contact.

Moreover, there were two important consequences as the result of his asking the woman for something. First, he aroused her interest. Dale Carnegie reminds us in his very successful book, *How to Win Friends and Influence People,* that the voice any person likes to hear best is his own. Jesus got the woman of Samaria talking. Her talking put her in a good mood (perhaps even changed her mood if, indeed she had arrived at the well shortly after being pushed off the path by Peter, as in an earlier study I indicated may have been the case). Out of her good mood the woman then clearly developed a favorable interest in Jesus. She must have found herself thinking, "My, what an interesting person this is! How polite! And what discrimination he must have to be interested in *me!*"

The second consequence of the Lord's asking her a question is that the woman found her curiosity aroused. He had asked her a question; she found it natural to begin to ask him a series of questions.

Let me state this again in a slightly different way. People are always full of questions, many of them religious questions. If you can get them to express these questions through yourself asking questions, by the grace of God you have already accomplished a great deal in your witness and God will use the aroused interest to point the one asking the questions to Jesus. Paul Little has written correctly about provoking such questions, "Once the non-Christian takes the first step in initiative, all pressure goes out of any conversation about Jesus Christ." He adds that thereafter "it can be picked up at the point where it is left without embarrassment."[2]

Something to Give

Third, *offer something relevant.* Jesus offered the woman something related quite directly to her need. In one sense the offer was always of himself, of course. Yet to aging Nicodemus Jesus spoke of himself as one who offers new life, a new beginning (John 3:3). He spoke of himself as light to the man who had been born blind (John 9:5). To the woman the same offer was couched in the metaphor of water. He said, "Everyone who drinks this water will be thirsty again, but whoever drinks the water I give him will never thirst. Indeed, the water I give him will become in him a spring of water welling up to eternal life" (vv. 13–14).

Most Christians need to learn from this principle. It will not do for us to witness about the transmission and reliability of the Bible if the person we are talking to is a young woman who isn't interested in that but who is afraid she will end up an "old maid" if she becomes a Christian. We must share Christ's offer to guide our lives and enrich them in whatever way he leads us. It will not be much use for us to speak about the power of Jesus Christ to deliver a person from the grip of drugs or alcohol if the man we are speaking to is a disciplined scientist whose greatest hang-up is his suspicion that other scientists have disproved Christianity. We need to offer him the challenge of searching the Scriptures himself to see whether these things are so and to encourage him to test Christ's claims. Above all we must not present our message in the language of the last century or in clichés that have no meaning to most of the non-Christian world.

Most people are thinking of their own needs. We must offer Jesus to them in ways that relate to those needs.

Good News

Fourth, *stress the good news.* Show that the gospel of Jesus Christ offers comfort. This does not mean, I am sure you realize, that we are totally to overlook sin. Jesus did not do that. He brought the woman to the point of recognizing her sin by his reference to the issue of her husbands. Nevertheless, even as he gently uncovered the sin he offered comfort, for he coupled his inquiry into her marital status with the invitation to come again to him (v. 16).

Unfortunately, it is true that we often do exactly the opposite in witnessing to non-Christians. The comfort of the gospel is there; but we forget the comfort, in our zeal to expose (and, I am afraid, often condemn) the sin. For instance, imagine a situation in which a non-Christian offers a Christian a drink at a party. Aren't there thousands of Christians who would immediately reply, "No, thank you. I don't drink. I'm a Christian"? They then think that they have offered a splendid witness to Jesus Christ, when actually they have really only succeeded in condemning the non-Christian. At the same time, they would have given him the wrong idea that nondrinking is somehow a very important part of Christianity. Nondrinking may be an important part of their Christian life. But the point I am making is that the statement "I don't drink; I'm a Christian" is no more intelligible to the unbeliever than his saying to you, when you ask him to go to a football game, "No thanks. I don't go to football games; I'm a non-Christian."

There are two real dangers in this. The first is the danger that in getting our witness tangled up in such issues, we miss the fact that our friend may be quite desperately lonely—perhaps that is why he drinks—and never suggest a cure for his loneliness. Or we may miss his feeling of guilt, sorrow, meaninglessness, or whatever it may be.

The second danger is that in focusing attention on some aspect of the nonbeliever's conduct, we may actually give the impression that he must improve himself before he can come to Jesus. This is quite wrong. We will never want to give the impression that when we come to Jesus we can do as we please, that we can sin that grace might abound. That would be untrue also. But neither do we want to suggest that there must be self-reformation before a man or a woman can come.

In England, in the early part of the nineteenth century, there was a woman who had heard the gospel but who had never been able to respond to it personally. She had come from a Christian home. She understood the faith. But still she could not come. She considered herself unworthy. One day she wandered into a very small church and sat down in the back. She was almost in despair and hardly heard the words of the elderly man who was speaking. Suddenly, right in the middle of his address, the preacher stopped and, pointing his finger at her, said, "You, Miss, sitting there at the back, you can be saved *now*. You don't need to do anything!" His words struck like thunder in her heart. She believed at once, and with her belief there came an unimagined sense of peace and real joy. That night Charlotte Elliott went home and wrote the well-known hymn:

> Just as I am, without one plea,
>   But that thy blood was shed for me,
> And that thou bidd'st me come to thee,
>   O Lamb of God, I come, I come.

If we are to witness for Jesus Christ, we must never give the impression that a person must first become worthy of the gospel. Nor should we forget that there is comfort in the gospel for sinners.

Point to Jesus

The fifth principle is that we must end by confronting the individual with his responsibility to decide for or against Jesus Christ. Jesus said, "I who speak to you am he" (v. 26). Well, was he or wasn't he? This was the decision placed before the woman. It must be the same in our witnessing. If we do not get to the point of focusing on Jesus himself, our witness is incomplete. It is not yet a full witness. If we do not get to the point of showing that a decision is necessary, our witness is inadequate.

These are the principles of how we should witness, from the story of Jesus' encounter with the Samaritan woman. First, be friendly. Second, ask questions. Third, offer that which most suits the individual's needs. Fourth, stress the good news. And fifth, show that the person must decide either for or against the Lord Jesus.

What will happen if you do that? I believe that the results will be similar to those that the Lord Jesus experienced in Samaria. The first obvious results were in the life of the woman. About midway through the conversation, the woman acknowledged her need, saying, "Sir, give me this water so that I won't get thirsty" (v. 15). A few moments later she confessed her sin, "I have no husband" (v. 17). Third, she began to show a quickening of spiritual intelligence: "I can see that you are a prophet" (v. 19). Fourth, she affirmed her faith in the Lord Jesus: "Could this be the Christ?" (v. 29). Finally, she took to her town the good news that she had received.

You may think that the people among whom you work or with whom you associate may be difficult specimens to speak to. That may be true. So was the woman. Yet she became the first great witness after John the Baptist. It may be that God will use your witness to reach one who in his turn may evangelize an entire generation.

52

The Secret of Satisfaction

John 4:31–34

Meanwhile his disciples urged him, "Rabbi, eat something."

But he said to them, "I have food to eat that you know nothing about."

Then his disciples said to each other, "Could someone have brought him food?"

"My food," said Jesus, "is to do the will of him who sent me and to finish his work."

In Spain there is a very old proverb that says, "All laws go the way that kings desire." Behind that proverb is a rather interesting story. About the beginning of the twelfth century, there was a debate about whether the country's churches were to use Gothic or Roman prayer books in their services. The question eventually came before Alfonso VI, who was king at the time. Alfonso decided to leave the matter to chance, so he threw a copy of both prayer books into a fire, declaring that the one that survived the ordeal should be chosen. However, when the Gothic missal survived the blaze, the king immediately threw it back into the fire and chose the Roman liturgies. Thus was the matter decided, and the proverb became popular throughout the country.

Many Christians treat the will of God in this manner. They say they want God's will. They declare that they are leaving the matter up to him. But then, when God reveals what they are to do, they continue trying to "find out his will," as they say, until events finally turn out to suit them. When they eventually do get their way—and, of course, find that it does not yield them the satisfaction they had hoped for—many of these persons become confused and desperately unhappy.

Unfortunately, such persons have never learned that true satisfaction in life comes from yielding totally to God's will in God's service and that knowing God's will consists in being willing to do it even before we know what it is.

The Will of God

If you have ever found yourself in the place of trying to get God's will to conform to your own—most of us have at one time or another—then you should be helped by the thoughts that the Lord Jesus Christ shared with his disciples on this subject.

We are told in the fourth chapter of John's Gospel that when Jesus and his disciples arrived in Samaria, where he was to meet the Samaritan woman, Jesus waited in the valley near Jacob's well while his disciples went up the hill to Sychar to buy food. While they were gone the woman came, and Jesus talked to her, leading her to faith. About the time the woman left her water jar to go up to the city to bring others to Jesus, the disciples had finished their errand and had returned. They were surprised that Jesus had been talking to the woman, but they were doubly surprised when Jesus showed no interest in the food they had purchased. He told them, "I have food to eat that you know nothing about." Peter and John and the others thought on the purely literal level, as Nicodemus and the woman had also both done, and began to wonder if someone had brought him food during their absence. At this point Jesus replied that the food he was talking about was not physical but spiritual. He said, "My food is to do the will of him who sent me and to finish his work" (v. 34).

This is a great sentence. It is even a "golden sentence," as Charles Haddon Spurgeon once described it. In essence these words are an expression of what was undoubtedly the keynote of Jesus' life, telling us that above all else Jesus lived to do God's will. They are the essence of his life. Moreover, they tell us that doing God's will gave Jesus complete satisfaction.

We shall understand a great deal more about the satisfaction that comes from desiring God's will and doing it when we compare the obedience of Jesus, recorded here and elsewhere, with the disobedience of Satan with which it forms a great contrast. In Isaiah 14 we are told in four verses of the thoughts that entered Satan's mind at the moment of his revolt against God and of the eventual results of this rebellion. The point of the verses is that Satan's revolt occurred in the area of the will, in desiring his will rather than God's, and resulted in dissatisfaction for Satan and his eventual judgment. Isaiah writes, "How you have fallen from heaven, O morning star, son of the dawn! You have been cast down to the earth, you who once laid low the nations! You said in your heart, 'I will ascend to heaven; I will raise my throne above the stars of God; I will sit enthroned on the mount of assembly, on the utmost heights of the sacred mountain. I will ascend above the tops of the clouds; I will make myself like the Most High.' But you are brought down to the grave, to the depths of the pit" (Isa. 14:12–15).

In these verses there are two interesting features in Satan's thought. The first is Satan's desire to climb above that station to which God had called him. He had already been given the highest position of any created being. According to Ezekiel he was "full of wisdom and perfect in beauty" (Ezek. 28:12). He was what we might call the king and high priest of the creation. Nevertheless, none of this was enough for Satan. Satan desired to rise into heaven . . . above the stars . . . to sit upon the mount of the assembly . . . above the heights of the clouds . . . to be like the Most High. In other words, he wanted to push God off the throne and receive the worship of the universe himself.

The second important feature of these verses is the strong assertion of Satan's own will. If you take time to count the occurrence of the phrase "I will" in these verses, you will see that Satan asserts his own will five times. He said, "I will . . . I will . . . I will . . . I will . . . I will." In time Satan's "I will" was multiplied many billions of times, first by the very distinct and equally rebellious "wills" of his followers and then by the "I wills" of billions of men and women. Satan's "I will" was the origin of sin in the universe; the results of sin show the tragic consequences of anyone's attempting to do things in any way other than that which God determines.

What were the results of this rebellion? When Satan caused Adam and Eve to sin in the Garden of Eden, God expressed the results of willfulness by telling Satan that it would be his fate to eat dust all the days of his life (Gen. 3:14). This symbolizes dissatisfaction. We might say that God told Satan that life for him would be dry, unnourishing, and tasteless. In Isaiah God describes the same thing in another way by describing Satan's end. "But you are brought down to the grave, to the depths of the pit."

How different was the obedience of the Lord Jesus Christ! Jesus declared, "I desire to do your will, O my God" (Ps. 40:8). Paul later wrote of his obedience, saying that Jesus "did not consider equality with God something to be grasped, but made himself nothing, taking the very nature of a servant, being made in human likeness. And being found in appearance as a man, he humbled himself and became obedient to death—even death on a cross! Therefore God exalted him to the highest place and gave him the name that is above every name, that at the name of Jesus every knee should bow, in heaven and on earth and under the earth" (Phil. 2:6–10).

It is a great contrast. Satan exalted his own will and found nothing but misery. He brought misery to others. Jesus submitted himself to the will of God and both found and brought blessing.

I wonder if you have been able to learn from this contrast. Do you see the benefits of submitting yourself to God's will? Are you willing to go in whatever direction he sends you? I am convinced that we know little about our own natures until we come to the point of recognizing that naturally we prefer our will to God's and that even at best, even after God works with us, we often only desire to know and to do his will halfheartedly.

Have you ever prayed to know God's will, surrendering yourself to him as best you know how, had his answer, but then had a heavy feeling as you set out to do as he directed? If so, isn't it true that you are acting like the little girl who wrote to her grandmother to thank her for her Christmas present? She wrote, "Dear Grandma, thank you for the pincushion. I have always wanted a pincushion, but not very much." We are all like that. We say, "Thank you, Lord, for having a will for my life. I have always wanted your will for my life." Yet if we are honest, we are forced to admit, ". . . but not very much." Thus it is that for many people one of the great steps in their spiritual growth comes when their will is first surrendered to God's will and they are enabled to say, as Jesus did, "My food is to do the will of him who sent me."

Doing the Will of God

That verse also leads to a second point in our study, for Jesus did not say, "My food is to *will* the will of him who sent me." That is important enough, but it is only part of the story. He actually said, "My food is to *do* the will of him who sent me." This is important for us, for it is often true that even when the will of God is revealed to us we fail to do it.

At one point in his ministry Jesus told a story involving a father and his two sons. The father owned a vineyard. He came to the first son and said, "Son, go work today in my vineyard."

The son said, "No, I won't." But afterward, Jesus reported, the son repented and went.

The father came to the second son and gave him identical instructions. This son said, "Yes, I'll work in the vineyard." But then he failed to do it.

Jesus asked those who were listening to him, "Which of the two did the will of his father?" When they pointed out that it was the first of the sons, in spite of the fact that initially he had refused, Jesus then showed that this was precisely the contrast between the religious leaders of his day who were always saying, "Yes, yes," to God but who were not obeying him, and the sinners of his day who initially disobeyed but after that repented.

The contrast is still valid. Do you say, "Yes, yes," but then not do what God instructs you to do? Or do you do his will and not merely talk about it?

I have always been impressed by the number of verses in the Bible that give us specific things to do. For instance, if you are not yet a Christian, there is a verse in the Sermon on the Mount that is specifically for you. Jesus said, "Enter through the narrow gate. For wide is the gate and broad is the road that leads to destruction, and many enter through it" (Matt. 7:13). If you are not yet a Christian, God's will for you is that you might believe in Jesus as your Savior.

If you are a Christian, there are hundreds of clear-cut statements for you to consider. Jesus said, "Let your light shine before men, that they may see your good deeds and praise your Father in heaven" (Matt. 5:16). He said, "Love your enemies and pray for those who persecute you" (Matt. 5:44). Peter wrote, "But in your hearts set apart Christ as Lord. Always be prepared to give an answer to everyone who asks you to give the reason for the hope that you have. But do this with gentleness and respect" (1 Peter 3:15). He wrote, "Humble yourselves, therefore, under God's mighty hand, that he may lift you up in due time. . . . Be self-controlled and alert" (1 Peter 5:6, 8). Paul declared, "Therefore, I urge you, brothers, in view of God's mercy, to offer your bodies as living sacrifices, holy and pleasing to God—this is your spiritual act of worship. Do not conform any longer to the pattern of this world, but be transformed by the renewing of your mind. Then you will be able to test and approve what God's will is—his good, pleasing and perfect will" (Rom. 12:1–2). A list of such verses could be almost endless, but this is enough for our purposes. Do you do such things? Do you work at them?

Let me share a challenge that the great Baptist preacher Charles Haddon Spurgeon had for the congregations of his day. Spurgeon wrote this about doing God's will: "Some of you good people, who do nothing except go to public meetings, and Bible readings, and prophetic conferences, and other forms of spiritual dissipation, would be a good deal better Christians if you would look after the poor and needy around you. If you would just tuck up your sleeves for work, and go and tell the Gospel to dying men, you would find your spiritual health mightily restored, for very much of the sickness of Christians comes through their having nothing to do. All feeding and no working makes men spiritual dyspeptics. Be idle, careless, with nothing to live for, nothing to care for, no sinner to pray for, no backslider to lead back to the cross, no trembler to encourage, no little child to tell of a Savior, no greyheaded man to enlighten in the things of God, no object, in fact, to live for; and who wonders if you begin to groan, and to murmur, and to look within, until you are ready to die of despair? Let us have practical Christianity."[1]

Finishing the Work

Finally, Jesus did not merely say, "My food is to *will* the will of him that sent me" or even "My food is to *do* the will of him that sent me." He said, "My food is to do the will of him who sent me *and to finish his work*." Unfortunately, many of us begin the work but then fail to finish it.

Before the incarnation, Jesus declared through David, "Here I am, I have come—it is written about me in the scroll. I desire to do your will, O my God; your law is within my heart" (Ps. 40:7–8). To do that, Jesus Christ assumed our humanity. Jesus was born in Bethlehem and was raised in the dirty little town of Nazareth and grew up in the carpenter shop of his earthly stepfather Joseph. In time he began his teaching ministry, a ministry that took him throughout all the towns and villages of Palestine. During these years, he looked ahead to the cross, which loomed ever larger before him. Finally, just before his crucifixion as he prayed in the garden, Jesus observed, "I have brought you glory on earth by completing the work you gave me to do" (John 17:4). One of his last cries from the cross was, "It is finished" (John 19:30).

Aren't you glad that the Lord Jesus Christ finished the work that God the Father gave him to do? It resulted in our salvation. Are you like him in that? Are you attempting to finish the work that you have been given?

Early in his life, George Müller, the founder of the well-known faith orphanages in England, made friendships with three men, none of whom was a Christian. Müller was burdened for these three friends and began to pray for them. He prayed for years, recording in his diary the fact that he was continuing to pray for them. Müller prayed throughout his lifetime and finally died without seeing any one of them come to faith. Nevertheless, after Müller's death, each of these three men believed, two of them well up in their seventies and one over eighty years of age.

The other story is told by Spurgeon of a missionary who had gone to the American Indians. As this man lay dying, the last thing he did was to teach a little child its letters so that the child might begin to read. Someone remarked how strange it was to see such a great man at such a seemingly insignificant work. But he replied that he thanked God that when he could no longer preach, he still had at least enough strength to teach the poor child. This man desired to finish his life's work. He wanted to brush in the final stroke that would complete the picture.

You have not finished the work that you have been given if you have merely put in a year at it, teaching a class, serving on a board. You have not finished the work if you have merely gone witnessing on a weekend. You have not finished your work merely by trying to help a child once and then dropping this great responsibility. The will of God is done for you only when your part is ended and the work itself is entrusted into the hands of your successor.

53

God's Harvest

John 4:35–38

"Do you not say, 'Four months more and then the harvest'? I tell you, open your eyes and look at the fields! They are ripe for harvest. Even now the reaper draws his wages, even now he harvests the crop for eternal life, so that the sower and the reaper may be glad together. Thus the saying 'One sows and another reaps' is true. I sent you to reap what you have not worked for. Others have done the hard work, and you have reaped the benefits of their labor."

There are few things in life so tragic as having missed a great opportunity. Let me give you an example.

During the first three days of July 1863, in the midst of America's great Civil War, the armies of the North and South clashed decisively at Gettysburg. For the first three days of the battle the fighting was inconclusive, but then the tide began to turn against General Lee and the Confederate forces. The northern troops under General G. G. Meade were winning. Lee began to retreat southward on the night of July 4, while storm clouds drenched the east coast with rain. When Lee reached the Potomac, he found that the river was swollen with rain. He could not cross it. Behind him was the victorious Union army. Before him was the river. He was trapped.

Here was the great, golden opportunity for General Meade. Meade could have attacked immediately, destroying Lee's army and, in effect, ending the Civil War. President Lincoln actually ordered him to attack. However, instead of attacking, Meade delayed. He held a council, then delayed again. Eventually the water of the river receded, and Lee escaped over the Potomac, from which ground he was able to extend the war by two more years. Meade never regained his lost opportunity, and it was to General Grant that Lee eventually surrendered on April 9, 1865.

This story shows us the tragedy of having missed a great opportunity. But if this principle is true in the physical realm, as we realize, it is certainly more true spiritually. The Bible recognizes this when it says, "What good will it be for a man if he gains the whole world, yet forfeits his soul?" (Matt. 16:26). Or again, "If it is burned up, he will suffer loss; he himself will be saved, but only as one escaping through the flames" (1 Cor. 3:15).

Apparently, the Lord Jesus Christ had been thinking along these lines as the result of the failure of the disciples to understand the need of the Samaritan woman. No doubt, as the disciples had started up the hill toward Sychar, the Lord had gazed after them. He had seen them pass the woman who was on her way down. She was the one to whom Jesus had come to Samaria to witness, but the disciples were unaware of her need. Perhaps they had even stood several abreast in the path and forced her to go around them with her water jar, while all this time Jesus looked after them from the well. After Jesus had spoken to the woman and the disciples returned, of what were they thinking? Once again, it was certainly not of her or her need. They had completed their errand. Now they wanted the Lord Jesus Christ to eat lunch.

Jesus must have smiled as he began to teach them, first, about the priority of spiritual things over physical things and, then, about their great opportunities. They had missed one opportunity, but Jesus did not chide them about that. Instead he began to teach them about their next opportunity so that they might not miss it.

He used a proverb to do it. The proverb said that after sowing seed a farmer needs to wait four months for the harvest. Jesus argued that in the present case that was not so: "Do you not say, 'Four months more and then the harvest'? I tell you, open your eyes and look at the fields! They are ripe for harvest. Even now the reaper draws his wages, even now he harvests the crop for eternal life, so that the sower and the reaper may be glad together" (vv. 35–36).

The development of the story shows that this was certainly true metaphorically. The hills of Samaria were spiritually ripe, for many of the Samaritans believed (vv. 39, 41). Nevertheless, it may even have been true in an observable sense. At any rate, I can imagine the woman returning with the men of the city even while Jesus was talking with the disciples so that, when he said that the fields were "ripe" to harvest, this was literally true as hundreds of the townspeople in their white robes began streaming down the hillside toward him.

The disciples had missed one opportunity; Jesus did not want them to miss this one. He was using the incident to show that there were now great opportunities for the spread of the gospel, and he was encouraging them on the basis of these opportunities to be missionaries.

Motivations for Mission

This was not to be the only motivation for their great assignment of bringing other men and women to the Lord, of course. Nor is it our only motivation. The first great motivation for evangelism is that the followers of Jesus Christ are not at liberty to set their own priorities. We are under marching orders, as the Duke of Wellington once said in answer to a similar question, and it is the Lord Jesus Christ, our commander-in-chief, who has issued them. What are the orders? The orders are that we are to go into all the world and preach the gospel to every creature, baptizing those who believe, in the name of the Father, Son, and Holy Spirit. This command, spoken to the disciples later, is given to us several times—once in the Gospels of Matthew, Mark, Luke, and John, and in the opening chapter of Acts.

In each case the emphasis is different. In Matthew's account, the account of Christ's commissioning of the disciples to world mission in Galilee, the *authority* of the Lord is emphasized. Here Jesus says, "All authority in heaven and on earth has been given to me. Therefore go and make disciples of all nations" (Matt. 28:18–19). In Mark the emphasis falls upon the *final judgment*. Luke presents the great commission as the fulfillment of *Old Testament prophecy,* for it is through the preaching of the cross that blessing is to come to the nations. In John's account Christ places the great commission in the context of *his own commissioning* by the Father. "As the Father has sent me, I am sending you" (John 20:21). Finally, in Acts the command is linked to a definite *program of world evangelization.* "But you will receive power when the Holy Spirit comes on you; and you will be my witnesses in Jerusalem, and in all Judea and Samaria, and to the ends of the earth" (Acts 1:8).

In light of these texts it should be evident that the command to evangelize the world is a command that touches each of us personally. It touched all Christ's disciples then. It touches all Christ's disciples now. The question is not *whether* you should go but *where* you should go. Wherever he sends you, there you are to be a missionary and an evangelist.

You may have to witness in your office. You may have to witness in your home. You may have to witness at school. You may be saying, "But I don't have the courage." Well, God knows that you lack it, but he has promised to supply all your need according to the riches of his glory in Christ Jesus. You may be saying, "But I have a family and children to take care of." Why should that hinder you? It certainly should not hinder you from giving a witness where you are today. It should not even deter you from work abroad if that is what God has called you to. Perhaps God will pick you up now and fill you with a yearning to spread his Word in a place you now know only by name but will one day come to love with a divine love and regard the place of your greatest labor for him.

Men Are Lost

The second motivation for world missions is that men and women are lost without Jesus Christ. This means that they are lost in this life as well as for eternity. Paul wrote to the Ephesians that before their conversion they were "separate from Christ, excluded from citizenship in Israel and foreigners to the covenants of the promise, without hope and without God in the world" (Eph. 2:12). Jeremiah wrote of men as "lost sheep" (Jer. 50:6). Jesus told pointed stories about a lost sheep, a lost coin, and a lost son (Luke 15). John wrote of Jesus, "Whoever believes in him is not condemned, but whoever does not believe stands condemned already because he has not believed in the name of God's one and only Son" (John 3:18). The same truths are taught in Revelation 20:11–15 where we are told about the judgment of the great white throne. At this judgment all are called to account, and those whose names are not found written in the Book of Life are lost.

Are men really lost? The great weight of theological opinion in our day is against this conclusion, but the Bible teaches it and we must stand with God's Word.

The various shades of universalism in the church are opposed to this teaching. It is probably universalism more than any other single factor that has blunted the cutting edge of evangelism and severed the lifeline of missions. The view of most anthropologists is against it. They tend to glorify primitive cultures. Often they teach that the spread of the gospel tarnishes an essentially beautiful religion. The truth of the matter is that although there may be and undoubtedly are some glimmerings of truth in paganism, the glimmers of truth that men may possess never lead them to God, and, as a result, there is always a great deal more of degradation and perversion in primitive cultures than nobility. The third ground on which the teaching of the Bible is opposed is religious relativism, the view that all men are on the same road to God and that the differences we see are only the differences between the various stages along it.

Are these views right? If they are right, then we may take our ease, leaving the world at peace. However, if they are wrong and the Bible is right, then we must give for the support of missions and we must go wherever God sends us.

Physical Needs

The third motivation for missions is found in the physical and social needs of large portions of the human race. The physical and social needs of men are not our prime motivation, for we know that it profits little if people gain the blessings of this world while losing their own souls. Yet these needs are a strong motivation, and they impel us onward. The Bible tells us that many times as the Lord looked upon the sick, poor, needy, and lonely, he had compassion upon them and healed their infirmities. He sat down with sinners. He touched the lepers. We are to follow his example.

I know that someone will reply, "But I am not sure that I want to do that. Doesn't it mean that I myself will get dirty?" In one sense, it does; but you are called to a life of such involvement.

When the great musician Johann Sebastian Bach was first called to the Sans-souci Palace in Potsdam by King Frederick the Great, he decided upon his arrival that he should first freshen himself from his journey. Instead, the king commanded an instant appearance, and Bach therefore arrived in the palace dirty and improperly attired. Some of the courtiers, with their court manners and habits, laughed at Bach's appearance. But the king instantly chided them for their insensitive contempt, and he had Bach play. Later, Zinzendorf, who knew the story, applied it to Christianity and Christian workers, saying, "Nothing is more beautiful than a dusty warrior." He was right. Nothing so commends the evangelist as an involvement with the persons whom he serves. Nothing in their need—be it spiritual, moral, social, or physical—should fail to impel him forward.

Fourth, the love of the Lord Jesus Christ impels us. Paul wrote, "For Christ's love compels us, because we are convinced that one died for all, and therefore all died. And he died for all, that those who live should no longer live for themselves but for him who died for them and was raised again" (2 Cor. 5:14–15).

A Ripe Harvest

Finally, we are motivated in the task of evangelism by the opportunities that each succeeding day thrusts upon us. Do we seize the opportunities as Christ did? Or do we do as the disciples did and walk by them?

We need to realize that the opportunities that are present today are present because of the coming of Jesus Christ and not because of any fortuitous arrangement of circumstances or because of our imagined ability to create them. This thought is suggested in the verses in a way that is not at once apparent to the casual reader. When Jesus quoted the proverb about the lapse of four months between sowing and harvest and disagreed with it, saying that the sowing and reaping could take place simultaneously, he was reminding the disciples of an Old Testament prophecy that had to do with the coming of the Messiah. According to the Old Testament the Messiah would usher in a period of great physical blessing for this earth. Amos had written, "'The days are coming,' declares the LORD, 'when the reaper will be overtaken by the plowman and the planter by the one treading grapes'" (Amos 9:13). Moses had written, "Your threshing will continue until grape harvest and the grape harvest will continue until planting" (Lev. 26:5). In a spiritual sense this had come true. The Messiah had come. Thus, the age of waiting had passed, and the period of perpetual reaping had dawned.

Are you aware of this harvest? Are you aware that God's Spirit is moving in our time? I am convinced he is. This is particularly evident in the student world. Let us ask ourselves: Are we awake to these opportunities and present to take advantage of them? Do we speak the Word in season? Are we available? If not, we must ask the Lord of the harvest to help us see the fields of ripe grain.

A Second Proverb

There is, however, one more proverb referred to by Jesus. It comes at the end of this section. It is true, said Jesus, that in the day of the Messiah, the reaper shall overtake the sower. But it is also true that at times the sower will not see the results of his labors. "One sows and another reaps," said Jesus. "I sent you to reap what you have not worked for. Others have done the hard work, and you have reaped the benefits of their labor" (John 4:37–38).

If you obey the Lord Jesus Christ and witness as he has commanded you to do, there is no guarantee that in every case you will see the results of your labors. Jesus will encourage you in your witness. You will probably see people come to faith in him. You will reap. But it is also true that, when you sow, some of the results of that sowing will appear only in an age when you are gone and that you will *not* see it. Do not be discouraged if that happens. We are harvesting fruit that is the result of the efforts of our predecessors. There will also be harvesting on the basis of the sowing that is going on today. We may see the results. We may not see the results. But whatever the case, we are to keep on with our commission.

The question for us is, "Do we sow the seed?" That is our job. We are to take the Word of the living God to those who need to hear it and thus allow the Lord Jesus Christ to use it to bring forth a harvest in their lives.

54

The Savior of the World

John 4:39–42

Many of the Samaritans from that town believed in him because of the woman's testimony, "He told me everything I ever did." So when the Samaritans came to him, they urged him to stay with them, and he stayed two days. And because of his words many more became believers.

They said to the woman, "We no longer believe just because of what you said; now we have heard for ourselves, and we know that this man really is the Savior of the world."

If ever there was a great spiritual climax to a story, that climax is found in the phrase with which John the evangelist ends his account of Christ's conversation with the woman of Samaria. The woman had believed in Jesus as the result of his conversation with her and had immediately gone off to her own city to tell others about him. These came and believed. They asked Christ to stay with them. When he did, others believed also. John's account of this miniature revival in Samaria is then rounded off with the concluding testimony of these new believers concerning Jesus: "They said to the woman, 'We no longer believe just because of what you said; now we have heard for ourselves, and we know that this man really is the *Savior of the world*'" (John 4:42).

This great phrase—"the Savior of the world"—concludes John's story and is therefore particularly significant. Of course, no one really wanted a Savior of the *world* in Christ's day. The Jews wanted a savior of Jerusalem. The Samaritans wanted a savior of Samaria, as their conduct at a later time indi-

330

cates (cf. Luke 9:52, 53). The Greeks wanted to save Greece; the Romans, to save Rome. But Jesus was not this kind of a savior. Jesus is the Savior of the *world.* Jesus appeared on earth for men of all races in order that he might die for them and be the means of their salvation.

It is because he did this that you and I, who are not Jews, have a Savior.

The Human Race

Before we look at this phrase—"the Savior of the world"—we need to look at the very important word "world." In Greek the word is *kosmos.* It occurs about 185 times in the New Testament, but what is highly significant for our study is that 105 of these 185 occurrences are in the books traditionally attributed to John. The word *kosmos* occurs 78 times in the Gospel of John, 24 times in John's epistles, and 3 times in Revelation. We get a sense of how unusual John's use of the word is when we realize that Matthew uses the word only 8 times and that it occurs just 3 times each in the Gospels of Mark and Luke. In other words, we are dealing here with one of the great concepts, or themes, of John's Gospel.

But what does the word *kosmos* mean? Initially the word probably denoted an ornament; that is, an object that was decorative or beautiful because it was well proportioned or well constructed. This usage appears many times in Homer and is preserved for us in our English word "cosmetic." From this original use, the word passed quite naturally into a word describing the universe because of its beauty and harmony. The universe is God's ornament. This sense of the word is retained in one of the three uses of it in John 1:10, which tells us that the world (meaning the universe) was made by Jesus Christ. Since the earth with its order and beauty was the most significant part of the universe for mankind, it was natural that the word *kosmos* should next be applied to this earth and, after that, to the men who live upon it.

This latter idea is the one normally used by John. In John the word *kosmos* most often means "the human race." In the later chapters of the Gospel particularly, the word denotes the human race in its opposition to God. Consequently, those who are called to faith in the Lord Jesus Christ are distinguished from it. We find John writing: "It was just before the Passover Feast. Jesus knew that the time had come for him to leave this world and go to the Father. Having loved his own who were in the world, he now showed them the full extent of his love" (John 13:1). Later, Jesus makes the distinction even clearer by praying on behalf of the disciples: "I pray for them. I am not praying for the world, but for those you have given me, for they are yours" (John 17:9).

In these later chapters the line of distinction is drawn between those who are Christ's and those who are merely "of the world." In the early chapters (that is, before Jesus has begun to do much of his work) the references deal with Christ's actions toward the human race generally.

God's Light

Let us look at some of these references. The first important one is John 1:9, which says, "The true light that gives light to every man was coming into the world."

What does that mean? If we are to understand this verse, we need to remember, first of all, that it does not refer to some imagined divine light or spark of divinity that is said to be innate to mankind. That is a view which has been held by the Quakers and peripheral Christian denominations, but it is not what the verse is teaching. We discussed this issue in one of our studies of John's first chapter. The "Light" of the verse really refers to the historical Jesus. The point of the verse is that Jesus shone upon all men—from the outside, as a spotlight shines upon the darkened front of an empty house—rather than there being any light shining forth from within.

The fact that Jesus shines upon all men is, however, important. It is important because it tells us that he is the light, rather than another. The verse says that he is the "true" or "genuine" light. It is important because we are told that the light is for all.

Do you realize that it is only because of the coming of the Lord Jesus Christ that you, a Gentile (if you are a Gentile), have spiritual light? Before Christ's coming, salvation was, as Jesus maintained, "of the Jews." To the Jews belonged the adoption, the glory, the covenants, the giving of the law, the service of God, and the promises (Rom. 9:4). That is true; it is a fact of our history. On one occasion, when Daniel O'Connell, a nineteenth-century Irish politician, taunted the great English statesman Benjamin Disraeli in the House of Commons about his being a Jew, Disraeli replied, "Yes, I am a Jew; and when the ancestors of this right honorable gentleman were brutal savages in an unknown island [he meant Ireland], mine were priests in the temple of Solomon and were giving law and religion to the world." It was a just rebuke. For centuries the true light of divine revelation was confined to Judaism. Now, however, through Jesus Christ the light of God's law and true religion have come to us Gentiles.

Have you recognized that the Lord Jesus Christ came to be your Light? If you will allow him to do so, he will use that light first to reveal the darkness of your heart and life to you and then to lead you into the light of his truth and righteousness.

The Lamb

The second important reference to the relationship of Jesus Christ to the world of men is that he came to be the world's Savior. That is the teaching of John the Baptist who declared, "The next day John saw Jesus coming toward him and said, 'Look, the Lamb of God, who takes away the sin of the world!'" (John 1:29). Jesus is only the Savior of those who believe on him, for salvation is through faith alone. "Without faith it is impossible to please

God," says the author of Hebrews (Heb. 11:6). Yet it is also correct to say that he died in order that all might come to repentance.

I wonder if you have ever pondered on all that is involved in that phrase, "the Lamb of God, who takes away the sin of the world." At the very least it referred to the sacrifices, as I pointed out in an earlier study. The sacrificial lamb had always figured highly in Israel's religious culture. Abel had sacrificed a lamb and thereby received God's blessing. Abraham had performed various sacrifices. The offering of lambs figured in the worship at the temple and was practiced daily. Thus, when John the Baptist termed Jesus the "Lamb of God," he was clearly identifying Jesus as the innocent substitute who would die in place of all those who have sinned.

However, John's phrase also referred to the culmination and far-reaching effect of the sacrifices. To understand the importance of this truth, we need to go back to the time when God first instituted sacrifices. There in the Garden of Eden, after man had sinned, God shed the blood of one animal for one person and then established this as a repeatable form of worship on the basis of which a sinful man might come to him. When Abel did that, God judged him righteous (Heb. 11:4). He rejected the more beautiful offering of Cain because it was not a sacrifice.

For thousands of years men lived with this basic one-lamb-for-one-person institution. The time came when the Jews were in slavery in Egypt and God was about to bring them out and lead them into their own land. At this time God instituted the Passover. Each family in Israel was to take a lamb and examine it for defects. Only a perfect lamb could be chosen. After three days, on the night of the Passover, the lamb was to be killed and eaten and its blood spread upon the lintel and side posts of the door of the house as a sign to the angel of death to pass over that house as it went through Egypt slaying the firstborn that night. One lamb for a person? Yes! But here God revealed that it could also be one lamb for one family.

The Exodus took place, and several months later the people were at Mount Sinai where God gave them the law. In the law were instructions for the Day of Atonement, on which the high priest was to kill a lamb for the nation and then take its blood within the veil into the Holy of Holies, where it was sprinkled upon the mercy seat beneath the wings of the cherubim. Here was the progression: one lamb for one person, one lamb for one family, one lamb for one nation. . . . But then Jesus came, and it was John's role to identify him as one lamb for this world.

For some years now I have been convinced that this was the primary meaning of Palm Sunday. Men who love liturgy and liturgical parades have seized upon this event, as men will, and have built it into a day of triumph in which Jesus supposedly presented himself as King to a warm and enthusiastic populace. But that is not what Palm Sunday is about. Jesus did not present himself as King to the people of Jerusalem only to be surprised several days later by their rejection of him. The day of crucifixion was the necessary prelude to Easter, and Palm Sunday was the necessary prelude to the day of the crucifixion. At Calvary Jesus died as God's Lamb. Palm Sunday was the day on which that Lamb was led into Jerusalem. Palm Sunday was the day on which Jesus offered himself as our substitute.

This was probably true in a very literal way. We must remember that the idea that Jesus was crucified on what we call Good Friday is a tradition inherited from a later period of church history and is therefore not necessarily accurate. In fact, recent studies have indicated that Jesus may have died just before sundown on Thursday of Passover week; that is, before a Friday Passover beginning on Thursday evening. According to this reckoning, there would have been two sabbaths in that particular Passover week, the regular Saturday Sabbath and the Friday Passover Sabbath. Thus, Jesus would have died on Thursday, would have spent three days and three nights in the tomb, as he foretold, and would have risen from the grave before sunrise on Sunday morning, which was (by Jewish reckoning) the first day of the week.[1]

The bearing that all this has upon the matter of the Passover lambs is readily apparent. For if Jesus was crucified on Thursday before a Friday Passover and if he entered Jerusalem on Sunday, as the Bible indicates, then Jesus was entering Jerusalem at the precise moment at which the thousands of Passover lambs were being led into the city to be taken into the thousands of Jewish homes. What better way could Jesus have dramatized the claim that he was God's Lamb? When he later died, as he did, at the precise moment when, according to John, the Jewish people were actually killing their lambs and feeding on them, the imagery was complete.

Do you realize that Jesus Christ truly is the Lamb of God who takes away the sin of this world? Do you realize that he came to die for you? Each of us should believe these things and commit ourselves to him.

God So Loved the World

The final important reference to the world in the opening chapters of the Gospel is in John 3:16. There we read: "For God so loved the world that he gave his one and only Son, that whoever believes in him shall not perish but have eternal life."

Where can a sinful human being such as you or I learn that God is love? You will not find it taught in books on human history. You will not find it in philosophy or in your own reasoning. You will not even find it in the other religions of this world. You will find this truth only in Christianity, at the cross of the Lord Jesus Christ. How do we know that God loves us? It is not because someone else tells us so. He may be mistaken. It is not because the universe is beautiful; the universe is also horrible at times. There is no love in space; space is nothingness. Even on earth we must admit that there are tidal waves and hurricanes, earthquakes and disease, just as there are gorgeous spring days and beautiful sunsets. How do we know that God loves us? Only because Jesus of Nazareth died for us! The Bible says, "But God demonstrates his own love for us in this: While we were still sinners, Christ died for us" (Rom. 5:8).

He died for us even when we were hostile toward him. What did men do when Jesus appeared as the Light? Men rejected the Light. What did men do when he appeared as the Lamb? Men crucified the Lamb. What did men do when Jesus appeared as the great and supreme manifestation of God's love? Men hated that love and despised it.

So we ask ourselves: Can God really love a race that rejects his Light, crucifies his Lamb, and despises his love? Everything within ourselves would say no. But the reality of the crucified Christ forces us to say yes, for he is indeed the Savior of such a sinful and rebellious world. Samuel Medley expressed this in a song written toward the middle of the eighteenth century:

> Awake, my soul, in joyful lays,
> And sing thy great Redeemer's praise:
> He justly claims a song from me,
> His loving-kindness is so free.
> He saw me ruined in the fall,
> Yet loved me notwithstanding all,
> And saved me from my lost estate;
> His loving-kindness is so great.

May the knowledge of the truth of the love of God for our race, found so long ago by the woman of Samaria and her friends, be yours as you come to know our great Savior.

55

Christ in Galilee

John 4:43–45

After the two days he left for Galilee. (Now Jesus himself had pointed out that a prophet has no honor in his own country.) When he arrived in Galilee, the Galileans welcomed him. They had seen all that he had done in Jerusalem at the Passover Feast, for they also had been there.

Not long ago a person complained to me that the Bible is difficult to understand. His objection was not only that the language of the Bible is difficult—I pointed out that there are very readable modern translations such as the American Bible Society's Good News for Modern Man or the New York Bible Society's New International Version—but that even then the concepts are difficult and that many passages contain contradictions. Because of this problem the person told me that in his opinion God was being difficult and unfair.

I answered this objection in two ways. I said that first of all it is really not right to charge that the basic message of the Bible is difficult to understand. It may be difficult to accept. I believe that no one ever does accept it unless God has already done a previous supernatural work in his mind and heart. Still this is not the same thing as saying that it is difficult to understand. "How, for instance, could God make John 3:16 any clearer?" I asked. "He simply tells us that he loves us so much that he sent his Son to die in our place so that anyone who commits himself to him will not be separated from him forever but will have new life. In other words," I said, "God has made the basic message of the Bible so clear that even a child can understand it," and, indeed, many do.

"On the other hand," I added, "it is also true that there are parts of the Bible that seem to contain contradictions and are difficult to understand.

But then, aren't we glad that the Bible contains statements that are deep enough to challenge our thought and keep us learning even through a lifetime of Bible study? The fact that this is true is one proof that the Bible is from God, for no other book would be so infinitely provocative and challenging. Moreover, I have personally learned, as have many others, that it is often the passages that seem difficult on first reading that yield the greatest harvest as the result of a deeper investigation."

The Problem

I give this particular introduction to these verses simply because they contain just such a difficulty and yet, upon a closer study, yield great blessing. The difficulty is apparent to anyone who reads them, and it becomes even more evident (at least initially) when these verses are compared with similar verses in the other Gospels.

Let me explain what I mean. John 4:43–45 says: "After the two days he left for Galilee. (Now Jesus himself had pointed out that a prophet has no honor in his own country.) When he arrived in Galilee, the Galileans welcomed him. They had seen all that he had done in Jerusalem at the Passover Feast, for they also had been there." Quite obviously, these verses are transition verses, taking the reader from the period of Christ's life spent in Samaria to the next stage of his ministry in Galilee, and they give a reason for Christ's decision to move to Galilee. The difficulty is that all the other Gospels also report the reason that John gives for Christ's move to Galilee, quoting Jesus as saying that a prophet has no honor in his own country, but in Matthew, Mark, and Luke, Jesus is quoted as saying this of Galilee as an explanation of why he had to go somewhere else (Matt. 13:57; Mark 6:4; Luke 4:24), while in John the move is reversed.

Moreover, there is a second difficulty that is apparent even without comparing the Gospels. In John Jesus says that he is going to Galilee because he will have no honor there. Yet the next verse tells us that "the Galileans welcomed him. They had seen all that he had done in Jerusalem at the Passover Feast."

What is the solution? Well, different answers have been given. First, some commentators have argued that Jesus went to Galilee to prove that his saying spoken earlier about not being received there was actually the case. The difficulty with this view is that, if this is what Jesus intended, he was mistaken, for he actually proved that even the Galileans would receive him. A second explanation is historical. Those who hold it argue that after the success Jesus had just known in Samaria, he wanted to slip away to a place where he would be able to rest. That sounds plausible, but it runs aground on the difficulty that Jesus had apparently determined to go back to Galilee even before he had the success that he did in Samaria (John 4:3), and, of course, even in this explanation he is mistaken. A third explanation is that to John "his own country" was actually Judea, rather than Galilee, and that in his view Jesus was returning to Galilee because the Jews in Jerusalem had not responded to his teaching. That would be a satisfactory explanation were it not for the fact that the other three Gospels all apply Christ's statement to Galilee.

If none of these explanations is adequate then, is there another that will do justice to both the literal meaning of the words and to the historical context? I believe that there is. Moreover, I believe that this view emerges precisely when we take the words at their face value. The explanation is simply that at this point Jesus Christ moved his ministry to Galilee precisely because he had not been received in Galilee previously, and it was therefore the Galileans above everyone else who needed him. In other words, Jesus went to Galilee because the Galileans needed the gospel. Doesn't that make sense? I believe that it does. I also believe that it gives a revelation of our Lord's own motivations in his ministry that can speak to us personally.

Regardless of Failure

Let me try to put this understanding of the verses in terms that we can easily appropriate and apply. What do we learn from this insight into the outlook on his ministry that motivated the Lord Jesus Christ? The first thing is this: Jesus had determined to do the will of God for his life regardless of the consequences. That is, he had determined to do God's will regardless of apparent success or failure.

We see that in a very graphic way in the light of Christ's previous rejection by his countrymen. The story of Jesus' initial appearance in Galilee is told in Luke. From Luke we learn that he had been so badly received by the Galileans that he was almost executed at their hands. Jesus had come to Nazareth, where he had been brought up, on the Sabbath. When he went into the synagogue on this particular day to worship, he was asked to take part in the service, as male Jews were often asked to do. He was given the task of reading the Scriptures, so he picked a prophecy from Isaiah that concerned himself. He read, "The Spirit of the Lord is on me, because he has anointed me to preach good news to the poor. He has sent me to proclaim freedom for the prisoners and recovery of sight for the blind, to release the oppressed, to proclaim the year of the Lord's favor" (Luke 4:18–19; Isa. 61:1–2).

He then began to teach them, beginning with the claim that the prophecy of Isaiah was being fulfilled on that precise day as he began his ministry. He ended with the prediction that most of the people would not receive him. At this point the citizens of Nazareth were so incensed that they led him to the top of a high cliff where they were about to cast him down to his death. We are told that Jesus simply passed through them and went his way.

This was the kind of reception Jesus had received in his own area of the country, and this would be fresh in his memory at the time of his return visit. Moreover, the favorable reception that he had received from the Samaritans would also be fresh, so that it would be a great temptation for him to simply remain where he was and work there. What did he do? He went to Galilee because he was determined to do God's will regardless of the consequences.

I wonder if we do that. If something does not work, isn't it true that we quickly throw it out and try something else, and that we do the same thing spiritually? If our witness is not readily received, we are quick to shake the dust off our feet and go elsewhere. Here the conduct of the Lord Jesus Christ should be helpful.

We are to keep hunting for effective means of presenting the gospel. No one would question that. Still, we are to learn from Christ's example that even when we have done our best and have not had success in our witnessing, we are to keep on trying.

Let me put it in another way. Your job as a witness to the Lord Jesus Christ is not to convert people. That is God's job. He will do the converting. Nevertheless, you have a job to do, and your job is to bring as many as you can into contact with the gospel. Moreover, you are not to stop doing your job even if the results from your own vantage point seem meager.

Man's Need

The second thing we learn from Christ's decision to go into Galilee is that he was motivated by an acute sense of man's need. He once used an illustration about a doctor to describe his activity. He said, "It is not the healthy who need a doctor, but the sick. I have not come to call the righteous, but sinners" (Mark 2:17). It was the need of men and women who were lost, without the gospel, that moved him.

Are you so motivated? Ask yourself these questions: "Whom do I know who is particularly needy? Whom do I know who is in need of physical help? Whom do I know who needs the gospel?" You might gain help along these lines by looking about for the most lonely person you know, the most introverted, the one who is most oppressed with guilt, sin, or distress. Speak to him or her. You might find an amazing openness to the gospel simply because you are (or could be) the only one who has ever taken time to listen to that person and share his problems.

Motivated by Scripture

The final lesson from the decision of the Lord Jesus Christ to enter Galilee is that Jesus was motivated by the specific statements of Scripture and that, therefore, we should be motivated by such specific statements too.

We see this not as much in John's Gospel as in Matthew's. In the early chapters of Matthew the author shows that Jesus' early ministry in Galilee was in direct response to a specific Old Testament prophecy about it. The prophecy is in the ninth chapter of Isaiah, which Matthew quotes as follows: "Leaving Nazareth, he went and lived in Capernaum, which was by the lake in the area of Zebulun and Naphtali—to fulfill what was said through the prophet Isaiah: 'Land of Zebulun and land of Naphtali, the way to the sea, along the Jordan, Galilee of the Gentiles—the people living in darkness have seen a great light; on those living in the land of the shadow of death a light has dawned'" (Matt. 4:13–16).

Clearly Jesus knew the Scriptures and studied them for the light they threw upon the course of his ministry. It was in response to this verse and many hundreds of verses like it that he made his decisions.

What does this have to do with us? A person might argue that the Bible does not contain such specific prophecies about what each of us is to do and about the course of our lives. That is true. Nevertheless, the Bible contains principles by which God instructs us how we are to organize our lives, fix our values, witness to others, and serve him. If we will read the Bible and allow God to interpret it and apply it to our own situation, then we will have the same type of direction that Jesus had and will be able to obey God on the basis of his written revelation.

That is the only way to any geniune blessing in the Christian life. Success, even in preaching the gospel, will not satisfy indefinitely. Neither will martyrdom. We will find blessing only when we allow God to speak to us through the Scriptures and obey him.

Martin Luther was a man who had come to learn this both theoretically and in practical experience. God had spoken to him through Scripture and had given peace to his soul. Scripture had kept him on course both in times of rejection and danger and in times of apparent success. Thus it was a study of Scripture that he recommended to others. On one occasion Luther was asked to autograph the flyleaf of a copy of the German Bible that he had translated, and he responded by writing a small testimony of his experience with this book. He first wrote John 8:25—"Who are you? . . . Just what I have been claiming all along." It was a claim on the part of Jesus Christ to divinity. Then Luther added, "They desire to know who he is and not to regard what he says, while he desires them first to listen; then they will know who he is. The rule is: Listen and allow the Word to make the beginning; then the knowing will nicely follow. If, however, you do not listen, then you will never know anything. For it is decreed: God will not be seen, known, or comprehended except through his Word alone. Whatever, therefore, one undertakes for salvation apart from the Word is in vain. God will not respond to that. He will not have it. He will not tolerate any other way. Therefore, let his book, in which he speaks with you, be commended to you; for he did not cause it to be written for no purpose. He did not want us to let it lie there in neglect, as if he were speaking with mice under the bench or with flies on the pulpit. We are to read it, to think and speak about it, and to study it, certain that he himself (not an angel or a creature) is speaking with us in it."[1]

It is true. The Bible is God's Word. In whatever circumstances we may find ourselves, it is not only an adequate source of information; it is also a treasure, the only absolutely necessary source of guidance for our lives.

56

The Second Miracle

John 4:46–54

Once more he visited Cana in Galilee, where he had turned the water into wine. And there was a certain royal official whose son lay sick at Capernaum. When this man heard that Jesus had arrived in Galilee from Judea, he went to him and begged him to come and heal his son, who was close to death.

"Unless you people see miraculous signs and wonders," Jesus told him, "you will never believe."

The royal official said, "Sir, come down before my child dies."

Jesus replied, "You may go. Your son will live."

The man took Jesus at his word and departed. While he was still on the way, his servants met him with the news that his boy was living. When he inquired as to the time when his son got better, they said to him, "The fever left him yesterday at the seventh hour."

Then the father realized that this was the exact time at which Jesus had said to him, "Your son will live." So he and all his household believed.

This was the second miraculous sign that Jesus performed, having come from Judea to Galilee.

It does not matter who you may be, sooner or later you are going to experience great sorrows or even tragedies in your life. You may be rich or poor, a man or a woman, black or white. Tragedy inevitably will become a part of your personal experience and there will be nothing you can do to avoid it.

That is not merely my own opinion, of course. It is a truth that has been recognized by many throughout history. One of the oldest pieces of literature in any language contains an expression of this that has become somewhat proverbial. It is from the Book of Job: "For hardship does not spring

341

from the soil, nor does trouble sprout from the ground. Yet man is born to trouble as surely as sparks fly upward" (Job 5:6–7). The Hebrew of this saying is beautiful; for the two Hebrew words translated by our one word "sparks" are literally "the sons of flame," and the thought is that men are born to endure the fires of this life and eventually perish in the burning.

We know it is true. Psychologists tell us that life begins with pain, as the child, who for the first nine months of its life has rested warmly and comfortably within the uterus of its mother, is suddenly pushed and pulled into a hostile environment in which his first independent act is to cry. The experience is one akin to strangulation as the baby gasps for its life. For a time after birth the mother cares for the baby's needs. Yet, as the child grows up, the years progressively knock away the props of life and the child is forced increasingly to depend on his own resources. He must learn to eat and clothe himself. Eventually he must go to school, then earn a living. In time there will be the failure of his plans and the dissolution of cherished relationships. There will be pain and sickness. Death will inevitably come to friends and family, and at last the person himself will face his own death and that which lies beyond.

I am not pointing this out to spread gloom. There is enough sorrow in this world without emphasizing it. Rather, I am writing in this way to start us thinking about how you and I will react to such events when they come to us. What will we do? Will we be beaten down by them? Or will we triumph over them in complete victory? The verses we end with show how we can have such victory and how the same solutions can enrich our lives even in the far more abundant times of joy and great happiness.

In Joy and Sorrow

The basis for arriving at such solutions comes from a story in the life of Jesus Christ. It is the story of a rich nobleman whose son was dying and who, out of his desperation, came to Jesus about it. By the end of the story we find that not only had the son been cured but in a far more wonderful way the rich man and his entire family had found a genuine faith in Christ.

The story begins by telling us that "once more he visited Cana in Galilee, where he had turned the water into wine" (John 4:46). It ends with the remark: "This was the second miraculous sign that Jesus performed, having come from Judea to Galilee" (v. 54). Why do we have this emphasis upon the place where Jesus performed the miracle? Why is this called the second miracle, when obviously many other miraculous things had been done by Jesus previously (cf. John 2:23; 4:45)? Why, in fact, is the former miracle of changing water into wine at Cana mentioned? Quite clearly, this is John's way of telling us that we are to put the two miracles—that of changing water into wine and that of healing the nobleman's son—side by side. In other words, we are to see them in relationship to each other and compare them.

What does the comparison show? In the first place it shows a number of similarities. Both were "third-day" miracles. Thus, the miracle at the wedding occurred three days after Jesus had left the area of the lower Jordan River to return to Galilee (2:1), while this miracle similarly occurred three days after Jesus had determined to leave Judea to return to Cana through Samaria (4:43). Both miracles contain an initial rebuke to the one who requested it. In the first case it was to Mary, Jesus' mother (2:4). In the second it was to the nobleman (4:48). Third, in each case Jesus performs the miracle at a distance, doing nothing but speaking a word (2:7, 8; 4:50). Fourth, the servants possess unique knowledge of what happened (2:9; 4:51). Finally, each account concludes with a statement that certain persons who knew of the miracle believed. Thus, in the earlier story we are told that "his disciples put their faith in him" (2:11), while in the second narrative we are told that the father "and all his household believed" (4:53).

These points reinforce the need of comparing the two stories. Yet the significant point of the comparison is not in the similarities but in their one great difference. What is the difference? Certainly that in the first the scene is one of joy, festivity, and happiness. The stage is a wedding. In the second the scene is fraught with sickness, desperation, anxiety, and the dreadful shadow of death. One is a picture of joy, the other of sorrow. In comparing the two we are clearly to see that life is as filled with the one as the other and that Jesus, the One who is the answer to all human need, is needed in both circumstances.

One writer has noted: "Jesus is more than equal to either occasion. He has a place in all circumstances. If we invite him to our times of innocent happiness, he will increase our joy. If we call on him in our times of sorrow, anxiety, or bereavement, he can bring consolation, comfort, and a joy that is not of this world."[1]

In pointing to this truth John is further documenting his claim that Jesus is indeed "the Savior of the world"; for Jesus is the Savior of all men, at all times, and in all circumstances.

Growth of Faith

The next fact we are told is that the man who came to Jesus at Cana was a nobleman. This is not the same word that is used in chapter 3 where Nicodemus is described as being a Pharisee, "a ruler of the Jews." The word that is used of Nicodemus is one that denotes preeminence of authority, however derived. In this case, the word is *basilikos*, which is related to the word for king and therefore denotes royalty. The word could even mean that the man was a petty king, but in this context it probably means that he was one of the royal officials at the court of Herod.

Moreover, the man had some means, for he had servants. Here was a nobleman, rich, no doubt with great influence. Yet neither his rank nor riches were able to exempt him from the common sorrows of mankind. Remember, as you think about those in positions of importance or power, that there is just as much sickness among them. And there is just as much of a need for Jesus Christ.

The wonderful thing, of course, is that this man sensed his need and its solution. When Jesus had performed his first miracle by changing water into wine, the miracle was at first known only to the disciples and to the servants who bore the wine to the master of ceremonies. Still, people being what they are, the news must have spread and have created a stir in Galilee. In time, some of the Galileans got to Jerusalem and learned of miracles that Jesus had been doing there. They told about these when they returned. It is part of the same picture that news of what Jesus was doing must have reached even Herod's court, for the nobleman had heard of Jesus and immediately remembered what he had heard when faced with the fact of his son's illness.

News came to the nobleman that Jesus was back in Galilee at Cana where the first miracle had been performed. Leaving home he made the four-hour trip (about twenty-five miles) from Capernaum, where he lived, to Cana. There he begged Jesus to accompany him back to Capernaum and heal his son.

There are two ways of looking at the man's faith at this point. The first way is to be surprised that he was exercising faith at all. Here was a man who was high in the court, where he doubtless exercised great authority, traveling twenty-five miles to request a miracle from a carpenter. It is true that desperation has driven many men and women to unusual actions, and that therefore we must not find this overly significant. Nevertheless, the man's faith is surprising. That is one way of looking at it. The other way of looking at the man's faith, however, is to look at it in the way in which Jesus looked at it and to realize that although it was real faith it was nevertheless quite weak. The man apparently believed that Jesus was able to heal his son. But he limited Jesus to the place—he thought it was necessary that Jesus should come down to Capernaum—and to a mode of operation. Presumably the nobleman thought that Jesus would have to touch his son to heal him, just as Jairus thought that Jesus would have to touch his daughter to heal her (Mark 5:23) and the woman with an issue of blood thought it would be necessary for her to touch the hem of Christ's garment (Mark 5:28). It therefore became Jesus' purpose to teach the nobleman and to help his faith to grow.

At first Jesus delivered a rebuke. He said, "Unless you people see miraculous signs and wonders, you will never believe" (John 4:48). That was the equivalent of calling him a curiosity seeker and was perhaps directed as much toward the crowd that had gathered as to the nobleman. It was a test of the man's faith or sincerity. How did he react? Fortunately, the nobleman proved himself to be truly noble, for he was not offended, nor did he seek to justify himself either before Jesus or the others. He simply stood his ground, reiterating his need and humbling himself to receive his answer in whatever way Jesus chose to give it to him.

Here then is the first answer to the way in which we can find triumph or victory in sorrow. It is to *trust Jesus enough to allow him to operate in whatever way he chooses.*

Believing Is Seeing

But there is also a second lesson to be learned, and it was this lesson that Jesus next began to teach him. Jesus taught that *one must believe first, then he will see the results.* Jesus had said, "Unless you people see miraculous signs and wonders, you will never believe." This statement was a true description of the thinking of vast numbers of men and women. The world even has it in a proverb, which says, "Seeing is believing." The teaching of Jesus was that in spiritual things the order is reversed and that believing is seeing, for it is only as one believes in Jesus that he sees spiritual things happening. Therefore, Jesus told the boy's father, "You may go. Your son will live" (v. 50). The nobleman was called upon to believe without sight. It was hard, but that is precisely what he did. The story goes on to say, "The man took Jesus at his word and departed."

Needless to say, if it had been a mere man speaking, the belief of the nobleman would have been absurd. No one believes without sight. Yet in spiritual matters it is entirely logical to do so—because we are dealing not with a man but with God. Jesus is God. Hence, to believe him is the most logical thing in the universe.

Moreover, to believe in Jesus is also the most effective way to set one's mind at rest, even when faced with sorrow. For we are told that having believed Jesus the nobleman simply continued on his way. The word used, plus the tense employed (imperfect), suggests that the nobleman believed Jesus so implicitly that he simply picked up his work where he had left it and went on about his business. At any rate, it is obvious that he did not rush home; for although the conversation took place about one o'clock in the afternoon and the journey was only four hours, the nobleman did not get back until the next day. When he did return it was to learn that his son had been healed instantly the day before at the very hour in which Jesus had spoken to him.

What a splendid story this is! And it is all the more splendid in that the man came to such strong faith from such a weak beginning. It is hard to read this story without thinking of that other similar story of the centurion who came to Christ requesting him to heal his sick servant. There are some noted similarities, so much so that some scholars have imagined these to be two versions of the same incident. Yet they are not the same, and the greatest of all differences is to be found in the attitudes of the two men involved. The centurion had the greatest faith. He said to Jesus, "Lord, I do not deserve to have you come under my roof. But just say the word, and my servant will be healed" (Matt. 8:8). Jesus praised his faith, saying, "I tell you the truth, I have not found anyone in Israel with such great faith" (v. 10). Still the centurion had this faith from the beginning, while the nobleman who sought out Jesus in Cana came to the same level of faith in a very short time through Jesus' teaching.

Truths for Everyone

The applications of this story to our own experiences are obvious. I am sure that you have already seen some of them. First, if Jesus acted as he did with this man and if his actions actually had the effect on him that the Bible tells us they did, then surely Jesus is the answer to our own anxieties also. The man came, talked to Jesus, and then went on his way without any tangible evidence that his request had been granted. Why? Because in meeting Jesus and in talking with him, his anxiety evaporated. It can be the same for you. You may be weighed down under great burdens. You may be crying inside. Just come to Jesus. Tell him about it. He will be delighted to ease your burdens and to take the weight of them all upon himself.

The second application is that the experience I have described may be true even though our actually seeing the results is postponed. They may even be postponed until after this life. We witness the death of a parent, friend, or child. We experience sorrow or sickness ourselves. We come to Jesus and find him saying, "I know what I am doing. I am working it all out." The Bible says, "And we know that in all things God works for the good of those who love him, who have been called according to his purpose" (Rom. 8:28). There will always be circumstances in which we will not *see* that this is true. Nevertheless, we are to go on about our business. We may have to pass through the night into the bright day of the next world before we see how our prayers are answered. Still we are to believe and know that Jesus has heard and that he has answered.

Finally, there is fact that these truths are for everyone. That is the burden of this first great section of John's Gospel. What has John done? He has shown Jesus at work in the three major sections of his world—Judea, Samaria, and Galilee. He has shown him with the rich and the poor, with the educated and the uneducated, with Jews and Samaritans, with religious leaders and those who show no religious orientation at all. He has shown him as the "light of the *world*," "the lamb that takes away the sin of the *world*," "the Savior of the *world*." In other words, he has shown us that the gospel is for everyone. Thus, the gospel is for you also, whoever you may be.

Jesus is speaking to you when he says, "Come now, let us reason together . . . though your sins are like scarlet, they shall be as white as snow; though they are red as crimson, they shall be like wool" (Isa. 1:18). He speaks to you when he says, "Come to me, all you who are weary and burdened, and I will give you rest" (Matt. 11:28).

Notes

Chapter 1: Introducing John's Gospel

1. A. M. Hunter, "Recent Trends in Johannine Studies," *Expository Times* 71 (1959), 166.
2. John A. T. Robinson, "The New Look at the Fourth Gospel," in *Twelve New Testament Studies* (London: SCM Press, 1962), 98–99.

Chapter 2: Jesus Christ Is God

1. Arthur W. Pink, *Exposition of the Gospel of John* (Grand Rapids: Zondervan, 1970), 10.
2. William Barclay, *The Gospel of John*, vol. 1 (Philadelphia: Westminster Press, 1958), 15.
3. Ibid.

Chapter 3: Jesus Christ Is Man

1. J. B. Phillips, *Ring of Truth: A Translator's Testimony* (New York: Macmillan, 1967), 88.
2. Martin Luther, *Luther's Works*, vol. 22, ed. J. Pelikan, trans. M. Bertram, (St. Louis: Concordia Publishing House, 1957).

Chapter 5: Jesus Christ Is Life

1. Donald Grey Barnhouse, *Genesis: A Devotional Commentary*, vol. 1 (Grand Rapids: Zondervan, 1970), 14.
2. Harry A. Ironside, *In the Heavenlies* (Neptune, N.J.: Loizeaux Brothers, 1937), 100–101.

Chapter 6: The Light of the World

1. E.M. Blaiklock, "New Light on Bible Imagery," *Eternity*, March 1967, 26–27.
2. Brooke Foss Westcott, *The Revelation of the Father* (London: Macmillan, 1884), 52.

348

3. Malcolm Muggeridge, *Jesus Rediscovered* (Garden City, N.Y.: Doubleday, 1969), 51.

Chapter 7: John the Baptist

1. James Montgomery Boice, *Witness and Revelation in the Gospel of John* (Grand Rapids: Zondervan, 1970), 81.

Chapter 8: Light for Every Man

1. Archibald Campbell. *The Seven Great "I Am's" and the Seven Miracles of Jesus in John's Gospel* (Fort Washington, Pa.: Christian Literature Crusade, 1968), 108.

Chapter 11: The Free Offer of the Gospel

1. Donald Grey Barnhouse, "Man's Answer," in *Epistle to the Romans*, part 60 (Philadelphia: The Evangelical Foundation, 1956), 16.

Chapter 14: Grace and Truth

1. C. S. Lewis, *The Screwtape Letters* (New York: Macmillan, 1956), 11.

Chapter 15: The Unique Christ

1. Donald Grey Barnhouse, *The Cross through the Open Tomb* (Grand Rapids: Eerdmans, 1961), 53–54.

2. The story of Hosea is told in full in connection with the exposition of John 3:16.

3. Barclay, *The Gospel of John*, 14–15.

Chapter 16: How to Witness for Jesus Christ

1. An argument supporting this view in this volume. There are, however, different ways of viewing the days. Most scholars note the division given here, though finding various meanings in it. L. Paul Trudinger ("The Seven Days of the New Creation in St. John's Gospel: Some Further Reflections," *The Evangelical Quarterly,* July-Sept. 1972, 154–58) eliminates the travel day, places the wedding at Cana on day six, and has Jesus resting with his family on day seven (2:12), which he regards as the Sabbath. This week early in Jesus' ministry corresponds with a similarly eventful week at the end.

2. Tertullian, *Apology*, chapter 37.

3. Edward Gibbon, *The Decline and Fall of the Roman Empire*, vol. 1, chapter 15.

4. Adolf Harnack, *The Mission and Expansion of Christianity in the First Three Centuries* (New York: Harper & Brothers, 1961), 368.

Chapter 18: Family Evangelism

1. There is a possibility that the hour was 10:00 A.M., based on the view that John employs the Roman rather than the Jewish method of reckoning time.

But this is uncertain. For a fuller discussion of the time notes in John, see under 19:14.

2. Donald Grey Barnhouse, "Winning Your Relatives to Christ," in *Share Your Faith*, ed. Russell T. Hitt (Grand Rapids: Zondervan, 1970), 57–58.

3. Donald Grey Barnhouse, "He First Found His Brother," in *First Things First* (Philadelphia: The Evangelical Foundation, 1961), 15–16.

Chapter 20: The Mark of the Christian

1. Watchman Nee, *The Normal Christian Worker* (Fort Washington, Pa.: Christian Literature Crusade, 1970), 14.

2. Francis A. Schaeffer, *The Church at the End of the Twentieth Century* (Downers Grove, Ill.: InterVarsity Press, 1970), 133.

Chapter 21: The Baptism of John

1. I owe the translation of this passage as well as certain points on the nature and meaning of baptism to Donald Grey Barnhouse (see *God's Freedom* [Grand Rapids: Eerdmans, 1958], 32–44, particularly p. 34).

Chapter 22: The Baptism of the Holy Spirit

1. John R. W. Stott, *The Baptism and Fullness of the Holy Spirit* (Downers Grove. Ill.: InterVarsity Press, 1964), 13.

2. Donald Grey Barnhouse, "Eternal Identification," *Epistle to the Romans*, part 30 (Philadelphia: The Evangelical Foundation, 1951), 32–33.

Chapter 23: Christian Baptism

1. Benjamin B. Warfield, *Selected Shorter Writings of Benjamin B. Warfield—I*, ed. John E. Meeter (Nutley, N.J.: Presbyterian and Reformed, 1970), 326.

2. Ibid., 327–28.

Chapter 25: What's in a Name?

1. Westcott, *The Revelation of the Father*, 7–8.

2. Emile Cailliet, *Journey into Light* (Grand Rapids: Zondervan, 1968), 18.

Chapter 26: The First Miracle

1. Charles Haddon Spurgeon, *Lectures to My Students* (Grand Rapids: Zondervan, 1970), 114, 170.

Chapter 27: Was Jesus Christ a Revolutionary?

1. Oscar Cullmann, *Jesus and the Revolutionaries*, trans. Gareth Putnam (New York: Harper & Row, 1970).

2. Tom Skinner, *Words of Revolution* (Brooklyn: Tom Skinner Associates, 1970), 74.

Chapter 28: He Gave Them a Sign

1. John Baillie, *The Idea of Revelation in Recent Thought* (New York: Columbia University Press, 1956), 140.

Chapter 29: Christ and the Heart of Man

1. For more on the fall of Adam, particularly the consequences of the fall, see chapter 31, "Intellectuals or New Men?"

2. I tell this story in similar words but at much greater length in *How God Can Use Nobodies* (Wheaton: Victor Books, 1974), 99–108.

Chapter 31: Intellectuals or New Men?

1. The fall of Adam is also discussed in chapter 29.

Chapter 33: Flesh and Spirit

1. Kenneth S. Wuest, "Great Truths to Live By," in *Word Studies in the Greek New Testament*, vol. 3 (Grand Rapids: Eerdmans, 1966), 57–58.

Chapter 34: The Breath of God

1. Edward E. Plowman, *The Jesus Movement in America* (Elgin, Ill.: David C. Cook, 1971), 15–16.

Chapter 35: Christ Speaks to Skeptics

1. H. A. Ironside, *Random Reminiscences from Fifty Years of Ministry* (New York: Loizeaux Brothers, 1939), 99–107.

Chapter 36: The Serpent in the Wilderness

1. Donald Grey Barnhouse, *God's Remedy* (Grand Rapids: Eerdmans, 1954), 219.

2. Ibid., 220–21.

Chapter 37: The Love of God

1. It is a characteristic of John's Gospel that speeches of Jesus pass into theological statements by the evangelist. But it is not always easy to tell where Jesus' words leave off and John's begin. In this chapter Jesus begins to speak in verse 10, but the dialogue is not ended, even though most commentators agree that John rather than Jesus is speaking later. Perhaps the dividing point is at this verse. In verses 14 and 15 the cross is being spoken of as a future event and the phrase "the Son of Man" occurs. Both make sense if Jesus spoke those words. At verse 16 the cross is spoken of as a past event, and there are indications in the style that John may be speaking.

2. The story of Hosea is told in this way by Barnhouse, *God's Freedom*, 187–92; *This Man and This Woman*, 21–26; and parts 37 and 38 of the published radio studies in the *Epistle to the Romans*.

Chapter 38: God's Greatest Gift

1. Watchman Nee, *Changed into His Likeness* (Fort Washington, Pa.: Christian Literature Crusade, 1967), 62.

Chapter 40: Condemned!

1. Plowman, *The Jesus Movement in America*, 48–51. In mid-1971 Hoyt abruptly joined the radical Children of God group.

Chapter 41: Last Words of a Humble Man

1. Pink, *Exposition of the Gospel of John*, vol. 1, 149.

Chapter 42: The Bride and the Bridegroom

1. Schaeffer, *The Church at the End of the Twentieth Century*, 118.
2. Donald Grey Barnhouse, *God's Methods for Holy Living* (Philadelphia: Eternity Book Service, 1951), 154–57.

Chapter 43: The Revealer Has Come

1. A. W. Tozer, *The Pursuit of God* (Harrisburg, Pa.: Christian Publications, 1948), 50.
2. Barclay, *The Gospel of John*, 136.
3. Michael Green, *Runaway World* (Downers Grove, Ill.: InterVarsity Press, 1969), 123.

Chapter 44: Christ at Sychar's Well

1. John R. W. Stott, *Christ the Controversialist* (London: Tyndale Press, 1970), 64.
2. Barclay, *The Gospel of John*, 147.
3. Donald Grey Barnhouse, *God's Wrath* (Grand Rapids: Eerdmans, 1953), 223–24.

Chapter 45: Living Water

1. Geoffrey T. Bull, *God Holds the Key* (London: Hodder and Stoughton, 1967), 70–71.

Chapter 48: How to Worship God

1. Tozer, *The Pursuit of God*, 9.
2. Barclay, *The Gospel of John*, 154.
3. C. S. Lewis, *Letters to Malcolm: Chiefly on Prayer* (New York: Harcourt, Brace & World, 1963), 4.

Chapter 49: "I Am He"

1. Donald Grey Barnhouse, *Man's Ruin* (Grand Rapids: Eerdmans, 1952), 45–47.
2. Westcott, *The Revelation of the Father*, 19–20, 25–27.

Chapter 51: Christ, the Soul Winner

1. Watchman Nee, *What Shall This Man Do?* (London: Victory Press, 1962), 37.

2. Paul E. Little, *How to Give Away Your Faith* (Downers Grove, Ill.: InterVarsity Press, 1966), 36.

Chapter 52: The Secret of Satisfaction

1. Charles Haddon Spurgeon, *Sermons on the Gospel of John,* comp. and ed. Chas. T. Cook (Grand Rapids: Zondervan, 1966), 35.

Chapter 54: The Savior of the World

1. See Roger Rusk, "The Day He Died," *Christianity Today,* 29 March 1974: 4–6; and Roy M. Allen, *Three Days in the Grave* (Neptune, N.J.: Loizeaux Brothers, 1942). The matter is discussed at greater length in volume 3.

Chapter 55: Christ in Galilee

1. Martin Luther, *What Luther Says: An Anthology,* vol. 1, comp. Ewald M. Plass (St. Louis: Concordia, 1959), 81.

Chapter 56: The Second Miracle

1. Campbell, *The Seven Great "I Am's,"* 57.

Subject Index

Abel, 202
Abraham, 39, 66, 112, 118, 145, 146, 157, 202, 305, 311; born again, 211, 212; descent from, 80; growth in faith, 244, 245; offering Isaac, 236–38; sought his own way, 68
Achilles, 67
Adam, 199; and Eve, 92, 182, 193, 204, 236, 305, 320; child of, 297; fall of, 182; first and last, 40
Adamic nature, 202
Adultery, spiritual, 259, 260
Aenon near Salim, 17
Aland, Kurt, 134
Albright, William F., 15
Alfonso VI, 318
"All who believe," 240–45
America, "Christian," 61, 63; decline of religion in, 212
Ancient of Days, 160
Andrew, 54, 116, 117, 120, 126, 152, 160, 163; brought others to Jesus, 119
Angels, 150–55
Anna, 305
Anthropology, 327
Anti-Semitism, 293
Apuleius, 101
Aramaic, 17
Aratus, 74
Aspirations and achievements, 239
Assurance, 123, 124
Assyrians, 284
Athens, 36
Atonement, 285; truth about, 96, 97
Augustine, 81, 85; second, 117
Authority, 75, 76

"Believing is seeing," 345, 346
"Book of Signs," 163
Babylonian captivity, 290
Bach, Johann Sebastian, 328
Baillie, John, 32, 178
Baptism, 12, 133–49; Christian, 144–49; for the dead, 136; into Christ, 141–43; of

John, 133–37; of the Holy Spirit, 138–43; water, 145
Barabbas, 171–73
Barclay, William, 12, 23, 24, 98, 101, 120, 166, 187, 200, 266, 297
Barnhouse, Donald Grey, 12, 40, 65, 77, 98, 117, 141, 256, 262, 303, 304,
Barth, Karl, 134, 227, 294
Beasley-Murray, G. R., 134
Belshazzar, 155
Bergman, Ingmar, 33
Bernard of Clairvaux, 299
Bernard, J. H., 57
Bethany, 16, 17
Bethesda, pool of, 17
Bethsaida, 16
Bible, 177, 216, 267, 307, 315; God's Word, 340; points to Christ, 23; principles in, 340. See also Scripture, Word of God
Bible Study Hour, 11
Birth from above, 198, 199
Blaiklock, E. M., 45, 46
Blake, Eugene Carson, 212
Blindness, spiritual, 64–66
Body, death of, 193
Body, soul and spirit, 192, 193
Boniface, 117
Born of water, 199–201
Breath of God, 209–13
Bride and bridegroom, 258–63
Bronze serpent, 224
Brotherhood of man, 74
Brunner, Emil, 102
Bull, Geoffrey T., 278
Bultmann, Rudolph, 242

"Come and See," 119, 120
Caesar, Julius, 300
Caiaphas, 172
Cailliet, Emile, 158, 159
Calvin, 80, 298
Campbell, Archibald, 60
Cana of Galilee, 89, 103, 180, 162–67, 342–44

Scripture Index

James Montgomery Boice is president and cofounder of the Alliance of Confessing Evangelicals, the parent organization of *The Bible Study Hour,* on which he has been the speaker since 1969. He is the senior pastor of Philadelphia's historic Tenth Presbyterian Church.